Aberdeenshire Library and Information Service
www.aberdeenshire.gov.uk/libraries
Renewals Hotline 01224 661511

KENDALL. Alan

The chronicle of classical
music

THE CHRONICLE OF CLASSICAL MUSIC

*An Intimate
Diary
of the Lives
and Music
of the
Great
Composers*

Alan Kendall

*with 388 illustrations
160 in colour*

Thames & Hudson

HALF-TITLE: Beethoven's study in the Schwarzpanierhaus, lithograph of 1827.

FRONTISPIECE: Painting of a court musician by Peter Jakob Horemans, 1772.

First published in the United Kingdom in 1994 by
Thames & Hudson Ltd, 181A High Holborn, London WC1V 7QX

www.thamesandhudson.com

First paperback edition 2000
Reprinted 2006

British Library Cataloguing-in-Publication Data
A catalogue record for this book is available from the British Library
ISBN-13: 978-0-500-28213-7
ISBN-10: 0-500-28213-7

Printed and bound in Singapore by Star Standard Industries (Pte) Limited

How to Use this Book

The core of this volume is a diary-style chronology of events, a four-part chronicle spanning the centuries from 1600 to the present day. It traces the development of Western Classical music, revealing the inside story of the composers' daily lives: their travels, encounters, great works, performances, patrons, friends, lovers, families, finances, struggles and ambitions – a kaleidoscope of facts through which you may follow your own lines of enquiry.

The four centuries are subdivided into periods, and, for each of these year-clusters, contemporary world events are also highlighted, setting the musicians' lives in a wider political and artistic context.

This rich store of information is complemented by a range of special features, which fall into the following categories, each flagged with a different symbol for easy reference:

 Key People, Key Works

The most important composers and librettists in the history of Classical music, and the genesis of their great works.

 Key Places

The different centres of musical energy from century to century, and the conditions which nurtured musical genius.

 Documents

Letters, diaries and articles in which you can hear the voices and opinions of the composers, their friends, patrons and critics.

 Issues, Events, Themes

The diverse influences on the changing style and form of music, and the development of instruments and of the orchestra.

These symbols are the cross-referencing signposts for you to trace the information you want. When a subject appearing in the chronology is followed by one of these signs, you can discover more about it by turning to the page indicated and looking for the feature with the appropriate symbol.

There are also cross-references within the chronological diary of events, which are signalled simply by the page number in brackets. In addition, there are links to information to be found in the captions to the illustrations: when you see the symbol ★ before a page reference, then you can turn to that page and look for the caption marked by a ★ .

If you encounter a word in small capitals in the text, you can look up its meaning in the **Glossary** of technical musical terms, which forms part of the extensive **Reference Section** beginning on p.257. This section includes everything the music-lover might need.

Throughout the book, the public and private worlds of the composers spring to life from a wealth of images; there are over three hundred and eighty illustrations, more than one hundred and fifty in full colour.

Contents

1900–Today
The Century of Modernism

Reference Data

INTRODUCTION

The Origins of Western Music

As Western Classical music emerges from the mists of antiquity, the church becomes the guardian of its future, although reluctantly because of music's association with the pagan past. Human joy in music-making cannot be stifled, however, and eventually the authorities realize that it is better to encourage and control the use of music than to outlaw it. As courtly establishments expand, music is no longer required solely for use in churches and chapels, but also for secular ceremonies and celebrations, for lavish banquets and intimate entertainment. Poets and musicians serenade their mistresses in the language of courtly love, and dancing becomes a favourite pastime. The music of the common people is rarely recorded, but as the centuries progress, a conscious effort will be made to provide music that is more accessible to them.

Angels with musical instruments, detail of a painting by Gaudenzio Ferrari, 1535-36.

The Origins of Western Music

Western Classical music, which has evolved over the centuries, now offers a richly varied repertoire of forms and styles, both vocal and instrumental, almost bewildering in its profusion, from the Baroque TRIO SONATA to the Romantic symphony or twentieth-century jazz opera. Access to this music through live performances, broadcasts on television and radio, and recordings on cassette and compact disc, provides us with unprecedented opportunities for extending and enhancing our knowledge and appreciation. Almost inevitably, a love of the works of a particular composer, or the repertoire of a particular instrument, will inspire the music lover to wish to know more. Why did the composer write a particular work in the first place? What were the influences at play on composers at the time? Why was it written in that way?

Our understanding of Classical music can be greatly strengthened by examining its origins, development and centres of excellence. Consider Italy, which we think of as a supremely musical land. A closer look reveals that for the last two hundred years, vocal music, and especially opera, constitutes almost the sum total of its composers' output. Yet no one can deny that from the Middle Ages to about 1800, Italy was the source of inspiration for successive generations of composers in Europe.

Just as musicians came and went from Italy, so the focus of musical life moved away from Naples, Rome and Venice to Vienna, Paris, London, Leipzig and Berlin, influenced by factors that were not simply musical. Politics, social and economic developments all played their part. Indeed, economics still affect music to a considerable degree; but whereas nowadays we tend to hold creative artists in esteem, even if we do not support them directly through our patronage, until the end of the eighteenth century composers were relegated almost to the status of servants by their employers and patrons (right). In the early days of Western music, however, the position of musicians was rather different.

The Legacy of Greece and Rome

We know from references in Homer and images on vases that music played an important role in the lives of the Ancient Greeks, and also the sort of instruments that were in use. The Greeks had four- and seven-stringed lyres, double pipes called *auloi*, panpipes called *syrinx* and trumpets called *salpinx*, but we know little about the music itself. From Etruscan and Roman times we have wall paintings and carved reliefs which show us that Greek instruments were used and adapted, and others introduced, such as an early kind of organ, a trumpet with a curved end, known by the Romans as *lituus*, and a horn, *cornus*. Once again, however, we cannot be sure about the precise nature of these instruments, or the music they played. In fact the earliest music to survive in a form that we may reasonably say sounded a certain way, is a section of a Christian hymn from the late third century AD on a papyrus fragment from Oxyrhynchus in Egypt, and even then scholars are not united in its transcription into a modern system of NOTATION.

Certainly it is to the Christian church that we owe the foundation of Western Classical music, and to the Western church in particular. Early writers such as St Jerome, St Ambrose and St Augustine all recognized the power of music, but had considerable reservations about its use in a religious context. Although singing was usually accepted, instrumental music was regarded with suspicion, because of its association with the theatre and paganism in general. Psalm-singing seems to have been practised throughout the church, thus continuing a Hebrew tradition; hymn-singing, which also had a Jewish precedent, was very popular, to the extent that the Council of Laodicea (360–81) ruled that only biblical texts might be sung as part of the LITURGY. This division of liturgical and non-liturgical elements was to become a preoccupation of the church.

Veronese's Marriage at Cana, *portrayed as a royal banquet in the second half of the sixteenth century, shows the importance of music at such an event. The instrumentalist in white (on the left) could be a self-portrait of the artist, and the man in red playing the bass (on the right) may be Titian.*

The account of a Spanish nun, Etheria, who went on pilgrimage to Jerusalem about 380, describes the principal offices or services of the Latin Church in the East. Around the same time these offices were used as models for the Roman church, when Pope Damasus was formulating the liturgy (below), assisted by St Jerome, who was an expert in Eastern liturgy. It was also during this period that the term *missa* began to be used to describe the Mass, from the closing Latin words 'Ite, missa est', meaning 'Go, it is over', though it was only later that the application of the term was restricted to the Mass itself, or indeed that the Mass was codified in the form that we know today.

Mediaeval Music

Towards the end of the ninth century a fundamental change took place in Western music when MONOPHONY, or 'one voice', gave way to POLYPHONY or 'many voices'. A monk called Hucbald (*c.*840–930), of the Abbey of St Amand in the diocese of Tournai, wrote the treatise *De harmonica institutione* (Concerning the Setting up of Harmony, that is, music), in the course of which he describes what is quite clearly simultaneous singing of different notes by different voices, or an early move in the direction of singing in parts.

Another important work to have survived from this early period is the tenth-century *Musica enchiriadis* (Music Manual), attributed to Hoger of Laon in France, from which we can see how the earliest polyphony was achieved. A chant is sung in its original form, and is reproduced simultaneously at the INTERVAL or space of a perfect fifth or fourth (five or four notes) below it. Both lines may be doubled (duplicated) by voices singing at the octave, or eight notes, above. This system, where the secondary voice or counterpoint is at a fixed distance from the chant, is called parallel or strict ORGANUM. A free style of organum is also described in *Musica enchiriadis,* however, where the chant and the additional voice begin and end on the same note, but in between use a limited number of different intervals.

In 1054 the two halves of the church were rent apart, thereby isolating the Orthodox church from subsequent developments in the West. Even within the Western church there were four 'dialects' of liturgical chant: Mozarabic (Spanish),

★ *An illustration from the Psalter of King Henry VI of England, which shows monks in their choir stalls intoning one of the eight offices or services that took place throughout the day from Matins at two in the morning, through Lauds, Prime, Terce, Sext, None and Vespers to Compline in the evening.*

Gallican (Frankish), Ambrosian (Milanese) and Roman. The Roman ultimately became the official chant of the whole Western church, and is known as GREGORIAN CHANT, after Pope Gregory the Great (reigned 590–604). However, it was largely due to the activities of Charlemagne, 'King of the Franks and Lombards and Patrician of the Romans', who was crowned 'Holy Roman Emperor' on Christmas Day, 800, that Gregorian chant (also known as PLAINSONG from a thirteenth-century term *cantus planus*) became the official chant of the church and Western music was ready to move into a new phase of its development.

It was another monk, a Benedictine named Guido (*c*.992–1050, right), from Arezzo in Italy, who took music forward another great step. He was credited with having invented the STAVE, the lines on which music is written, and of using different colours for the lines to indicate different levels of PITCH, that is whether the notes are high or low. More importantly, however, he devised a system called SOLMIZATION to indicate the degrees of the musical scale, which in his system was the HEXACHORD or six notes. Guido took the first six lines of a Latin hymn to St John the Baptist, in which each of the lines begins a note higher than its predecessor. The first syllable of each line thus gave him the names of a sequence of six notes Ut, Re, Mi, Fa, So, La:

Ut quant laxis/**Re**sonare fibris/**Mi**ra gestorum/**Fa**muli tuorum
Solve polluti/**La**bi reatum/**S**ancte **I**ohannes;

(Holy John, cleanse our polluted and ensnared lips, so that your children might properly sing your great deeds). The initials of Sancte Iohannes were later taken to provide an additional note designated Si. Guido used the convenient diagram of the open left hand, so that the teacher could point to it with the right. In this system G (*So*) is the tip of the thumb, A (*La*) the joint of the thumb, and B (*Si*) the root of the thumb. The fingers are treated in the same way.

From manuscripts dating from the late eleventh and early twelfth centuries, thought to have originated in the monastery of St Martial at Limoges in France, an interesting practice is now seen. The notes of the original chant occur in an extended form as a lower or TENOR line (from the Latin *tenere*, to hold), with an added upper voice or DUPLUM where several notes correspond to only one of the chant, which it uses as a kind of tonal anchor. What is happening is that the upper voice is now assuming more importance than the original chant, which eventually loses all effective meaning, as we can no longer hear it as a melody.

Although the vast majority of mediaeval music was in the hands of the church (even musical drama originated in a liturgical context, such as the acting out of the Easter and Christmas stories), we do know that plays written by *goliards*, or wandering scholars, sometimes in vernacular languages such as French or Czech, were performed outside the church,

A thirteenth-century version of the system, devised by the monk Guido of Arezzo, and known after him as the Guidonian Hand, to help memorize the pitch of notes in relation to each other. The sections of the thumb and fingers of the hand each correspond to a note in a scale or melody, but the starting point is not fixed, so that the pitch is only relative, and the system is therefore of limited application. Nevertheless, the Guidonian Hand remained the basis of learning the art of singing until about 1600.

13

The Minnesinger *Heinrich von Meissen (c.1320) known as* Frauenlobe, *or Praiser of Women, with some of his colleagues. The instruments from left to right are a tabor, a cornett , a shawm ◆ (p.73), two bowed fiddles or* vielles, *a psaltery and a set of bagpipes. The* Minnesänger *were the German equivalent of French* troubadours *and* trouvères *and English minstrels, and sang of courtly love.*

in monastic schools, although the earliest to survive with its music intact is *The Play of Daniel,* from Beauvais in France, dating from about 1230. There were secular songs before this, but we know little about their music or the circumstances of their performance. We do know of a tradition of aristocratic vernacular song at the court of Aquitaine in southern France. Duke William IX, on his return from the First Crusade, entertained guests in the role of a *troubadour* with accounts of his misfortunes, known as *chansons de geste.* Under his granddaughter Eleanor, queen of France, then of England, we see the rise of the ideal of courtly love, which was emulated by the Minnesänger (left) and *trouvères* in Germany and Northern France. In addition there were wandering professional entertainers, of lower social standing, known as *jongleurs,* whom the church deplored.

French mediaeval aristocratic culture not only produced beautiful music, but also wrote it down in exquisite form, as shown in this heart-shaped collection known as the Chansonnier Cordiforme *of Jean de Montchenu (below).*

In general, however, the church still took the initiative as far as music was concerned. This was the age of the early Gothic cathedral building in England and France and the new developments in music can be identified above all with the cathedral of Notre Dame in Paris, begun in 1163, whose high altar was consecrated in 1182. It is almost as if music expanded to fill those soaring Gothic vaults, and ORGANUM alone was no longer sufficient – a new kind of POLYPHONY was required. Steps were taken in this direction by the men we know as Leoninus and Perotinus, who worked at Notre Dame in the late twelfth and early thirteenth centuries, developing the form known as the MOTET.

One collection of music carries us right through this period. Known as the Montpellier Codex, it is of Parisian origin, and roughly covers the years 1280 to 1310. The music in the codex moves from secular texts with a Latin PLAINSONG TENOR, to the use of secular tenors; even the cries of Parisian street sellers appear towards the end. The name of Adam de la Halle (*c.*1237–88) occurs in this later part. A native of Arras, Halle studied in Paris, and applied the techniques of current polyphony to many of the existing secular forms of music. He is remembered for composing the earliest pastoral comic opera, *Le Gieus [Jeu] de Robin et de Marion* (The Play of Robin and Marion).

The fourteenth century saw the dawn of a new kind of music called *Ars nova* – the New Art. The invention of the term is usually credited to Philippe de Vitry (1291–1361), from his treatise of this title dating from around 1320, though there is also an earlier *Ars novae musicae*. Philippe de Vitry was both musician and poet, churchman and statesman. Music was now a free art form, composed according to its own laws, liberated from the constraints of poetry or religion, and, although Pope John XXII (reigned 1316–34) complained bitterly that words had become simply a pretext for music, he could not suppress the new spirit that was abroad. Indeed, it is in this period in Italy that some scholars place the start of the great movement known as the Renaissance.

The New Art was brought to a splendid climax in the person of Guillaume de Machaut (*c*.1300–77) who, rather like Philippe de Vitry, combined the attributes of poet and composer, churchman and diplomat, and is also known as the last of the *trouvères* (opposite above). Machaut's attitude towards music is wonderfully summed up in his own words: 'Et musique est une science/Qui vuet [*sic*] qu'on rie et chant et dance' (Music is a science that wants people to laugh and sing and dance, above). Although he wrote a great deal of secular music, he is also remembered as the composer of the first complete polyphonic setting of the Ordinary of the Mass, that is to say the parts that may not alter, which for musical purposes means the Kyrie, Gloria, Credo, Sanctus (and Benedictus), and Agnus Dei.

An illuminated capital letter from a mid-fifteenth-century manuscript (above). As befits a drinking song, wine is being drawn from a cask and served to the assembled company.

In Italy during this period there was virtually no polyphonic church music, and the work of the great Florentine organist Francesco Landini (*c*.1335–97), who was blind, is most notable for the polyphonic *ballate* in two or three parts, often with one of the parts instrumental, related to the French form known as the *virelai*. He wrote a few MADRIGALS too, though the early madrigal was very different from what we tend to think of as madrigals today. England was still in touch with the more advanced music of France at this time, because of the political situation, and in John Dunstable (*c*.1380–1453) had a composer of international standing. Dunstable probably served the Duke of Bedford, Regent of France, in Paris between 1422 and 1435, which would explain why so much of his music found its way into continental sources. The Duke of Bedford's brother-in-law was Philip the Good, Duke of Burgundy, and it was no doubt at the Burgundian court that Dunstable's music came to the attention of the Walloon from Cambrai, Guillaume Dufay (*c*.1400–74).

Maximilian I, who became Holy Roman Emperor in 1493 and ruled over a vast empire, invited many of the best musicians of the time to his court. This woodcut by Hans Burgkmair of 1513, shows him among his musicians and clearly depicts the instruments that were played at this time.

Dufay is typical not only of the Franco-Flemish School, but also of the new international Western European musician of his day. He was working in Italy by the time he was twenty, first in Pesaro, then Bologna, after which he became a singer in the papal chapel. When the Pope fled from Rome to Florence in 1435 Dufay went too, and the following year composed a MOTET for the consecration of Brunelleschi's cathedral there, whose proportions are thought to be mathematically related to the proportions of the dome. If any single composer may be said to act as a bridge between the Middle Ages and the Renaissance, it is Dufay. Indeed, in many respects it was he who evolved a musical language for the Renaissance.

Renaissance

It is hard to cite any particular date or event as marking the beginning of the Renaissance, for there is no unanimity amongst scholars. In Italy it arrived much earlier than elsewhere – certainly in the fourteenth century – but for countries beyond the Alps, and for European musical history, too, one might conveniently take the Fall of Constantinople in 1453, which in turn led to Philip the Good organizing the Feast of the Oath of the Pheasant in February 1454, intended as a prelude to a crusade to recapture the city, and for which Dufay wrote some music.

Philip the Good died in 1467, and his son, Charles the Bold, fell in combat at Nancy in January 1477, leaving only one daughter, Mary, as heiress to the extensive Burgundian dominions. On her marriage to the Habsburg Maximilian Archduke of Austria in August that year, Mary of Burgundy took with her to Innsbruck Franco-Flemish musical influence, so extending its orbit considerably, and drawing southern Germany and Austria into the mainstream of European development.

In the person of Henricus Isaac (*c.*1450-1517) we see another example of synthesis of the musical culture of the time. His early life is largely undocumented, but we find him in Florence after 1480, in the service of Lorenzo the Magnificent. After the death of Lorenzo in 1492, Isaac was made court composer to Maximilian I (above) in 1496, though he returned several times to Florence, finally retiring there for the last three years of his life. His output is staggering, and includes Mass settings and motets, German *Lieder,* French *chansons,* Italian carnival songs and *frottole* (simple settings of secular poems) and, at the end of his life, the monumental *Choralis constantinus* – the earliest complete cycle of POLYPHONIC LITURGICAL compositions for the ecclesiastical year. In fact it was incomplete on Isaac's death, and was finished by one of his pupils.

Undoubtedly the most famous master of the Franco-Flemish school was Josquin Desprez (des Prés, *c.*1440-1521, below), and few composers can have exercised such enormous influence in their own day. He was born in St Quentin, but made his way to Milan, where he sang in the cathedral from 1459 until 1474 before entering the service of Cardinal Ascanio Sforza, with whom he went to Rome, singing in the papal chapel choir from 1486 until 1499. He directed the music of the Este court at Ferrara for about a year in 1503–04, but eventually returned to his homeland. Possibly Josquin's greatest legacy to posterity was his concern to make his music express the inner meaning of the words.

What we know of secular music at this time was still very much the music of an aristocratic, and therefore closed, society, though we can infer something of its nature from references in literature, illustrations from manuscripts, and certain carvings in wood and stone. What must

Josquin was possibly the greatest of the Franco-Flemish composers. He is thought to be the figure on the right in this allegorical painting of Music (on the left), who holds a small portative organ.

be considered is that professional musicians, whether employed by a spiritual or secular authority, performed all kinds of music, even if their primary function tended to be the fulfilment of their religious duties. In earlier times, and in less advanced countries, the two functions were indeed hard to separate, which is reflected in the music and in its performance. It is questionable whether musicians saw any such dichotomy in their art, unless they were in religious orders, despite periodic attempts by church rulers to enforce it. With early English CAROLS, for example, the border between sacred and secular was very fine, since some originally seem to have been round dances, and their performance involved movement by a group of performers during the refrains, with a pause whilst a soloist sang the verse and everyone else stood still. Not all carols were sacred, so that they would be performed at dinner or some similar suitable occasion. For more intimate occasions there was a growing use of clavichords ◆ (p.51) and early harpsichords at court and in the wealthier private homes, though much of this music was not written down, since a talented musician such as Isaac, was expected to improvise, and only less able performers were thought to need written or printed music.

One of the most important new factors in the dissemination of the works of composers was the rise of music printing. In Venice Ottaviano dei Petrucci published Josquin Masses, *Misse Josquin*, in 1502, and five Masses by Isaac *Misse henrici Izac*, in 1506. Of these last five works, four take their compositional point of departure not from plainsong CANTUS FIRMI, but from secular *chansons*. Isaac was not unique in this practice, and one tune in particular, 'L'homme armé' (The Armed Man) was used by several composers, including Josquin, and the Scots composer Robert Carver (1487-*c.*1546), whilst Carissimi ■ (p.33), in a twelve-part Mass setting, even carried it into the seventeenth century.

Reformation and Counter-Reformation

Although the movement towards Reformation of the Western church probably became most crucially evident with the appearance of Luther before the Diet of Worms in 1521, voices had been raised within the church itself a century before that. Cardinal Pierre d'Ailly (1350–1420), in his *Tractatus super Reformatione Ecclesiae* (Tract on the Reform of the Church, 1416) rued the increasing number of highly decorated churches being built; the proliferation of saints, holy days and festivals; and the introduction of new hymns and prayers. The formal Catholic response to the Protestants was not issued until the Council of Trent ended in December 1563. For church musicians the most important result of the council was the declaration that words must be intelligible, prompting the Franco-Flemish composer Jacobus de Kerle (*c.*1532–91) to write a set of special prayers for the council, *Preces speciales.* Kerle's prayers were sung thrice weekly almost every week towards the end of the council. They were composed in a simple kind of POLYPHONY, with little overlapping of the voices, ensuring that the text was intelligible.

Kerle's compositions were somewhat in the style of a much greater contemporary, Giovanni Pierluigi da Palestrina (1525–94), whose rather conservative works became the model for Tridentine church music, that is that required by the Council of Trent. His *Missa Papae Marcelli* (Mass of Pope Marcellus) may well have been one of the Masses given in the home of Cardinal Vitellozzo Vitellozzi on 27 April 1565, when various works were given the church's seal of approval. One work so approved, somewhat ironically, was Lassus's Mass (below) based on a madrigal by Cipriano de Rore (1516-65) entitled 'Qual donna attende'.

Lassus depicted directing the choir in the court chapel at Munich where, after a period of some twelve years in Italy, he served for almost forty years from 1556. Although it was not unusual for musicians to be well thought of by their employers, Lassus enjoyed a degree of patronage and esteem accorded to relatively few other musicians.

Elsewhere in Italy things were different. In Venice Andrea Gabrieli (*c.*1515–86) and his nephew Giovanni employed instruments and voices to their fullest effect in St Mark's, so developing the concertato style, and in Bologna musical opulence was acceptable in San Petronio. Even in Rome itself, the Oratorian movement founded by St Philip Neri ★ (p.33), to provide music for the ordinary people, including spiritual songs known as *laude,* began producing something entirely different, ORATORIO ■ (p.33), which, had they forseen its evolution, would have incited the Tridentine fathers to ban every vestige of music from church services.

The world was changing. The divisions between sacred and secular, aristocrat and peasant, were becoming blurred, and a new educated middle class was emerging, who demanded music that might be played and sung in the home, with the accompaniment of lute and viol (opposite), or performed on clavichord and virginal. The ability to sing or play an instrument was regarded as a

Domestic music-making in the sixteenth century shows a trio of young ladies performing Claudin de Sermisy's setting of Jouissance vous donnerai (I Will Give Your Happiness), *a highly popular Renaissance song (opposite). The singer is accompanied by transverse flute ◆ (p.73) and lute, whose open case hangs behind them.*

necessary accomplishment for any person with pretension to education, as can be seen from the testimony of the English composer Thomas Morley in 1597: 'Supper being ended, and music books (according to the custom) being brought to the table, the mistress of the house presented me with a part, earnestly requesting me to sing; but when, after many excuses, I protested unfainedly that I could not, every one began to wonder. Yea, some whispered to others, demanding to know how I was brought up: so that, upon shame of mine ignorance, I go now to seek out mine old friend, master Gnorimus, to make myself his scholar'.

A detail from a painting dating from c.1595, showing in the foreground players at a masque ◆ (p.35) for the wedding of Sir Henry Unton, who was the special envoy of Elizabeth I of England to Henri IV of France. The tendency in the Renaissance was to utilize extended families of instruments of strings, brass or woodwind, but where families were mixed, as here, then the ensemble was known as a broken consort.

This demand for music was created, and stimulated, by the rise of music printing in Venice ◆ (p.29), to which reference has already been made. Pierre Attaingnant set up in Paris in 1528, and Jacques Moderne in Lyons in 1532. Georg Rhaw started publishing in Wittenberg in 1538 and Berg and Neuber in Nuremberg after 1542. Susato took music publishing to Antwerp in 1543 and Phalèse to Louvain in 1545. Songs and dance music flowed from their presses, arranged so that they might be played in almost any combination of instruments and voices available, though the underlying music was still almost always thinly disguised traditional POLYPHONY.

Composers very often responded to this outlet, since it increased their fame and income, even if there was a degree of pandering to popular taste. What was about to happen, however, was that the old form of polyphony was no longer able to hold in its embrace both religious and secular music – certainly not the more sophisticated variety – under the impact of new techniques developed by the rise of keyboard and other instruments, the determination of composers to marry their music ever more closely to their chosen texts, and the revolutionary concept of contrast and spatial effects. Ironically, as it was the rise of the great Gothic cathedrals that probably gave impetus to the development of polyphony, it was a fascination with the very concept of architectural and acoustic space that finally shattered it. It was as if composers such as Palestrina (above) and Victoria, having developed the ideal form of polyphonic music, had exhausted the possibilities of the language.

In Italy change was in the air; in Venice a very different approach to instrumental music appeared, and the basic relationship between vocal and instrumental music was radically altered as polyphony began to disintegrate. In the secular field one of the direct consequences of this collapse was a revival of interest in MONODY, which in turn led to the birth of opera (p.24). In 1579 the Florentine aristocrat Count Giovanni de'Bardi ◆ (p.25) devised a MASQUE for the wedding of Francesco I, the music of which included a song composed along these 'new' lines by Piero Strozzi and sung by Giulio Caccini (*c*.1550–1610).

Bardi again devised the dramatic musical entertainments, known as *intermedi*, for the wedding of Ferdinando I and Cristina of Lorraine in 1589. Included were several MADRIGALS and COLORATURA vocal solos from the hands of Marenzio (*c*.1553–99), Caccini, Bardi, Emilio de' Cavalieri (*c*.1550–1602) and Jacopo Peri (1561–1633), who sang, accompanied by a chitarrone, a kind of bass lute with metal strings running along a neck that might be two metres long. The instrumental TIMBRES must have been captivating, since we know that in addition to the chitarrone, lyres, harps, soprano, tenor and bass viols ◆ (p.39), large and small lutes, psalteries (flat, plucked stringed instruments with metal strings), trombones, cornetts, transverse flutes, citterns (pear-shaped plucked stringed instruments) and mandolas (small guitars) were all employed at different points in the proceedings. From here it was clearly but a short step to opera, once the final ingredient of RECITATIVE had been added.

The title page of Palestrina's First Book of Masses, *which was published in Rome in 1554. The composer is shown presenting his music on bended knee to Pope Julius III, who raises his hand in benediction. As papal legate, Julius III had opened the Council of Trent, which reformed music in the Catholic church.*

1600-99

The Flowering of Baroque Music

The seventeenth century sees Italy – and Venice, Rome and Naples in particular – setting the pace for almost all that is new in musical development. Traditional forms, such as church music, continue to be developed in ever more exciting ways, but there are brand-new forms, too, such as opera and oratorio which, when exported beyond the confines of Italy, will eventually capture the imagination of music lovers all over Europe. There are important developments in the making and playing of instruments, and a new interest in musical theory and practice. The expansion of the music printing industry makes composers' works available to a wider audience than ever before, though the patronage of temporal and ecclesiastical rulers still remains of vital importance to musicians. Outside Italy, Germany's development is impeded by a long period of war and unrest, and France tends to resist assimilating too rapidly what Italy has to offer.

The sense of hearing is represented allegorically as domestic music-making in this seventeenth-century French painting.

1600-04
The Birth of Opera in Italy

Under the inspiration of a Florentine aristocrat, Count Giovanni de' Bardi, a group of professional musicians, gifted amateurs, curious intellectuals and dedicated scholars share their thoughts on a wide range of topics – the sciences, music, poetry and Greek drama – and the art form of opera is born.

Opposite: The Concert *by Bartolommeo Manfredi. This painting of the pleasures of music-making probably shows a concert at the Florentine court where this Roman artist was much in favour.*

The title page of Cavalieri's La rappresentazione di anima e di corpo, *performed in Rome in February 1600. Unlike the Florentine composers, Cavalieri was not trying to recreate the style of Greek tragedy. His is a morality play set to music, with recitative, ensembles, choruses and dances, in which Soul and Body, and allegorical personifications, such as Time, Intellect and Worldly Existence, contrast the brevity of earthly pleasure with the lasting joys of Heaven.*

1600 Caccini, a member of the Camerata ◆ (p.25), completes his opera *Euridice* ◆ (p.49).

• **February** The first performance of Cavalieri's *La rappresentazione di anima e di corpo* (The Representation of Soul and Body, left and ★ p.33) is given in the oratory of the church of Santa Maria in Vallicella in Rome. It is the earliest known drama with music throughout and the first time a FIGURED BASS features in a printed score.

• **6 October** Peri's opera *Euridice* ◆ (p.49) is performed in the Palazzo Pitti in Florence to celebrate the marriage of Maria de' Medici (known subsequently as Marie de Médicis) and Henri IV of France.

1601 Luzzaschi's book of MADRIGALS for one, two and three sopranos, doubtless composed for the famous trio of singing ladies at the court of Ferrara, is published in Rome. This collection of madrigals is the first to be published with a written-out keyboard accompaniment.

• In London Morley publishes his anthology of twenty-nine madrigals by twenty-four composers, *The Triumphes of Oriana*, in honour of Elizabeth I.

• Hassler produces two new works: *Sacri concentus* (Sacred Harmonies), a collection of church music in four to twelve parts, and *Lustgarten neuer teuscher Gesäng* (Pleasure Garden of New German Song), thirty-two German songs and eleven instrumental ballet pieces.

• Monteverdi is made director of music to the Gonzaga court in Mantua.

1602 Caccini's collection of solo songs using the ideals of the Camerata ◆ (p.25), *Le nuove musiche* (The New Music), is published in Florence.

• Viadana brings out the first part of his collection of church MOTETS, *Cento concerti ecclesiastici* (One Hundred Church Compositions in the Concertato Style), in Venice. In this influential publication Viadana shows that it is possible to adopt the new style of writing, with an organ OBBLIGATO, for sacred as well as secular use.

• **10 April** Monteverdi is made a citizen of Mantua.

• **5 December** Caccini's *Euridice* ◆ (p.49) is performed for the first time in the Palazzo Pitti, Florence.

1603 Monteverdi publishes his Fourth Book of Madrigals.

1604 Sweelinck (right) publishes his first book of settings of the metrical Marot-Bèze (Geneva) Psalter in Amsterdam.

• Frescobaldi enters the Accademia di Santa Cecilia in Rome as organist and singer.

• Dowland brings out his *Lachrimae or Seaven Teares*, a set of instrumental pieces for viols ◆ (p.39) and lute.

★ *Sweelinck, whose portrait (right) was painted by his brother in 1606, succeeded his father as organist of the Oude Kerk in Amsterdam, and was in turn succeeded by his son. He formed a bridge between English virginalists such as Bull (p.30) and Venetian organists such as Merulo and Giovanni Gabrieli, and created, through his German pupils, a Baroque school of organ music.*

OTHER EVENTS

1600 Giordano Bruno burned at the stake in Rome as a heretic
• The English East India Company founded
• Tycho Brahe elaborates his planetary system

1601 English East India Company's first voyage
• Founding of the University of Parma
• Shakespeare: *Hamlet*

1602 Galileo Galilei investigates the laws of falling bodies, gravitation and oscillation (until 1604)
• Dutch East India Company founded
• War between Persia and Turkey (until 1627)

1603 Accademia dei Lincei founded in Rome
• Elizabeth I of England dies and is succeeded by James I

1604 Sigismund III of Sweden deposed; Charles IX becomes king
• Annibale Carracci: *The Flight into Egypt*

◆ *The Florentine Camerata*

The term 'camerata' (meaning salon) was originally used for the association of scholars, intellectuals and musicians, both amateur and professional, who met in the salon of Count Giovanni de' Bardi in Florence between about 1573 and 1587. It was then extended to the group who, in the last decade of the century, experimented with the concept of music drama under the impulse of the aristocrat, composer and writer Jacopo Corsi, and which led directly to the production of Peri's Dafne *in 1598 and* Euridice *in 1600.*

Although Camerata was not an official title, Caccini used the term to describe the circle around Bardi in the dedication of the score of his Euridice ◆ *(p.49). In addition to Caccini and Bardi himself, we find Vincenzo Galilei (father of Galileo Galilei), who was researching into Greek music in correspondence with the humanist scholar Girolamo Mei in*

Rome. It would seem that by 1573 Mei had examined every source of information relating to Greek music then in existence.

In 1582 Galilei composed some songs in what he believed to be the ancient Greek style, which are lost, but we have an account from Caccini in which he describes singing such songs for the Camerata in a style which he calls 'speaking with melody'. Galilei summed up his views in a treatise entitled Dialogo della musica antica et della moderna *(Dialogue between Ancient and Modern Music), the fundamental principle of which was that the words should be set as clearly as possible for the listener, in order to convey directly the sentiments expressed by the performer. Possibly more significant for the future of operatic development was the view put forward by Galilei that the Greek dramas had been sung continuously, and that all the text was therefore to be sung throughout the work.*

1605-16
Venice: Musical Capital of the World

Although Venice no longer enjoys genuine political power, its geographical situation ensures that it still retains all the outward trappings of a great maritime state. Foreigners flock to the Most Serene Republic and its cultural life, underpinned by the stability of its institutions, dazzles the eyes and charms the ears of all.

1605 Monteverdi publishes his Fifth Book of Madrigals (p.24).

• Praetorius is working in Wolfenbüttel, where he will remain until 1610, and begins producing his monumental collection of church music entitled *Musae Sioniae* (Songs of Sion), which will take five years to complete.

• Victoria's Requiem, composed for the funeral service of Empress Maria of Austria, is published in Madrid.

• Byrd (left) completes his first book of *Gradualia* (Graduals) for the different feast days and seasons of the church year.

1606 Agazzari writes his pastoral opera *Eumelio*. Book Four of his collection of MOTETS with CONTINUO, *Sacrarum cantionum* (of Sacred Songs), is published in Rome and Milan. Agazzari is now choirmaster of the Jesuit Roman Seminary.

Portrait of William Byrd which bears the description Inglese Compositore *(English Composer). This shows Byrd's significance as one of the greatest composers of the Renaissance, not only in his native country, but throughout Europe.*

1607 Publication of the second part of Viadana's collection of *Cento concerti ecclesiastici* (p.24) in Venice.

• Agazzari's treatise on THOROUGH BASS, *Del sonare sopra il basso* (Concerning Performance over a Bass), is published in Siena. Through Praetorius's translation of the work in Book Three of his *Syntagma musicum* (Music Collection, p.29), Agazzari's influence will extend far into Germany.

• Gagliano becomes one of the founder members of the Accademia degli Elevati in Florence, with the sobriquet *L'Affanato* (The Agitated). His opera *Dafne* ◆ (p.49) is completed, and will be published in Florence in 1608.

• Byrd's second book of *Gradualia* is brought out in London.

• Monteverdi publishes his *Scherzi musicali* (Musical Jokes or Light Compositions) in Venice.

• **24 February** Monteverdi's opera *L'Orfeo* ◆ (p.49) is performed before the Accademia degli Invaghiti in Mantua.

• **10 September** The death of Monteverdi's wife, who had been a court singer in Mantua, leaves him with two infant sons.

1608 Bataille begins publication of his six books of lute songs, *Airs de différents autheurs* (Airs by Different Composers), in Paris. The task will take him until 1615.

• Hassler publishes his sacred collection entitled *Kirchengesänge* (Church Songs) in Nuremberg.

• **28 May** Monteverdi's opera *L'Arianna* ◆ (p.49) and dramatic ballet *Il ballo delle ingrate* (The Ballet of the Ungrateful Women) are shown in Mantua, in celebration of the marriage of Francesco Gonzaga to Margherita of Savoy. All the music of the opera is now lost ◆ (p.29).

Right: A bass player in the service of the Doge of Venice ● (p.27), whose chapel was the Basilica of St Mark's, which traditionally supported a large establishment of organists, composers, singers and instrumentalists.

OTHER EVENTS
1605 Camillo Borghese elected as Pope Paul V
• Guy Fawkes is arrested for trying to blow up the Houses of Parliament in London

1606 Galileo invents the proportional compass
• Shakespeare: *Antony and Cleopatra*

1607 Founding of first English settlement on American mainland at Jamestown, Virginia
• Charles IX crowned king of Sweden

1608 Champlain founds a French settlement at Quebec
• Telescope invented by Lippershey

1609 Start of the Twelve Years' Truce between Spain and the Netherlands
• Hudson explores Hudson River and Delaware Bay

apart from one ARIA, Ariadne's lament, which Monteverdi will later arrange as a five-part MADRIGAL in his Sixth Book of Madrigals (p.29); he will also publish the solo version with CONTINUO in 1623.

• **21 July** Frescobaldi becomes organist of St Peter's, Rome.

1609 Schütz ■ (p.31) goes to Venice to study with Gabrieli.

• Schein ★ (p.30) publishes his collection of vocal and dance music *Venus Kräntzlein* (Venus's Little Garland) in Wittenberg.

• Peri brings out his collection of songs *Le varie musiche* (The Various or Different Songs) in Florence.

• Viadana publishes the third part of his *Cento concerti ecclesiastici* (p.24) in Venice.

• Tregian begins the transcription of some three hundred pieces of keyboard music, known as the *Fitzwilliam Virginal Book* (left), while he is detained in London's Fleet Prison for recusancy.

★ *'O Mistris Myne' by Byrd, from the* Fitzwilliam Virginal Book, *a collection including almost every English composer of virginal music in the early seventeenth century. The fact that it also has music by Sweelinck ★ (p.24) testifies to the extent of both his fame and of the contact between English and Dutch composers at this time.*

A ceremony taking place at the high altar in St Mark's, Venice, in the seventeenth century. In the top right-hand corner can been seen instrumentalists, who would be matched by a similar group on the opposite side. The existence of these galleries in St Mark's had a profound effect on the music composed for the Basilica, especially the use of individual groups of singers and instrumentalists placed around the building, either performing alone, antiphonally (across the building from side to side), or unanimously at the climaxes, thus filling the great spaces with echoing sound.

● *Venice: A Musical Magnet*

For generations, aspiring musicians from all over Europe had been drawn to Venice, either to learn the art of composition and then to return to their homelands, or to put their talents as performers at the service of the Republic. There were a great many opportunities in the scores of ecclesiastical institutions and among the aristocratic patrons living in the city, but the focus of talent was the Chapel of the Doge (the Head of State), St Mark's Basilica (right).

The role of St Mark's required that its services should be conducted with the sumptuous magnificence that characterized almost everything to do with the official face of the Venetian Republic. The building itself, with its several galleries where choirs could be stationed, and its shimmering mosaics covering almost every inch of walls and ceilings, cried out for great music to fill its vast spaces. Small wonder, then, that Venice drew musicians of the highest calibre and inspired some of the finest music of the age.

1610 Monteverdi completes his Vespers, which is published in Venice.

• Dowland's son brings out his *Musicall Banquet*. This includes songs in the style advocated by the Camerata ◆ (p.25), showing how rapidly the Italian influence has travelled through the rest of Europe.

1611 Byrd completes his *Psalmes, Songs and Sonnets*, published in London.

• Schütz ■ (p.31) publishes his first book of madrigals in Venice. It is dedicated to his sponsor the Landgrave of Hesse.

• Praetorius completes his collection of sacred vocal and organ pieces entitled *Hymnodia Sionia* (Hymns of Sion).

• Gesualdo, Prince of Venosa, composer of some of the most harmonically advanced music of his day, completes his *Responsories*. He is notorious for having ordered the murder of his first wife and her lover in 1590.

★ *A painting from the lid of a German spinet of 1615. The central instrument is a virginal ◆ (p.51); around it is a consort of viols ◆ (p.39) indicating the survival of an earlier tradition whereby performers preferred to combine instruments from the same family. As the orchestra developed, however, the tendency was to bring together instruments of different families, such as wind or brass, though the string quartet survives intact for chamber music.*

1612 Dowland publishes *A Pilgrimes Solace*, a mixture of sacred and secular lute songs, in London.

• Praetorius publishes his collection of 312 dances, entitled *Terpsichore* (the name of the Muse of Dance).

• *Parthenia* (below), a collection of keyboard music by Byrd, Bull and Gibbons, is published late this year in London.

• **30 July** Monteverdi is dismissed unexpectedly from his post at Mantua (p.24) by Francesco Gonzaga, successor to Duke Vincenzo.

• **12 August** Schütz ■ (p.31) is bequeathed a ring by Gabrieli, who died earlier this month.

• **28 October** Dowland is appointed musician for the lutes to James I.

1613 Sweelinck publishes the Second Book of the Marot-Bèze Psalter (p.24) in Amsterdam.

• Praetorius goes to Dresden as temporary director of the court chapel, and remains there until 1616.

• Schütz leaves Venice and is appointed court organist in Kassel.

• **19 August** Monteverdi is appointed to St Mark's, Venice ● (p.27), as director of music, having left Mantua. His annual salary is now three hundred ducats, and he is given fifty ducats' travelling expenses.

• **October** Monteverdi is robbed at gunpoint by highwaymen as he returns to Venice to take up his appointment.

1614 Sweelinck publishes the Third Book of the Marot-Bèze Psalter.
• Monteverdi publishes his Sixth Book of Madrigals in Venice (opposite).

• The Medicean Gradual, begun during the life of Palestrina on the orders of Pope Gregory XIII, is finally completed. This revision of the music for the liturgy is to remain current for almost three centuries.

OTHER EVENTS

1610 Henry IV of France allies with the German Protestant Union, and is subsequently assassinated; his son Louis XIII succeeds him, but Marie de' Médicis is regent until 1617
• Death of Caravaggio

1611 Publication of the *King James Bible*
• Charles IX of Sweden dies, Gustavus II elected king

1612 Last recorded burning of heretics in England
• Tobacco planted in Virginia

1613 Accession of the Romanov dynasty in Muscovy
• Elizabeth, daughter of James I of England, marries Frederick V, Elector Palatine
• Rubens: *The Descent from the Cross*
• Death of El Greco

1614 Napier publishes his tables of logarithms
• John Webster: *The Duchess of Malfi*

1615 Galileo first faces the Inquisition

1616 Richelieu made French minister of state for foreign affairs and war
• Deaths of Shakespeare, Cervantes and Scamozzi

The title page of Parthenia, *the first collection of printed keyboard music in England, published in 1612.*

• Caccini's collection of songs with a preface concerning musical theory entitled *Nuove musiche e nuova maniera di scriverle* (New Music and New Methods of Composing) is published in Florence.

1615 Praetorius publishes Book One of his *Syntagma musicum* (Music Collection) in Wittenberg. ★ (p.30).

• Frescobaldi ★ (p.33) brings out his TOCCATAS and RICERCARI for organ in Rome.

• Gabrieli's *Symphoniae sacrae* (Sacred Compositions), Book Two, and *Canzoni e Sonate* (Songs and Sonatas), which are mainly specified instrumental compositions, are published posthumously in Venice.

• Schein finishes a set of thirty MOTETS on Latin and German texts in the POLYCHORAL Venetian style, entitled *Cymbalum Sionium* (Sion's Cymbal).

• Schütz is sent to Dresden on loan to the Elector of Saxony.

• Bataille completes publication of his *Airs de différents autheurs* (p.26).

1616 Praetorius leaves Dresden.

• Belli publishes his *Libro dell'arie* (Book of Songs) in Venice, pronounced 'unsingable' by critics, and finishes his opera *Orfeo dolente* (Grieving Orpheus), the music of which is now lost ◆ (p.29), for the Carnival season in Florence.

• Franck completes his collection of four-part secular music, *Lilia musicalia* (Musical Lilies), which is published in Nuremberg.

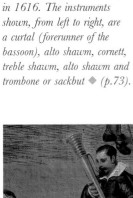

Detail from a painting of a religious procession in Antwerp on the feast day of the Rosary in 1616. The instruments shown, from left to right, are a curtal (forerunner of the bassoon), alto shawm, cornett, treble shawm, alto shawm and trombone or sackbut ◆ (p.73).

Below: The title page from Monteverdi's Sixth Book of Madrigals, first published in 1614. This edition, also published in Venice, dates from 1620, proving the success of the work. Most of the madrigals are in five parts, with one piece in seven parts. The provision of a thorough bass indicates that they may be accompanied by a keyboard and other instruments.

◆ *Music Printing in Italy*

With so much music being written, sung and played in Italy, it is not surprising that certain cities, and Venice in particular, supported a thriving music-printing industry, which was only overtaken by Paris and Amsterdam as the century drew to a close. Publication of a composer's works not only had the very practical purpose of providing performers with printed scores rather than manuscripts to decipher, but it also established his status and gave proof to the world at large of his graduation into the ranks of the recognized masters of the profession. A dedication to a noble or distinguished patron could be an expression of gratitude for his or her interest and protection, but it also helped to confer status on the composer by association, especially if the composer was able to describe himself as 'Court Composer', 'Director of Music', or some such title.

There was an unfortunate exception to music printing: the scores of operas tended to be altered frequently, sometimes for each performance, depending on the singers and instrumental forces available. Conditions varied enormously from place to place, and the composer took his score with him, in its constantly modified state. Moreover, opera houses and theatres generally were notoriously prone to fires, and in this way many early opera scores have perished.

1617-23
The Early German Baroque

The close proximity of southern Germany to Venice encourages both commercial and cultural traffic across the Alps. Hassler is the first German composer of importance to study in Italy, but it is primarily to Schütz, Schein and Scheidt that German music owes its excellence. Indeed, Schütz is often referred to as the father of German music.

★ *A plate from Praetorius's* Syntagma musicum *(right) shows the blowing of organ bellows on a large scale. The illustrated supplement to Book Two,* Teatrum instrumentorum, *provides useful, if sometimes fanciful, details about German practice and instruments of the day.*

1617 Marini, a violinist at St Mark's, Venice ◆ (p.27), publishes *Affetti musicali* (Musical Affections or Moods) – pieces for violin and CONTINUO.

• Schein (below) publishes his set of twenty, five-part instrumental variation SUITES entitled *Il banchetto musicale* (The Musical Banquet).

• **12 February** Schütz ■ (p.31) becomes director of the Court Chapel in Dresden.

• **29 December** Bull, after having left England in 1613 for the Low Countries, is appointed organist of Antwerp Cathedral.

1618 Part One of Schein's collection entitled *Opella nova* (New Little Works) is published in Leipzig. Schein uses BASSO CONTINUO for the first time in these thirty sacred MOTETS, which are for three to five voices, based on Lutheran chorales, and clearly inspired by Viadana. In bringing the Italian influence to German music, Schein is pioneering a new form.

• Praetorius publishes Book Two of *Syntagma musicum* (p.29).

★ *A portrait of Schein (below), painted in 1620, when he was thirty-four, four years after he had taken up his appointment as cantor in Leipzig. Although he never left Saxony, Schein assimilated Italian influences through studying the works of masters such as the Gabrielis, Monteverdi and Viadana.*

1619 Praetorius publishes Book Three of *Syntagma musicum* and *Polyhymnia caduceatrix et panegyrica* (Polyhymnia, Muse of the Art of Mime, as Herald and Offering Praise), a collection of magnificent POLYCHORAL works.

• Sweelinck composes his five-part vocal pieces with basso continuo – *Cantiones sacrae* (Sacred Songs). The inclusion of certain texts would seem to imply that towards the end of his life he turns to Catholicism.

• Monteverdi publishes his Seventh Book of Madrigals.

• Schütz ■ (p.31) publishes the first collection of his *Psalms of David* in Dresden.

• Landi's opera *La morte d'Orfeo* (The Death of Orpheus, ◆ p.49) is possibly the first opera given in Rome.

• Anerio publishes his *Teatro armonico spirituali di madrigali* (Musical and Spiritual Theatre of Madrigals) in Rome. This collection of ninety-four MADRIGALS is an important step in the development of ORATORIO in the vernacular.

• The *Fitzwilliam Virginal Book* is completed (p.27).

1620 Praetorius publishes his *Teatrum instrumentorum* (Theatre of Instruments), a supplement to Book Two of *Syntagma musicum* (above right).

• Coelho publishes the earliest surviving collection of printed Portuguese keyboard music, *Flores de Musica* (Flowers of Music), in Lisbon.

• Filippo Vitali's *L'Aretusa* is performed in Rome, one of the earliest performances of opera in that city.

OTHER EVENTS
1617 Calvin's collected works published in Geneva posthumously

1618 Outbreak of the Thirty Years' War
• Electorate of Brandenburg acquires Prussia

1619 Marie de' Médicis attempts to overthrow Louis XIII of France but is defeated
• First black slaves arrive in North America

1620 Pilgrim Fathers leave Plymouth for North America in *Mayflower*, land at Cape Cod, found New Plymouth

1621 Death of Philip III of Spain, accession of Philip IV
• End of the Twelve Years' Truce between Holland and Spain – war resumed

1622 Richelieu is created a Cardinal

1623 Shakespeare's First Folio published
• Raphael cartoons bought by Prince Charles of England

• **17 November** Grandi is made deputy director of St Mark's, Venice ● (p.27), a post he will hold until 1627.

1621 Schein publishes the first part of his *Musica boscareccia* (Woodland or Rustic Music), fifty settings of his own poems for voices or instruments, in Leipzig. Part Two will follow in 1626, and Part Three in 1628.

• Sweelinck publishes Book Four of the Marot-Bèze Psalter (p.24).

• Franck's vocal collection *Newes Teutsches Musicalisches Fröliches Convivium* (New German Musical Happy Gathering), is published in Coburg.

'In forty-four days the work was begun and ended, the music written and the parts distributed and learned, the performers coached and rehearsed and the work finally performed.'
The preface to the libretto of Vitali's *L'Aretusa.*

• Scheidt publishes his collection of SUITES entitled *Paduana, Galliarda, Couranta, Alemande, Intrada, Canzonetto* (Pavan, Galliard, Courante, Allemand, Intrada, Little Canzonet) in Hamburg.

• **15 February** Death of Praetorius in Wolfenbüttel.

• **16 October** Death of Sweelinck in Amsterdam.

1622 Widmann publishes his *Musicalischer Studentenmuth* (Musical Student Spirit), a collection of songs, in Nuremberg.

• Scheidt completes the first part of his sacred choral collection *Concertus sacrorum* (Sacred Harmony), published in Hamburg.

1623 Schütz completes his oratorio *The Resurrection Story* ■ (below).

• Schein publishes his *Fontana d'Israel* or *Israelis Brünnlein* (Israel's Fountain), twenty-six settings of biblical texts in the manner of the Italian madrigal.

• Titelouze publishes his *Hymnes de l'Eglise* (Church Hymns) in Paris.

• Carissimi ■ (p.33) becomes a singer at the cathedral in Tivoli, where he is later to be appointed organist.

• **4 July** Death of Byrd at Stondon Massey in Essex.

A portrait of Schütz at the age of forty-two, when he was director of music to the Elector of Saxony, and shortly before he paid his second visit to Italy to experience at first hand the new developments in Monteverdi's music, though there is no record of his having taken lessons from the great Venetian composer.

■ *Schütz in Dresden*

The Thirty Years' War, which raged across Europe from 1618 to 1648, took a huge toll on German cities and human life. Initially, however, Dresden was little touched by the war, and Schütz was able to settle into his recently acquired post of director of the Court Chapel, introducing some of his own polychoral music in the Venetian manner.

Schütz's innovative *Resurrection Story* of 1623, for Vespers on Easter Day, was his first narrative work. Drawing on the text used by Scandello fifty years before in Dresden, he also followed tradition by giving the role of the Evangelist to a tenor, but he introduced the accompaniment of four viole da gamba ◆ (p.39), and, for the words of Christ, Mary Magdalene and the other characters an accompaniment of organ basso continuo.

In 1625 Schütz's wife died, and it seems that his long life (he lived to be eighty-seven) took a sad direction; his parents, his two daughters and his beloved only brother all predeceased him. Schütz's personal tragedy, and that of the German people, is reflected in the music of these later years. Although he wrote the first German opera, *Dafne* ◆ (p.49), in 1627 (p.32), his output was mainly religious, and we see the composer standing physically and figuratively apart, keeping alive the flame of musical and intellectual endeavour in a darkened world.

Schütz directing the chapel choir at Dresden. The building is shown after its restoration in 1662, when Schütz had effectively ceased being in charge of the music, but the composer continued to write for the chapel virtually to the end of his life.

1624-29
Carissimi and the Oratorio

During the papacy of Urban VIII, opera is established in Rome; there is also considerable expansion in the work of the oratories, founded by St Philip Neri in the previous century, in which music plays a large part. With the arrival of Carissimi in Rome, oratorio is developed even further, and virtually becomes the sacred counterpart of opera, with music just as dramatic.

The music beneath this portrait of Scheidt is a four-part canon to the closing words of the Te Deum: 'In thee, Lord, have I trusted: let me never be confounded.'

1624 Berti, a tenor at St Mark's, Venice ● (p.27), publishes the first part of his vocal collection, *Cantade et Arie* (Songs and Arias), in Venice. The second part will follow in 1627.

• Schein publishes his collection of secular vocal music, *Diletti pastorali* (Pastoral Delights).

• Monteverdi composes the dramatic dialogue *Il combattimento di Tancredi e Clorinda* (The Fight between Tancred and Clorinda) which will be published in 1638 as part of his Eighth Book of Madrigals (p.36). For the first time Monteverdi uses the CONCITATO STYLE, with its pronounced rhythms and theatrical gestures.

• Scheidt (left) publishes his *Tabulatura nova* (New Tabulature) for organ in Hamburg. This three-volume compendium of music for the Lutheran services contains song and dance arrangements, sets of VARIATIONS, FANTASIAS, TOCCATAS, FUGUES and liturgical items that are often based on PLAINSONG.

• **September** Berti is made second organist at St Mark's ● (p.27).

1625 Francesca Caccini completes her opera-ballet *La liberazione di Ruggiero* (The Liberation of Ruggiero) for the reception of the future Wladyslaw IV of Poland at the Medici Villa at Poggio Imperiale, near Florence. It becomes possibly the first wholly Italian opera to be heard outside Italy when it is performed in Warsaw in 1682.

• Schütz ■ (p.31) publishes his collection of Italianate Latin MOTETS entitled *Cantiones sacrae* (Sacred Songs) in Freiburg.

1626 Titelouze publishes his organ *Versets* for the Magnificat. These solo pieces, which have the feeling of EXTEMPORIZED meditations, are composed with interweaving parts over the eight plainsong tones which act as a foundation, and are to be played at appropriate places in the liturgy.

• Schein publishes Part Two of his *Opella nova* (p.30), a pioneering work in German music. There are twenty-seven motets to German texts, five to Latin, and only about a third based on CHORALES. He uses contrasting solo vocal and choral passages, BASSO CONTINUO, and OBBLIGATO instruments.

1627 Schütz composes his opera *Dafne* ■ (p.31), ◆ (p.49), the first German opera, for the wedding of a daughter of the Elector of Saxony at Torgau. The music has since been lost.

• Schein completes the *Leipziger Cantional* (Leipzig Songbook), a collection of more than two hundred chorales.

• Monteverdi composes his full-length comic opera *La finta pazza Licori* (The Feigned Madness of Licoris) for Mantua, but the work is never performed and the music is now lost.

OTHER EVENTS
1624 Cardinal Richelieu assumes power in France
• Outbreak of war between England and Spain
• Frans Hals: *The Laughing Cavalier*

1625 Death of James I of England; accession of Charles I
• Death of Maurice of Nassau, accession of Frederick Henry in the Netherlands
• Defeat of French Huguenots under Soubise, who flees to England

1626 Peace of La Rochelle temporarily ends Huguenot revolt in France
• Dutch colony of New Amsterdam founded
• Manhattan Island purchased by Peter Minuit

1627 Death of Vincenzo II, Duke of Mantua; Charles I of England purchases the Duke's art collection
• New outbreak of Huguenot revolt, Cardinal Richelieu besieges La Rochelle

1628 Dutch occupy Java and the Moluccas
• Capture of La Rochelle, end of Huguenot power in France
• Taj Mahal begun

1629 Bernini appointed architect of St Peter's, Rome

- Frescobaldi publishes his second book of toccatas in Rome (p.29).

1628 Carissimi is director of music at the cathedral in Assisi.

- Gagliano and Peri's opera *La Flora* is performed in Florence in honour of the wedding of Duke Odoardo Farnese and Margherita de' Medici.

- Schütz ■ (p.31) pays his second visit to Venice, where he studies the music of Monteverdi, and publishes his second set of the *Psalms of David* (p.30) in Freiberg.

- **22 February** Scheidt is appointed director of music at the Marienkirche, Halle (a post created specially for him), but is dismissed two years later following a dispute with the rector of the grammar school over the availability of the choristers for singing.

- **March** Bull dies in Antwerp aged about sixty-six.

1629 Schütz publishes the first book of his *Symphoniae sacrae* (Sacred Symphonies) in Venice.

- Marini publishes his SONATAS for instruments in Venice.

- Carissimi ■ (below) is appointed director of music at the Jesuit German College in Rome.

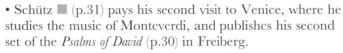

★ Frescobaldi aged thirty-six. Born in Ferrara, Frescobaldi was first appointed organist at St Peter's, Rome, in 1608. He subsequently held posts in Mantua and Florence, but returned to St Peter's for the last decade of his life, until his death in 1643.

Below: The Church of Santa Maria in Vallicella in Rome, where Cavalieri's La rappresentatione di anima e di corpo *(p.24) was first performed, marking a crucial stage in the development of oratorio. Next to the church is the Oratory of St Philip Neri, built in the name of the founder of the Oratorian Order, who advocated beautiful music to encourage worship.*

■ *Carissimi and Oratorio*

Before he went to Rome Carissimi had held posts in Tivoli and Assisi, so it is not surprising that he pursued a career in church music. He composed several CANTATAS, but is chiefly remembered today for his ORATORIOS, which represent only part of his extant output, since a good deal was regrettably destroyed in a fire.

Most of Carissimi's oratorios were written for the Oratorio del Crocifisso in Rome, which may explain why he composed to Latin texts rather than Italian. In fact, of the fifteen or so oratorios by Carissimi that we know of, only two are in Italian, and this at a time when the vernacular was increasingly preferred for oratorio. The congregation at the Oratorio del Crocifisso had a reputation for being more sophisticated, however, and preferred to listen to motets set to Latin texts rather than take part in the more popular Italian laudi or spiritual songs favoured elsewhere.

One consequence of Carissimi's preference for Latin texts was that his influence was much less felt in his homeland, Italy, than abroad; his immediate successors included his pupils

Bernhard in Germany and Charpentier in France. Nevertheless, the oratorio was by now so well established that its popularity gathered momentum and it quickly began to put down roots almost all over Europe, merging with local influences, diversifying and so taking on its own development.

1630-36
On Distant Shores

In Italy musical life continues to flourish, but in Germany there seems no end to the devastation and dislocation. Schütz eventually flees Dresden for a time and makes his way to Copenhagen. In England the influence of Italy is slow to arrive, but at the Stuart court there is a tradition for elaborate masques that develops into a new degree of elegance and splendour, if not musical excellence.

Bernini's design for Landi's opera Il Sant'Alessio *(St Alexis), performed in Rome in 1632 in the theatre built specially for opera by the Barberini family. The pope, Urban VIII, was a Barberini, two of his nephews were cardinals, and all were patrons of music.*

1630 Monteverdi composes his opera *Proserpina rapita* (The Abduction of Proserpine), of which only a TRIO survives, to celebrate the wedding of Giustiniana Mocenigo, daughter of a Venetian senator, and the Roman commentator Lorenzo Giustiniani.

• Frescobaldi's collection of accompanied songs, *Arie musicale*, is published in two volumes, in Florence.

• **7 January** Cavalli marries Maria Sosomeno, a wealthy widow some years his senior.

• **19 November** Death of Schein from plague. Schütz ■ (p.31) composes the motet *Ie gewisslich wahr* (Ever Certainly True) in memory of his compatriot and friend.

1631 9 January Ben Jonson and Inigo Jones devise the English court MASQUE *Love's Triumph through Callipolis* ◆ (p.35).

• **22 February** Jonson and Jones produce the court masque *Chloridia* ◆ (p.35), their last collaborative work.

1632 Monteverdi takes holy orders. Also this year his second book of *Scherzi musicali* (p.26) is published in Venice.

• **21 February** Landi's opera *Il Sant'Alessio* (St Alexis) is given in Rome to celebrate the opening, in the Palazzo Barberini, of the first Roman opera house (above). This is the first opera to be based on both an historical subject and the life of a saint.

• **28 November** Birth of Lully ■ (p.53) in Florence.

1633 2 February First performance of Rossi's opera *Erminia sul Giordano* (Herminia on the Jordan, right), based on Tasso's epic romance, in the Palazzo Barberini, Rome.

• **12 August** Peri dies in Florence.

• **September** After the closure of the Dresden Court Chapel, Schütz ■ (p.31) goes to Copenhagen where he works as director of music at court until 1635.

Right: *The title page of Michelangelo Rossi's opera* Erminia sul Giordano, *dating from 1637, and dedicated to the Barberini family in whose palace the opera had been presented four years earlier, with Rossi playing the role of Apollo.*

OTHER EVENTS

1630 Treaty of Madrid ends Anglo-Spanish war
• Puritans establish Boston
• Gustavus Adolphus of Sweden invades Germany

1631 German Protestant princes ally with Gustavus Adolphus, who occupies Würzburg and Mainz

1632 Gustavus Adolphus is killed at Lützen, Queen Christina succeeds him
• Rembrandt: *The Anatomy Lesson*

1633 Outbreak of plague in Bavaria leads to passion play vow in Oberammergau

1634 Swedish army defeated at Nördlingen

1635 Peace of Prague signed uniting the House of Habsburg against France and Sweden
• Foundation of Académie Française

1636 Founding of Harvard College

1634 Revival of Rossi's *Erminia sul Giordano* and Landi's *Il Sant'Alessio* in Rome (opposite) with scenery designed by Bernini.

• **29 September** Lawes composes the music for the masque *Comus* ◆ (below) to a text by Milton, for performance at Ludlow Castle, Shropshire.

1635 Albert, a cousin and pupil of Schütz ■ (p.31), as well as of Schein ★ (p.30), composes his opera *Cleomedes* for Königsberg. Only two ARIAS have survived.

• Schütz returns to Dresden (p.34).

• Frescobaldi's volume of sacred music, *Fiori musicali* (Musical Flowers), is published in Venice. This somewhat heterogeneous collection embraces VERSETS for organ for the Kyrie and Christe of the Mass, CANZONI to be played after the Epistle, RICERCARI after the Credo, and TOCCATAS after the Elevation. There are also some four-part pieces in the volume. Two of the ricercari are prefaced by toccatas, an arrangement which anticipates the later PRELUDE AND FUGUE form perfected by Bach.

1636 Marin Mersenne begins his illustrated treatise *Harmonie universelle* (Universal Harmony, right), which gives full descriptions of all contemporary musical instruments.

• Schütz composes his *Musikalische Exequien* (Musical Requiem), the first so-called German Requiem, for the funeral of his friend Prince Heinrich of Gera. He also publishes Book One of his *Kleine geistliche Concerten* (Little Sacred Concertos) for one to five voices with organ and string BASSO CONTINUO, in Leipzig.

'In Queen Elizabeth's time, gravity and state were kept up. In King James's time things were pretty well. But in King Charles's time there has been nothing but trenchmore and the cushion dance, Omnium gatherum, tolly polly, hoyte come toyte.'

John Selden, *Table Talk*, 1634-54

A plate from Mersenne's Harmonie universelle showing two plucked instruments: a lute and a theorbo, with details of the length and thickness of the strings. Mersenne was a pioneer of acoustics, and his work includes descriptions of the sounds and functions of the various instruments.

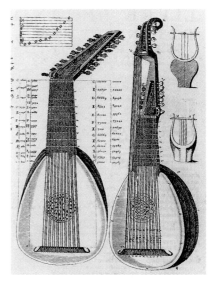

Costume design by Inigo Jones for one of the twelve masquers, led by the queen herself, in The Masque of Blackness. *The spectacles included an artificial sea with tritons and mermaids, presided over by the Moon seated on a silver throne in the clouds.*

◆ *The Stuart Court Masque*

In England in 1629 Charles I decided to rule without Parliament, for the period known as the Eleven Years' Tyranny. As if to underline the significance of the Divine Right of Kings, the year 1631 opened with two masques in which first the king and then the queen were prominent. In Love's Triumph through Callipolis *(p.34)* the king appeared as Heroic Love attended by his lords as other aspects of exemplary love. Platonic ideals such as love and virtue were made expressions of autocratic power, leaving no hint of uncertainty, no room for opposition.

The second masque, Chloridia *(p.34)*, took up the same story, this time making the queen a point of focus as Chloris enshrined in a garden in full bloom. The climax of the work was a symbolic renaissance of the arts and a celebration of the royal couple and their perfect union. It is interesting to note that the production of Chloridia saw the first appearance of female professional singers on the English stage.

Unfortunately, Chloridia marked the end of the collaboration between Jonson and Jones. The latter objected, as the designer, to his name appearing underneath that of Jonson on the title page. Although both men were known to nurse large egos (the papal agent described Jones as a 'very vain and very boastful man'), the incident cost Jonson dearly as it resulted in his losing royal patronage.

1637-42
The Triumph of Italian Opera

With the opening of the first public opera house in Venice in 1637, an art form that began as the result of intellectual curiosity and aristocratic desire for entertainment is suddenly available to all. It is no accident that this should happen in Venice, where hardly a day passes without some kind of ceremony or celebration.

1637 Virgilio Mazzocchi and Marazzoli write their opera *Fiametta* or *Il Falcone* (The Falcon), which is revived two years later as *Chi soffre speri* (He who Suffers has Hope).

• **1 January** Froberger, appointed to the Imperial Chapel in Vienna, goes to Rome to study with Frescobaldi (right) until 1641.

• **6 May** The Teatro San Cassiano, the first public opera house in Venice, opens with Manelli and Ferrari's *L'Andromeda*. By 1651 there will be six opera houses in the city.

• **August** Schütz ■ (p.31) returns to Copenhagen where he remains until 1638.

1638 Monteverdi publishes his Eighth Book of Madrigals, entitled *Madrigali guerrieri et amorosi* (Madrigals of War and Love).

• Schütz's pupil Kittel publishes a collection of songs entitled *Arien und Cantaten* (Songs and Cantatas) in Dresden, and so introduces the use of the term CANTATA into Germany.

• Albert begins publication of his collection of songs, *Arien*, in eight parts, which will continue until 1650.

• Domenico Mazzocchi publishes his book of madrigals for five voices in Rome.

'Arianna, the most praised of dramatic compositions in Italian theatres, returns to the stage in Venice, the work of Signor Claudio Monteverdi, most celebrated Apollo of the century and the greatest intelligence in the heaven of harmony.'
From the dedication of the reprint of the libretto of *Arianna* for its Venetian revival in 1640.

1639 Schütz publishes the second book of his *Kleine geistliche Concerten* (Little Sacred Concertos) (p.35) in Dresden.

• Vittori's opera *La Galatea* is given in Rome.

• Monteverdi's lost opera *Adone* is given at the Teatro San Cassiano, Venice.

• **23 January** Cavalli becomes second organist at St Mark's, Venice ● (p.27).

• **24 January** Cavalli's first opera *Le nozze di Teti e Peleo* (The Marriage of Thetis and Peleus) is performed at the Teatro San Cassiano in Venice.

• **27 February** Virgilio Mazzocchi and Marazzoli complete the first comic opera with their *Chi soffre speri*, which has its first performance at the Barberini Theatre in Rome. Milton and Cardinal Mazarin are in the audience.

1640 The Bay Psalm Book is printed in Cambridge, Massachusetts.

• The Teatro San Moisè in Venice opens for opera performances with a revival of Monteverdi's *L'Arianna* (p.26).

• Luigi Rossi publishes his collection *Arie spirituali* (Spiritual Songs).

A caricature by Bernini, dating from 1640–45, thought to be of Frescobaldi, ★ (p.33), in the last years of his life. Frescobaldi was the founder of a new school of organ playing, drawing together elements from Ferrara, Naples and Venice, but he also composed masses, motets and secular music.

Opposite: *Bernardo Strozzi's portrait of Monteverdi painted around 1640, near the end of the composer's life. It is a face marked with weariness and even suffering, but also shows patience and dignity, integrity and intelligence.*

A view of Lübeck in the mid-seventeenth century. The historic city boasted a rich musical tradition, and was especially proud of its organists at the Marienkirche: only two men held the post for a period of more than sixty years – Tunder from 1641 until his death in 1667, and Buxtehude from 1668 until the early years of the next century.

The title page of Monteverdi's Selva morale e spirituale, *dedicated to Eleonora Gonzaga, wife of Emperor Ferdinand II. Despite his dismissal from the court of Mantua (p.28), and his appointment to a much more prestigious post in Venice, Monteverdi never entirely escaped from the influence of the Gonzaga family.*

• Monteverdi completes his opera *Il ritorno d'Ulisse in patria* (Ulysses's Homecoming, ◆ p.49) for the Teatro Santi Giovanni e Paolo, Venice.

1641 Cavalli's opera *La Didone* (Dido) is given at the Teatro San Cassiano, Venice.

• Sacrati composes his opera *La finta pazza* (The Feigned Madwoman) for the opening of the Teatro Novissimo in Venice.

• Monteverdi completes his opera *Le nozze d'Enea con Lavinia* (The Marriage of Aeneas and Lavinia), now lost ◆ (p.29), for the Teatro Santi Giovanni e Paolo, Venice, and publishes his collection of religious music entitled *Selva morale e spirituale* (Moral and Spiritual Collection).

• **29 September** Tunder is appointed organist of the Marienkirche in Lübeck (above), where he founds the famous *Abendmusiken* (Evening Music), at first only as organ recitals, but subsequently they become concerts with CANTATAS for solo voices and instruments.

1642 Monteverdi composes *L'incoronazione di Poppea* (The Coronation of Poppea, ◆ p.49) for the Teatro Santi Giovanni e Paolo, Venice.

• Hammerschmidt, a follower of Schütz ■ (p.31), publishes the first book of his secular vocal *Oden* (Odes) in Freiburg.

• **22 February** Luigi Rossi's opera *Il palazzo incantato d'Atlante* (The Enchanted Palace of Atlas) is produced at the Barberini Theatre in Rome.

• **May** Schütz ■ (p.31) is once more in Copenhagen as director of music at court.

OTHER EVENTS

1637 Death of Ferdinand II; Ferdinand III succeeds him as Holy Roman Emperor
• Death of Ben Jonson

1638 Elector of Brandenburg moves his capital to Königsberg

1639 Poussin: *The Gathering of the Manna*
• Mazarin enters Richelieu's service

1640 Portugal gains independence from Spain
• Elector George William of Brandenburg dies; Frederick William succeeds him

1641 Dutch take Malacca and establish supremacy in East Indies
• Descartes: *Meditationes de Prima Philosophis*
• Death of Van Dyck

1642 Start of English Civil War. All theatres in England closed by the Puritans
• Death of Richelieu; Cardinal Mazarin becomes first minister of France
• Rembrandt: *The Night Watch*
• Death of Galileo

◆ *Viols to Violins*

A cursory glance at the evolution of stringed instruments in the first half of the seventeenth century seems to give the impression that the softer sounding viol family slowly gave way to the newer, more dynamic, violin family. Although in general terms this was true, in reality the process was not as straightforward.

Firstly, viols and violins existed side by side, certainly from the middle of the sixteenth century, and famous Italian instrument makers such as Gasparo da Salò of Brescia and Andrea Amati of Cremona were producing both instruments. In theory therefore a composer was able to choose either, according to his preference. Secondly, the idea that a composer might have certain sonorities in mind when writing a work is one that only gradually evolved from the end of the Renaissance period onwards.

By the middle of the sixteenth century composers were beginning to write for specific combinations of instruments, their directions becoming increasingly comprehensive until by the end of the century we find music that can only be played on the instruments for which it is written. In the case of the string family the determining factor was still usually the purpose for which the music was written – music for masques ◆ (p.35), operas and dancing was normally assigned to the more tonally and rhythmically dynamic violins; the more intimate consort music, often employing strings and voices together, to the viols. In other words, viols were used for domestic (and this often implies amateur) music-making, of the sort later known as chamber music, ★ (p.28), whereas violins were used for orchestral groups, dance music and, by and large, what tended to be the more professional aspects of instrumental music.

A plate from Athanasius Kircher's Musurgia universalis *(p.42), published in Rome in 1650, showing several possible ways of stringing instruments, as well as the marked difference between the shape of the violin (left) and the viol (centre).*

Left: *Brueghel's visual allegory of the sense of hearing depicts bowed instruments. On the music stand to the right is music by the Englishman Peter Philips, who became court organist in Brussels in 1597.*

1643-48
France and the Italian Influence

Cultural and dynastic links between France and Italy are much strengthened when an Italian protégé of Cardinal Richelieu, Giulio Mazarini, enters the service of the French Crown, becomes a naturalized Frenchman in 1639 and a cardinal in 1642. Following the death of Richelieu and Louis XIII, Mazarin becomes head of the king's council and effectively the most powerful man in France.

The interior of St Peter's in Rome reflects the magnificence of Urban VIII, the Barberini pope, who died in 1644. Bernini's great canopy over the high altar was made from bronze taken from the Pantheon, leading to the comment that the Barberini had done what the barbarians had failed to do. Nevertheless, St Peter's set an ideal for liturgical music for the whole of Christendom.

1643 Cavalli's opera *L'Egisto* (Aegisthus) is performed at the Teatro San Cassiano, Venice.

• Hammerschmidt publishes his second set of *Oden* (Odes) in Freiburg (p.38).

• **1 March** Frescobaldi dies in Rome. Rival parishes San Lorenzo and Santi Apostoli vie to receive his body. The latter church wins.

• **29 November** Death of Monteverdi, aged seventy-six, in Venice, where he is buried in the Church of the Frari.

1644 The Barberini Pope Urban VIII dies and his family, exiled from Rome, flee to Paris. As a result the Barberini Theatre (p.34) closes.

• Cavalli composes his *Messa concertata* (Mass in the Extended Concertato Style, p.45).

• Rovetta succeeds Monteverdi as director of music at St Mark's, Venice ● (p.27).

1645 Schütz ■ (p.31) composes his oratorio *The Seven Last Words*.

• **14 December** Sacrati's *La finta pazza* (p.38) is given in Paris at the request of Mazarin ● (p.41).

1646 Lully ■ (p.53) is brought to Paris by the Chevalier de Guise and enters the service of the king's cousin, Anne Marie Louise d'Orléans.

• **February** Cavalli's *L'Egisto* is given at the Palais-Royal, Paris ● (p.41).

• **7 October** Benevoli becomes director of music at the Cappella Giulia of St Peter's, Rome.

1647 Crüger, CANTOR at the Nicolaikirche in Berlin, completes his book of CHORALES, *Praxis pietatis melica* (The Lyric Practice of Piety).

• Schütz ■ (p.31) completes his second volume of *Symphoniae sacrae* (p.33) and presents a manuscript of the work to the Crown Prince of Denmark.

• Luigi Rossi's newly commissioned opera *L'Orfeo* (Orpheus, ◆ p.49) is given in Paris at the Palais-Royal ● (p.41).

1648 Schütz completes his set of twenty-nine MOTETS in five, six and seven parts entitled *Geistliche Chor-Musik* (Sacred Choral Music). Some of the motets are in the old German choral style, and some in the more modern Italian style for solo voice and instruments.

OTHER EVENTS
1643 Death of Louis XIII and accession of his five-year-old son Louis XIV
• Molière founds Illustre Théâtre in Paris

1644 Chinese Ming dynasty falls, Mandarins established
• Milton: *Areopagitica* for the freedom of the press
• Bernini: *The Ecstasy of St Theresa*

1645 Turkish Venetian War
• Founding of the University of Palermo

1646
• Parliamentarians win first part of English Civil War

1647 Frederick Henry of Orange dies; William II of Orange succeeds him

1648 Outbreak of the Fronde in France
• Treaty of Münster finally gives independence to the Netherlands
• Treaty of Westphalia brings to an end the Thirty Years' War

A portrait of Cardinal Mazarin seated in his palace, with a view of his art gallery behind him, indicating to what extent this cultured prelate fostered the arts in France.

● *The Birth of French Opera*

The history of the introduction of opera into France consists of attempts by Cardinal Mazarin to impose his own artistic vision on his adopted country. From the outset he had to embrace an existing tradition of court ballets – a synthesis of music, poetry, acting, costumes and scenery, and only partially choreography. The cardinal failed to appreciate fully what a difficult task he had set himself when, in 1645, Sacrati's *La finta pazza* (p.40) was given in Paris. Its success on this occasion was owed more to the scenic effects produced by Giacomo Torelli than to Sacrati's music. By the time Cavalli's *L'Egisto* (p.40) was given the following year at the Palais-Royal, the audience was patently bored to tears. Nonetheless, Mazarin commissioned yet another Italian opera, Rossi's *L'Orfeo* (p.40), with Torelli providing the sets and stage effects. The composer and a company of Italian singers were brought to Paris, including two CASTRATI, Marc-Antonio Pasqualini and Panfilo Miccinello. The opera's reception was varied, with the mixture of tragedy and comedy, the choreography, and the stage machinery all appealing to the audience, the orchestral music considered acceptable, but the RECITATIVES, the most Italian feature, disliked. Also, the use of castrati offended French ideas of propriety, and the fashion never caught on.

'6 February:
In the evening, came
Signor Alessandro, one of the
Cardinal Mazarine's musicians…
to visit my wife, and sung before
divers persons of quality in my chamber.
1 March: I went to see the masquerados,
which was very fantastic; but nothing
so quiet and solemn as I found
it at Venice.'
John Evelyn, *Diary*,
1650

Over the next one hundred and fifty years a native French opera was forged in the face of the enormously popular Italian opera, and France stood aloof from current fashion elsewhere in Europe. Cardinal Mazarin cannot take the full responsibility for this rejection of Italian opera, since there was a firmly established tradition of court entertainment that was well able to absorb Italian influences without being overwhelmed by them, and there was the national pride in the French language which meant that it was unlikely to take second place to Italian as the language of song. Ironically, it was to be another Italian who became a naturalized Frenchman, namely Lully, who devised a form of opera that was acceptable to the French, and who indeed convinced them that they were as capable as the Italians of producing singers and operas.

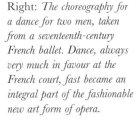

Right: The choreography for a dance for two men, taken from a seventeenth-century French ballet. Dance, always very much in favour at the French court, fast became an integral part of the fashionable new art form of opera.

1649-52
Music for All Occasions

The ending of the Thirty Years' War in 1648 sees Germany gradually resuming musical life, though it is Italy that continues to lead the way. Venice reigns supreme, not only in opera, but also in church music. Indeed music becomes a necessary accompaniment to almost all social activities.

Schütz ■ (p.31), painted by Christoph Spetner about 1650, when the composer, disgusted with the state of music at the court in Dresden, addressed a letter to his employer to tell him so.

1649 Cesti's first opera, *Orontea*, is given at the Teatro Santi Apostoli in Venice, and in Lucca the following year, with the composer appearing in one of the roles ◆ (p.43). Since Cesti is a Franciscan friar, certain people are offended.

• Luigi Rossi composes his CANTATA *La Fortuna* (Fortune), with its reference to the execution of Charles I of England on 30 January this year.

• Hammerschmidt publishes the third book of his *Oden* (Odes, p.38) in Leipzig.

• **5 January** Cavalli's opera *Il Giasone* (Jason) is given at the Teatro San Cassiano, Venice.

1650 First performance of Carissimi's ■ (p.33) ORATORIO *Jephte* (Jephthah) in Rome, though composed prior to this.

• Scheidt completes his set of one hundred CHORALES for organ known as the *Görlitzer Tabulatur-Buch* (The Görlitz Book of Keyboard Music).

• Kircher publishes his treatise on music, *Musurgia universalis*, in Rome (below).

• Schütz (left), ■ (p.31), publishes the third set of his *Symphoniae sacrae* (p.33) in Dresden.

• **20 February** Cavalli's opera *L'Orimonte* is performed for the first time at the Teatro San Cassiano, Venice.

1651 Monteverdi's Ninth Book of Madrigals is published eight years after his death.

• Playford publishes his collections entitled *The English Dancing Master*, with descriptions of country dances, and *A Musicall Banquet*, containing pieces for viols ◆ (p.39) and ROUNDS and CATCHES for voices, in London.

• Cavalli's new opera *La Calisto* is given late this year or early next year at the Teatro Sant'Apollinare, Venice.

1652 Cavalli's opera *Eritrea* is first performed at the Teatro Sant'Apollinare in Venice.

• **29 September:** A magnificent concert is given in Paris at the Convent of the Jacobins, in honour of Froberger (p.36) who is visiting the city. Although such concerts later become common, it is unusual at this time for a musician to be held in such high regard by his contemporaries.

OTHER EVENTS

1649 Charles I executed; England declared a Commonwealth
• Descartes: *Traité des passions de l'âme*

1650 Tea drunk for the first time in England
• Death of Descartes

1651 First Navigation Act gives monopoly to English shipping and starts Anglo-Dutch War
• Dutch found Cape Town at Cape of Good Hope

1652 Von Guericke invents the air pump
• Death of Inigo Jones

A design for a mechanical organ, to be operated by water power, from Kircher's Musurgia universalis, *published in Rome in 1650.*

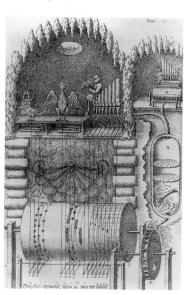

◆ *Music in Church and at Court*

The relationship between sacred and secular music had always been an uneasy one, especially for the church authorities who were constantly aware of the tendency for secular music to invade the realm of the sacred. Indeed, there were many clerics who would have been happy to have had no church music at all. The spirit of the Reformation by no means deplored the use of music in church ceremonies, and Luther for one encouraged it and felt that it was an essential part of devotion. Such an approach influenced the attitude of the Catholic Church during the Counter-Reformation, for it did not abolish music entirely, though it did place considerable restrictions on its use and application. As the development of the Oratorian movement shows, however, there were musical energies which the Catholic Church could not ignore, and indeed was able to channel to its advantage.

> *'Venice…*
> *this city which in every aspect exceeds the limits of the marvellous.'*
> From *Il cannocchiale* (The Telescope), 1641, on the opera *La finta pazza.*

By the middle of the seventeenth century the distinction between the nature and character of sacred and secular music had again become somewhat vague, though perhaps less so in its application. In Rome, for example, the divide between opera and oratorio was musically a fine one, though subject matter made it perfectly plain which was secular and which was sacred. We see clerics writing LIBRETTOS, composing secular music and even taking part in opera, as in the case of Cesti (p.42). In Venice the situation was rather different, since church music still tended to be fairly conservative, and opera was a more recent phenomenon. It is significant that oratorio made little impact in the city. Even so the composers, singers and instrumentalists tended to find themselves engaged in both sacred and secular events and the struggle to keep the two domains separate continued into the next century.

It is clear that, as the demand for music increased, so did the employment opportunities for musicians: a pattern which was repeated across Europe. The existence of a musical establishment at court conferred status on the ruler, from the humblest German prince to the opulent French king, who retained several different groups of musicians for clearly defined functions. In such a situation, questions of succession, seniority and politics come to play an increasingly important role in the provision of music.

Top Right: *The title page of Praetorius's* Musarum Sioniar[um] Motectae et Psalmi Latini, *(1607). This and the illustration on the right give an insight into the performing conditions of the time at a princely court.*

Right: *A trompe l'oeil ceiling in Rosenborg Castle, Copenhagen, showing musicians at the court of Christian V. The instruments shown are lutes (bottom), viols (left), cornetts (top) and trombones or sackbuts (right).*

1653-63
Lully Arrives in France

The Florentine-born Giovanni Battista Lulli, pupil of Carissimi, arrives at the French court and soon gains the favour of the young king. The composer's metamorphosis into Jean-Baptiste Lully is more than a superficial gesture. He observes, listens, waits for the moment, and emerges as the man who gives French music in general, but opera in particular, much of its individual character that will set France apart from the rest of Europe for the next century and a half.

Scene e Machine preparate alle Nozze di Teti Balletto REALE rapresentato nella sala del piccolo Borbone et da Giacome Torelli Inuentore dedicate all Eminentissimo Prencipe. CARDINAL MAZZARIN.

Decorations et Machines apreftées aux de Tetis Ballet ROYAL: Representées en du petit Bourbon par Iacques Torelle Inuenteur Dedicée a l'Eminentissime Princeſ. CARDINAL MAZZARIN.

An engraving, dedicated to Cardinal Mazarin ● (p.41), illustrating Torelli's set for the royal ballet Le nozze di Peleo e Theti, performed in Paris in 1654. The ballet had been commissioned the year before by the cardinal from the Roman composer Caproli.

1653 With the Barberini family now back in Rome (p.40), Marazzoli and Abbatini's comic opera *Dal Male il Bene* (Good Comes from Bad) is given at the family theatre for the wedding of Maffeo Barberini, Prince of Palestrina, and Olimpia Giustiniani.

• **17 February** Birth of Corelli in Fusignano.

• **23 February** Lambert's *Ballet royal de la Nuit* (Royal Ballet of the Night), in which both Lully ■ (p.53) and the fifteen-year-old Louis XIV take part, is given at the French court.

• **16 March** Lully ■ (p.53) becomes instrumental court composer in Paris.

• **1 September** Pachelbel is baptized in Nuremberg.

1654 The Teatro San Bartolomeo opens in Naples.

• **24 March** Death of Scheidt in Halle.

• **14 April** The opera-ballet, *Le nozze di Peleo e Theti* (The Marriage of Peleus and Thetis), commissioned by Cardinal Mazarin ● (p.41) from Caproli, is performed at the Petit Bourbon in Paris (left). Again both Lully and the king dance in almost all the ENTRÉES. The music of the work has since been lost.

1655 Legrenzi ■ (p.57) publishes his collection of MOTETS and psalm settings entitled *Harmonia d'affetti devoti* (Music of Devotional Moods), in Venice. They are his first published work.

• **12 January** Cavalli's opera *Xerse* is performed at the Teatro Santi Giovanni e Paolo, Venice.

• **22 January** La Guerre composes for the French court his pastorale *Le Triomphe de l'Amour* (The Triumph of Love), which is lost. The original feature of this work was the inclusion of a sung dialogue in the form of songs for one or more voices, the work being sung throughout.

• **4 November** Cesti's opera *L'Argia* is performed in Innsbruck, where he is in the service of the Archduke Ferdinand Carl.

OTHER EVENTS
1653 Oliver Cromwell dissolves the Long Parliament and becomes Lord Protector

1654 Coronation of Louis XIV of France

1655 Outbreak of the first Northern War

1656 Velasquéz: *Las Niñas*

1657 Huygens designs first pendulum clock

1658 Cromwell dies; his son, Richard, succeeds him

A portrait of Sir William Davenant, reputedly the natural son of William Shakespeare. Under Cromwell, Davenant evaded the ban on stage-plays by representing his productions as 'music and instruction'.

1656 Cesti's opera *Orontea* (p.42), in revised form, is performed in Innsbruck for the archducal court.

• Cavalli publishes his *Messa concertata*, an accompanied Mass in the choral and orchestral Venetian tradition, dating from 1644 (p.40).

• The Teatro della Pergola, the city's first public theatre, opens in Florence.

• Lawes and Locke contribute music to *The Siege of Rhodes* by William Davenant (left), which is performed at Rutland House in London. It has claims to be the first English opera, though without the music – only the LIBRETTO and set designs survive – its significance lies more in the fact that through Davenant the nascent English opera-masque ◆ (p.35) moves away from the court and becomes a public entertainment.

1657 Krieger, a pupil of Scheidt, publishes in Leipzig his set of fifty songs or *Arien* for one to three voices accompanied by strings.

• **January** The Residenz Theater in Munich opens with Kerll's opera *L'Oronte*, the music of which is lost.

1658 14 February Lully ■ (p.53) finishes composing his ballet *Alcidiane*.

• **12 June** Cavalli's opera *Hipermestra* (above) is given in Florence at the newly-opened Teatro degli Immobili.

Above: '*The Burning of the City of Argos*', *a scene from Cavalli's opera* Hipermestra, *staged in Florence in 1658.*

1659 Cambert composes *La Pastorale d'Issy* (The Pastoral of Issy), the music of which is lost, as is that of his opera of the same year, *Ariane ou le Mariage de Bacchus* (Ariadne or the Marriage of Bacchus ◆ (p.49). Although the opera is rehearsed, it is never performed at the time because of the death of Cardinal Mazarin in 1661. A private performance will take place at the home of the Duc de Nevers in 1669 or 1670.

'The incomparable M. de Lully'

Molière in his preface to *L'Amour médecin*, 1665

• Birth of Purcell in London.

1660 Cardinal Mazarin ● (p.41) invites Cavalli to Paris to mount his opera *Xerse* (p.44) in the Louvre for the wedding festivities of Louis XIV and the Spanish Infanta Maria Theresa.

• **2 May** Birth of Alessandro Scarlatti in Palermo.

• **5 December** Hidalgo composes the earliest surviving example of a Spanish opera, *Celos aun del aire matan* (Jealousy, even of the Air, Kills), to a LIBRETTO by Pedro Calderón.

1661 Cesti's opera *La Dori*, originally composed for Innsbruck in 1657, is given in Florence for the wedding of Grand Duke Cosimo III de' Medici and Marguérite Louise d'Orléans.

• The Académie Royale de Danse is founded by Louis XIV.

• Locke is made court composer to Charles II.

• **9 March** The death of Cardinal Mazarin ● (p.41) effectively puts an end to Italian operatic influence in Paris.

• **16 May** Lully (right), becomes superintendent of music to the king, as well as composer of CHAMBER MUSIC, and is therefore effectively in control of music at the French court.

• **23 July** With ballet in France enjoying a resurgence of popularity after the death of Mazarin, Lully ■ (p.53) gives his ballet *Les Saisons* (The Seasons) at Fontainebleau.

1662 D'Anglebert, a pupil of Chambonnières, is appointed personal harpsichordist ◆ (p.51) to Louis XIV.

• **7 February** Cavalli's opera *Ercole amante* (Hercules in Love), originally commissioned by Mazarin for the wedding of Louis XIV two years earlier, is given in the Tuileries Palace, Paris, though the Venetian Ambassador says that no one is able to hear it because of the bad acoustics of the new theatre.

1663 Legrenzi ■ (p.57) publishes his third book of SONATAS in Venice.

• **8 January** Lully's *Ballet des Arts* (Ballet of the Arts) is performed at the Palais-Royal, Paris.

Lully ■ (p.53) had a dazzling rise to fame at the French court. When barely twenty, he had secured the favour of the young Louis XIV, and at his wedding in 1662, the king, queen and queen mother all signed the marriage contract. Within ten years he had obtained a total monopoly on all theatre music in France.

OTHER EVENTS
1659 Treaty of the Pyrenees between France and Spain

1660 Restoration of Charles II of England
• Pepys begins his *Diary*
• Death of Velasquéz

1661 First American edition of the Bible

1662 Louis XIV begins to enlarge the palace at Versailles
• Molière: *L'Ecole des femmes*

1663 Turks declare war on the Holy Roman Empire
• Bernini: Scala Regia, St Peter's, Rome

▲ *The Magnificence of Louis XIV*

We saw the whole equipage and glorious cavalcade of the young French Monarch, Louis XIV, passing to Parliament, when first he took the kingly government on him, now being in his fourteenth year, out of his minority and the Queen Regent's pupillage. First, came the captain of the King's Aids, at the head of fifty richly liveried; next the Queen Mother's light horse, one hundred, the lieutenant being all over covered with embroidery and ribbons, having before him four trumpets habited in black velvet, full of lace, and casques [helmets] of the same. Then, the King's Light Horse, two hundred, richly habited, with four trumpets in blue velvet embroidered with gold, before whom rid the Count d'Olonne coronet [cornet], whose belt was set with pearl. Next went the grand Prévôt's company on foot, with the Prévôt on horseback; after them the Swiss in black velvet toques, led by two gallant cavaliers habited in scarlet-coloured satin, after their country fashion, which is very fantastic; [the Prévot] had in his cap a pennach [plume] of heron, with a band of diamonds, and about him twelve little Swiss boys, with halberds. Then, came the Aide des Cérémonies; next, the grandees of court … and the whole troop, covered with gold, jewels, and rich caparisons, were followed by six trumpets in blue velvet also … lastly, appeared the King himself on an Isabella barb [Barbary horse] …; the King, … like a young Apollo, was in a suit so covered with rich embroidery, that one could perceive nothing of the stuff under it; he went almost the whole way with his hat in hand, saluting the ladies and acclamators, who had filled the windows with their beauty, and the air with Vive le Roi. He seemed a prince of a grave yet sweet countenance.

John Evelyn, Diary, *7 September 1651*

When Louis XIV assumed absolute power in 1662 at the age of twenty-three, an entertainment was mounted to celebrate the occasion. The king led the 'Romans', whilst the Duc de Guise led the 'Indians', as illustrated below.

1664-68
Schütz and the German Oratorio

As Schütz comes to the autumn of his long career he returns to a more serene, contemplative style that is ascetic in character and profound in feeling, owing much to an old tradition of intoning the gospel stories in church. From these years, a bridge stretches into the next century, leading to the monumental Passions of Bach.

1664 Lully ■ (p.53) writes a double-choir setting of the Miserere.

• Schütz ■ (p.31) publishes his *Christmas Story* in Dresden.

• **29 January** Lully ■ (p.53) works with Molière to produce the *comédie-ballet, Le Mariage forcé* (The Forced Marriage), which is given in the Louvre, Paris.

• **9 February** Cavalli's opera *Scipione affricano* (Scipio Africanus) plays at the Teatro Santi Giovanni e Paolo, Venice.

1665 Schütz ■ (p.31) composes his *St John Passion*.

1666 Schütz composes his *St Matthew Passion*.

• Antonio Stradivari's first surviving dated violin is labelled in his workshop in Cremona.

• **1 January** Pallavicino's first opera, *Demetrio*, is given at the Teatro San Moisè, Venice.

• **20 February** Cavalli's opera *Pompeo magno* (Pompey the Great) opens the Teatro San Salvatore, Venice.

• **2 December** Lully's *Ballet des Muses* (Ballet of the Muses, ■ p.53), libretto by Molière, is given at the palace of St Germain-en-Laye.

An engraving of a scene from Cesti's opera Il pomo d'oro, *designed by Burnacini. Here the mouth of hell is represented, with Charon's boat on the River Styx and, in the background, a burning city. By now opera has evolved from its Venetian origins, and Cesti's work is a five-act court opera of the type that is expected for state occasions.*

Buxtehude's autograph of one of his chorales written out in new German tablature. The most important German composer between Schütz and Bach, it was as an organist that Buxtehude achieved his fame.

1667 Rosenmüller publishes a set of twelve five-part instrumental *Sonate da camera à 5 stromenti* (Chamber Sonatas for Five Instruments).

• **19 February** Cesti's opera *Le disgrazie d'Amore* (The Misfortunes of Love) is performed in Vienna.

• **May** Froberger dies at Héricourt.

1668 Tomkins's church music is published posthumously as *Musica Deo sacra* (Music Sacred to God).

• De Bacilly publishes his treatise *Remarques curieuses sur l'art de bien chanter* (Interesting Remarks on the Art of Good Singing), a famous singing teacher's theory of technique, which provides interesting information about current practice.

• **11 April** Buxtehude is elected organist of the Marienkirche, Lübeck, and on 3 August marries the daughter of his predecessor, Tunder.

• **13 and 14 July** Cesti's opera *Il pomo d'oro* (The Golden Apple, left) is performed in Vienna to celebrate the wedding of Leopold I of Austria. It exemplifies Italian court opera as adopted by most countries in Europe.

OTHER EVENTS
1664 New Amsterdam becomes New York

1665 Accession of Charles II of Spain
• Plague in London
• Spinoza: *Ethics* (published posthumously)
• Newton begins to elaborate differential calculus and laws of universal gravitation

1666 Great Fire of London
• Thévenot invents the spirit level

1667 Peace of Breda ends second Anglo-Dutch War
• Milton: *Paradise Lost*

1668 Perrault designs the Louvre colonnade (east front)
• La Fontaine begins his *Fables*

◆ *The Stories of Baroque Opera*

One of the strongest influences on the birth of opera was the interest of the Camerata ◆ *(p.25)* in Greek theatre and music, and their desire to recreate the world of Classical antiquity. In the mythology of Greece they found the ideal opera plot in the story of Orpheus (who could charm the very stones with his music) and his wife Euridice. The tale of Apollo and Daphne provided similar inspiration, and we see Monteverdi, for example, taking up the mythological themes with his L'Orfeo *(p.26)*, L'Arianna *(p.26)* and

Il ritorno d'Ulisse *(p.38)*. Soon, however, composers turned to other stories, some from history, such as Monteverdi himself with L'incoronazione di Poppea *(p.38)*, and once this threshold was crossed, then almost anything that seemed exotic or remote was deemed suitable for an opera plot. With the demise of the old mythological themes the aspiration to a higher plane of expression also disappeared, and sadly the opera became a vehicle for the singers to display their prowess and the scenic designers their mechanical and decorative skills.

'Half Olympus sat enthroned on a cloud, Neptune's sea horses stamped their way through the foaming main, churches split open at the impact of an earthquake. Dragons spitting fire flew down from the sky, the earth yawned to disgorge Charon the ferryman from the burning realm of Pluto and send him across the fiery flood.'
Contemporary account of a performance of *Il pomo d'oro* in Vienna.

Above: *Three figures from the* Commedia dell'arte, *an elusive form of Italian theatre, often improvised, which gave to posterity the characters of Harlequin, Punch and Columbine and ultimately influenced the development of comic as opposed to serious opera.*

Left: *Titian's* Bacchus and Ariadne, *painted c.1523, is typical of the interest in mythological subjects that would, in the closing years of the sixteenth century, inspire the birth of opera.*

1669-80
Lully Reigns Supreme

Over the next five years Lully increases his hold on the music of the French court, and in 1672 the king issues letters patent giving the composer what amounts to a dictatorship over all public performances involving music in any way, throughout the whole of France.

Louis XIV is depicted in this painting by Jean Garnier at the heart of artistic endeavour, and it is true that the king was to make the French court at Versailles a brilliant focus of the arts ★ (p.52). The prominence of musical instruments in the painting reflects the essential part that both vocal and instrumental music played in court life, whether for religious ceremonies, intimate chamber music, or the sumptuously mounted mixture of opera and ballet preferred by the French court.

1669 13 February Lully's *Ballet de Flore* (Ballet of Flora, ■ p.53) is performed in the theatre of the Tuileries Palace, Paris.

• **June** The Académie Royale de Musique is founded in Paris under a royal patent.

1670 Chambonnières publishes two books of keyboard works entitled *Pièces de clavessin*.

• **14 October** Lully ■ (p.53) and Molière collaborate on a performance of *Le Bourgeois Gentilhomme* (The Commoner Gentleman) at Chambord. Lully plays the role of the mufti in the Turkish ceremony scene.

1671 Schütz ■ (p.31) composes his German Magnificat.

• Corelli leaves Bologna for Rome, where he remains for the rest of his life.

• **3 March** Cambert's pastoral-opera *Pomone* inaugurates what will become known as the Paris Opéra in the Salle du Jeu de Paume de la Bouteille with great success.

1672 Death of Chambonnières in Paris, aged about seventy.

• Alessandro Scarlatti comes to Rome, and possibly studies with Carissimi.

• Charpentier is approached by Molière to write music for his plays after the latter's quarrel with Lully.

• **April** Lully ■ (p.53) is given control of the Académie Royale de Musique, and with it the effective control of opera, and eventually all forms of music and channels of professional musical life in France.

• **6 November** Death of Schütz ■ (p.31) in Dresden.

• **15 November** Lully's pastiche-pastorale *Les Fêtes de l'Amour et de Bacchus* (The Festival of Love and Bacchus) is given at the Opéra in Paris.

1673 27 April Lully's tragic opera *Cadmus et Hermione* is given at the Opéra in Paris ■ (p.53).

• Buxtehude begins his *Abendmusiken* (Evening Music) concerts at Lübeck.

1674 The Teatro San Giovanni Grisostomo opens in Venice.

• Stradella composes his SERENATA *Lo schiavo liberato* (The Freed Slave).

• **12 January** Death of Carissimi ■ (p.33) in Rome, aged sixty-eight.

• **19 January** Lully's opera *Alceste* is given at the Opéra, Paris ■ (p.53).

• **10 December** Pallavicino's opera *Diocletiano* (Diocletian) is performed at the Teatro Santi Giovanni e Paolo, Venice.

OTHER EVENTS
1669 Aurangzeb prohibits Hinduism in India
• Last entry in Samuel Pepys's diary
1670 England and France sign Treaty of Dover
• Pascal: *Pensées* (published posthumously)
1671 Turks declare war on Poland
• Milton: *Paradise Regained*
1672 Britain and France declare war on the Dutch
1673 Test Act: Catholics excluded from public office in England
• Death of Molière
1674 Death of Milton

◆ *Keyboard Instruments*

Keyboard instruments may use a variety of means to produce sound. Although an organ incorporates a keyboard, it is in fact the air in the pipes that produces the sound, and the function of the key is to give the air access to the pipes. Percussion is used in the mediaeval precursors of the piano mechanism, where the hammer strikes the string; prior to the development of the piano itself, the most popular instrument to use percussion is the clavichord, where a metal tangent is brought into contact with the string to produce the sound. Although a certain amount of expression may be obtained from a clavichord, it is essentially a very quiet instrument. However, the instrument probably most associated with the non-organ keyboard music of the seventeenth century is the harpsichord ('clavecin' in French), where the strings are plucked rather than struck.

Within the plucked-string keyboard group there are certain questions of nomenclature. In England, for example, the term virginal or virginals was used to refer to all such plucked-string instruments, whereas strictly it should have been reserved for an oblong instrument, with strings running parallel to the keyboard. The virginal tended to have only one set of strings to each note, and a four-octave compass, in common with the spinet.

What distinguished the spinet was its shape, which was usually an uneven hexagon, and the strings might run parallel to the keyboard along the longest side of the hexagon, or diagonally across the interior.

Because of their nature, tonal and dynamic contrasts were impossible on the plucked-string keyboard group, therefore touch and articulation were of prime importance. Later harpsichord makers gave their instruments two manuals or keyboards in an attempt to produce a variety of sounds, but it was inevitable that as the much more expressive piano was developed and improved, from the end of the seventeenth century onwards, it would begin to replace its softer cousins.

The three main types of plucked-string keyboard instrument are shown here. On the left is a spinet from one of the plates for the Encyclopaedia of Diderot and d'Alembert. Below, is the title page from Chambonnières's first book of harpsichord pieces, published in 1670, showing on the left a two manual harpsichord, and on the right a virginal. Chambonnières was the first composer of the French tradition which blossomed in the seventeenth century.

★ *The splendour of the French court is demonstrated by this engraving of a ball given at Versailles in 1678, for which a temporary pavilion was erected in the park.*

One of Jean Bérain's costume designs for the Indians in Lully's opera-ballet Le Triomphe de l'amour, *with text by Quinault, performed on 21 January 1681 at St Germain-en-Laye. This was the last time that courtiers danced on stage, at least in public, for when it was repeated in Paris on 16 May the same year, a professional corps de ballet was formed, with female dancers.*

1675 Legrenzi's opera *Eteocle e Polinice* (Eteocles and Polynices) ■ (p.57) plays at the Teatro San Salvatore, Venice.

• **12 January** Lully's opera *Thésée* (Theseus) is performed at the palace of St Germain-en-Laye, near Paris ■ (p.53).

• **31 March** Stradella's ORATORIO *San Giovanni Battista* (Saint John the Baptist) is performed in the church of San Giovanni dei Fiorentini in Rome with Corelli playing in the orchestra.

1676 Cavalli completes his double-choir Requiem.

• Legrenzi ■ (p.57) publishes his vocal collection entitled *Cantate e canzonette* (Cantatas and Canzonets) in Bologna.

• **10 January** Lully's opera *Atys* is given at St Germain-en-Laye ■ (p.53).

• **14 January** Death of Cavalli in Venice.

1677 Stradella's comic opera *Il Trespolo tutore* (Trespolo the Tutor) is performed in Genoa.

• Pope Innocent XI revives a sixteenth-century edict against women appearing on the theatrical stage, which greatly affects Roman opera.

• Lully composes his Te Deum.

• Purcell becomes composer to the king's violins ★ (p.59).

• Stradella elopes from Rome with Ortensia Grimani, but is wounded in Turin by the assassins hired by her husband. He flees to Genoa where he will be stabbed to death five years later (p.54).

• **January** Sartorio's opera *Antonino e Pompejano* (Anthony and Pompey) is produced at the Teatro San Salvatore, Venice.

1678 Legrenzi ■ (p.57) publishes his collection of songs entitled *Echi di riverenza* (Echoes of Reverence) in Bologna.

• **2 January** Hamburg's first opera house opens, the Gänsemarkt Theater ● (p.61).

• **4 March** Birth of Vivaldi in Venice.

1679 Corelli ■ (p.55) is appointed first violinist at the Teatro Capranica in Rome.

• Purcell succeeds his teacher Blow ★ (p.56) as organist at Westminster Abbey.

• **31 January** Lully's opera *Bellérophon* plays at the Opéra, Paris ■ (p.53).

• **5 February** Alessandro Scarlatti's first opera *Gli equivoci nel sembiante* (Mistaken Identities) is produced at the Teatro Capranica, Rome.

• **11 November** Pallavicino's opera *Le Amazoni nelle isole fortunate* (The Amazons in the Fortunate Isles) is performed to celebrate the opening of the Teatro Contarini at Piazzola sul Brenta near Venice.

1680 Stradavari makes his earliest known cello.

• **3 February** Lully's opera *Prosperine* is given at the palace of St Germain-en-Laye, near Paris ■ (p.53).

OTHER EVENTS

1675 Wren begins St Paul's Cathedral, London
• Spinoza finishes *Ethics*

1676 Pope Clement X dies, Benedetto Odescalchi becomes Pope Innocent XI
• Hooke invents universal joint to turn astronomical instruments in any direction

1677 Racine: *Phèdre*
• Death of Spinoza

1678 Peace of Nijmegen between France, Spain, the Netherlands and the Holy Roman Empire
• French court moves to Versailles
• Murillo: *The Mystery of the Immaculate Conception*
• Bunyan starts *The Pilgrim's Progress*

1679 Habeas Corpus Act in England gives protection against arbitrary arrest

1680 Death of Bernini

Opposite: *A painting by Puget of a gathering of French musicians in the late seventeenth century. It has been suggested that the seated figure in the left foreground represents Lully ■ (p.53), whose primary instrument was the violin.*

■ *Lully and French Opera*

When Lully took control of the Académie Royale de Musique he ruthlessly formed an institution that was the envy of many other nations. From the LIBRETTI of his operas, most of which were by Philippe Quinault, we may assume that, in addition to the principal singers and dancers, he had at his disposal between twenty and thirty singers and some twenty dancers. The orchestra probably consisted of about thirty musicians, roughly a third of whom were wind players. Carlo Vigarani first supplied the décor and stage machinery, and was followed by Jean Bérain ★ (p.56).

Lully's tragedies are sung throughout, with airs or arias, as in Italian operas, but the composer's great innovation was his style of RECITATIVE. Instead of having a *secco* recitative, in which the singer speedily delivers the words with a minimum of accompaniment, Lully's recitative has considerable variety of TEMPO, alternating DUPLE and TRIPLE TIME, with expressive pauses or more lyrical, song-like sections. It is only fair to add that Lully's airs tend to be of less interest. However, his orchestral passages (which are often used to set the scene) and his majestic overtures are an additional element in what was a total spectacle, and a recipe that was copied faithfully from Lully to Rameau.

1681-84
Corelli and the Violin Tradition

Probably the greatest violin teacher of his age, Corelli introduces new standards of excellence into orchestral playing, and into his own compositions. His influence reaches well into the next century, and far beyond the confines of Italy.

1681 Corelli ■ (p.55) publishes his first TRIO SONATAS in Rome as his Opus One, setting a tradition that composers will adopt in the future.

• Stradella's ORATORIO *Susanna* is performed in Modena.

• **5 January** Legrenzi ■ (p.57) becomes deputy director of music at St Mark's, Venice ● (p.27).

• **14 March** Birth of Telemann in Magdeburg.

1682 Corelli ■ (p.55) becomes director of music at the Church of San Luigi dei Francesi, Rome.

• Rosenmüller publishes his last work, a set of sonatas for one, two, three and five instruments in Nuremberg.

• The Salzburg Festival Mass, originally assigned to 1628, when the cathedral there was first consecrated, is now believed to have been written this year (below). Fifty-four STAVES are required to accommodate the music for two choirs and orchestra. The composer is thought to be Biber.

• Purcell is appointed organist at the Chapel Royal ● (p.59).

• **25 February** Stradella (p.52) is murdered in Genoa.

• **18 April** Lully's opera *Persée* (Perseus) plays at the Opéra, Paris ■ (p.53).

1683 Charpentier composes his *Orphée descendant aux Enfers* (Orpheus descending to the Underworld), one of the earliest French CANTATAS. This year he also competes for one of the four posts of assistant director of the Chapel Royal, Paris, but is seriously ill and so unable to take part in the final stage. He is granted a pension by way of compensation.

• Legrenzi ■ (p.57) completes his most successful opera, *Guistino* (Justinian), for the Teatro San Salvatore, Venice.

• Pachelbel publishes his sets of harpsichord VARIATIONS on hymn tunes, intended for performance in the home ◆ (p.51), entitled *Musicalische Sterbens-Gedancken* (A Musical Meditation on Death), in Erfurt.

• **25 January** Alessandro Scarlatti composes his *opera seria*, ◆ (p.67), *Il Pompeo* (Pompey) for the Teatro Colonna, Rome.

• **22 November** Purcell's *Ode for St Cecilia's Day* – 'Welcome to all the Pleasures' ● (p.59), is performed for the first time in London.

1684 Vitali publishes his sacred string sonatas, *Sonate da chiesa* (Church Sonatas), in Venice.

• **February** Alessandro Scarlatti becomes director of the Teatro San Bartolomeo, Naples.

• **October** Kuhnau is appointed organist at the Thomaskirche in Leipzig.

> '...At last Corelli's concertos came, all which are to the musicians like the bread of life.'
> The musicologist Roger North on the arrival of Corelli's music in England.

OTHER EVENTS
1681 Academy of Sciences, Moscow, founded

1682 Accession of Peter the Great of Russia
• Exploration of the Mississippi by La Salle
• Death of Ruisdael

1683 First German settlers in North America
• First coffeehouses in Vienna

1684 Bunyan finishes *The Pilgrim's Progress*

Salzburg Cathedral, rebuilt in the baroque style, was reconsecrated in great pomp with a Mass for two choirs in eight parts and a large instrumental ensemble including organ, with two additional groups of wind instruments, including cornetts, trombones, trumpets and drums.

Corelli and the Influence of the Italian Violin School

Corelli is often called the father of Italian violin playing. Through his pupils he can be said to have created the violin school that bears his name and spread across Europe. He handed on his high ideals through his teaching, and an unbroken succession of masters and pupils has kept his principles alive to the present day.

He was regarded during his lifetime as one of the leading musicians in Italy, and contemporaries spoke of his brilliance of interpretation, wonderful singing tone and remakably supple technique. He enjoyed great esteem among the Roman aristocracy, principally under the patronage of Cardinal Ottoboni, and was regarded with something little short of reverence. At the very least he was a remarkable personality, and one of those rare musicians of whom one hears not a word of scandal or jealousy, least of all from colleagues.

Corelli was a harsh critic of his own compositions, which is why he published relatively little, but through his works he laid the foundations for both the solo sonata and the CONCERTO GROSSO, for which both Bach and Handel are indebted to him.

Left: The musician in this portrait is shown as both violinist and a composer. Although some argue that the lock of red hair poking from under the wig reveal the sitter to be Vivaldi (who was known as il prete rosso – *the red-headed priest), others believe him to be Corelli.*

Below: The entrance of Cardinal Pietro Ottoboni into Rome. A great patron, particularly of opera for which he wrote libretttos, he employed Corelli as the leader of his orchestra.

1685-88
Legrenzi in Venice

The arrival of Legrenzi at the head of the musical establishment of St Mark's heralds an increase in the size of the choir and orchestra to record numbers, and a marked improvement in standards. By perfecting the late baroque style in Italy, he influences a whole generation of young composers who follow him.

1685 Blow's opera *Venus and Adonis* is performed in London (left).

• Corelli ■ (p.55) publishes his Trio Sonatas Op.2, in Rome.

  • **18 January** Lully's tragic opera *Roland* ■ (p.53) is performed at Versailles.

    • **23 February** Birth of Handel in Halle.

    • **21 March** Birth of Bach in Eisenach.

     • **23 April** Legrenzi succeeds Monferrato as director of music at St Mark's, Venice ■ (p.57).

     • **26 October** Birth of Domenico Scarlatti in Naples.

   1686 15 February Lully's final operatic masterpiece, *Armide,* (below, ■ p.53), is performed at the Paris Opéra.

  1687 Pallavicino's last opera *La Gierusalemme liberata* (The Liberation of Jerusalem) is given in Venice at the Teatro Santi Giovanni e Paolo.

  • Corelli ■ (p.55) is appointed director of Cardinal Pamphilj's orchestra in Rome.

  • **2 February** Pallavicino's *La Gierusalemme liberata* plays at the Hoftheater, Dresden ● (p.61).

• **22 March** Death of Lully ■ (p.53) from gangrene after striking his foot with his staff when conducting his Te Deum on 8 January. It is common practice for time to be beaten with raps on a lectern or the floor, especially where large forces are required for the performance of a work, but Lully chooses a particularly big staff on this occasion.

• **Late July** Birth of Benedetto Marcello in Venice.

1688 Kuhnau publishes his dissertation *De juribus circa musicos ecclesiasticos* (Concerning the Laws regarding Church Musicians) in Leipzig. This year he also founds a Leipzig Collegium Musicum for public concerts.

• Stradella's ORATORIOS *Santa Pelagia* (St Pelagia) and *San Giovanni Battista* (St John the Baptist) are given in Modena.

★ *John Blow was recruited as a choirboy to the Chapel Royal and became organist both there and at Westminster Abbey. His* Venus and Adonis *was an attempt to create a court opera similar to those enjoyed by Charles II during his exile in France.*

OTHER EVENTS

1685 James II crowned king of England
• Revocation of the Edict of Nantes

1686 France annexes Madagascar

1687 Newton begins his *Philosophiae naturalis principia mathematica*

1688 James II's reign ends with the Glorious Revolution

★ *Set design by Bérain for Lully's final opera* Armide, *the scene of the destruction of Armide's palace. Ironically it marks the end of such spectacles in France, for with Lully's death the king turned to piety, and music and dance were left to the smaller courts.*

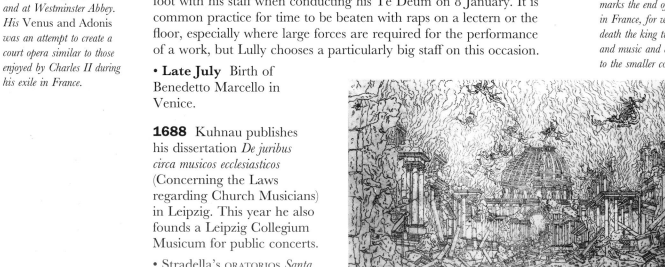

■ *Legrenzi at St Mark's*

Legrenzi was a worthy successor to Monteverdi and Cavalli at St Mark's, Venice ● (p.27), and his career illustrates the nature of the personality required to fill this important post, as well as the demands made on its incumbent. His initial reforms imply that not only had standards fallen before his arrival, but also that more and more was being demanded of the musical establishment of St Mark's.

'For his virtuous and commendable application in the continued decorous service of the Chapel, to give him in silver or another gift, 200 ducats.'
Decree of the Procurators of St Mark's for Legrenzi, 10 July 1689

In common with many of the holders of such posts in Venice, and indeed all over Italy, at this time, he had taken holy orders, but this did not prevent him from composing operas. He also taught music at one of the female orphanages in the city ■ (p.71), that of the Mendicanti, and had a number of private composition pupils of whom the most famous was probably Lotti.

Accounts of Legrenzi's life reveal that as respite from St Mark's, he enjoyed nothing more than an impromptu concert at home, such as the musical evening depicted below.

Legrenzi seems to have kept open house for visitors to Venice, and from contemporary reports there was always music of some kind being performed there. In March 1688, for example, a trio of young French sisters came to sing some of Lully's compositions to him, he in turn provided a STRING CONCERTO of his own, and the concert was rounded off with a performance by an Italian guitarist.

Legrenzi was held in great affection and esteem by those who worked with him, and in his will, dated 12 May 1689, he showed that he was equally appreciative of his friends, pupils and colleagues, who had not only assisted him, but also given him so much fulfilment.

1689-94
Purcell, the British Orpheus

In Henry Purcell, British music finds one of its most brilliant and inspired exponents. His untimely death robs the country of one of its greatest composers, leaving it wide open to the influx of continental musicians, and British music will, after the departure of Handel, sink into virtual oblivion for almost two centuries.

Purcell, in the portrait by Clostermann. Although there are many gaps in our knowledge of Purcell's life, it is known that as a Chapel Royal chorister he received some lessons from Blow (p.56), then the organist at Westminster Abbey. Blow surrendered his post to his brilliant young pupil, who later became organist at the Chapel Royal and keeper of the king's instruments.

1689 Purcell's opera *Dido and Aeneas* is first performed at a girls' boarding school, Josias Priest's Chelsea School for Young Ladies, in London.

• Corelli ■ (p.55), now director of Cardinal Ottoboni's orchestra, publishes his third set of TRIO SONATAS in Rome.

• D'Anglebert publishes his keyboard collection *Pièces de Clavecin* (Pieces for Harpsichord, below).

1690 Foundation of the Accademia dell'Arcadia in Rome, which will greatly influence musical aesthetics.

• Purcell's *The Prophetess, or The History of Dioclesian* ● (p.59) is performed at the Dorset Garden Theatre, London.

• **5 January** Alessandro Scarlatti's opera *La Statira* is performed in the Teatro Tordinona, Rome.

• **27 May** Legrenzi ■ (p.57) dies in Venice.

1691 Legrenzi's collection of dance music for strings and BASSO CONTINUO entitled *Balletti e Correnti* is published posthumously in Venice.

1692 Torelli publishes his set of six *Sinfonie a tre* and six *Concerti a quattro*, three- and four-part instrumental works, in Bologna, thus confirming the rise of the city in musical importance.

• Keiser ● (p.61) is appointed to the ducal chamber at Brunswick.

• Kuhnau's second part of *Neue Clavier-Übung* (New Keyboard Music), includes sonatas, the first time this Italian form appears in German music.

• **22 November** Purcell's *Ode for St Cecilia's Day*, 'Hail! Bright Cecilia', is performed in London.

1693 Alessandro Scarlatti composes his first version of the ORATORIO *La Giuditta* (Judith).

• Pachelbel publishes a set of eight CHORALES to be played by way of preamble, entitled *Choräle zum praeambulieren*, in Nuremberg.

• Couperin becomes organist to the king of France.

• **18 September** Vivaldi is tonsured in Venice.

1694 Perti's *Passione del Redentore* (Passion of the Redeeemer) is performed in Bologna.

• Corelli's fourth set of trio sonatas is published.

• Albinoni publishes his first set of trio sonatas as his Opus One, thus copying Corelli's example.

Right: The frontispiece to D'Anglebert's collection for harpsichord published in 1689. On the left is a harpsichord ◆ (p.51), and on the right a small organ, which represents the five fugues for organ that also appear in the edition. Appointed harpsichordist to Louis XIV of France in 1662, D'Anglebert held the post for almost thirty years.

OTHER EVENTS
1689 William III and Mary joint sovereigns in Britain
• Peter the Great becomes Czar of Russia

1690 Battle of the Boyne in Ireland; James II defeated by William of Orange
• Papin invents a machine run by steam
• Locke: *An Essay concerning Human Understanding*

1691 Racine: *Athalie*

1692 Duke Ernst August of Hanover becomes Elector of the Holy Roman Empire

1693 Kingston, Jamaica, founded

1694 Foundation of the Bank of England
• Birth of Voltaire

British music after the Restoration

During the Commonwealth period in Britain there was considerable dislocation of the usual channels of musical life. With the restoration of the monarchy came the resumption of official music, but it took time to recruit singers and instrumentalists and re-establish the royal musical household which, together with the choirs of Westminster Abbey and St Paul's Cathedral, tended to form the focus of musical activity in London at that time. Furthermore, the fact that Charles II had spent his exile in France meant that there were bound to be changes of direction, both of style and emphasis, as well as the inevitable reaction to the years of Puritanism.

Purcell himself was well aware that things had to change. Recruited as a boy chorister when the Chapel Royal was re-established, he grew up in this new atmosphere, and was attuned to the new currents coming across the English Channel from Europe. As he wrote in the preface to his *Dioclesian* of 1690: 'Musick is yet but in its Nonage [infancy], a forward Child which gives hope of what it may be hereafter in England... 'Tis now learning Italian, which is its best Master, and studying a little of the French Air, to give it somewhat more of Gayety and Fashion. Thus being further from the Sun, we are of later growth than our Neighbour Countries, and must be content to shake off our Barbarity by degrees.'

A string orchestra playing during the banquet in Westminster Hall which, according to tradition, followed the coronation of James II on 23 April, 1685. It is quite possible that at least some of the violinists shown here were members of the Twenty-four Violins established by Charles II on his return from exile in France, where he had seen Louis XIV's Vingt-quatre violons, as well as his group of younger musicians, the Petits violons, at first hand. Both Blow and Purcell wrote anthems for the coronation service itself in Westminster Abbey. Until the establishment in the early part of the eighteenth century of professional opera companies, whose members tended to be imported from Italy, the vast majority of both sacred and secular music-making in London was centred on Westminster Abbey, the Chapel Royal and St Paul's Cathedral.

1695-99
Keiser and Opera

Keiser, first and foremost a man of the theatre, brings the influence of Lully from France and Steffani from Italy to Hamburg, where he establishes an important centre which will draw Handel, among others, to experience its musical riches. Head and shoulders above his contemporaries, Keiser has an innate lyricism and excels in expressive recitative and orchestration.

Below: *An extract from Orpheus Britannicus, a collection of Purcell's music published after his death by his son, the first volume in 1698 and the second in 1702. The figured bass line indicates that the singer might be accompanied by organ, harpsichord or theorbo lute.*

'He [Purcell] is much lamented, being a very great Master of Musick.'
The Post Boy, 26-28 November 1695

1695 Charpentier composes his *divertissement*, *La Descente d'Orphée aux Enfers* (The Descent of Orpheus into the Underworld) for the French court.

• Keiser moves to the Hamburg Opera ● (p.61), where he is not made official director until 1703.

• Bach's father dies and he goes to live with his elder brother, organist at Ohrdruf.

• **21 November** Purcell ● (p.59) dies in London possibly from tuberculosis, aged only thirty-six, having written over five hundred works.

1696 Keiser's opera *Mahumet II* plays in Hamburg ● (p.61).

• Couperin is granted a coat of arms. Since 1690 he has called himself Lord of Crouilly, as did his father.

• Kuhnau composes *Frische Clavier-Früchte, oder sieben Suonaten* (Fresh Fruit for the Piano, or Seven Sonatas), with sonatas containing several contrasting movements.

• **27 December** Bononcini's opera *Il trionfo di Camilla* (The Triumph of Camilla) is performed at the Teatro San Bartolomeo in Naples.

1697 24 October Campra's first opera *L'Europe galante* is performed in Paris.

1698 A collection of Purcell's music ● (p.59) is published posthumously in London and entitled *Orpheus Britannicus*.

• Torelli publishes his twelve four-part concertos, *Concerti musicali a quattro*, in Augsburg.

• Charpentier is finally admitted to the Chapel Royal (p.54), despite not being in holy orders, in recognition of his ability.

• **16 April** Fux is appointed court composer by Leopold I in Vienna.

1699 Pachelbel publishes his six sets of variations for keyboard ◆ (p.51) entitled *Hexachordum Apollinis* (Apollo's Hexachord) in Nuremberg.

A painting dating from 1693 of a ballet sequence from an Italian opera entitled Camilla generosa, *produced in a German theatre, which testifies to the rapid spread of the art form throughout Germany.*

OTHER EVENTS
1695 University of Berlin founded

1696 Letters between Scottish and English secretaries of state use envelopes for first time

1697 Treaty of Ryswick
• Birth of Canaletto

1698 Tax on beards introduced in Russia

1699 Treaty of Karlowitz; Austria obtains Hungary, Poland and regains Podolia

Peter Schenck's engraving of Hamburg from Totius orbis terrarum, *published in Amsterdam in 1702, where it is described as the most distinguished and the most flourishing emporium in the whole of Germany, to which its rich secular and religious musical life bore witness.*

● *Music Flourishes in Northern Germany*

Although European musicians continued to be drawn to Italy ● (p.27) to work and study and Italian composers and musicians still migrated to the rest of Europe, during the second half of the seventeenth century other centres of musical excellence began to spring up across the continent. France, as we have seen ● (p.41), was content for the most part to develop its own style, and, as a result of this, its influence on other countries was restricted. In Germany, however, and especially Hamburg, composers remained in touch with developments elsewhere in Europe while still nurturing their own talent, thus enabling them to remain within the mainstream of musical progress.

Keiser moved to Hamburg in 1693. Although he was official director to the Opera only between 1703 and 1707, he remained its artistic driving force until the last decade of his life, producing over one hundred stage works which established him as the central figure in German baroque opera. A colleague of Keiser's was Mattheson, the majority of whose compositions, which had remained in manuscript, were destroyed in World War II. Nevertheless, Mattheson deserves his place in the history of music as one of the first musical journalists and, by extension, musicologists. More familiar perhaps to today's music lovers are Telemann and Handel, both of whom benefited from Keiser's example. This gradual departure from Italian domination was to be the history of musical development throughout the next century, though the Italian ideal would persist in people's minds and fade only gradually and with great reluctance.

1700-99

From Baroque to Classicism

Initially eighteenth-century musical life continues to be concentrated in the courts, palaces and civic institutions of Europe where musicians depend, for the most part, on a succession of appointments in order to pursue their careers. In general the movement away from exclusively religious functions for composers persists. Although individual composers may be highly esteemed, the general perception of the musician is still essentially that of some kind of artisan. As the century advances, however, and music finds patrons outside exclusively royal and aristocratic circles, composers are more able to follow their own dictates, especially in the opera house, where there are paying audiences, and in the steadily growing taste for public concerts. Finally, as revolution in France shakes the established order towards the end of the century, a totally new expressive spirit begins to find its way into music.

Music-making at court celebrates an Austrian royal wedding in the eighteenth century.

1700-05
Enter Bach and Handel

The presence of Alessandro Scarlatti in Naples and Vivaldi in Venice ensures that Italy continues to enjoy its position as the home of musical excellence. In Germany, however, two composers appear who will, in very different ways, challenge Italian dominance.

1700 Cristofori invents a prototype piano, which produces sound when the strings are struck with hammers, rather than plucked as in the harpsichord ◆ (p.51). He calls it a *gravicembalo col piano e forte* (harpsichord with soft and loud), from which the modern instrument gets its name.

• **March** Bach wins a singing scholarship to the Michaeliskirche in Lüneburg (opposite).

• **18 September** Vivaldi is ordained deacon, aged twenty-two, in Venice.

1701 Handel ■ (opposite) at the age of sixteen, first makes contact with Telemann (below) and they initiate a lifetime's friendship. The latter enrolls as a law student in Leipzig.

• Kuhnau is made CANTOR of the Thomasschule and director of music at Leipzig. He gives up the law to concentrate on music.

• Domenico Scarlatti becomes organist at the royal chapel in Naples.

1702 Telemann revives the Collegium Musicum in Leipzig, originally founded by Kuhnau (p.56).

• **10 February** Handel begins to study law at Halle University. The following month, aged seventeen, he is appointed organist of the city cathedral.

• **Summer** Bach leaves Lüneburg and applies for the post of organist of the Jacobikirche, Sangerhausen. In November he wins the vacancy, but the Duke of Sachsen-Weissenfels intervenes and imposes an older man.

1703 Handel gives up his legal studies and goes to Hamburg ● (p.61), where Mattheson helps his recognition as an organist. He becomes second violinist in the opera house orchestra under Keiser's direction.

• Alessandro Scarlatti ★ (p.68) becomes assistant organist at Santa Maria Maggiore in Rome. He devotes himself to writing church music and chamber CANTATAS.

• **March** Bach goes to work for Duke Johann Ernst of Weimar as a liveried string player, dubbed 'Laquey Bach'. He decides to leave as soon as possible.

• **23 March** Vivaldi is ordained priest in Venice.

• **August** Handel goes to Lübeck as a prospective successor to Buxtehude at the Marienkirche, but since this would entail marrying the latter's daughter, Handel does not apply for the post.

• **September** Vivaldi takes up his appointment as violin master at the Pietà orphanage in Venice ■ (p.71).

• **September** Bach becomes organist at the Bonifatiuskirche in Arnstadt.

Telemann went to Leipzig in 1701 to study law, but his musical talent impressed the city council so much that they very soon offered him a commission to write cantatas for the Thomaskirche, in competition with Kuhnau, and appointed him director of the opera.

OTHER EVENTS
1700 Charles II of Spain dies; Philip V, grandson of Louis XIV of France is heir to the throne

1701 Accession of Frederick I of Prussia
• Start of war of Spanish Succession
• Founding of Yale College at New Haven

1702 Accession of Queen Anne of England

1703 Peter the Great founds St Petersburg
• Death of Samuel Pepys

1704 Stanislas Leczinski elected King of Poland

1705 Emperor Leopold I dies; his son Joseph I succeeds him

'Handel in those days set very, very long arias…he was a stranger to melody.'
Mattheson writing about Handel on his arrival in Hamburg.

1704 17 March Vivaldi's salary for his first six months at the Pietà is thirty ducats ■ (p.71). Five months later he gets a pay rise in recognition of his teaching the *viola all'inglese* ◆ (p.39).

• **5 December** Handel and Mattheson quarrel over the playing of the harpsichord ◆ (p.51) in the latter's opera *Cleopatra*. In the ensuing duel Handel is saved by a coat button. They resolve their differences on the thirtieth of the month.

1705 Vivaldi publishes his twelve trio SONATAS ◆ (p.127) as his Opus One in Venice.

• Telemann (opposite) abandons his legal studies and becomes director of music to Prince Promnitz at Sorau.

• **8 January** Handel's first opera *Almira* is performed in Hamburg and is very well received.

• **25 February** First performance of Handel's second opera, *Nero*. The composer leaves the Hamburg Opera, and begins teaching private pupils.

• **October** Bach takes a month's leave, which he overstays, and goes to Lübeck on foot to hear Buxtehude play.

■ *The Early Years of Handel and Bach*

Despite their very different musical personalities, the early careers of Bach and Handel share a common theme, namely the search for a place in which to develop and exercise their respective talents.

By now the roles of church and court composer were very separate ◆ (p.43), and we see the two men taking divergent paths, meeting various obstacles before reaching their goals.

Handel was always drawn towards opera, so it is not surprising that when he decided to give up studying law at Halle University, he moved to Hamburg ● (p.61), home of the first public opera house outside Italy. With a number of successful operas behind him, he then travelled to Italy itself, to experience at first-hand what

he had assimilated. He hesitated at one point, and cast his eyes in the direction of Lübeck, where the venerable Buxtehude was looking ahead to his retirement from the Marienkirche (p.64). The fact that marriage to the organist's daughter was one of the conditions of the post (as Buxtehude himself had been obliged to marry the daughter of his predecessor) cannot have been the only deterrent for Handel – he was never destined to be a church organist, despite the fact that he was perfectly able to fulfil that function.

Unlike Handel, Bach felt that he had a true vocation for church music. He too made the pilgrimage to Lübeck, though via Lüneburg (left), Sangerhausen, Weimar and Arnstadt, and one may see his appointment at Leipzig ■ (p.77) as the culmination of years of working towards that goal. Unfortunately, his creative genius was constantly at war with the mundane demands of his various posts (as choirmaster he was responsible for the rowdy boys from the high school, p.66), and though he was known as a virtuoso organist, his profound musical ability was never appreciated by his employers.

Interior of the Michaeliskirche in Lüneburg. Bach became a pupil in the choir school here in late March 1700. When his voice broke he continued to make music as a violinist and organist, and may well have studied with Böhm, organist of the Johanniskirche in the city. We also know that Bach would go on foot to Hamburg to hear Reincken play the organ of the Catharinenkirche.

1706-13
Handel Takes Italy by Storm

Handel has developed a taste for Italian music in general and opera in particular, and decides that he must experience it at first hand. He therefore leaves Hamburg and heads south, where he takes the musical world by storm and triumphs in Venice.

1706 Handel ■ (p.65) is invited to Florence by a patron, Prince Gian Gastone de'Medici. He arrives in the autumn and is introduced to Prince Ferdinando de'Medici at Pratolino, near Florence (below).

• Complaints are made in Arnstadt about Bach's lack of control over the choirboys, who 'fight, play games in the classroom and even in the church, drink, gamble and at night roam through the streets shouting' ■ (p.65).

• Rameau publishes the first volume of his monumental *Pièces de clavecin* (Keyboard Pieces) in Paris.

• **Autumn** Telemann becomes court orchestral leader and subsequently director of music at Eisenach.

• **September** Handel meets Alessandro Scarlatti at Pratolino, near Florence (below).

• **11 November** Bach refuses to take choir practice in Arnstadt (left), which prompts the authorities to observe: 'If he does not think it shame to attend church and take his salary, he ought not to be ashamed of music-making with the choir'.

1707 Alessandro Scarlatti's opera *Il Mitridate eupatore* (Mithridates Eupator) is given at the Teatro San Giovanni Grisostomo, Venice, for the Carnival season.

• **January** Handel leaves Florence for Rome, where he composes some psalm-settings and probably begins work on his first ORATORIO, *Il trionfo del tempo e del disinganno* (The Triumph of Time and Disenchantment), completed by May this year to a text by Cardinal Pamphilj.

• **Easter** Bach ■ (p.65) plays the organ at the Blasiuskirche in Mühlhausen and so impresses the authorities that he is offered the post of organist, vacant since the death of Ahle the previous December.

• **9 May** Death of Buxtehude, aged about seventy, in Lübeck ■ (p.65).

• **15 June** Bach signs the receipt for the last portion of his salary earned in Arnstadt, and leaves the city.

• **July** Handel returns to Florence, where *Rodrigo*, his first Italian opera, is given with great success. He goes on to Venice.

• **August** Bach receives a legacy from his uncle, enabling him to marry his cousin Maria Barbara on 17 October.

OTHER EVENTS
1706 The French are defeated by the British and Dutch at the Battle of Ramillies

1707 Act of Union between England and Scotland creates Great Britain

1708 Peter the Great divides Russia into eight administrative districts

1709 *The Tatler* founded
• The ancient Roman theatre at Herculaneum is discovered

Record of quarterly payment to Bach dated 15 September 1706 for his services as organist in Arnstadt. At this time he was already looking for an appointment elsewhere, and the following year he moved to Mühlhausen.

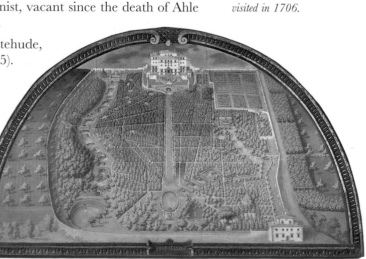

The Medici villa at Pratolino, near Florence, which Handel visited in 1706.

1708 In Venice Handel meets Domenico Scarlatti and Lotti. On his return to Rome, he visits the Arcadian Academy ◆ (below), where he meets Corelli ■ (p.55) and Benedetto Marcello ★ (p.74).

• **4 February** Bach ■ (p.65) writes his first real commission, a CANTATA to mark the elections to the town council of Mühlhausen.

• **8 and 9 April** Handel's ORATORIO *La Resurrezione* is given two sumptuous semi-staged performances in Rome. Corelli is leader of the orchestra of some forty-five players.

• **Autumn** Bach leaves Mühlhausen and enters the service of the Duke of Sachsen-Weimar as court organist.

1709 About this time Handel and Domenico Scarlatti engage in a keyboard duel at the Ottoboni palace in Rome ★ (p.69). Scarlatti is pronounced better on the harpsichord, Handel on the organ.

• Vivaldi ■ (p.71) publishes a set of twelve violin sonatas (left) as his Opus Two, which he dedicates to Frederik IV of Denmark.

• **24 February** Vivaldi is voted out of office at the Pietà.

• **26 December** Handel's opera *Agrippina* is given at the Teatro San Giovanni Grisostomo, Venice, with enormous success.

An Allemanda (left) from Vivaldi's set of twelve sonatas for violin and keyboard, published by Bortoli in Venice in 1709 and then by Roger in Amsterdam. By this time the Venetian printing was becoming old-fashioned by comparison with Dutch engraving.

A caricature (below) of the male soprano Bernacchi, in an elaborate costume typical of Baroque opera. His trills travel over the campanile of St Mark's in Venice, where he enjoyed considerable popularity.

◆ *Opera Seria*

During the lifetime of Bach at least eighty Italians worked in London at one time or another, over one hundred in Vienna, twenty-five at St Petersburg, forty at Dresden and, perhaps most surprising of all, as many as fifty visited Paris.

Their contribution to European music was immense, and was most noticeable in the theatre.

For the first half of the eighteenth century Italian opera continued to enjoy the supremacy which it had won in the seventeenth. With the vogue for Italian composers went that for Italian singers. CASTRATI such as Farinelli and Caffarelli enjoyed a success which has been compared to that of the great movie stars in the heyday of Hollywood.

The classic style of Italian opera was known as opera seria. *The plot, usually on an historical or mythological theme ◆ (p.49), became of little importance. The form was essentially a series of*

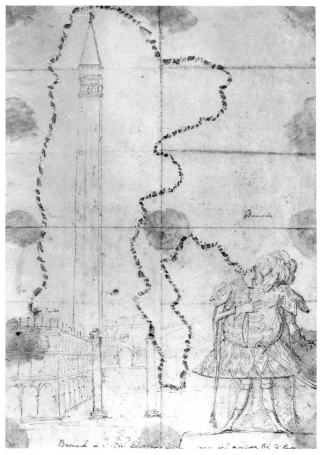

florid ARIAS linked in the most tenuous manner by passages of RECITATIVE, intended to recount the development of the story, but in fact generally regarded by the audience as periods of relaxation. Orchestral interludes served, like the recitatives, primarily as intervals between the arias, while the chorus was almost entirely dispensed with. The aria acquired a three-part form, where the opening section was followed by a contrasting one and then was repeated. Known as the da capo aria, *this was the dominant formal element in* opera seria.

In the eighteenth century opera seria *was the target of both the Arcadian Academy (intellectuals who strived for a return to the classical ideals of Aristotle) and those who felt opera was taking itself too seriously, and encouraged lampoon and pastiche. Despite this, however, the serious convention held its own both in Italy and abroad.*

1710 Handel meets Prince Ernst of Hanover and Baron Kielmansegge in Venice, who encourage him to go to London. He journeys via Hanover, however, where he is appointed music director by Elector Georg Ludwig.

• **8 February** Alessandro Scarlatti's opera *La principessa fedele* (The Faithful Princess) is given at the Teatro San Bartolomeo, Naples (below).

• **16 June** Handel takes up his appointment at the Court of Hanover, with immediate leave to pay a visit to England.

• **17 June** Campra's *Les Fêtes vénitiennes*, designated an *opéra-ballet comique*, is given for the first time in Paris.

• **Autumn** Handel visits his mother in Halle and leaves for London, where he is presented to Queen Anne. Aaron Hill ★ (p.85), manager of the Queen's (later King's) Theatre, proposes that he write an opera to an Italian libretto by Rossi. Handel completes the work, entitled *Rinaldo* ▲ (opposite), in a fortnight.

1711 Vivaldi publishes his set of twelve violin CONCERTOS *L'estro armonico* (The Soul of Music).

• **24 February** Handel's opera *Rinaldo* ▲ (opposite) is first heard at the Queen's Theatre in London, and receives fifteen performances before the season ends on 2 June, after which the composer returns to Germany.

'I was not a little astonished to see a well-dressed young Fellow, in a full bottom'd Wigg, appear in the midst of the Sea, and without any visible Concern taking Snuff.'
Sir Richard Steele on a performance of Handel's opera *Rinaldo*, 1711.

• **July** Handel studies English and is in touch with the poet John Hughes, whose cantata *Venus and Adonis* he sets to music. He also writes a series of duets for Princess Caroline of Ansbach and some oboe CONCERTOS.

• **27 September** Vivaldi ■ (p.71) regains his position as violin master at the Pietà in Venice (p.67).

1712 Handel requests permission to return to England. The Elector of Hanover agrees, on condition that the composer 'return within a reasonable time', but when he arrives in London later in the year, Handel will settle in the British capital for good.

• Alessandro Scarlatti's opera *Il Ciro* (Cyrus) is given at the Ottoboni Theatre at the Palazzo della Cancellaria, Rome (opposite).

1713 The Earl of Burlington invites Handel to live in his house in Piccadilly, London.

• Couperin publishes the first of four books of keyboard SUITES entitled *Pièces de clavecin*. Each dance has a programmatic title.

• **8 January** Corelli ■ (p.55) dies in Rome, aged fifty-nine, and is buried in the Pantheon.

• **10 January** Handel's *Teseo* is produced at the Queen's Theatre, but after the second showing the new manager absconds with the takings, leaving Handel and the cast unpaid.

• **30 April** Vivaldi is granted a month's leave from the Pietà and goes to Vicenza, where his first opera, *Ottone in Villa*, is performed at the Teatro delle Grazie in May.

• **November** Domenico Scarlatti becomes assistant director of music at the Cappella Giulia of St Peter's, Rome.

OTHER EVENTS

1710 George Berkeley (1685-1753) completes *A Treatise concerning the Principles of Human Knowledge*

1711 Charles V becomes Holy Roman Emperor (d.1740)
• Alexander Pope (1688-1744) publishes his *Essay on Criticism*
• Foundation of *The Spectator*

1712 The Act of Toleration is passed in England
• Pope completes *The Rape of the Lock*

1713 The Peace of Utrecht ends the War of Spanish Succession
• The Pragmatic Sanction reserves the Hapsburg succession to Maria Theresa

★ *Alessandro Scarlatti (below) left Naples in 1703, but failed to find a suitable post elsewhere. He was assistant organist at Santa Maria Maggiore in Rome for a short time (p.64), but returned to Naples at the end of 1708. He wears here the insignia of knighthood bestowed on him by the pope in 1715.*

★ *An engraving of the Palazzo della Cancellaria in Rome, scene of the competition between Handel and Domenico Scarlatti ★ (p.67) and home of Cardinal Ottoboni ★ (p.55). Ottoboni was a highly cultured Venetian, whose love of opera resulted in the production at his palace of works by Bononcini, Pollarolo and Alessandro Scarlatti.*

▲ *Two Accounts of the Genesis of Handel's* Rinaldo

I resolv'd to frame some *Dramma*, that, by different *Incidents* and *Passions*, might afford the *Musick* Scope to vary and display its *Excellence*, and fill the Eye with more delightful *Prospects*, so at once to give two *Senses* equal Pleasure.

I could not chuse a finer Subject that the celebrated Story of Rinaldo and Armida.... I have, however...vary'd from the Scheme of Tasso... for the better forming a Theatrical Representation.

It was a very particular Happiness, that I met with a Gentleman so excellently qualify'd as Signor Rossi, to fill up the Model I had drawn ...that if my Translation is in many Places to deviate, 'tis for want of Power to reach the Force of his Original.

Aaron Hill ★ (p.85) in his preface to *Rinaldo*, 1711.

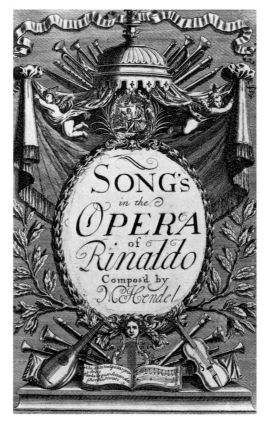

The title page (right) of the first edition of Handel's opera Rinaldo, published by Walsh at 'the Harp and Hoboy in Katherine Street, near Somerset House in the Strand' and also at 'the Viol and Flute in Cornhill near the Royal Exchange'.

S ignor Hendel [sic], the Orpheus of our Age, in setting to music this lay from Parnassus [Greek myth], has scarcely given me time enough to write it, and I have beheld, to my great astonishment, an entire opera harmonized to the last degree of perfection in the short space of a fortnight by this sublime genius (p.68).

I pray you then, discreet reader, to receive my rapid work and, if it does not merit all your praises, at least do not refuse it your compassion, I would rather say your justice, remembering how short a time I have had to write it.

Giacomo Rossi, from his libretto of *Rinaldo*, 1711. Handel wrote the opera so quickly by using material from previous works.

1714-16
Vivaldi and Venice

Although destined to be remembered for his concertos, Vivaldi is drawn to opera, that supremely Venetian institution, for which he composes numerous works. Despite being in holy orders, he acts as his own impresario, extending his activities far beyond the city.

1714 Vivaldi begins his association with the Teatro Sant'Angelo in Venice and publishes his set of concertos entitled *La stravaganza* (The Extravaganza or Unconventional).

• Bach is promoted to director of the orchestra at Weimar (below).

• **26 September** A Te Deum by Handel is sung at St James's Palace in the presence of the new king, George I, the former Elector of Hanover.

• **Autumn** Vivaldi's opera *Orlando finto pazzo* (Orlando Driven Mad) is given at the Teatro Sant'Angelo, Venice.

1715 Geminiani, a violin virtuoso, insists on Handel accompanying him on the harpsichord ◆ (p.51) when he performs before the London court.

• First Opéra-comique founded in Paris.

• **4 February** A German visitor to Venice, Johann von Uffenbach, hears Vivaldi play the violin and is amazed at his skill. On 6 March he commissions some *concerti grossi* from the composer.

• **March** Bach's salary is increased to match that of the director and assistant director of music at Weimar.

• **2 June** Vivaldi ■ (p.71) is voted a special payment by the governors of the Pietà for composing works for the chapel of the orphanage.

• **October** Handel ■ (p.65) receives his salary for six months from the treasury in Hanover.

A portrait thought to be that of Bach, painted around 1715, after he had been promoted to orchestral leader at Weimar. Bach's initial appointment in 1708 had been as organist to the court of Duke Wilhelm Ernst of Sachsen-Weimar, which meant that he composed no cantatas or liturgical music for at least five years between leaving Mühlhausen and his promotion in 1714.

1716 Vivaldi publishes a set of six SONATAS and a set of six CONCERTOS in five parts.

• **29 March** Vivaldi is voted out of office by the governors of the Pietà, who are disturbed by the amount of time he is devoting to opera.

• **24 May** Vivaldi is reinstated at the Pietà as director of the orchestra.

• **20 June** Handel adds 'two New Symphonies' (orchestral interludes) to his opera *Amadigi*, including an extract from a concerto, later to be published as part of his Opus Three.

• **July** Handel visits Ansbach, where he persuades an old friend, Johann Christoph Schmidt, to work for him. Father and son, anglicized as John Christopher Smith ★ (p.96), will serve Handel until his death.

• **1 December** The death of Samuel Drese, director of music at Weimar, leads Bach to hope that he will be appointed in his place. Instead Drese's son, deputy director, is advanced, and Bach decides to leave Weimar.

OTHER EVENTS
1714 Accession of George I of England
• Gottfried Leibniz: *Monadologie*, expounding his metaphysical doctrine.
• Fahrenheit constructs mercury thermometer

1715 Accession of Louis XV of France
• First Jacobite rebellion in Scotland

1716 *Diario di Roma*, first Italian newspaper, founded

'Vivaldi played a solo accompaniment... but I cannot say it pleased me, for it was not so pleasant to listen to as it was skilfully performed.'

Johann von Uffenbach on Vivaldi's playing, 4 February, 1715.

■ *Vivaldi and the Ospedali: Music for Venice's Orphans*

During the first half of the eighteenth century in Venice, orphaned girls were housed and educated in establishments known as *ospedali*. Musical standards in the *ospedali* were extremely high, with distinguished and accomplished musicians such as Vivaldi – himself on the staff of the Ospedale della Pietà from 1703 – engaged to teach the girls.

The pupils at the *ospedali* gave concerts of vocal and instrumental music, which soon become the rage of Venetian music lovers and an obligatory part of any foreigner's visit to the city. Contemporary accounts, such as those of the German Johann von Uffenbach in 1715 (opposite), or the Frenchman Charles de Brosses in 1739 and 1740, provide us with valuable information about the organization of the musical life of the day. The girls, according to de Brosses, play 'the violin, the recorder, the organ, the oboe, the cello, the bassoon; in short, no instrument is large enough to frighten them', and their abilities extend to clarinets, horns and timpani.

Private as well as public money was forthcoming to maintain the many fatherless children in a Venice of vast maritime commerce, but proceeds from the concerts

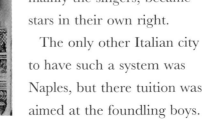

helped greatly to underwrite the running of the *ospedali*. Pupils were encouraged to be as versatile as possible, and for an innovator and experimenter such as Vivaldi, they rovided an unequalled pool of talent, erforming his works to perfection, and also inspiring him to try out new and unusual instrumental and orchestral effects.

The choice of a musical education for the orphans was a wise one, considering the demand for singers and players, and although many pupils took the veil, some, mainly the singers, became stars in their own right.

The only other Italian city to have such a system was Naples, but there tuition was aimed at the foundling boys.

Longhi's painting (above) of a singing lesson shows the important place occupied by music in eighteenth-century Venice. The city boasted four female orphanages whose most gifted singers enjoyed the sort of adulation usually reserved for opera stars. The girls might be known by their Christian name, followed by that of the particular institution to which they belonged, and they were also asked to give recitals outside Venice.

Concerts of instrumental and vocal music by the girls of the ospedali were usually given in the chapels or churches of their own orphanages, and because these foundations were run by religious orders, they performed from galleries, behind grilles (left), which can still be seen in Venice today at the Pietà and the Ospedaletto.

1717-21
The Genius of Bach

Bach moves from Weimar to Cöthen, where his genius is more clearly recognized. Vivaldi, too, finds a new appointment in Mantua. In England, Handel consolidates his position, and embarks on the most ambitious enterprise of his career so far.

A portrait of Prince Leopold of Anhalt-Cöthen, who was only twenty-three when Bach left Weimar in December 1717 to take up his appointment as director of music. Since Cöthen was a Calvinist state, only the plainest music without instruments was used in church services, for which Bach was not even required to play the organ. He therefore devoted himself to secular instrumental composition at this time, and any cantatas that he composed were for secular occasions, such as the prince's birthday.

1717 Couperin publishes the second book of his *Pièces de clavecin* (p.68) and his keyboard tutor *L'art de toucher le clavecin* (The Art of Playing the Harpsichord), in Paris. The latter also contains six PRELUDES for keyboard.

• Vivaldi leaves the Pietà ■ (p.71).

• Lotti's opera *Giove in Argo* (Zeus in Argos) is given in Dresden where the composer has taken up residence with his wife, the singer Santa Stella.

• **5 January** Handel's opera *Rinaldo* ▲ (p.69), revised by the composer, is revived at the King's Theatre, London.

• **29 June** The King's Theatre, London, closes for opera and will not reopen for almost three years, except for concerts, balls and French comedies.

• **17 July** Handel's *Water Music* is played in a barge on the Thames by some fifty musicians following the king's barge up the river from Whitehall to Chelsea. Although the king had requested the music, it is provided at the expense of Baron Kielmansegge.

• **August** Bach's wife and four children are installed in Cöthen, where the composer intends to take up residence at the court of Prince Leopold (below), earning twice the salary, but his current employer in Weimar will not release him from his contract.

• **25 September** The Earl of Carnarvon reports that Handel has written two ANTHEMS for him, and is working on two more.

• **6 November** Bach is imprisoned by his employer until 2 December for demanding to be released from his service in Weimar. He is now finally free to go to Cöthen.

1718 Vivaldi goes to Mantua as director of chamber music to the Prince of Hesse-Darmstadt.

• **May** Handel's English masque *Acis and Galatea* ◆ (p.35) is performed at Cannons, near London.

• Bach accompanies the Prince of Anhalt-Cöthen to the spa at Karlsbad, where it is possible that he meets the Margrave of Brandenburg, to whom he will dedicate the six *Brandenburg* Concertos (p.75).

1719 A Royal Academy of Music in London is planned, with the intention of securing a constant supply of operas. The Proposal reads: 'Opera's [*sic*] are the most harmless of all

> *'I thought that the art was dead, but I see that it lives once more.'*
> Johann Adam Reincken, in his hundredth year, hearing Bach improvise in Hamburg in 1720

Frontispiece and title page of Hotteterre's manual for the flute, recorder and oboe (opposite), which was originally published in Paris in 1707, but went through several editions and revisions, such as the one here dating from 1720.

OTHER EVENTS
1717 Inoculation against smallpox introduced in England
• Watteau: *The Embarkation for the Island of Cythera*

1718 Quadruple Alliance formed between Holland, Britain, France and the Holy Roman Empire
• Sicily becomes an Austrian possession and the Duke of Savoy obtains Sardinia in exchange

1719 Defoe: *Robinson Crusoe*

◆ Developments in Woodwind Instruments

In France the woodwind instruments, including shawms (ancestors of the oboe), curtals (later bassoons), crumhorns, bagpipes and fifes, formed part of the Grande Ecurie (literally the royal stables) and were used for processions and ceremonies 'because of the great noise they make'. A group of composers, players and craftsmen from the Grande Ecurie, chief among them Jean Hotteterre (below) and André Philidor, redesigned some of the instruments during the seventeenth century, making them suitable for indoor use. Their principal improvements were made to the transverse flute, oboe and bassoon.

The main problems with wind instruments were that they were often out of tune, difficult to play, and very raucous. By dividing the instrument into several sections instead of using one piece of wood, as had been the case hitherto, the finger holes could be placed accurately, making the INTONATION more precise, while fine tuning could be achieved by lengthening the instrument at the joins. The remaining problems were alleviated by reducing the diameter of the fingerholes, thus making them easier to cover, and reducing the bore size, thereby softening the TONE.

Improvements to the transverse flute included the abandonment of the cylindrical for a conical bore, which was shortly followed by the provision of a B-flat key. This design was used until Böhm made his modifications in the nineteenth century. It is interesting to note that in Germany the recorder continued to be favoured above the flute by many composers including Bach.

It was to the oboe or 'hautbois' that most improvement was made. By reducing the bore slightly throughout, the instrument produced a full, sweet tone which blended well with strings, while the subsequent addition of keys gave greater flexibility and range. The oboe seems to have made its debut in a ballet by Lully in the late 1650s.

The bassoon was also modified by the Hotteterre group, who, by dividing the body into four segments and altering the position of the holes, developed the instrument which was used throughout the eighteenth century.

A firework display given in Dresden in September 1719 for the marriage of the future Elector Frederick Augustus to Maria Josepha, daughter of the Holy Roman Emperor. Such lavish celebrations were greatly favoured as a means of marking important dynastic events in the eighteenth century.

publick Diversions. They are an Encouragement and Support to an Art that has been cherished by all Polite Nations.'

• **20 February** Handel writes to his brother-in-law in Germany that he must postpone his visit to his mother in Halle: 'I find myself kept here by affairs of the greatest moment, on which (I venture to say) all my fortunes depend.'

• **14 May** The Lord Chamberlain issues a warrant for Handel to travel abroad and engage singers for the Royal Academy.

• Handel visits Düsseldorf and Halle, where he narrowly misses Bach, who is travelling from Cöthen to try and see him.

• **July** Handel is in Dresden, where he tries to induce the CASTRATI Berselli and Senesino to come to London.

• **September** Lotti's opera *Teofane* (Theophanes) is given in Dresden to celebrate the wedding of the Elector of Saxony to Maria Josepha, daughter of Emperor Joseph I of Austria (above). Handel retains a copy of the libretto, which he will utilize for his opera *Ottone* (Otho).

• **30 November** Handel is appointed 'Master of the Orchestra with a Sallary [unspecified]' for the Royal Academy.

1720 The directors of the Royal Academy approach Bononcini (opposite) in Rome 'to know his Terms for composing and performing in the Orchestra'.

• Vivaldi returns to Venice from Mantua. His opera *Gli inganni per vendetta* (The Deceptions for Revenge) is given at the Teatro delle Grazie, Vicenza.

• **2 April** The Royal Academy opens in London with Porta's *Numitore* (Numitor). Handel's *Radamisto* (Radamistus) is held back until the king can attend.

• **27 April** Handel's *Radamisto*, dedicated to the king, opens in London to enormous enthusiasm.

• **May** Bach attends Prince Leopold in Karlsbad for several weeks, during which time his wife dies and is buried. He first learns of her death on his return home.

• **19 November** The second opera season begins in London with Bononcini's opera *Astarto* (Astartes), starring the castrati Berselli and Senesino. For the next few years London becomes the operatic capital of Europe, with the best singers, composers, set and costume designs.

★ *Benedetto Marcello (above) and his older brother Alessandro were well-to-do members of the Venetian ruling class, and composed music chiefly for their own enjoyment and that of their immediate circle, which is why Benedetto poured scorn on what he saw as the commercialism of Vivaldi and his associates.*

• **November** Bach travels to Hamburg and plays the organ for nearly two hours in front of the town dignitaries. While there he applies for the post of organist at the Jacobikirche in Hamburg, but on the day of the auditions decides to 'return to his Prince' at Cöthen.

• **December** Benedetto Marcello's satirical pamphlet on Vivaldi and his associates, *Il teatro alla moda* (The Theatre in Fashion), ridicules the composer's activities in the opera house (above left).

OTHER EVENTS
1720 The 'South Sea Bubble', an English speculation craze, bursts
• John Law's Mississippi Company fails, leading to French national bankruptcy
• Palatinate court moves to Mannheim

1721 Peter the Great is proclaimed Emperor of All the Russias
• The Treaty of Nystadt gives Russia control of the Baltic coastline and a tacit protectorate over Poland
• Cabinet government established in Britain
• Baron de Montesquieu: *Lettres persanes*

1721 Bach dedicates the six Brandenburg Concertos, of a type known as *concerti grossi*, to the Margrave of Brandenburg. The works are notable for their richly varied instrumentation.

• **15 April** The opera *Muzio Scevola* (Mucius Scaevola) opens at the King's Theatre in London. The theatre's three resident composers, Amadei, Bononcini (right) and Handel each compose an act, and that of the latter is found to be the best.

• **4 June** Telemann moves to Hamburg and takes up the position of CANTOR at the Gymnasium Johanneum.

• **1 November** The third season of the Royal Academy of Music opens.

• **3 December** Bach marries his second wife, Anna Magdalena Wülcken, the daughter of a trumpeter in the service of the prince of Saxe-Weissenfels, and herself an accomplished harpsichordist, singer and copyist.

▲ *Bach Competes for a Post in Hamburg in 1720*

I remember, and doubtless other people still remember also, that some years ago a great musician [Bach], who since then has, as he deserves, obtained an important appointment as cantor [in Leipzig], appeared in a certain town of some size [Hamburg], confidently performed on the largest and finest instruments, and drew universal admiration by his skill. At the same time, among other lesser performers, there presented himself the son of a comfortable artisan, who was able to play better with thalers [coins] than with his fingers, and the appointment went to him, as may easily be assumed, although nearly all were angered by it. It was close to Christmas, and an eloquent preacher [Erdmann Neumeister], who had not been party to this act of simony [bought preferment], expounded very elegantly the gospel about the angelic music at the birth of Christ, which very naturally gave him the occasion of expressing his opinions about the recent event concerning the rejected artist, and of ending his sermon with this noteworthy epiphenomenon: He believed quite certainly that if an angel from Bethlehem came down from heaven, played divinely and wished to be organist of the Jacobikirche, if he had no money he would have no alternative but to fly away again.

Johann Mattheson
Der musikalische Patriot, *1728*

Bononcini studied and later worked in Bologna before he joined the orchestra of Cardinal Pamphilj in Rome, and then moved on to Vienna. After working at the Imperial court for more than a decade he returned to Italy, by now a highly experienced operatic composer, and it was in this capacity that he was invited to work in London in 1720, where he become Handel's chief competitor in the theatre.

Bach's many compositions for organ, and keyboard in general, remained at the heart of his life and work, and his ideal was to dedicate himself to the service of God. Appropriately inscribed above the keyboard of the organ here is the last verse of Psalm 150: 'Let everything that breath, praise the Lord'. The engraving also shows some interesting features of contemporary music making such as the rolled sheets of music with which the conductor directs the players, and the pike-nose bows used by the string players.

1722-25
Bach Moves to Leipzig

Bach applies for the vacant position of director of music at Leipzig. Though he is not the first choice, he is appointed in due course. For Bach the move is a conscious decision to dedicate his talents to the service of the church. Sadly, he is destined to be disillusioned.

1722 Bach completes the first book of his keyboard collection *The Well-Tempered* (or *Tuned*) *Clavier*, twenty-four PRELUDES and FUGUES in all MAJOR and MINOR keys. The work will not be published during his life.

• Rameau publishes his *Traité de l'harmonie* (Treatise on Harmony), in Paris.

• Couperin completes the third volume of his *Pièces de clavecin* (p.68).

• **5 June** The death of Kuhnau in Leipzig opens the way for Bach to apply for the post of CANTOR ■ (p.77), though Telemann (p.75) is the first choice of the councillors.

• **August** Telemann is appointed to Leipzig.

• **October** Telemann's salary is increased in Hamburg, and he decides not to leave.

• **December** Graupner is the new choice for cantor at Leipzig, but accused of trying to improve his situation at Darmstadt, he withdraws, recommending Bach in his place.

• **20 December** Domenico Scarlatti's serenata *Le nozze di Baco e Arianna* (The Marriage of Bacchus and Ariadne) is performed in Lisbon, in preparation for the composer taking up his post there.

1723 12 January Handel's *Ottone* is performed at the King's Theatre. Despite her initial reluctance to sing one of the ARIAS (left), the soprano Francesca Cuzzoni takes the house by storm.

• **25 February** Handel is appointed 'Composer of Musick for His Majesty's Chapel Royal'.

It is thought that the central standing figure (above) may be Handel. When introduced to the music of Ottone, *Cuzzoni refused to sing Handel's aria 'Falsa imagine', whereupon the composer threatened to throw her out of the window. In the event the aria assured her triumph.*

• **30 May** Bach makes his debut as cantor at Leipzig's Thomasschule.

• **2 July** The governers of the Pietà ■ (p.71) engage Vivaldi to provide two concertos monthly and direct two or three rehearsals in person.

• **18 July** Bach's funeral motet *Jesu meine Freude* (Jesu my Joy) is given at the memorial service for the wife of the postmaster of Leipzig.

• **Christmas** Bach's Magnificat is first heard in Leipzig.

1724 20 February Handel's opera *Giulio Cesare* is performed for the first time at the King's Theatre, London.

• **7 April** Bach's *St John Passion* is given its first hearing at the Nikolaikirche, Leipzig.

• **Autumn** Vivaldi first hears the contralto Anna Girò at the Teatro San Moisè in Venice, and she subsequently becomes the star of his operas and his close companion (p.86).

OTHER EVENTS
1722 Afghan-Persian War Persia dismembered by Turks and Russians
• Austrian East India Company founded

1723 Louis XV attains majority
• Voltaire: *La Henriade*
• Christopher Wren dies

1724 Paris Bourse opens
• China closes to Westerners and missionaries expelled
• Birth of Immanuel Kant

1725 Peter the Great dies and is succeeded by his wife, Catherine I
• St Petersburg Academy of Science is founded

1725 The *Concert spirituel* is inaugurated in Paris, one of the first series of regular public orchestral and choral concerts that will increase general interest in, and demand for, music and raise professional standards.

• Fux (left), director of music at the Viennese court, publishes his important treatise on music, *Gradus ad Parnassum*, which will be translated into German, Italian, English and French.

• **13 February** Handel's *Rodelinda* is a great success at the King's Theatre, running for fourteen performances. Cuzzoni is the toast of London, and women imitate her dresses.

• **Summer** The directors of the Royal Academy of Music decide to invite the soprano Faustina Bordoni ★ (p.78) to London, in addition to Cuzzoni, as a lure for audiences.

• **22 October** Alessandro Scarlatti ★ (p.68) dies in Naples at the age of sixty-five.

• **14 December** The *Gazette d'Amsterdam* announces the publication of Vivaldi's Twelve Concertos Op.8, under the title *Il cimento dell'armonia e dell'inventione* (The Contest between Harmony and Invention), containing the four concertos known as *The Four Seasons*. The title implies the striking of a balance between the more cerebral aspect of composition (Harmony) and the powers of imagination (Invention).

★ *Fux was typical of the career musician in the early eighteenth century. After working for the Archbishop-Primate of Hungary he was appointed court composer in Vienna in 1698 (p.60), then went to study in Rome with Pasquini, and on his return to Vienna was both a court musician and organist of St Stephen's Cathedral, becoming director of music to the court in 1715. In addition to his church music and chamber music he also wrote several operas.*

■ *Bach's Appointment at Leipzig*

When Bach was being considered for the post of cantor in Leipzig, few of the members of the appointing committee – if indeed any of them – could have known that they were dealing with one of the greatest musical geniuses of the day, or indeed of any age. They were aware that he was a virtuoso organist, and well informed about keyboard and other instruments. Playing the organ and writing music were, however, only part of the duties expected of the person they eventually chose, and if they had knowledge of Bach's difficulties in the past in dealing with unruly choirboys, they did well to hesitate to appoint him, or even put him on their short list (p.66).

In addition to performing and composing, Bach was expected to teach music and act as a kind of housemaster at a boarding school, taking his turn with three other members of staff in being in charge for a week at a time, when he was responsible for taking morning and evening prayers, supervising meals, paying calls to the sanatorium and seeing that the boys came back from weddings and funerals in a sober and orderly manner. It must also be remembered that some of the boys might have been approaching twenty.

A view of Leipzig (below) during the time that Bach lived and worked in the city, painted from a spot close to his home. In the gardens across the river the composer's birthday cantata for King Augustus II of Saxony is said to have been performed on 12 May 1727.

The school trained choristers for four Leipzig churches; the best sang at the Nikolaikirche and Thomaskirche, and the others at the Neukirche and Peterskirche. Under the terms of his contract, Bach was not allowed to leave Leipzig without permission from the mayor.

1726-28
The International Perspective

As Italian opera becomes an internationally practised form, composers and singers become celebrities in their own right, travelling extensively to the cities where their services are required, and commanding large fees for doing so. Only France remains aloof for the time being.

1726 Rameau publishes his treatise *Nouveau système de musique théorique* (New System of Music Theory) in Paris, underlining the expansion in musical theory and education now taking place.

• Bach completes his earliest printed keyboard work, a PARTITA for harpsichord, which he publishes at his own expense.

• **5 May** Handel produces his new opera, *Alessandro* (Alexander), with roles for the CASTRATO Senesino and the prima donnas Cuzzoni and Bordoni (left). Rivalry breaks out between the sopranos, and Dr Burney writes: 'It seems impossible for two singers of equal merit to tread the same stage, *a parte equale* [on equal footing], as for two people to ride on the same horse, without one being behind.'

• **13 October** A private contract between the singer Lucrezia Baldini and Vivaldi, names the latter as director of the Teatro Sant'Angelo, Venice.

★ *Faustina Bordoni was born into a noble Venetian family, and in her youth had had Benedetto Marcello ★ (p.74) as her mentor. In 1724 she sang in Vienna in operas by Caldara and Fux ★ (p.77) and was on intimate terms with members of the Imperial family. She had already an international reputation, therefore, when she arrived in London in 1726.*

1727 13 February Handel applies to become a naturalized British subject. Royal assent is given a week later.

• **May** Vivaldi's opera *Siroe, re di Persia* (Cyrus, King of Persia), the first Metastasio libretto to be set by the composer ■ (opposite), is given at the Teatro Pubblico in Reggio Emilia.

• **6 June** The rivalry between Cuzzoni and Bordoni (above) reaches its climax when the prima donnas come to blows on the stage, in the presence of the Princess of Wales. The audience is delighted, but the opera season is brought to a close.

• **11 October** Handel composes four ANTHEMS for the coronation of George II, including *Zadok the Priest* (right), which will be sung at every future British coronation.

• **11 November** The future of the Royal Academy is in doubt. Mrs Pendarves tells her sister: 'The subscription is expired and nobody will renew it.'

1728 Vivaldi meets Emperor Charles VI, who is said to give him a large sum of money and 'spoke more to him in private in a fortnight than he speaks to his ministers in two years'.

• **29 January** Gay's *The Beggar's Opera*, an English riposte to Italian opera, runs for sixty-two performances at the Lincoln's Inn Fields Theatre.

• **17 February** Handel uses a libretto by Metastasio ■ (p.79) for the first time in his new opera, *Siroe, re di Persia* (Cyrus, King of Persia).

• **15 May** Domenico Scarlatti, forty-two, marries Maria Catarina Gentili, sixteen, in the church of San Pancrazio, Rome.

• **1 June** The Royal Academy closes.

OTHER EVENTS
1726 First circulation library established in Edinburgh by Ramsay
• Voltaire, banished from France, flees to England
• Swift: *Gulliver's Travels*

1727 George I of England dies; George II suceeds him
• Isaac Newton dies

1728 Dutch explorer Vitus Behring finds Behring Strait

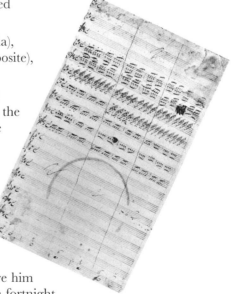

The opening orchestral bars of Handel's autograph score of the coronation anthem Zadok the Priest, in which Handel portrayed the solemn dignity of the occasion, using extracts from works already composed in Italy, but in so doing he created a style uniquely suited to the occasion.

The castrato Farinelli, in the centre of the painting, holding one of his own songs, was the greatest operatic star of the age, creating a sensation whenever he sang. He took part in a famous contest with Bernacchi ★ (p.67) in Bologna in 1727, from which the two men emerged great friends. At his shoulder is the artist, Amigoni, and at his side the soprano Teresa Castellini. The person in clerical dress at the left is the librettist Metastasio ■ (below).

■ *Pietro Metastasio: Librettist*

Of all the writers who produced operatic librettos, or whose works were used as the basis for librettos, Metastasio is one of the most important. Born Pietro Trapassi in Rome on 3 January 1698, he first studied law, but his interest in the theatre of Classical antiquity induced him to use the Greek translation of his name, and embark on a literary career.

On the death of his protector, a wealthy lawyer and writer called Gravina, Metastasio went to Naples. Here he realised his interest in theatre music, writing texts for Porpora, Feo and Sarro. He was appointed court poet in Vienna in 1730, where he stayed until his death in 1782. As a measure of Metastasio's success as a librettist, his *Alessandro nell'Indie* (Alexander in India) was set no less than sixty-eight times between 1729 and 1824, *Artaserse* (Artaxerxes) eighty times between

1730 and 1795, and *La Clemenza di Tito* (The Clemency of Titus) forty-one times between 1734 and 1839, with Mozart using it in 1791.

Metastasio was not a passive contributor to the evolution of opera, for he had very precise ideas on the structure of operas, and the roles of librettist and composer. For example, his love of Classical drama led him to reintroduce the chorus, especially at the climax of an opera; he preferred using accompanied RECITATIVE to SECCO believing it to be more expressive; he reduced the number of acts from five to three, condensing the action and increasing the work's impact; and he decided that six was the perfect number for a cast. Above all, his language was simple and ideal to set to music.

Illustration and start of the cast list for a Metastasio libretto on the story of Semiramide, which Vinci set as La Semiramide riconosciuta *(Semiramide Recognized) for Rome in 1729. Although Gluck also used it, it did not prove as popular with composers as certain others that Metastasio wrote.*

1729-36
A Time for Reflection

As the third decade of the century unfolds, what once seemed certain becomes less sure. In London Handel is faced with the fact that Italian opera is less popular. In Leipzig Bach is disenchanted with the church he has served for so long, and even contemplates leaving the city, while in Venice Vivaldi plans to seek his fortune abroad.

1729 Vivaldi publishes the first known Concertos for Flute and Strings Op.11, as well as his twelve Violin Concertos Op.12.

• Bach becomes director of the Collegium Musicum refounded in Leipzig by Telemann in 1702 (p.64).

• **January** In a double wedding, the Spanish Infanta marries Don José of Portugal, and the Crown Prince of Spain marries Maria Barbara of Portugal, whom Domenico Scarlatti serves as music master. He follows his mistress to Spain, where he will spend the rest of his life.

• **18 January** The directors of the Royal Academy in London let the King's Theatre to Handel and John James Heidegger (left), 'to carry on operas without disturbance for five years'. They also will lend them costumes, scenery and stage machines, so that existing operas may be cheaply revived.

• **February** Handel goes to the Continent in search of singers, and visits Venice and Rome.

• **Good Friday** First whole performance of Bach's *St Matthew Passion* in the Thomaskirche, Leipzig.

• **June** Handel visits his mother in Halle for the last time, and goes on to Hanover, returning to London at the end of the month.

• **30 September** Vivaldi's father applies for a year's leave from St Mark's Venice, to accompany his son to Bohemia.

• **26 November** The French ambassador in Rome celebrates the birth of the dauphin, son of Louis XV, with a performance Vinci's *La contesa dei Numi* (The Contest of the Gods), based on a text by Metastasio (opposite).

• **2 December** Opening of the first Handel-Heidegger opera season in London with a new opera by Handel, *Lotario* (Lothario), which runs for only ten performances and is never revived.

1730 Handel now resorts to revivals of his own and other composers' operas, or compilations known as pasticcios, to maintain his venture with Heidegger.

• Bordoni ★ (p.78) marries the composer Hasse.

• **24 February** With his new opera *Partenope* (Parthenope), Handel moves away from *opera seria* ◆ (p.67) to a form of ironic comedy, but this fails to please, and the work runs for only seven performances.

• **August** Bach's employers accuse him of neglecting to take singing lessons and of having unauthorized leave of absence ▲ (p.83).

Heidegger, the impresario of Swiss origin whom Handel met when he first visited London, and with whom he collaborated as musical director to Heidegger's manager when the Royal Academy of Music was set up in 1719 to provide Italian opera in London. When that company failed, the two men set up their own company from 1729 until 1734.

OTHER EVENTS
1729 The name Methodists is first given to members of Charles Wesley's Holy Club at Oxford
• Founding of Baltimore

1730 Prince Frederick of Prussia (the future Frederick the Great) tries to escape to the English court and is imprisoned by his father

1731 Treaty of Vienna between England, Holland, Spain and the Holy Roman Empire
• Hogarth: *A Harlot's Progress*
• Abbé Prévost: *Manon Lescaut*

'He shows no disposition to work.'
The mayor of Leipzig after speaking to Bach in August 1730

• **28 October** Bach writes to Georg Erdmann, Russian consul in Gdansk, asking for a post there ▲ (p.83). However, the rector in Leipzig dies, and his replacement by a friend of Bach's, Johann Matthias Gesner, leads to a temporary improvement in relations. Bach now more or less abandons church compositions and devotes his attention to the Collegium Musicum.

• **25 November** The *Mercure de France* reports that Louis XV has commanded an impromptu performance of Vivaldi's violin concerto *La primavera* (Spring) at court.

1731 Bach completes the six PARTITAS (p.78) for harpsichord that constitute the first part of the *Clavierübung*, a collection of keyboard music that will eventually appear in three sections.

• **2 February** A new Handel opera, *Poro, re dell'Indie* (Porus, King of India), whose libretto is adapted from Metastasio's ■ (p.79) *Alessandro nell'Indie*, achieves sixteen performances.

• **Good Friday** Bach's *St Mark Passion*, made up from existing works, including the *Funeral Ode*, is performed in Leipzig.

• **13 September** Hasse is appointed director of music to the King of Poland and Elector of Saxony.

A magnificent costumed cantata, Vinci's La contesa dei Numi, *was performed in the palace of the Cardinal de Polignac, French Ambassador in Rome, to celebrate the birth of the Dauphin in 1729. The courtyard of the palace was turned into a theatre for the occasion, and the setting depicts Olympus, with the chariot of the sun, and statues of five great French kings in the colonnade.*

Handel, painted around 1730, deep in thought, seated next to a harpsichord and working on a composition. Handel may have commissioned the portrait himself from Mercier, who was also working for the Prince of Wales ★ (p.84) at this time, since the composer kept it in his possession for some fifteen years, and no other version is known.

1732 January Vivaldi's opera *Semiramide* (Semiramis), to a Metastasio ■ (p.79) LIBRETTO, is heard at the Teatro Arciducale, Mantua.

• **15 January** Handel experiences the lowpoint of his operatic career with his new opera *Ezio* (Aetius) which runs for only five performances.

• **15 February** Handel's next opera, *Sosarme, re di Media* (Sosarmes, King of Media), is better received, lasting eleven performances. In it he cuts the unpopular recitatives, thus making the plot incomprehensible without a summary in the libretto. This practice becomes more usual in London, further jeopardizing Italian opera.

• **23 February** The first of three private performances of Handel's ORATORIO *Esther* is given at the Crown and Anchor Tavern in London. This, the birth of British oratorio, is such a success that Princess Anne ★ (p.84) requests that it be transferred to the King's Theatre.

• **31 March** Haydn is born at Rohrau.

• **2 May** A performance of *Esther* is given by Handel at the King's Theatre. The oratorio is not acted as the Bishop of London forbids the representation of a sacred subject in the opera house.

• **28 September** Pergolesi composes his three-act comic opera *Lo frate 'nnamurato* (The Lovelorn Brother) for the Teatro dei Fiorentini in Naples, marking a growing trend for dialect comic opera.

• **5 December** Handel's old associate, Aaron Hill ★ (p.85), begs him to compose to English texts. Handel declines to do so for the time being.

• **7 December** John Rich opens a theatre at Covent Garden in London.

1733 27 January Handel gives his new opera, *Orlando*, one of his most powerful and impressive works, which runs for ten performances.

• **17 March** Handel's new oratorio *Deborah* opens at the King's Theatre. Handel doubles the ticket price on the first night (which is badly attended), for which he is criticized adversely by the public.

• **9 June** Senesino (right), whose relations with Handel have become strained, makes a farewell speech to the audience on the last night of the opera season.

• **15 June** With the encouragement of the Prince of Wales, who is in opposition to his father the king, an Opera of the Nobility is set up. Events will prove that London cannot support two such opera companies.

• **27 July** Bach petitions the new Elector of Saxony for a post in Dresden.

OTHER EVENTS

1732 King Frederick I of Prussia settles 12,000 Salzburg protestants in East Prussia
• John Gay dies

1733 War of Polish Succession starts
• Founding of Savannah, Georgia
• Pope: *Essay on Man*

1734 Boucher: *Rinaldo and Armide*
• Voltaire: *Lettres philosophiques*

1735 Linnaeus: *Systema naturae*
• Hogarth: *The Rake's Progress*

1736 Linnaeus: *Bibliotheca botanica*
• Manufacture of glass begins in Venice at Murano

The castrato Senesino left England towards the end of 1735, having made a large amount of money, as the engraving (below) indicates on the right. Men were delighted but the ladies lamented over the departing singer, as the words of the ballad indicate.

• **August** The comic INTERMEZZO *La serva padrona* (The Maid Turned Mistress) from Pergolesi's serious opera, *Il prigionier superbo* (The Proud Prisoner) takes on an independent life, becoming a landmark in the history of comic opera.

• **12 September** Death of Couperin in Paris, aged sixty-four.

• **1 October** Rameau's first opera, *Hippolyte et Aricie* (Hippolytus and Aricia, ★ p.85), is condemned by the Lullists when given at the Opéra.

• **29 December** The Opera of the Nobility launch their season at the Lincoln's Inn Fields Theatre with Porpora's *Arianna in Nasso* (Ariadne on Naxos), whose cast is largely poached from Handel's company.

1734 26 January Handel's new opera, *Arianna*, has seventeen performances, and attendances at the theatre improve.

• **6 July** The season at the King's Theatre closes, ending the Handel-Heidegger partnership. The latter lets the theatre to the Opera of the Nobility, so Handel moves to Covent Garden (p.82).

• **25 October** Pergolesi produces his serious opera *Adriano in Siria* (Hadrian in Syria) at the Teatro San Bartolomeo in Naples, with a comic intermezzo *Livietta e Tracollo*.

• **29 October** The Opera of the Nobility opens at the King's Theatre with the renowned CASTRATO Farinelli, and so steals a march on Handel.

▲ *Bach Expresses his Disillusionment in Leipzig*

I remember that you kindly condescended to ask for some news of my fate; this shall now most obediently be done. The vicissitudes from my youth on are well known to you, as far as the change that took me to Cöthen as director of music. There I had a gracious prince who loved music as much as he knew it, and I thought that I would end my career at his court. But … the said prince married a princess of Berenburg, and it began to seem as if his musical leanings grew lukewarm, chiefly because the new princess seemed to be rather empty-headed. So God willed that my vocation should be that of musical director and CANTOR *at the Thomasschule here [in Leipzig], although in truth, initially I found it difficult to envisage being changed from a director of music into a cantor. So I put off making my decision for three months. However, the post was described to me in such glowing terms that*

finally (particularly because it seemed favourable to my sons' studies) I decided in the name of God to travel to Leipzig, go through the audition and, in the end, move. Here, by the will of God, I still am. However, since 1) I find the post much less desirable than it had been described to me, 2) many perquisites due to me in my situation are denied to me, 3) it is very expensive here and 4) those over me are capricious and have little feeling for music so I have to live in almost continuous frustration, envy and persecution, I perceive that, with the aid of the Almighty, I must seek elsewhere for my fortune. Should your Highness know of a position for an old and devoted servant in your town, I would most obediently ask you to favour me with a recommendation.

Bach to Georg Erdmann, 28 October 1730

• **9 November** For his first season at Covent Garden, Handel produces a choreographed version of *Il pastor fido*. There is a ballet in each act danced by the French ballerina Marie Sallé and her company, and a unique one-act opera-ballet prologue entitled *Terpsichore*.

• **7 December** Handel publishes his set of six CONCERTI GROSSI as his Opus Three.

• **Christmas** Bach completes his *Christmas Oratorio*, a set of CANTATAS to be performed on separate days from Christmas Day to Epiphany.

1735 8 January Pergolesi's opera *L'Olimpiade*, to a Metastasio ■ (p.79) libretto, has a disastrous reception at the Teatro Tordinona, Rome, and the composer returns to Naples.

• **26 March** Handel gives three performances of *Deborah* (p.82) at Covent Garden. According to the *London Daily Post*, he plays 'a large new Organ, which is remarkable for its Variety of curious Stops; being a new Invention, and a great Improvement of that Instrument'. The composer writes four organ CONCERTOS, a new art form, which he plays during the intervals.

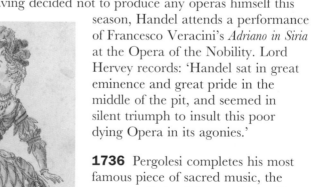

• **16 April** Handel produces a 'magic' opera with ballet, *Alcina*, for Covent Garden. It is the composer's last great operatic success, though the London audiences are scandalized at the costume of Marie Sallé, and his later performances, so that she forsakes England.

• **Spring** Vivaldi collaborates with Carlo Goldoni ▲ (p.87) on the opera *Griselda* at the Teatro San Samuele, Venice.

• **5 August** Vivaldi is re-engaged at the Pietà in Venice ■ (p.71) as leader of the orchestra at a salary of one hundred ducats.

• **28 August** Rameau completes his *opéra-ballet Les Indes galantes* ★ (below), eventually one of his most popular works, for Paris.

• **25 November** Having decided not to produce any operas himself this

One of Boquet's costume designs for Rameau's Les Indes galantes, produced at the Opéra in Paris on 28 August 1735. The role of Emilie was sung by one of the stars of the Opéra at this time, Marie Pélissier, who enjoyed a rivalry with Nicole Le Maure similar to that between the Italian prima donnas in London.

season, Handel attends a performance of Francesco Veracini's *Adriano in Siria* at the Opera of the Nobility. Lord Hervey records: 'Handel sat in great eminence and great pride in the middle of the pit, and seemed in silent triumph to insult this poor dying Opera in its agonies.'

1736 Pergolesi completes his most famous piece of sacred music, the sequence Stabat Mater, which will later be described by Bellini as a 'divine poem of grief'.

• **17 January** Covent Garden is awaiting a new CASTRATO singer, so Handel composes a non-operatic work for the opening of the season – a setting of John Dryden's 1697 St Cecilia's Day Ode, *Alexander's Feast*.

Frederick, Prince of Wales and his sisters in the Banqueting House at Hampton Court, painted about 1733 by Mercier. The prince plays the cello, which he took up this year, and Anne, Princess Royal, is seated at the harpsichord. Princess Caroline plucks a mandora, and Princess Amelia listens, a copy of Milton on her lap. The apparent harmony is entirely superficial, however. The prince and his sister Anne were sharply at odds, since she loyally supported Handel, and he the composer's rivals.

• **19 February** The first performance of Handel's *Alexander's Feast* at Covent Garden is well attended; there were 'at least 1300 Persons present and it is judg'd that the Receipt of the House could not amount to less that £450' *(London Daily Post)*.

• **16 March** Pergolesi dies, aged twenty-six, of consumption. He is buried near Naples.

• **27 April** Handel's anthem *Sing unto God* is performed at the wedding of the Prince of Wales ★ (p.84) to Princess Augusta Saxe-Gotha. The Earl of Egmont notes in his diary that it 'was wretchedly sung…'.

• **12 May** King George, apparently tired of the wrangles between the London companies, has lost interest in opera. Handel, vying for the favour of the only remaining royal patron, dedicates his new opera, *Atalanta*, to the Prince of Wales. When performed at Covent Garden the work's special effects, including a firework display, cause 'uncommon Delight and Satisfaction'.

• **12 August** Bach and the new rector of the Thomasschule, Johann August Ernesti, argue over who should appoint choir prefects. The composer appeals to Leipzig town council, insisting that the choice should be his, but the council take Ernesti's part, leading to two years of open war and mutual sabotage.

▲ Handel Ignores an Appeal for English Opera

Having this occasion of troubling you with a letter, I cannot forbear to tell you the earnestness of my wishes, that, as you have made such steps towards it, already, you would let us owe to your inimitable genius, the establishment of musick, upon a foundation of good poetry; where the excellence of the sound should be no longer dishonour'd, by the poorness of the sense it is chain'd to.

My meaning is, that you would be resolute enough, to deliver us from our Italian bondage; and demonstrate, that English is soft enough for Opera, when compos'd by poets, who know how to distinguish the sweetness of our tongue, from the strength of it, where the last is necessary.

I am of the opinion, that male and female voices may be found in this kingdom, capable of every thing, that is requisite; and, I am sure, a species of dramatic Opera might be invented, that, by reconciling reason and dignity, with musick and fine machinery, would charm the ear, and hold fast the heart, together.

Such an improvement must, at once, be lasting, and profitable, to a very great degree; and would, infallibly, attract an universal regard, and encouragement.'

Aaron Hill, writing to Handel
5 December 1732

1737-39
The Apotheosis of Vivaldi

Vivaldi encounters hostility and even outright condemnation, not only in Venice but elsewhere in northern Italy, both for his compositional practices and his professional and private conduct. Outside Italy, however, he is revered as one of the greatest composers of his day, and is invited to Amsterdam to celebrate the centenary of its theatre.

1737 Johann Gottlieb Goldberg, a ten-year-old harpsichord virtuoso, takes some lessons from Bach (p.89).

• **January** Vivaldi negotiates to produce opera in Ferrara.

• **16 February** Handel produces a new opera, *Giustino* (Justinus) at Covent Garden, which has nine performances, though it is never revived.

• **March** The first performance of Vivaldi's opera *Catone in Utica* (Cato in Utica), with a libretto by Metastasio ■ (p.79), is a huge success in Verona.

• **13 April** Handel suffers from either a stroke or severe rheumatism, and is unable to play or conduct. His mind is also affected.

• **18 May** Handel's new opera, *Berenice*, opens at Covent Garden. All the royal family are present, but the composer does not make an appearance.

• **11 June** The Opera of the Nobility closes in a state of financial collapse.

• **September** Handel takes the waters at Aix-la-Chapelle, makes a remarkable recovery, and returns to London in October.

• **18 October** Bach writes to the king of Prussia asking him to support him in his row with Leipzig town council (p.85).

• **24 October** First performance of Rameau's *Castor et Pollux* (Castor and Pollux) at the Paris Opéra.

• **November** The papal governor refuses Vivaldi permission to put on opera in Ferrara, on the grounds that he was a priest who did not say Mass and that Anna Girò (p.76) was his mistress.

• **4 November** The San Carlo opera house, built between March and October, opens in Naples.

1738 Haydn is sent to the school of a distant relation in Hainburg, where he studies reading, writing and music.

• Bach completes his *Mass in B Minor*.

• **3 January** Handel's new opera *Faramondo* has only eight performances at the King's Theatre, though the London public is glad to see his return.

• **7 January** Vivaldi, aged sixty, is invited to lead the orchestra for the celebration of the centenary of the Schouwburg Theatre in Amsterdam.

• **15 April** Handel's *Serse*, which includes the famous 'Largo', is produced at the King's Theatre, but achieves only five performances.

OTHER EVENTS
1737 The Grand Duke of Tuscany, the last of the Medici, dies
• Licensing Act restricts number of London theatres and subjects them to censorship

1738 Voltaire: *Discours sur l'homme*

1739 Anglo-Spanish War of Jenkins' Ear begins
• David Hume: *A Treatise of Human Nature*

'The invitation to Mira, requesting her company to Vauxhall Garden' testifies not only to the popularity of the pleasure garden itself, but to the honour accorded to Handel, whose seated statue shown here was erected during his lifetime.

> '*Here my opera is in the heavens.*'
> Vivaldi writing from Verona, 3 May 1737

• **2 May** Handel's statue by Roubiliac is unveiled in Vauxhall Gardens, London, probably the first such tribute to a living composer (opposite).

• **23 July** Handel begins composing his ORATORIO, *Saul*. The text is by Charles Jennens ★ (p.88), the first time that the pair work together.

• **12 September** Keiser dies in Hamburg ● (p.61), aged sixty-five.

• **27 September** Handel finishes *Saul* (right) and begins another ORATORIO, *Israel in Egypt*, which he completes on 1 November.

• **4 October** Handel's first set of six organ CONCERTOS, transcribed for solo keyboard, are published as his Opus Four.

1739 Bach publishes the third part of his *Clavierübung* (p.81), which is described as 'comprising various preludes on the Catechism, and other hymns, for the organ'.

• Mattheson, unable to continue performing because of his deafness, publishes his treaty on conducting *Der vollkommene Capellmeister* (The Complete Music Master).

• Vivaldi's opera *Siroe* is produced in Ferrara, but the composer is unable to attend (p.86).

• **16 January** Handel's *Saul* has six performances.

• **4 April** Handel's *Israel in Egypt* is a failure with only three performances, possibly because of the use of biblical texts in the theatre.

• **Autumn** *Feraspe*, possibly Vivaldi's last opera, is given in Venice. It is not a success.

• **30 October** Handel completes composition of his twelve Grand Concertos for Strings, Op.6.

The indenture, bearing Handel's signature, for the loan of kettledrums from the Royal Ordnance for use in a performance of his oratorio Saul *in 1739.*

▲ *Vivaldi and Goldoni*

Goldoni's first play, Belisario, *was given in Verona on 24 November 1734, so he was a brilliant new talent when he was chosen to work with Vivaldi in the following year.*

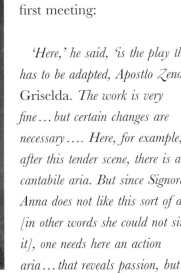

By the age of twenty-six, Carlo Goldoni had made a name for himself as a librettist in Venice, and was chosen to write to a SCORE by Vivaldi for the spring opera season of 1735. The following is Goldoni's account of their first meeting:

'Here,' he said, 'is the play that has to be adapted, Apostlo Zeno's Griselda. *The work is very fine … but certain changes are necessary …. Here, for example, after this tender scene, there is a cantabile aria. But since Signora Anna does not like this sort of aria [in other words she could not sing it], one needs here an action aria … that reveals passion, but not pathos, and is not cantabile.'*

'I understand,' I replied. 'I will endeavour to satisfy you. Give me the libretto.'

'But I need it for myself,' replied Vivaldi. 'When will you return it?'

'Immediately,' I replied. 'Give me a sheet of paper and a pen ….'

'What! Your Lordship imagines that an opera aria is like an intermezzo aria!'

I was furious and replied to him insolently. He gave me the pen and took a letter from his pocket, from which he tore a sheet of white paper ….

He went back to his worktable and began to say his breviary. I then read the scene carefully. I analyzed the sentiment of the cantabile aria, and turned it into one of action and passion. I took my work to him. With his breviary in his right hand and my paper in his left, he began to read gently. When he had finished he threw the breviary into a corner, got up and embraced me.

1740-43
Handel's 'Messiah'

As Handel finally, if reluctantly, abandons Italian opera and concentrates his energies on oratorio, he finds inspiration in a text that presents in a direct and vivid manner the basic Christian belief of the life of Christ, and creates one of his most enduring works.

Charles Jennens, who provided Handel with the texts he set for both Saul *and* Messiah, *has often been unerestimated by posterity, but it is clear that in* Saul *he provided Handel with a strong, dramatic text that gave the composer ample opportunity to use the talents that Jennens recognized in him.*

1740 Mattheson publishes his *Grundlage einer Ehren-Pforte* (Foundation for a Gate of Honour) a collection of biographies of famous musicians.

• C. P. E. Bach ▲ (p.97) is made harpsichordist to Frederick the Great, a post he will hold with distinction for twenty-seven years.

• Haydn enters the court chapel in Vienna, as a choirboy.

• **21 March** Vivaldi contributes a SINFONIA and three CONCERTOS to a SERENATA entitled *Il coro delle muse* (The Choir of the Muses), given by the girls of the Pietà ■ (p.71), on the Prince Elector of Saxony's visit to Venice.

• **29 April** At a meeting of the governors of the Pietà ■ (p.71) it is anounced that Vivaldi is leaving Venice for Vienna, and it is suggested that they buy some of his concertos. The vote, however, goes against this.

• **12 May** The governors of the Pietà change their minds and purchase twenty concertos from Vivaldi for seventy ducats and twenty-three lire.

• **8 November** Handel publishes his second set of organ concertos four of which are arrangements of the Opus Six concertos (p.87).

1741 Gluck composes his first opera, *Artaserse* (Artaxerxes), to a Metastasio libretto ■ (p.79).

• Quantz ▲ (p.93) becomes court composer to Frederick the Great.

• Stamitz arrives in Mannheim ▲ (p.93).

• Rameau publishes five chamber-music works for the harpsichord, violin, and viol, in which some of the movements are portraits of friends and patrons.

• **13 February** Death of Fux ★ (p.77) in Vienna.

• **28 July** Vivaldi dies a pauper in Vienna, of an 'internal inflammation'.

• **22 August** Handel begins composing his ORATORIO *Messiah* ■ (opposite), to a libretto by Charles Jennens (above). He finishes in twenty-five days.

• **29 October** Handel completes his first version of *Samson* ■ (opposite).

• **18 November** Handel arrives in Dublin following an invitation from the Lord Lieutenant of Ireland to attend the winter season.

'Handel is the greatest composer that ever lived. I would uncover my head, and kneel down at his tomb.'
Beethoven to Edward Schulz in 1823

1742 Bach publishes the fourth part of his *Clavierübung* (p.81) known as the 'Goldberg' Variations, said to have been composed for Goldberg (p.86) to play to his employer when he suffered from insomnia.

• **13 April** *Messiah* ■ (below) is performed for the first time in the Music Hall, Dublin. An estimated 700 people are present, and the sum of £400 is raised for charity.

• **13 August** Handel leaves Dublin to return to England. He agrees with Rich to mount an ORATORIO season at Covent Garden during Lent, 1743.

1743 18 February Handel's *Samson* ■ (below) is given at Covent Garden, and enjoys eight performances. English ORATORIO is now firmly established as an art form, though not without prejudice against it.

• **23 March** *Messiah* ■ (below) is given at Covent Garden, but fails to win success because of public disapproval of the singing of sacred texts in a theatre.

• **April** Handel has a mild stroke.

• **4 July** Handel completes *Semele*, a secular ORATORIO, whose music demonstrates that the composer has lost none of his powers.

The entrance to the Music Hall in Fishamble Street, Dublin (above), where Handel's Messiah *had its first public performance. The enthusiasm of the public was such that ladies were requested in advance not to wear hoops in their skirts, and gentlemen were subsequently asked to leave their swords at home.*

Right: Rehearsal of an oratorio, possibly in the presence of Handel. It was clear from the rehearsal of Messiah *in Dublin that the oratorio would be a huge success, though initially in London it failed to create much enthusiasm.*

■ *The Impact of Handel's Oratorios*

Although *Messiah* has an ecstatic reception in Dublin where it is first heard, and is destined to become one of the world's best known and best loved ORATORIOS, it fails, in the short term, to please London audiences. In fact Horace Walpole, writing to Sir Horace Mann on 24 February 1743, a month before *Messiah's* first London performance, but a few days after *Samson* at Covent Garden, has this to say: 'Handel has set up an Oratorio against the Operas, and succeeds. He has hired all the goddesses from farces and the singers of *Roast Beef* [a popular ballad] from between the acts at both theatres, with a man with one note in his voice, and a girl without ever an one; and so they sing, and make brave hallelujahs; and the good company encore the recitative, if it happens to have any cadence like what they call a tune.'

Walpole is of course a dilettante, a snob, and a supporter of Italian opera. Moreover, enjoyable as his snide references to the singers Mrs Clive, Thomas Lowe, John Beard and Mrs Cibber may be, *Samson* is the one oratorio that Handel has composed to date that does not contain a single Hallelujah. Under these circumstances, Handel's oratorios may be said to be successful, and, in due course, *Messiah* above all.

1744-50
Bach's Last Works

Despite his discontent in Leipzig, Bach remains in his post and distils the fruit of his long years of patient work into a series of compositions, mostly for keyboard, that are destined to remain some of the highest expressions of the art of music. Meanwhile a new star is rising in the firmament, the composer Gluck, who will bring a new vision to the world of opera.

This portrait of Bach was made by Haussmann in 1746 for the Mizler Society for Musical Science in Leipzig and shows Bach holding a copy of a six-part canon triplex. In 1747 he wrote for the society the canonic variations on the Christmas hymn Von Himmel hoch *(From Heaven Above), which is not only a suitably erudite work for the learned society, but also a very beautiful piece of music.*

1744 Bach (left) publishes the second part of his set of PRELUDES and FUGUES for keyboard known as *The Well-Tempered Clavier* (p.76).

• C.P.E. Bach dedicates a set of keyboard SONATAS to the Duke of Württemberg, by whose name they are now known. Being left-handed C.P.E. Bach was better at playing keyboard instruments than strings, and it is for his compositions for the former that he is best remembered. His keyboard sonatas, which are in classic form, bridge the gap between his father and Haydn.

• **10 February** Handel's *Semele* (p.89) is given at Covent Garden. The work's secular content leads some to boycott it, and it only runs for four performances.

• **3 November** Handel hires the King's Theatre for a run of ORATORIO subscription concerts ■ (p.89). The series is a disaster, ending on 23 April 1745 with only sixteen of the projected twenty-four concerts given. Handel will never again conduct oratorios in the opera house.

1745 Rameau writes his COMÉDIE-BALLET, *La Princesse de Navarre* (The Princess of Navarre), to celebrate the wedding of the Dauphin and the Infanta Maria Theresa at Versailles.

• **Autumn** Gluck is asked to compose opera for the troubled Haymarket Theatre in London. He meets Handel, who says of him 'he knows no more of contrapunto [COUNTERPOINT], as mein cook'. However, the younger composer makes a study of Handel's work, which proves to be the turning point in his career

• **14 November** Handel's new patriotic *Song for the Gentlemen Volunteers of the City of London* ('Stand round my brave boys'), is sung at the Drury Lane Theatre, thus firmly demonstrating the composer's support for the Hanoverian dynasty during the Jacobite Rebellion.

OTHER EVENTS
1744 Hogarth: *Marriage à la Mode*

1745 Second Jacobite Rebellion in Scotland
• Prussia obtains Silesia by the Treaty of Dresden
• Tiepolo: frescoes for the Palazzo Labia in Venice

1746 Accession of Ferdinand VI of Spain
• Charles Stuart, the 'Young Pretender', is defeated at Culloden and flees to France
• Boucher: *The Toilet of Venus*

1747 Voltaire: *Zadig*

1748 The Peace of Aix-la Chapelle marks the end of the War of the Austrian Succession
• Montesquieu: *L'esprit des lois*

1749 Fielding: *Tom Jones*

1750 Georges Buffon: *Histoire naturelle*
'Capability Brown' designs Warwick Castle's gardens

An autograph page of Handel's Occasional Oratorio, *which he compiled in the wake of the Scottish rebellion. He did not date the work precisely, as was his usual practice; this, and the general untidiness of the score, together with the fact that he did not copy out the borrowed material, indicates the speed at which he produced the work.*

1746 Bach, whose eyesight is failing, publishes the six 'Schübler' CHORALES for organ. Five of these are TRANSCRIPTIONS from earlier CANTATAS, hardly altered.

• **January–February** Handel compiles his *Occasional Oratorio* (left), an extended ANTHEM in celebration of the Jacobites' retreat. The first performance takes place on 14 February at Covent Garden.

• **25 March** Handel and Gluck perform together at a benefit concert in London.

• **July–August** Frederick, the Prince of Wales, commissions Handel to compose his ORATORIO *Judas Maccabaeus* in celebration of the victory of the Duke of Cumberland over the Jacobites at Culloden.

1747 Rousseau composes his OPERETTA *Les Muses galantes*, which leads to his correspondence with Voltaire and acquaintance with Diderot ◆ (p.95).

• Bach's eldest son, Wilhelm Friedemann, receives the appointment of organist at the Liebfrauenkirche in Halle.

• **1 April** Handel's *Judas Maccabaeus* is first performed at Covent Garden. Its patriotic subject matter ensures that it is an instant success.

• **May** Bach visits his son, Carl Philipp Emanuel, at the court of Frederick the Great (right), in Berlin. The meeting is later recorded by his son: 'His Majesty himself played his a theme for a fugue, which he at once developed, to the particular pleasure of the Monarch, on the pianoforte. Hereupon, His Majesty demanded to hear a fugue with six voices, which command he also fulfilled, to the astonishment of the King and the musicians there present, using a theme of his own. After his return to Leipzig, he set down on paper a three-voiced and a six-voiced so-called RICERCAR together with several other intricate little pieces, all on the very theme that had been given him by His Majesty, and this [the *Musical Offering*] he dedicated, engraved on copper, to the King.'

> *'Our Bach was the greatest organ and clavier player that ever lived.'*
>
> Obituary notice for Bach

1748 Stamitz ▲ (p.93) becomes director of instrumental music at the court of Mannheim.

• **5 May–13 June** Handel composes his oratorio *Solomon* which includes the SINFONIA *The Arrival of the Queen of Sheba*.

• **14 May** Gluck's opera *Semiramide riconosciuta* is outstandingly successful when performed at the reopening of the Burgtheater in Vienna.

1749 Bach completes *The Art of Fugue*, his last work, and a magisterial exploration for keyboard of the possibilities of the fugue.

• **27 April** Handel's *Music for the Royal Fireworks* is performed in Green Park, London. The fireworks fail to go according to plan, but the music is a great success.

Frederick the Great, King of Prussia, for whom Bach composed his Musical Offering *as a result of his visit to the king at Sanssouci, his palace at Potsdam.*

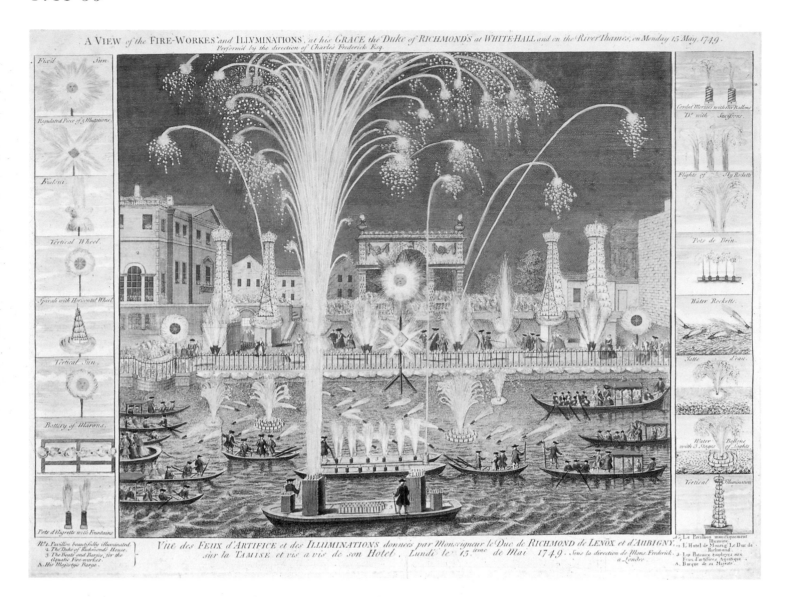

A VIEW of the FIRE-WORKES and ILLUMINATIONS, at his GRACE the Duke of RICHMOND'S at WHITE-HALL and on the River Thames, on Monday 15 May 1749.
Performed by the direction of Charles Frederick Esq.

VUE des FEUX d'ARTIFICE et des ILLUMINATIONS données par Monseigneur le Duc de RICHMOND de LENOX et d'AUBIGNY
sur la TAMISE et vis a vis de son Hotel, Lundi le 15.eme de Mai 1749. Sous la direction de Mons. Frederick
a Londre.

The celebrations for the Peace of Aix-la-Chapelle in 1749 inspired one of Handel's best known compositions, the Music for the Royal Fireworks, given in Green Park, London, on 27 April that year. Another firework display was given on the Thames on 15 May in the presence of the king (above).

• **August** Bach makes his last known appearance as director of music at the Thomaskirche in Leipzig when he directs the CANTATA *Wir danken dir, Gott* (We Thank Thee, God).

• **November** Haydn is dismissed from the cathedral choir school of St Stephen's as his voice has broken. He possesses three shirts, a coat and no money. He takes a garret in the Michaelerhaus, and is therefore living in the same house as Metastasio ■ (p.79).

• **5 December** Rameau completes the first version of his lyric tragedy *Zoroastre* (Zoroaster), destined to be his last such work to be performed.

1750 Bach's eyesight is very weak, so he undergoes two operations, one in March and one in April, by a travelling occulist. Both are a failure, leaving him totally blind and affecting his general health.

• Quantz composes his flute CONCERTOS for Frederick the Great of Prussia ▲ (p.93), who is a former pupil.

• **August** Handel pays his last visit to Germany.

• **22 July** Bach takes his last communion at home.

• **28 July** Death of Bach in Leipzig, aged sixty-five.

• **15 September** Gluck marries Maria Anna Bergin, whose family are well connected at the Viennese Imperial court.

Frederick the Great playing his flute, accompanied by strings and harpsichord (right). From 1728 Quantz went from Dresden to Potsdam twice a year to give lessons to Frederick, but in 1741 the flautist went to live in Potsdam, where he remained for the rest of his life.

▲ *Frederick the Great on the Effect of Quantz's Flute*

Frederick the Great was a highly cultured man, who, thanks to the instruction of Quantz, was of almost professional standard on the flute (right). On 2 January 1736 when still prince, he wrote to his sister Wilhelmine. The letter, written in French, was delivered by Quantz and shows the virtuoso's influence:

Carl Theodor, Elector Palatine (below), whose orchestra at Mannheim became one of the musical wonders of Europe under the direction of Stamitz. Distinguished musicans flocked to work there, and eventually the musical establishment included some eighty persons.

I wish that Quantz's flute, which speaks much better than himself, might tell you in its most mellow and touching notes, by the most pathetic of adagios, all that my heart tells me I should feel towards you. If you feel that you are moved by these masters of our senses, think for a little about the whole extent of my tenderness and about all that I would tell you concerning it if I were so happy as to be entertaining you. The fire of his allegros are the living symbol of the happiness I shall experience the moment I shall be in your presence.

▲ *The Amazing Orchestra at Mannheim*

Charles Burney, a well-known musicologist, travelled in Europe from 1770–73 collecting material for his *General History of Music* (p.107). On visiting Mannheim he was amazed by the orchestra there, formed some thirty years earlier by Stamitz:

It has not been merely at the Elector's great opera that instrumental music has been so much cultivated and refined, but at his concerts, where this extraordinary band has 'ample room and verge enough', to produce great effects without the impropriety of destroying the greater and more delicate beauties, peculiar to vocal music; it was here that Stamitz first surpassed the bound of common opera overtures, which hitherto had only served in the theatre as as kind of court cryer, with an 'Oh Yes!' in order to awaken attention, and bespeak silence, at the entrance of the singers. Since the discovery which the genius of Stamitz first made, every effect has been tried which such an aggregate of sound can produce; it was here that the Crescendo *and Diminuendo had birth; and the* Piano, *which was before chiefly used as an echo, with which it was generally synonymous, as well as the* Forte, *were found to be musical colours which had their shades, as much as red or blue in painting.*

1751-58
Opera War in Paris

The revival of an opera by Pergolesi in Paris ignites a fuse that has been smouldering for some time and which now causes the explosion known as the 'Querelle des bouffons' or War of the Comic Opera, and which is in effect the manifestation of a desire for change, and a break with the tradition established by Lully in the previous century.

1751 Francesco Geminiani, a violin virtuoso in the Italian style, publishes his treatise *The Art of Playing the Violin* in London. The text is short, but includes his views on musical performance as well as technique.

• 21 January Handel begins his last ORATORIO, *Jephtha*, but is obliged to break off on 13 February because the eyesight is failing in his left eye. He resumes work with difficulty on 23 February.

• 30 August Handel completes his oratorio *Jephtha*, despite having lost all vision in his left eye.

1752 Quantz ▲ (p.93) publishes his treatise on flute playing entitled *Versuch einer Anweisung die Flöte traversiere zu spielen* (Essay on a Course for Playing the Transverse Flute), which will be translated into French, Dutch, Italian and English.

• 26 February Handel manages to conduct the first performance of *Jeptha* at Covent Garden, even though the sight is now deteriorating in his right eye.

Interior of an eighteenth-century French opera house. The stage scenery closely resembles that of Rousseau's Le Devin du village, *when it was given at the Royal Academy of Music in Paris in 1753.*

• August Gluck goes to Naples to mount his opera *La clemenza di Tito* (The Clemency of Titus) to a libretto by Metastasio ■ (p.79).

• 1 August Pergolesi's *opera buffa, La serva padrona* (p.83), is revived in Paris, where it had failed in 1746, and causes a sensation, which sparks off the contest between French and Italian music known as the *Querelle des bouffons* ◆ (p.95).

• 17 August The *General Advertiser* reports that Handel 'was seized…by a Paralytick Disorder in his Head, which has deprived him of Sight'.

• 18 October Rousseau's opera *Le Devin du village* (The Village Seer, right and opposite) is performed at Fontainebleau in front of the king. The OVERTURE and RECITATIVES, however, are not his own. The work will move to the Royal Academy of Music in Paris next year (above).

• 3 November Handel has an unsuccessful operation on his eyes at Guy's Hospital, London.

OTHER EVENTS
1751 Benjamin Franklin: *Experiments & Observations on Electricity*
• British Parliament changes New Year to 1 January
• Voltaire begins his *Siècle de Louis XIV*

1752 Britain adopts Gregorian calender
• Voltaire: *Micromégas*

1753 Foundation of Vienna Stock Exchange

★ *The title page of Rousseau's opera* Le Devin du village, *which was given twice at Fontainebleau in the autumn of 1752 and then at the Opéra in Paris the following March.*

◆ *The Querelle des bouffons*

*A*lthough usually dated to the revival of Pergolesi's opera
La serva padrona *(p.83) in Paris on 1 August 1752,*
the controversy began at the beginning of the year, when an
opera by Destouches entitled Omphale *was performed. Baron*
Friedrich Melchior Grimm, a German aristocrat who had
settled in Paris, published his Lettre sur Omphale,
attacking French opera, though praising Rameau's Platée
and Pygmalion, *and the Italian opera he had seen in*
Dresden. This began the war of pamphlets, and in April,
Jean-Jacques Rousseau, a friend of Grimm, contributed
an anonymous Lettre à M. Grimm *in which he damned*
Rameau with faint praise. It was then that the performances
of La serva padrona, *given by an Italian company at the*
Opéra, created their sensation. The company gave another
season the following year, including works by Pergolesi and
Jommelli, that kept the controversy alive. Rousseau contributed
his Lettre sur la musique française – *a critique of the*
general aesthetic of French opera, focusing on the recitative
as practised by Lully and Rameau – and Grimm his Le
Petit prophète de Boemisch-Broda, *which is a rather*
unedifying skit. Ultimately Rameau himself reluctantly
replied in 1754 with his own Observations *(p.96).*

The controversy coincided with the start of the publication
in 1751 of the great encyclopaedia, directed by D'Alembert
and Diderot, which was to run to thirty-three volumes.

The work was a survey of the current state of knowledge and
development in all intellectual domains, and the contributors –
including Rousseau and Voltaire – became known as the
Encylopaedists. For such open and enquiring minds the
'new' form of opera was understandably greeted as a
welcome breath of fresh air.

★ *Illustration from Rousseau's*
Le Devin du village *(above),*
which brought a new sense of
realism and simplicity into
French opera for the first time,
and an attempt to portray basic
human sentiments on stage.

Philosophers at Table:
an imaginary meeting of the
Encyclopaedists. Voltaire raises
his left hand; Père Adam is
seated on the right in a tricorne
hat; on the far left is Abbé
Mauri; D'Alembert is in
the left foreground; Condorcet
has his back to the viewer;
Diderot is on Voltaire's left,
and La Harpe on his right.

Goupy's caricature, published in 1754, depicting Handel, 'The Charming Brute', as a glutton, though there is no evidence whatsoever that the composer ever behaved in such a way.

1753 C.P.E. Bach publishes his treatise on keyboard playing entitled *Versuch über die wahre Art das Clavier zu spielen* (Essay on the Correct Method of Playing the Clavier ▲ p.97).

• Rousseau, keeping the opera war in Paris alive ◆ (p.95), publishes his attack on French opera composed by Lully and Rameau entitled *Lettre sur la musique française* (Letter on French Music).

• **23 January** Handel (left) is now totally blind. From now on John Christopher Smith (p.70 and below) will write down his dictations.

• **1 March** Rousseau's *Le Devin du village* ★ (pp.94 and 95) is given at the Opéra in Paris, this time with his own RECITATIVES and perhaps his own overture. It advocates a return to nature, unsophisticated sentiments and justice for ordinary people.

• **29 May** Haydn's *Singspiel, Der krumme Teufel* (The Crooked Devil) is a success when performed in Vienna.

1754 Galuppi and Goldoni ▲ (p.87) collaborate on the comic opera *Il filosofo di campagna* (The Country Philosopher).

• Rameau, in his contribution to the pamphlet war ◆ (p.95), publishes his reply to Rousseau's attack entitled *Observations sur notre instinct pour la musique* (Observations on Our Instinct for Music).

• Stamitz ▲ (p.93) visits Paris and conducts concerts in various salons and at the establishment of Rameau's patron La Pouplinière.

• Gluck's opera *Le Cinesi* (The Chinese), to a Metastasio LIBRETTO ■ (p.79), is given before the Viennese court, and the composer is appointed house composer to the Burgtheater in Vienna.

• **June** Count Durazzo, who, with Gluck, is interested in opera reform, is appointed director of the court theatres in Vienna.

'The characters in an opera never say what they ought. The actors generally sing in maxims and proverbs, and perform madrigal after madrigal. When each one has sung two or three couplets, the scene ends and the dancing resumes. If it did not, we should all die of boredom.'
Baron Grimm, *Correspondance littéraire*, 1757

1755 Algarotti publishes his *Saggio sopra l'opera in musica* (Treatise on Opera), in which he states that drama should dominate all other elements in opera.

• **12 May** Therese Keller, the woman with whom Haydn is in love, takes the veil. The composer is devastated, but performs and conducts his own works during the ceremony.

1756 Duni sets Goldoni's play *La Cecchina* (Cecchina, based on Samuel Ricardson's *Pamela*) and arrives in Paris.

• **27 January** Mozart is born in Salzburg, his parents' seventh, but second surviving child.

1757 Haydn is working in Weinzierl, near Vienna, for a Baron von Fürnberg.

• **27 March** Stamitz ▲ (p.93) dies in Mannheim.

• **23 July** Death of Domenico Scarlatti in Madrid.

1758 August–September Handel is in Tunbrige Wells, where it is likely that the same oculist who failed to cure Bach (p.92) performs an unsuccessful operation on him.

OTHER EVENTS

1754 Thomas Chippendale: *The Gentleman and Cabinet-Maker's Directory*
• Anglo-French boundary war in North America

1755 Lisbon earthquake kills 30,000
• Moscow University is founded
• Gotthold Lessing: *Miss Sara Sampson*, the first important domestic tragedy in German
• Samuel Johnson begins his *Dictionary of the English Language*

1756 120 British soldiers imprisoned and die in the 'Black Hole of Calcutta'
• Porcelain factory founded at Sèvres
• Voltaire: *Essai sur les moeurs*
• Piranesi: *Antichità romane*, engravings of ancient Rome

1757 Battle of Plassey; British gain control of Bengal

1758 Diderot: *Le Père de famille*

★ *John Christopher Smith, Handel's amanuensis after he became blind. Smith's father, Johann Christoph Schmidt, had been a student friend of the composer's in Halle, but came to England to be his copyist and secretary and anglicized his name. Between them the father and son served Handel for some forty years until his death.*

▲ *C.P.E. Bach on Ornaments for Keyboard Playing*

Bach's second son, Carl Philipp Emanuel, received much greater recognition for his abilities as composer and performer during his own lifetime than his father. Deeply respected for his keyboard works, in 1753 he published a treatise on the correct way to play the clavier. The following extract from his *Versuch über die wahre Art das Clavier zu spielen* (Essay on the Correct Method of Playing the Clavier) displays his attitude towards ornaments; the musical embellishments prevalent during the eighteenth century.

Surely no one has ever questioned the need for ornaments, which is why they occur in abundance. It is certain that they are completely necessary if we but stop and think of their usefulness; they bind together the notes; they enliven them; they give them a special, expressive quality and weight, where necessary. They make them pleasant and so engage attention; they help to explain their intention ... an indifferent composition may be thus improved, whilst the finest melody must seem hollow and clumsy without them.

Carl Philipp Emanuel Bach, standing, with Hamburg Pastor Sturm at right, and the artist at left.

1759-62
Haydn: Composer in Residence

With the disappearance of Handel from the scene, the focus of European music moves away from London towards Austria, where two of the greatest composers – Mozart and Beethoven – are destined to dominate the scene for the rest of the century and beyond, though during their lifetimes one will die in poverty and the other only achieve international fame in middle age.

1759 Jean d'Alembert, one of the Encyclopaedists ◆ (p.95), publishes his *De la liberté de la musique* (On the Freedom of Music), in which he proposes that Italian musical idiom be adapted to French dramatic forms.

• **6 April** Handel attends and performs at a rendition of *Messiah*, but is taken ill afterwards.

• **14 April** Handel dies in London, aged seventy-four. Newspapers report that he was worth over £20,000.

• **20 April** Handel is buried in Westminster Abbey, in the presence of some 3000 people.

Mozart and his sister Nannerl in the court costumes given to them by Empress Maria Theresa in the autumn of 1762. The one given to Mozart had been made in the first place for Archduke Maximilian, who later became Archbishop of Cologne and a patron of the young Beethoven.

1760 Haydn has probably composed the ten STRING QUARTETS, known as Opus One and Opus Two from a pirated Paris edition, landmarks in one of the most important musical forms.

• Piccinni's opera *La Cecchina, ossia la buona figliuola* (Cecchina, or the Good Girl), set to Goldoni's libretto ▲ (p.87) on Samuel Richardson's *Pamela*, is given in Rome.

• **26 November** Out of a feeling of gratitude towards her generous father, Haydn marries Maria Anna Keller in St Stephen's Cathedral, Vienna. His bride is the daughter of a wig-maker and sister of his real love, Therese (p.96). The couple are incompatible, and the marriage is not a happy one.

1761 Duni becomes director of the Comédie-Italienne, Paris.

• **1 May** Haydn's appointment as deputy director of music to the Esterházy family at Eisenstadt takes effect, though he may already be in service there ■ (p.99). He composes his Symphonies Nos. 6, 7 and 8, known as *Morning*, *Noon* and *Evening*.

• **17 October** *Don Juan*, Gluck's action ballet, is choreographed and danced by Gasparo Angiolini before the court in Vienna.

1762 Johann Christian, Bach's youngest son, is invited to London to write Italian operas.

• **12 January** Mozart and his sister (above), who are aged six and ten respectively, are taken by their father to Munich, where they play before the Elector of Bavaria.

OTHER EVENTS
1759 Wolfe captures Quebec from French
• The British Museum in London opens to the public
• Voltaire: *Candide*
• Laurence Sterne begins *Tristram Shandy*

1760 Russians occupy and burn Berlin
• Accession of George III as King of England
• Jean Fragonard: *The Garden of the Villa d'Este at Tivoli*
• James Macpherson: *Ossian*, literary fraud

1761 Death of Samuel Richardson

1762 Catherine the Great succeeds as Empress of Russia on the death of her husband, Peter III
• Rousseau: *Le contrat social, Emile, Pygmalion*

- **March** Prince Paul Anton Esterházy, Haydn's employer, dies and is succeeded by his brother Nicolaus, known as 'The Magnificent'.

- **10 July** A monument to Handel by Roubiliac is unveiled in Westminster Abbey.

- **5 October** Gluck's opera *Orfeo ed Euridice* (Orpheus and Euridice), strictly speaking an *azione teatrale* or 'theatrical event' involving choreography, is performed before the court in Vienna to celebrate the emperor's birthday. It represents Gluck's first attempt to reform opera ▲ (p.107).

- **13 October** Mozart and his sister play for the Empress Maria Theresa, her husband Francis I and their daughter Maria Antonia, the future Queen Marie-Antoinette of France, at the Schönbrunn Palace in Vienna.

- **31 December** The Mozarts leave Vienna for Salzburg.

> *'There was no one near me to upset or torment me, so I was forced to become original.'*
>
> Haydn on his life at Esterháza.

■ *Haydn's Duties at Esterháza*

When Haydn first went to Esterháza he was responsible for all music-making throughout the prince's establishment, with the exception of the chapel. This was still under the control of the incumbent director Gregorius Werner, who was already old and infirm, though he would live another five years. It was agreed that Haydn would eventually assume total control in the event of Werner's demise.

Haydn's contract, dated 1 May 1761, gives an insight into the life of a court composer during the eighteenth century, and lists his duties as follows: to dress in a uniform of white stockings, white linen, powder and either a pigtail or a tiewig whenever the orchestra was performing; to behave with decorum, refraining from vulgarity in eating, drinking and speech; to compose music exclusively for the prince (this restriction was later lifted); to be present twice daily for instructions as to performances; to oversee the musicians, solving small disputes personally, and referring larger ones to the prince; to be responsible for the purchase and maintenance of instruments and provision of music; to provide vocal instruction as required, and to teach any instrument with which he was familiar. For this he received a salary of 400 florins, plus board.

The frontispiece and list of characters for Haydn's opera La vera costanza *(True Constancy), which was first performed at Esterháza in 1779, and then revised for its revival in 1785. On the right are some of the folios in which were kept materials necessary for the performance of operas by Guglielmi, Cimarosa and Paisiello.*

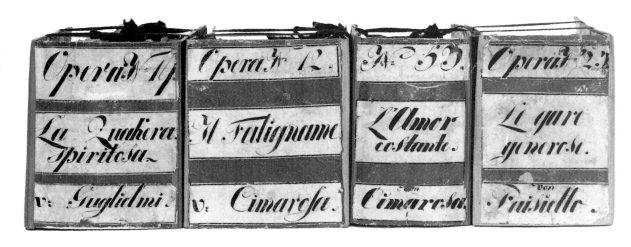

1763-66
The Mozart Touring Prodigies

In 1763 the Mozart family sets out on a tour of Europe that will keep them away from Salzburg for more than three years. It is Leopold Mozart's wish to present his daughter and son in the courts of Europe so that their talents might be recognized and suitably rewarded, and eventually, perhaps, appropriate status may be conferred on them.

1763 19 February J.C. Bach's opera *Orione* is performed at the King's Theatre in London (p.98). It proves so succesful that it runs for three months, and is followed in May by the equally successful *Zanaida*. Except for brief visits to the continent he remains in London for the rest of his life and becomes known as the 'English Bach'.

> '*My children have taken almost everyone by storm.*'
> Leopold Mozart writing to a friend in Salzburg, from Versailles, December 1763.

• **9 June** The Mozarts set out from Salzburg on a journey across Europe that will last until 29 November 1766.

• **18 November** The Mozarts arrive in Paris.

1764 1 January The Mozarts are present for dinner at the French court. Although the royal family treats them kindly, Mme dc Pompadour (the king's mistress) remains aloof. Their father subsequently receives 1200 livres or fifty *louis d'or*.

• **7 January** Gluck's OPÉRA-COMIQUE, *La Rencontre imprévue* (The Unexpected Meeting, known as The Pilgrims to Mecca) is given in Vienna. It is the composer's most frequently performed work, and through a translation becomes influential in the revival of German opera.

• **February** Gluck visits Paris and Frankfurt, and then resigns from the Burgtheater in Vienna.

• **March** Mozart dedicates his two Sonatas Op.1, to Princess Victoire, second daughter of the French king.

Mozart playing the harpsichord at a thé à l'anglaise (English teaparty) in 1766 in the salon of the Prince de Conti known as the Salon des Quatre Glaces from its four huge wall mirrors.

• **10 April** The Mozarts leave Paris for London, where they arrive on

23 April ▲ (p.101). On 27 April Wolfgang and Nannerl play before King George III and Queen Charlotte, for which their father receives twenty-four guineas. They are received again on 19 May and 25 October.

• **12 September** Rameau dies in Paris, aged eighty.

1765 18 January Mozart dedicates six Sonatas for Harpsichord and Violin Op.3, to Queen Charlotte.

• **24 July** The Mozarts leave London, stay in Kent and reach Dover on 1 August, whence they sail to Calais.

OTHER EVENTS
1763 Canada is ceded to England
• Treaty of Paris

1764 Imposition of Stamp Tax by Britain on American colonies
• Stanislas Poniatowski made King of Poland by Catherine the Great
• Voltaire: *Dictionnaire philosophique*
• Johann Winckelmann: *Geschichte der Kunst des Altertums*

1765 Robert Clive's reforms in India
• Accession of Joseph II as Emperor of Austria

1766 Lessing publishes his *Laokoon*, a critical essay on the limits of the various arts
• Oliver Goldsmith: *The Vicar of Wakefield*

• **4 September** After a month spent in Lille, the Mozarts travel via Ghent, Antwerp and Rotterdam to The Hague. Both the Mozart children fall ill in turn with intestinal typhoid.

1766 Haydn is described by a Viennese publication, the *Wienerisches Diarium*, as 'the darling of our nation', indicating that his fame has spread to the capital.

• **22 January** The Mozart children are well enough to play in a concert in The Hague. They travel to Amsterdam, where they perform in public on 29 January and 26 February. They then return to The Hague, where they remain for most of March, performing at court on 11 March.

• **3 March** Haydn's superior, Werner, dies, and he is promoted to the post of director of music ■ (p.103).

• **April** The Mozarts perform again in Amsterdam, then travel to Paris via Utrecht, Antwerp, Malines and Brussels. They reach Paris on 10 May, where they stay until 9 July. On 20 August they move to Geneva, then go on to Lausanne, Berne and Zürich, where they remain until 10 October.

• **8 November** On the last lap of their tour, the Mozarts reach Munich and then return to Salzburg on 29 November.

An engraving made in 1763 showing Mozart playing the harpsichord, with his father on violin and his sister, Nannerl, singing.

▲ *Mozart in London*

At the Great Room in Spring-Garden near St James's Park, Tuesday, June 5, will be performed a grand Concert of Vocal and Instrumental Music. For the Benefit of Miss Mozart of Eleven, and Master Mozart of Seven Years of Age, Prodigies of Nature; taking the Opportunity of representing to the Public the greatest Prodigy that Europe or that Human Nature has to boast of. Every Body will be astonished to hear a Child of such a tender Age playing the Harpsichord in such a Perfection – It surmounts all Fantastic [sic] and Imagination, and it is hard to express which is more astonishing, his Execution upon the Harpsichord, playing at Sight, or his own Composition. His father brought him to England, not doubting but that he will meet with Success in a Kingdom, where his Countryman, that late famous Vertuoso [sic] Handel, received during his Life-time such particular Protection.

Tickets at Half a Guinea each; to be had of Mr. Mozart, at Mr. Couzin's, Hair-Cutter, in Cecil Court, St. Martin's Lane.

The Daily Advertiser, 31 May 1764.

1767-69
Haydn, 'Darling of the Nation'

Although Haydn's chief concern is for the music of Esterháza in all its different types — chamber music, church music and operas — he nevertheless finds time to work out his ideas about the development of musical form, especially in relation to the symphony and the string quartet, and he is not isolated from musical life in Vienna.

Emperor Joseph II and his brother Leopold, grand duke of Tuscany, painted in Rome in 1769. The previous summer the emperor had asked Mozart to compose an opera La finta semplice, but its performance was stopped by the impresario Affligio, who had drawn Gluck into financial difficulties.

1767 Haydn composes his Symphonies Nos.35 to 38, and his *Stabat Mater*.

• Gluck writes his opera *Alceste* to Calzabigi's LIBRETTO, which is a new and direct challenge to traditional *opera seria* ◆ (p.67).

• Rousseau publishes his *Dictionnaire de musique* (Dictionary of Music) in Paris, in which he rails against the new instrumental music.

• **25 June** Telemann dies, aged eighty-six. His godson, C.P.E. Bach ▲ (p.97) succeeds him as CANTOR of the Gymnasium Johanneum and director of music in Hamburg (p.75).

• **11 September** The Mozarts journey from Salzburg to Vienna, which they reach four days later, and then set off for Brno on 23 October. They go on to Olmütz, where Mozart develops smallpox, which has been raging in Vienna. Mozart is cured by 11 November, but the family remains in Olmütz until 23 December They return to Brno on Christmas Eve.

1768 Haydn writes his *Applausus* Cantata.

• Duni's opera *Les Moissonneurs* (The Harvesters), based on the Biblical story of Ruth, is given at the Comédie-Italienne in Paris, marking a move from *opéra-comique* towards *comédie larmoyante*, influenced by Diderot ◆ (p.95).

• **9 January** The Mozarts leave Brno and return to Vienna where, ten days later, they are once more received at court.

• **18 March** It is noted in the Salzburg court archives that unless Leopold Mozart returns during the following month, his salary will be witheld. The warning is ignored and Leopold receives no money from his patron from April until December this year.

• **May–June** At the request of Emperor Joseph II Mozart composes the opera *La finta semplice* (The Feigned Madwoman), but its performance is obstructed by intrigues (left).

OTHER EVENTS
1767 Rousseau settles in England with a pension
• Laurence Sterne: *Tristram Shandy*

1768 France buys Corsica from Genoa
• Leonhard Euler: *Lettres à une princesse d'Allemagne*
• Royal Academy of Art founded in London
• Laurence Sterne dies

1769 James Watt patents a separate condenser for the steam engine
• Nicolas Cugnot invents a three-wheeled steam-driven artillery carriage

'Do they imagine that after mingling our tears with those of a mother who mourns over the death of her son, we shall accept their world of fantasy, with their insipid mythology and mawkish madrigals?...Fiddlesticks!'

Denis Diderot on current opera, in *Le Neveu de Rameau*

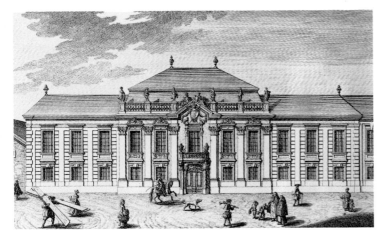

The Schönbrunn Palace, Vienna, was principally a summer residence for the imperial family, though they spent a great deal of time there, and the Mozarts were received twice in 1762 (p.99).

- **5 August** Haydn's new opera *Lo speziale* (The Chemist) inaugurates the new opera house at Esterháza.
- **September–October** Mozart's one-act German *singspiel*, *Bastien und Bastienne* (Bastien and Bastienne) is given at the house of Dr Anton Mesmer, the founder of mesmerism.
- **28–29 December** The Mozarts leave Vienna once again, travelling through Melk and Linz.

1769 5 January The Mozarts arrive back in Salzburg.

- **1 May** Mozart's *La finta semplice* is possibly performed in Salzburg on the archbishop's name day.
- **27 November** The Mozarts, father and son, are given 120 ducats by the Archbishop of Salzburg towards their forthcoming visit to Italy, and Wolfgang (aged fourteen) is appointed one of three leaders of the orchestra.
- **13 December** Leopold and Wolfgang Mozart travel to Verona via Innsbruck, Bolzano, Trento and Rovereto. They arrive on 27 December.

■ *Haydn Assumes Control*

In 1766 Haydn's output at Esterháza took on a new dimension. The death of Werner (p.99) meant that he could begin composing church music again after a break of five years, and this event coincided with Prince Nicolaus's transformation of his hunting lodge into a one-hundred-and-twenty-six-bedroomed castle at Esterháza. Improvements made to the building included the addition of two theatres; a large one for the performance of Italian operas (which opened in 1768), and a smaller German marionette theatre (inaugurated five years later). In addition to his previous duties, which included providing chamber music and incidental music to plays, Haydn now had to provide music for the two theatres, while the demand for music to accompany special events, such as an outdoor fireworks display, was ever increasing.

By 1776, Haydn was in charge of one of the most active opera houses in Europe. Not for him the difficulties experienced by so many composers during the eighteenth century,

from Vivaldi to Mozart, in getting their works commissioned or performed. Although Haydn was somewhat cut off from the outside world (both culturally and geographically), he had at his disposal a ready-made theatre, orchestra, vocal company and audience. Therefore, despite the many restrictions of patronage, he was able to reserve his energies for his music, and to experiment with, and perfect, a variety of new forms and combinations of instruments.

The final scene of Haydn's Italian opera L'incontro improvviso (The Unexpected Meeting), given at Esterháza with the composer directing a band of some twenty or so musicians from the keyboard in the pit. From 1766 Haydn was responsible for the production of such operas, as well as German operas for a marionette theatre, rehearsal schedules, and the overall provision of music, musicians and instruments.

1770-72
Mozart's Italian Years

Just as Handel and many less well known composers decided to experience music first-hand in Italy, Mozart, guided as ever by his watchful and determined father, now sets out on the journey south. It brings honours from the pope and the musical establishment, but most of all it confirms Mozart as a composer of opera.

1770 5 January Mozart gives his first concert in Italy at the Accademia Filarmonica in Verona. Five days later he leaves for Mantua, and Milan.

• 7 February Mozart plays for the Austrian Governor General of Lombardy, whose guests include Sammartini.

• 15 March The Mozarts leave Milan for Bologna. Wolfgang composes his first string quartet, which is possibly modelled on Sammartini's.

• 26 March Mozart plays in a concert in Bologna attended by Padre Martini. Three days later he leaves for Rome via Florence.

The interior of the Teatro Regio Ducal, Milan, during festivities to celebrate the birth of Peter Leopold, Archduke of Austria, in 1747. It was here in 1770 that Mozart's opera Mitridate *(below) was heard for the first time.*

> 'Here ends the German idiot and the Italian one begins.'
> Mozart to his sister, 7 January 1770, from Verona

• Ash Wednesday, 11 April In Rome Mozart hears Allegri's Miserere in the Sistine Chapel, and later writes it out perfectly from memory. On 8 May the Mozarts travel to Naples.

• 25 June The Mozarts leave Naples post-haste and reach Rome in twenty-seven hours.

• 5 July Mozart is made a Knight of the Golden Spur by Cardinal Pallavicini ▲ (opposite). Three days later Mozart, wearing the insignia, is presented to the pope in the Palazzo Santa Maria Maggiore. Although both Gluck and Ditters von Dittersdorf have previously received the order, they are of a lower grade than Mozart, and only one musician, Orlando di Lasso, has ever been appointed to the same grade.

• 10 July The Mozarts leave Rome for Bologna.

• 9 October Mozart is elected to the Accademia Filarmonica of Bologna. He subsequently leaves the city for Milan.

• 16 December Beethoven is born in Bonn.

• 26 December Mozart's opera *Mitridate* (Mithridates) is first heard in the Teatro Regio Ducal, Milan. The work has twenty-two consecutive performances, with the composer himself conducting the first three from the harpsichord (which last some six hours) .

1771 Haydn composes his second setting of the Salve Regina.

• 5 January Mozart is nominated an honorary director to the Accademia Filarmonica of Verona. The following month he journeys to Venice.

• 4 March Mozart is commissioned to write another opera for Milan, entitled *Lucio Silla* (Lucius Sulla), by October 1772.

OTHER EVENTS
1770 James Hargreaves patents his spinning jenny
• Thomas Gainsborough: *The Blue Boy*

1771 Jean Houdon: *Diderot*
• First edition of *Encylopaedia britannica* is published

1772 First partition of Poland by Russia, Prussia and Austria
• Choderlos de Laclos: *Les Liaisons dangereuses*

• **12 March** The Mozarts leave Venice for Padua. Wolfgang is asked to compose an oratorio *La Betulia liberata* (The Liberation of Bethulia), to a text by Metastasio ■ (p.79).

• **28 March** The Mozarts return to Salzburg.

• **13 August** The Mozarts begin their second visit to Italy. They arrive in Milan on 21st.

• **17 October** Mozart's serenata *Ascanio in Alba* (Ascanius in Alba), commissioned to celebrate the wedding of Archduke Ferdinand of Austria to Princess Maria Beatrice d'Este of Modena, is given at the Teatro Regio Ducal in Milan.

• **5 December** The Mozarts leave Milan for Salzburg.

• **16 December** Archbishop Schrattenbach dies (right).

1772 Haydn composes his String Quartets Op.20, and the St Nicholas Mass.

• **14 March** The new Archbishop of Salzburg is elected, who will prove to be less indulgent as an employer than his predecessor.

• **29 April** The new archbishop takes up his see, and shortly afterwards Mozart's SERENATA *Il sogno di Scipione* (Scipio's Dream) is given in his honour.

• **24 October** The Mozarts, father and son, set off on their third visit to Italy. They reach Milan on 4 November.

• **26 December** *Lucio Silla*, Mozart's three-act opera, has the first of twenty-six performances at the Teatro Regio Ducal in Milan. The first night lasts from 8 pm until 2 am.

Sigismund Christoph von Schrattenbach, Prince-Archbishop of Salzburg, and employer of the Mozarts father and son.

▲ *The Astonishing Mozart*

After seeing a Church or two in my way, I went to San Giovanni in Monti to hear the Philharmonic performances. There was a great deal of company there ...and among the rest who should I spy but the celebrated little German Mozart who

A portrait of Mozart wearing the insignia of a Knight of the Golden Spur, conferred on him by Pope Clement XIV in 1770 during his Italian visit. As the legend on the painting indicates, Mozart was also a member of the philharmonic academies of Bologna and Verona.

three or four years ago surprised everybody in London by his premature musical talent. I had a great deal of talk with his father ... The little man has grown a good deal but is still a little man. He is engaged to compose an opera for Milan. His father has been ill here these five or six weeks. The Pope has knighted the little great wonder.

Taken from Dr Burney's Italian diaries (30 August 1770, ★ p.108). In a later version he added:

He astonished the Italian musicians wherever he stopt. He is now at the age of twelve [he was fourteen] ingaged to compose an opera for Milan ....There are to be three new Operas composed on this occasion. I ... shall be curious to know how this extraordinary boy acquits himself in setting words in a language not his own. But there is no musical excellence I do not expect from the extraordinary quickness and talents, under the guidance of so able a musician and intelligent man as his father.

1773-78
Gluck Reforms Opera

The first performance of Gluck's first grand opera in French in 1774 marks a return to the ideals of the first composers of opera, though he has in fact already introduced his reforms in his operas with Italian text such as Orfeo ed Euridice *and* Alceste. *He matches his music to the drama, and the simpler the dramatic situation, the better his music tends to be.*

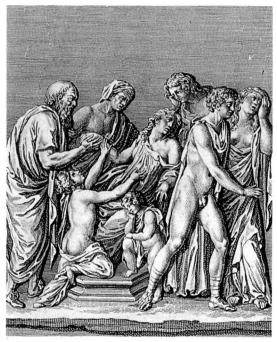

An illustration from Calzabigi's libretto to Gluck's Alceste ▲ *(opposite), first given in Vienna in 1767, published two years later, and then revised for Paris in 1776. The almost neo-Classical character of the scene is a pointer to the way Gluck's ideas about opera now turned.*

1773 17 January Mozart's MOTET for solo voice, *Exsultate, jubilate,* is first sung by the CASTRATO Venanzio Rauzzini in Milan.

• **13 March** The Mozarts return to Salzburg.

• **12 July** Death of Quantz ▲ (p.93), aged seventy-six, in Potsdam.

• **14 July** The Mozarts leave for Vienna, where they are received in audience by the empress on 5 August. When the Archbishop of Salzburg arrives in Vienna a week later, he extends their leave of absence. They return to Salzburg on 26 September.

• **26 July** Haydn's opera *L'infedeltà delusa* (Faithlessness Deluded), written to celebrate the name day of the Dowager Princess Maria Anna, is performed at Esterháza.

• **5 October** Mozart completes his Symphony No.25, which has parts for four horns.

1774 Haydn dedicates his first authorized publication, a set of six keyboard sonatas, to Prince Nicolaus Esterházy.

• **4 April** Mozart's incidental music to Baron Gebler's play *Thamos, König in Ägypten* (Thamos, King in Egypt) is given for the first time in Vienna.

• **19 April** Gluck's opera *Iphigénie en Aulide* (Iphigenia in Aulis) receives an enthusiastic reception at the Opéra in Paris ◆ (p.109).

• **28 August** The French version of Gluck's opera *Orfeo ed Euridice* (p.99), *Orphée et Euridice,* is given a triumphant production at the Opéra in Paris.

• **6 December** The Mozarts leave Salzburg for Munich.

1774–75 Haydn composes his ORATORIO *Il ritorno di Tobia* (The Return of Tobias), commissioned for the new season by the Vienna Tonkünstler-Sozietät, a charitable organization for widows and orphans of musicians.

1775 Gluck's comedy *Cythère assiégée* (Cythera Beseiged) is badly received in Paris ◆ (p.109).

• **13 January** Mozart's three-act OPERA BUFFA, *La finta giardiniera* (The False Gardening Lady) has its first performance in Munich. The Mozarts return to Salzburg on 7 March.

• **23 April** Mozart's SERENATA *Il rè pastore* (The Shepherd King) is performed in Salzburg.

OTHER EVENTS

1773 Dissolution of the Jesuit Order by Pope Clement XIV
• The Boston Tea Party

1774 The first Continental Congress takes place in Philadelphia
• Accession of King Louis XVI of France
• Joseph Priestley discovers oxygen
• James Watt, in partnership with Matthew Boulton, completes an experimental steam engine

1775 Alessandro Volta invents the electric battery
• Start of American Revolution
• Pierre Beaumarchais: *Le barbier de Séville*

1776 American Declaration of Independence
• Discovery of hydrogen
• Thomas Paine: *Common Sense*
• Adam Smith: *The Wealth of Nations*

1777 Articles of Confederation in America
• Richard Sheridan: *The School for Scandal*

1778 War of Bavarian Succession
• Death of Rousseau

1776 Sir John Hawkins's *General History of the Science and Practice of Music* is unfortunately overshadowed by the first volume of Dr Charles Burney's *General History of Music* ★ (p.108), when both are published in London.

• **March to May** Gluck is in Paris for the production of his opera *Alceste* (p.102) at the Paris Opéra on 23 April ▲ (below).

> *'Whatever talent the musician may have, he will never produce any other than mediocre music if the poet does not stimulate in him that enthusiasm without which the manifestations of all the arts remain weak and lifeless.'*
> Gluck writing to the *Mercure de France* in February, 1773

• **21 July** Mozart's *Haffner* SERENADE, is performed at the wedding celebrations of Marie Elizabeth Haffner, daughter of the mayor of Salzburg and a friend of the composer.

• **Late 1776** Piccinni arrives in Paris ◆ (p109).

1777 May Gluck is in Paris for the production of his opera *Armide* at the Opéra on 23 September.

• **28 August** In response to a request from Mozart for further leave of absence, the Archbishop of Salzburg grants permission to both father and son 'to seek their fortune elsewhere'. In the event Leopold Mozart stays in his post, but Wolfgang is eventually dismissed.

• **23 September** Mozart and his mother leave Salzburg for Paris, via Munich and Mannheim, where the composer falls in love with the singer Aloisia Weber, his host's daughter.

Gluck set out to reform opera from within, and this portrait (below), painted in Paris in 1775, conveys something of the idealism with which he set about his task and the patience with which he faced opposition.

▲ *Gluck's Manifesto*

I have tried to restrict music to its true role of serving poetry through expression and by following the situation of the story, without interrupting the action or smothering it with useless, superfluous ornaments; and I believe that it should do this in the same way that telling colours affect a correct and well organized drawing, by a well matched contrast of light and shade, which animates the figures without altering their shapes.

Therefore, I have not seen fit to arrest an actor in the heat of dialogue to make him wait out a tedious RITORNELLO, *or to stop him in mid-word over a favourable vowel, or to show off the nimbleness of his fine voice by means of a lengthy passage, or to purchase time with the Orchestra while he took breath for a cadenza...in short I have endeavoured to banish all those abuses against which common sense and reason have for so long cried out in vain.*

Gluck writing in the 1769 publication of the score of his opera *Alceste*. In fact, when he revised *Alceste* for Paris in 1776 he repeated a similar claim, though the work was to lose something of its original grandeur in the process.

★ *A musical evening at the house of Dr Burney, whose massive* General History of Music *was published in four volumes between 1776 and 1789. The musicologist had travelled extensively in Europe between 1770 and 1773, gathering information.*

1778 Piccinni's first French opera, *Roland*, is given in Paris ◆ (opposite).

• **1 January** Karl Theodor, Elector Palatine, becomes Elector of Bavaria too, which will entail the eventual removal of the court music establishment from Mannheim to Munich.

• **14 March** Mozart and his mother leave the Webers and journey to Paris, where they arrive nine days later. There, Mozart meets the Duc de Guines, an admirable flautist. The nobleman's daughter, who plays the harp, studies composition with Mozart, and the duke commissions Mozart to write the Concerto for Flute and Harp.

• **26 March** Beethoven, aged seven, is presented by his father as a musical prodigy at a concert in Cologne.

• **11 June** *Les Petits Riens* (The Little Nothings), a ballet by Jean Georges Noverre with music by Mozart, is given at the Opéra in Paris in the same programme as a Piccinni opera, *Le finte gemelle* (The False Twins). It is repeated six times.

• **12 June** Mozart's *Paris* Symphony is performed in the house of the Ambassador of the Palatinate (Mannheim), and six days later the work opens the *Concert spirituel* (p.77) in Paris.

• **19 June** Mozart's mother falls seriously ill, and dies on 3 July, aged fifty-seven. Mozart writes to his father that evening, telling him of her illness, but does not reveal that she has died until six days later.

• **27 July** Baron Grimm condemns Mozart in a letter to his father: 'He is too trusting, too lazy, too easy to catch, too little interested in the means that may lead to fortune. In order to make an impression here one has to be cunning, enterprising and daring. To make his fortune I wish he had only half his talent and twice as much shrewdness, and then I should have no worries for him.'

Plan of the ground floor of the new opera house of La Scala, Milan (right), rebuilt after a fire in 1776, and intended to be the finest in the world.

• **2 August** La Scala opera house in Milan (strictly Teatro alla Scala, right) opens with a performance of Salieri's opera *Europa riconosciuta* (Europe Rewarded). The Teatro Regio Ducal was destroyed by fire in 1776; Empress Maria Theresa then ordered the architect Foligno to build a new opera house that would be the most magnificent in the world.

• **September** Fridolin Weber moves with the court orchestra from Mannheim to Munich, where his daughter Aloisia (p.107) is engaged at the opera.

• **26 September** Mozart leaves Paris.

• **November** Six sonatas for violin and clavier ◆ (p.127) by Mozart are published in Paris as his Opus One.

• **November** Gluck is in Paris again ◆ (below).

• **6 November** Mozart arrives in Mannheim.

• **25 December** Mozart arrives in Munich and stays with the Weber family. His father demands his return, and secures him the post of orchestral leader and court organist at Salzburg.

Piccinni (below), who was summoned to Paris as a rival to Gluck in 1776 (p.107).

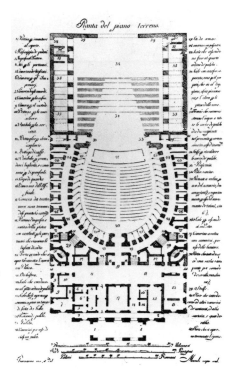

Pianta del piano terreno.

◆ *The Second Opera War in Paris*

Although Gluck had been warmly received in Paris with Iphigénie en Aulide *and* Orphée et Euridice *in 1774, his comedy* Cythère assiégée *of 1775 failed to please, and* Alceste *of 1776 drew absolutely no enthusiasm from the Parisian opera lovers* ▲ *(p.107). So the opera war that had been threatening in a minor way since 1774 now broke out in the press in earnest. The traditionalists, against Gluck, maintained that tragedy ought to be the concern of spoken drama, and that opera ought to limit itself to the type of magical drama, which was a synthesis of poetry, music and stage spectacle. As Gluck stated in his preface to the French version of* Alceste *in 1776, however: 'When I undertook to set the opera of* Alceste *to music, I resolved to avoid all those abuses which had crept into Italian Opera through the foolish vanity of singers*

and the mistaken compliance of composers, and which had made it tedious and ridiculous instead of being what it once was, the grandest and most important theatre of our day.' To show how this might be achieved, Gluck then set about composing Armide, *to a French libretto by Philippe Quinault, with hardly any changes to the original poem, and it was even said that Gluck's production used the same sets as those provided for Lully's version of 1686 (p.56). It was argued now that Gluck was basically a traditionalist who was trying to reform French music on Italian lines, so it was better, therefore, to keep the French forms but use an Italian composer. Piccinni was therefore brought to Paris at the end of 1776. He was probably the most successful composer in Italy at the time, but he barely understood French, and his first Parisian opera,* Roland, *was not ready until the beginning of 1778. Gluck had started to compose* Roland, *too, but he destroyed it when he heard that Piccinni had been commissioned as well. The Opéra were still able to stage a contest of sorts, by commissioning Piccinni to write an* Iphigénie en Tauride *(Iphigenia in Taurus), but whereas Gluck's was produced in 1779 (p.110), Piccinni's was delayed until 1781. Gluck was to write one more French opera,* Echo et Narcisse *(Echo and Narcissus, p.110), which was a failure. Broken in health, he decided to return to Vienna.*

1779-81
Mozart Dismissed

Mozart finds the restrictions imposed on him by his employer increasingly irksome, and he provokes the rupture that leads to his dismissal. His subsequent failure to earn enough to keep his family without the support of a permanent post highlights the difficulties surrounding the creative artist in society.

1779 Haydn signs a new contract which gives him much more freedom of movement and control over his compositions.

• **7 January** Mozart presents his Violin Sonatas Op.1 (p.109) to Electress Maria Elisabeth, dedicated to her, in Munich.

• **15 January** Mozart returns to Salzburg. He receives his new contract as court organist (p.109).

• **18 May** Gluck's opera *Iphigénie en Tauride* is first performed at the Paris Opéra . Later in the year his final French opera, *Echo et Narcisse* is a disaster, and he returns to Vienna ◆ (p.109).

• **September** The Weber family leave Munich for Vienna, where Aloisia (p.107) is engaged at the German Opera.

1780 1 May Mozart's *La finta giardiniera* (p.106) is performed in Augsburg, probably the first time that one of his operas is given on a stage for which it has not been written.

• **31 October** Aloisia Weber marries an actor, Joseph Lange, in Vienna.

Costume design for Mozart's Idomeneo. *In contemporary accounts the scenery by Quaglio and the singers came in for more mention than Mozart himself.*

• **5 November** Mozart goes to Munich for performances of his opera *Idomeneo* (left). He has official leave from Salzburg until 18 December.

1781 Haydn dedicates his new String Quartets Op.33 to Grand Duke Paul of Russia.

• **29 January** Mozart's *Idomeneo* is performed at the court theatre in Munich (later known as the Residenztheater), after two postponements.

• **12 March** Mozart is summoned to Vienna by the Archbishop of Salzburg.

• **3 April** Mozart makes his public début in Vienna as composer and pianist at a charity concert in aid of the musicans' benevolent fund at the Kärntnertor Theatre.

• **9 May** Mozart quarrels with the Archbishop of Salzburg, and submits his resignation to the chief steward, Count Arco, the following day.

• **9 June** Mozart is literally kicked out of the archbishop's palace by Count Arco ▲ (opposite).

• **15 December** Mozart writes to his father of his plans to marry Constanze Weber ★ (p.112).

• **24 December** Mozart takes part in a piano contest with Muzio Clementi before Emperor Joseph II in the Hofburg, Vienna.

The last section of a letter from Mozart, dated 10 May 1779, to his cousin Maria Anna Thekla Mozart, with sketches by the composer. The letter is written in the rather bawdy and scatological language that was used between the members of the family.

OTHER EVENTS
1779 Lessing: *Nathan der Weise,* a plea for religious tolerance
• Sheridan: *The Critic*

1780 Scheller invents the first fountain pen

1781 Lord Cornwallis surrenders at Yorktown, marking an end to the British cause in America
• Immanuel Kant: *Critique of Pure Reason*
• Jean Houdon: *Bust of Voltaire*

▲ *Mozart's Account of his Unceremonious Exit*

*S*o this is the way to influence people and attract *them! To refuse petitions out of innate stupidity, not to say a word to your master for want of courage and a delight in obsequiousness, to keep a man hanging about for four weeks, and finally, when he is forced to present the petition in person, instead of even granting him admittance, throw him out of the room and give him a boot on the backside – that is the Count [Arco] who, according to your last letter, has my interests so much at heart – and this is the court in which I am supposed to continue working – the place where anyone who wishes to make a written request, instead of being helped to deliver it, is treated in this manner!*

In this letter to his father in Salzburg, written from Vienna on 9 June 1781, Mozart relates the events following his resignation from the service of the Archbishop of Salzburg. In all fairness to Count Arco, and as Mozart's father was perfectly well aware, the count, who held an important position in the archbishop's household, was hoping that by delaying Mozart's petition there might be a time for reflection on the composer's part and an improvement in the general situation which would allow him to continue in the archbishop's employ, but this was not to be.

A portrait of the Mozart family painted in the winter of 1780–81, when Mozart and his sister were no longer the darling child prodigies of the aristocratic salons. Their mother, who looks down from the wall, had died in Paris two years earlier.

1782-83

Beethoven Makes his Appearance

Although Beethoven is not a child prodigy of Mozart's calibre, and lacks a father with the talent and education of Leopold Mozart, he nevertheless impresses those around him with his ability. It gradually becomes clear that the somewhat restricted horizons of provincial Bonn will be too narrow for him, and that he must take his place on a much larger stage.

1782 1 January J.C. Bach dies in London, aged forty-six.

• **12 April** Pietro Metastasio ■ (p.79) dies in Vienna.

• **16 July** Mozart's opera *Die Entführung aus dem Serail*, (The Abduction from the Harem, opposite) is first performed at the Burgtheater, Vienna. It becomes his greatest stage success during his lifetime.

• **4 August** Mozart and Constanze Weber (below) are married in St Stephen's, Vienna.

• **27 October** Birth of Paganini in Genoa.

1783 2 March Beethoven's teacher Neefe writes: 'This young genius deserves support to enable him to travel. He would be sure to become a second Wolfgang Amadeus Mozart, if he progressed as he has begun.'

• **11 March** Mozart takes part in a concert in the Burgtheater, Vienna, with his sister-in-law Aloisia. Gluck sits in the box next to Mozart's wife and Joseph Lange (p.110). They all lunch with Gluck five days later.

• **23 March** Mozart holds a successful concert of his music, including two piano concertos, in the Burgtheater in the presence of the emperor.

OTHER EVENTS
1782 Montgolfier brothers invent air balloon
• Schiller: *Die Räuber*
• Rousseau: *Confessions* (posthumous)
• Fanny Burney: *Cecilia*

1783 The Peace of Versailles: recognition of the American Republic
• France renounces India
• Civil marriage and divorce made possible in Austria

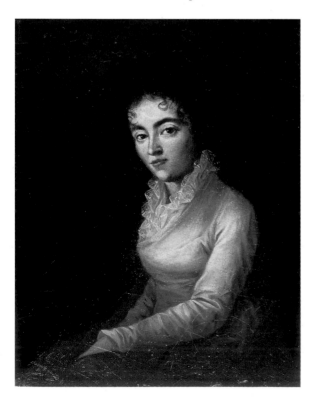

★ *Constanze Weber in 1782, the year of her marriage to Mozart, very much against the wishes of his father, since he felt that his son had not the means to support a family, which was true, and that his career would inevitably suffer before he had time to establish himself in Vienna.*

• **26 April** Beethoven, aged thirteen, is appointed keyboard player in the court orchestra in Bonn.

• **8 May** Mozart's opera *Die Entführung aus dem Serail* is performed in German in Warsaw.

• **17 June** The Mozarts' first child, Raimund Leopold, is born, but dies at his foster mother's in Vienna on 19 August.

• **29 July** The Mozarts are in Salzburg so that Constanze may meet Leopold Mozart. It is possible that they do not learn of their son's death until their return to Vienna.

• **26 October** In fulfilment of a vow made before his wedding, Mozart celebrates his marriage and reconciliation with his father with a performance of his unfinished Mass in C Minor in Salzburg, with his wife as one of the soloists. The following day the couple leave Salzburg for Linz.

• **4 November** Mozart's *Linz* Symphony, written for a concert in the country town whose name it bears, is first performed.

Das Sarail. Le Sérail.

A scene fom Mozart's opera Die Entführung aus dem Serail *first performed in 1782, showing Bassa or Pasha Selim (in the event a non-singing role) in his harem. The work became one of Mozart's most successful operas, though initially some of the more sophisticated music lovers felt that he had wasted his talent on inferior material.*

◆ *Composers and Patrons*

As the example of Mozart shows all too clearly, it was virtually impossible for a composer to exist during the eighteenth century without some sort of appointment, salary or pension. With a personality such as that of Haydn, and an employer who appreciated the worth of his director of music, then the system of patronage could work well, though it must be said that Haydn's first contract was fairly restrictive ■ *(p.99), and would not have suited Mozart.*

Mozart's great daring was to hope that he could manage to exist financially by fulfilling commissions, giving lessons, concerts and recitals, and publishing his music by subscription, thereby ensuring that a much greater share of the proceeds went to him, and not to his publisher. He was not averse to the title bestowed by an appointment, but he found it intolerable if the title imposed what he regarded as unreasonable restrictions on his ability to pursue his career as he saw fit. Herein lay the

great intractable problem. The time had not yet arrived for the composer to be regarded as much more than an employee, and it would require a change in society, an expansion of the concert-going public, the increased importance of instrumental, especially symphonic music, and a personality like Beethoven's to establish composers as creative artists in their own right.

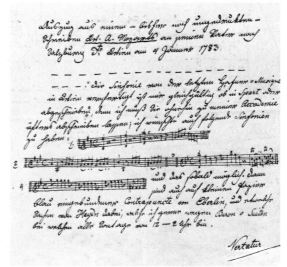

A letter from Mozart and his wife to the composer's father, dated 4 January 1783, in which they send belated New Year greetings and the composer asks for the scores of five of his compositions to be sent to him.

1784-85
Mozart and Haydn

Through the medium of the string quartet, a friendship is cemented between Mozart and Haydn that has a deep underlying significance. Two generations combine in a symbolic way, setting the seal on the supremacy of Viennese music in Europe at this time.

1784 Grétry's masterpiece, his opera *Richard Coeur de Lion* (Richard the Lionheart, ■ opposite), is given in Paris.

• **9 February** Mozart begins a thematic catalogue of his works, which he keeps until his death.

• **17, 24 and 31 March** Mozart holds three subscription concerts, on Wednesdays during Lent, in Vienna ◆ (p.113).

• **1 April** Mozart holds a benefit concert in the Burgtheater, Vienna.

• **1 July** W.F. Bach dies in poverty in Berlin.

• **23 August** Mozart attends the first night of Paisiello's opera *Il rè Teodoro in Venezia* (King Theodore in Venice) at the Burgtheater, but is taken ill during the performance with a severe attack of colic. He develops a kidney infection, which lasts until September.

• **21 September** The Mozarts' second child, Karl Thomas, is born. He will survive the whole family.

• **14 December** Mozart is received as apprentice (first grade) in the Viennese Masonic lodge 'Zur Wohlthätigkeit' ('Beneficence').

Mozart's fortepiano, now in the Salzburg Mozarteum, which was made in 1780 and acquired by the composer four years later. Several of his piano concertos were written for Mozart to perform as virtuoso.

1785 Haydn (right) has been asked to write six new symphonies for the *Concert de la Loge* 'Olympique' (Concert for the 'Olympic' lodge), a fashionable Masonic lodge in Paris. He begins these, his *Paris* Symphonies.

• **7 January** Mozart is promoted to journeyman in the 'Zur wahren Eintracht' ('True Concord') lodge.

• **15 January** At his apartment in Vienna, Mozart and his friends perform some of the six String Quartets, Op.10, subsequently dedicated to Haydn, in the latter's presence.

• **3 February** The first performance of the Beaumarchais play *The Marriage of Figaro* in Vienna is announced ▲ (p.117) but is immediately prohibited. The official censor has allowed the words to be published but not performed, because of the potentially seditious nature of the work.

Haydn (right) recognized in Mozart a genius very different from his own, and was generous in his response to it. Mozart was quick to acknowledge his debt to the older man.

OTHER EVENTS
1784 Pitt's India Act: the East India Company's power transferred to the British Government
• Schiller: *Kobale und Liebe*

1785 Thomas Jefferson completes his design for the Virginia State Capitol
• Rozier's balloon crashes when he attempts to cross the English Channel by air

- **11 February** Mozart petitions the musicians' benevolent society for membership but is refused because he is unable to produce his birth certificate.

- **12 February** Mozart arranges a second performance of his string quartets for Haydn. In a letter to his daughter, dated 16 February, Leopold Mozart relates Haydn's comments on his son: 'Before God and as an honest man I tell you that your son is the greatest composer known to me, either personally or by name.'

'He has taste and, in addition, the deepest knowledge of composition'

Haydn, talking on Mozart to his father on 12 February 1785

- **10 March** Mozart gives a benefit concert at the Burgtheater, Vienna, when he plays his Piano Concerto in C Major, No.21 (opposite).

- **1 September** Mozart's String Quartets Op.10 are published, with a dedicatory letter to Haydn (right): 'Here they are then, great man and my dearest friend, these six children of mine. They are indeed the fruit of long and laborious work.'

- **17 November** First performance of Mozart's Masonic CANTATA *Die Maurerfreude* (The Masons' Joy), specially composed to commemorate two deceased brothers.

- **24 December** Mozart's silhouette appears in a calendar in Vienna, along with those of Haydn, Gluck and Salieri.

The dedication, in Italian, of Mozart's string quartets to Haydn, dated 1 September 1785 – ample testimony to Mozart's recognition of his debt to his senior.

■ Grétry's 'Richard Coeur-de-Lion'

Although Grétry was probably gifted with more imagination than talent as an operatic composer, his work is significant in that it provided pointers to the way that Parisian opera was to develop in the next century. From Gluck he had absorbed much that helped him on his way, while at the same time noting the success of the naïve type of opera going back to Rousseau ◆ (p.95). What resulted was a form of opera which, on the one hand contained an element of the noble, and even exotic, in the location of the plots of some of his works, and on the other depicted the lives and emotions of ordinary people.

Grétry's masterpiece, *Richard Coeur-de-Lion*, was highly innovative in its approach. Not only was it one of the earliest rescue operas, a convention which Beethoven was later to employ in his *Fidelio*, but also the minstrel Blondel's song 'Une fièvre brûlante' ('A Burning Fever') is one of the earliest examples of a motif being repeated in various forms through an opera, to signal a character. As Grétry said, 'it is the pivot on which the whole opera turns'. The opera contains spectacle, too (in the final assault on the castle), a feature which was to become an important element in 'grand opera' of the Parisian school.

Grétry, in a miniature dating from 1790.

1786-87
'Figaro' and 'Don Giovanni'

Mozart excels in many different musical forms, but it is the theatre that draws from him some of his most enduring music. Yet in spite of the enthusiastic reception given to his operas in Vienna and Prague, Mozart still finds it almost impossible to make a living, and is contemplating making the journey to London where his talents might be better appreciated and rewarded.

A memorandum from Joseph II to Count Orsini-Rosenberg, Lord Chamberlain and director of the court theatres, concerning payment for entertainment provided at Schönbrünn on 7 February 1786. Salieri, whose name comes first, received one hundred ducats and Mozart fifty, but whereas the first provided a small opera buffa, Mozart only wrote an overture and four songs for a German play.

1786 7 February Mozart composes incidental music for a German play *Der Schauspieldirektor* (The Stage Manager), given before the court at Schönbrunn, for which he receives fifty ducats (left). The companion piece is Salieri's *Prima la musica, poi le parole* (First the Music, then the Words).

• **1 May** Mozart's *The Marriage of Figaro* is first performed at the Burgtheater in Vienna ▲ (p.119), having been postponed from 28 April. The composer himself directs the first two performances from the harpsichord. Five numbers are encored at the second performance and seven at the third, inspiring the emperor to impose an edict that only solo ARIAS may be repeated in operas. In all the opera is given nine times this year.

• **Autumn** Mozart contemplates going to England with his wife, but his father refuses to have their son Karl (p.114) to live with him in Salzburg, since he already has Nannerl's son Leopold.

• **18 October** The Mozarts' third child, Johann Leopold, is born. He dies of suffocation on 15 November.

• **Early December** Mozart's *The Marriage of Figaro* is performed in Prague, by 11 December at the latest, to great acclaim ★ (p.118).

• **18 December** Birth of Weber, cousin to Constanze Mozart, née Weber ★ (p.112).

1787 8 January Mozart and his wife leave Vienna for Prague, where they arrive on 11 January.

• **19 January** Mozart conducts his *Prague* Symphony in the National Theatre in Prague, and on 22 January conducts a performance of *The Marriage of Figaro* there.

• **8 February** Mozart leaves Prague with a commission to write an opera, and returns to Vienna on 12th.

• **14 February** Haydn makes a STRING QUARTET arrangement of his orchestral composition *The Seven Last Words of Our Redeemer from the Cross*, which is possibly given its first performance in Vienna on 26 March.

• **March** Mozart's father is taken seriously ill.

• **7 April** Beethoven, aged sixteen, goes to Vienna to take lessons from Mozart. He possibly returns home two weeks later, as his mother is ill.

OTHER EVENTS
1786 Accession of Frederick William II of Prussia
• Robert Burns: *Poems Chiefly in the Scottish Dialect*
• Joshua Reynolds: *Duchess of Devonshire*

1787 American Constitutional Convention
• Schiller: *Don Carlos*
• Goethe: *Iphigenie auf Tauris*

★ *Title page from the 1785 edition of Beaumarchais's play* La Folle journée, ou Le Mariage de Figaro, *which ultimately provided the libretto for Mozart's opera. The count discovers Cherubino, who has been hiding in a covered chair, and has therefore heard his master's approaches to the countess's maid, Susanna.*

▲ Da Ponte on the Libretto of 'The Marriage of Figaro'

The length of time considered usual for dramas, the number of characters usually included in them, and other wise considerations and requirements imposed by morality, place and audience, were the reasons why I did not make a translation of this excellent comedy [Beaumarchais's play], but rather an adaptation or, shall we say, an extract from it.

With this in mind I reduced the number of characters… and cut out, in addition to an entire act, many delightful scenes and a number of good jokes, in place of which I had to put CANZONETTAS, arias, choruses and other pieces, and words suitable to be set to music…. Nevertheless in spite of all efforts and application and care taken by the composer and myself to be brief, the opera will not be one of the shortest to come on to the stage, for which we hope that sufficient excuse will be found in the various strands from which the action of this play is woven, the scope and grandeur of it, the many musical numbers necessary so as not to leave the actors too long with nothing to do… and to express… the various emotions that are shown, but above all in our wish to give as it were a new kind of spectacle to a public of such refined taste and just comprehension.

Da Ponte's preface to the libretto of *The Marriage of Figaro*, 1 May 1786.

• **28 May** Mozart's father dies in Salzburg, leaving his son 1000 gulden.

• **17 July** Beethoven's mother dies in Bonn of tuberculosis.

• **1 October** Mozart and his wife go to Prague to rehearse *The Marriage of Figaro* (above). They arrive three days later.

• **14 October** Mozart's *The Marriage of Figaro* is revived at the National Theatre in Prague under the composer's direction in place of *Don Giovanni*, planned to celebrate the marriage of Archduchess Maria Theresa and Prince Anton Clemens of Saxony. The bride and her brother, Archduke Franz, are present.

• **29 October** Mozart's *Don Giovanni* receives its first performance in Prague and is greeted with great enthusiasm.

• **Mid-November** Mozart returns to Vienna.

• **15 November** Death of Gluck, aged seventy-three, in Vienna.

• **December** Requested by a Prague official to compose an opera for the city, Haydn replies that he will provide an unstaged opera, but suggests that Mozart would be a more suitable choice for a staged work: 'It makes me angry to think that this unique Mozart has not yet found a post at some imperial or royal court. Forgive me if I wander from my path. I love the man too much.'

• **7 December** Mozart is appointed a court chamber musician in Vienna at a disappointingly low salary of 800 gulden (for the same appointment Gluck had received 2000 gulden). The only requirement, and it is an informal one, is to compose dances for the court masked balls held during the winter months.

• **27 December** The Mozarts' fourth child, Theresia, is born, but will live only six months.

★ *A set design by Joseph Platzer for the garden scene at the end of Mozart's* The Marriage of Figaro *in the 1786 Prague production. Mozart himself conducted the revival of the opera in Prague the following year.*

Silhouettes of six members of the original cast of The Marriage of Figaro *(clockwise from top left): Michael Kelly ▲ (p.121), Don Basilio and Don Curzio; Francesco Bussani, Dr Bartolo and Antonio; Maria Piccinelli-Mandini, Marcellina; Dorotea Sardi-Bussani, Cherubino; Luisa Laschi-Mombelli, the Countess; and Stefano Mandini, Count Almaviva.*

Mich: Okelly

Franz Bussani

Maria Piccinelli Mandini

▲ *What the Critics Said:*

Herr Mozart's music was generally admired already by connoisseurs at the first performance, apart from those whose love of self and their conceit will not permit them to find merit in anything that was not written by themselves.

The public, however (and this is often the case with the public), did not really know on the first day where it stood. It heard lots of bravos from unbiased connoisseurs, but unruly louts in the gallery employed their hired lungs with all their strength to deafen both singers and audience with their St! and Pst!; so that opinion was divided at the end of the work.

Apart from that, it is accurate to say that the first performance was not one of the best, because of the difficulty of the composition.

Now, however, after several performances, one would be taking part in the cabal or subscribing to lack of taste if one maintained that Herr Mozart's music is anything other than a work of art.

It contains so many beautiful things, and such a wealth of ideas, as can only be drawn from the source of inherent genius.

From the *Wiener Realzeitung*, 11 July 1786

Stephano Mandini

Luisa Laschi Mombelli

Sardi Bussani

1788-90
Vienna: Musical Focus of Europe

As Mozart's career draws to its magnificent but tragic close, Haydn, finally released from his long period of service in Esterháza, basks in national and international fame, and the young Beethoven decides to leave Bonn and go to Vienna, now the musical capital of Europe and the Western world.

1788 Haydn composes his String Quartets Op.54 and Op.55.

• **7 May** Mozart's *Don Giovanni* is first performed in Vienna, and will have fifteen performances by the end of the year. Certain critics find the music too difficult for the singers, and after this year it is never again performed during the composer's lifetime.

• **26 June–10 August** Mozart's last three Symphonies Nos.39 to 41, are composed in six weeks. As the conclusion of his quest for perfection in this form, they are among the most important instrumental pieces composed during the eighteenth century

• **15 December** Death of C.P.E. Bach, aged seventy-four, in Hamburg.

1789 6 March Handel's *Messiah*, in Mozart's orchestration, is performed for the first time at Count Johann Esterházy's palace in Vienna.

• **8 April** Mozart leaves Vienna with Prince Karl Lichnowsky for Prague, Dresden, Leipzig and Berlin.

• **4 June** Mozart returns to Vienna.

> *'Mozart, a star of the greatest magnitude in the current musical firmament.'*
> *Vaterlandschronik,*
> Stuttgart,
> 1788

★ *The St Michael Square in Vienna, showing the old Burgtheater, which became the National Hoftheater. Here were given the first performances of Mozart's* Die Entführung aus dem Serail, The Marriage of Figaro *and* Così fan tutte.

• **29 August** Mozart's *The Marriage of Figaro* ▲ (p.117) is revived at the Burgtheater (opposite) in Vienna.

• **16 November** The Mozarts' fifth child Anna Maria is born, but lives for only an hour.

• **22 December** Mozart's clarinet QUINTET, performed by Anton Stadler, the clarinettist for whom the piece is composed, is included at a concert of the Tonkünstler-Societät (the Musicians' Benevolent Society) in Vienna.

1790 26 January Mozart's new opera *Così fan tutte* (So Do All Women) is performed at the Burgtheater, Vienna (opposite). It is generally well received, with ten performances this year.

• **23 September** Mozart sets out for Frankfurt (below), where Emperor Leopold II is to be crowned on 9 October. Salieri is in the imperial retinue, and Mozart is simply an onlooker. After giving an unsuccesful concert there on 15 October, he returns to Vienna in November.

• **Late September** On the death of Prince Nicolaus Esterházy, his successor dismisses the musical establishment and closes the palace. Haydn is persuaded by the impresario Johann Peter Salomon to go to London.

• **14 December** A farewell dinner, at which Mozart is present, is given in Vienna for Haydn by Salomon on the eve of the composer's departure for London. When taking his leave Mozart says to Haydn, 'We are probably saying our last adieu in this life.'

• **25 December** Beethoven is among the court musicians at Bonn entertained to dinner by Haydn who is on his way to London.

▲ *Mozart Remembered*

He was a remarkably small man, very thin and pale, with a profusion of fine fair hair, of which he was rather vain. He gave me a cordial invitation to his house, of which I availed myself, and passed a great part of my time there. He always received me with kindness and hospitality. He was remarkably fond of punch, of which beverage I have seen him take copious draughts. He was also fond of billiards, and had an excellent billiard table in his house. Many and many a game have I played with him, but always came off second best. He gave Sunday concerts, at which I was never missing. He was kind-hearted, and always ready to oblige; but so very particular, when he played, that if the slightest noise were made, he instantly left off. He one day made me to sit at the piano, and gave credit to my first master, who had taught me to place my hand well on the instrument. He conferred upon me what I considered a high compliment. I had composed a little melody to Metastasio's canzonetta 'Grazie agl' inganni tuoi' ['Thanks to Your Deceptions'], which was a great favourite wherever I sang it. It was very simple, but had the good fortune to please Mozart. He took it and composed variations upon it, which were truly beautiful; and had the further kindness and condescension to play them whenever he had an opportunity.'

Michael Kelly ★ (p.119), *Reminiscences*, 1826

This portrait by an unknown artist (right) was bought by the music historian Albi Rosenthal in the early 1970s, and bears a striking resemblance to late portraits of Mozart. Scholars agree that it could well be a likeness of the composer, perhaps made during Mozart's visit to Frankfurt in 1790.

1791-99
Haydn Goes to England

After a relatively quiet existence in the country, with intermittent visits to the capital, at the age of fifty-eight Haydn finds himself honoured not only in Vienna but also abroad. The warmth of his reception in London is comparable to that accorded to Handel.

1791 21 February Czerny is born in Vienna.

• **11 March** Salomon's concert series (p.121) begins in London with a performance every Friday evening until early June. Hadyn's symphonies feature largely in the programmes, and his Symphony No.94, known as the *Surprise*, becomes especially popular.

• **Spring** Mozart is commissioned to compose a Requiem anonymously by a person who is acting for Count Franz Walsegg-Stuppach.

• **9 May** Mozart is appointed unpaid assistant director of music at St Stephen's Cathedral, Vienna, with the promise of the post of director when it falls vacant.

• **4 June** Constanze Mozart ★ (p.112) goes to Baden, a spa near Vienna. Mozart joins her and composes the MOTET *Ave verum corpus* on 18 June.

• **July** At the instigation of Dr Burney ★ (p.108), Haydn is awarded an honorary doctorate by Oxford University. He performs the Symphony No.92, which becomes known as the *Oxford*, in the city.

★ This coloured engraving of the twenty-eighth scene from Act Two of Mozart's The Magic Flute, *shows Tamino before the Gates of Terror, awaiting his next trial to win the hand of Pamina.*

OTHER EVENTS
1791 Declaration of the Rights of Man

1792 France is declared a republic; the guillotine is first used in Paris

1793 The 'Reign of Terror' begins in France. Louis XVI and Marie-Antoinette are executed
• Second partition of Poland

1794 Slavery is abolished in the French colonies

1795 Third and final partition of Poland

By the end of the eighteenth century, Haydn (opposite) had achieved renown throughout Europe and had settled in Vienna where this portrait was painted in 1799.

Cimarosa, a product of the Neopolitan tradition, made his debut there as a composer of opera in 1772, and went on to conquer Italy. In 1791 he went to Vienna, where Leopold II is said to have asked him to set Bertati's Il matrimonio segreto *to music. On his return to Naples he was thrown into prison for composing anti-royalist songs, but was allowed to leave the city and end his days in Venice.*

• **26 July** Mozart's sixth child, Franz Xaver Wolfgang, is born.

• **Late August** Mozart and his wife leave for Prague, where Leopold II is to be crowned king of Bohemia.

• **2 September** Mozart's *Don Giovanni*, possibly conducted by the composer, is given before the emperor in Prague.

• **5 September** Birth of Meyerbeer in Vogelsdorf near Berlin.

• **6 September** Mozart's new opera *La clemenza di Tito* (The Clemency of Titus) is first heard in Prague as part of the coronation celebrations.

• **30 September** Mozart's opera *The Magic Flute* ★ (p.122) is first performed in the Theater an der Wieden, Vienna, and enjoys growing success, being performed almost daily during October.

• **20 November** Mozart is taken ill. There is a slight improvement in his condition on 3 December, and the next day he is able to sing some of the unfinished Requiem, later completed by his pupil Süssmayr.

• **5 December** Mozart dies before finishing his Requiem ▲ (opposite).

1792 Cimarosa's masterpiece of comic opera, *Il matrimonio segreto* (The Clandestine Marriage), is performed in Vienna (above left).

• **29 February** Rossini is born in Pesaro.

• **3 May** Haydn has a benefit concert in London, which is the highlight of the musical season.

• **June** Haydn begins his return journey to Vienna.

• **November** Beethoven leaves Bonn for Vienna, to study with Haydn.

• **18 December** Beethoven's father dies.

1793 July The house of Artaria publishes Beethoven's early set of twelve VARIATIONS for piano and violin on Mozart's 'Se vuol ballare' ('If You Wish to Dance') from *The Marriage of Figaro*, an important landmark in the young composer's career.

1794 19 January Haydn embarks on his second visit to London, where he is again received with great acclaim. Beethoven therefore begins taking lessons from Albrechtsberger (which he continues for about a year and a half) and shows settings of Italian texts to Salieri.

• **10 February** Salomon's new concert series opens in London.

• **31 May** Paganini makes his debut in Genoa, aged eleven.

1795 The Paris Conservatoire is founded, assuring standards of training for young French musicians for generations to come.

• Beethoven allegedly proposes marriage to the singer Magdalena Willmann, who refuses his offer.

• **29 March** Beethoven makes his first public appearance in Vienna playing the Piano Concerto in B-flat major, Op.19.

OTHER EVENTS

1796 Edward Jenner introduces a vaccination against smallpox
• Accession of Paul I of Russia
• Napoleon in Italy. Battle of Lodi

1797 The Treaty of Campo Formio confirms the French victory in Italy
• François Gérard: *Cupid and Psyche*
• Samuel Taylor Coleridge: *Kubla Khan*
• Schlegel begins to translate Shakespeare into German

1798 Napoleon in Egypt. The British destroy the French fleet at Aboukir
• Charles Bulfinch designs the Massachusetts State Capitol in Boston

1799 Napoleon becomes First Consul
• Schiller: *Wallenstein*

▲ *Mozart's Last Day Remembered*

Iwent into the kitchen; the fire had gone out. I had to light a candle and make a fire. I was thinking of Mozart constantly. The coffee was ready and the candle was still burning…I stared right at it and thought to myself, 'I wonder how Mozart is?', and while I was thinking this and staring at the candle, it went out, as if it had never been alight…I shivered, ran to our mother and told her everything. She said, 'Very well, take off your good clothes and go into town, but come back straight away and tell me how he is. Don't be long.' I went as fast as I could. Oh how frightened I was when my sister, who was almost in despair, but trying to keep control, came out and said, 'Thank God you've come, dear Sophie. He was so ill last night that I didn't think that he would still be alive this morning. Stay with me today, for if he has another bad turn he will not survive the night. Go and see him for a little while, and see how he is.' I tried to keep control of myself… and went to his bed. He called to me at once and said, 'Oh, dear Sophie, how good of you to come. You must stay tonight and see me die.' I tried hard to be strong and assure him of the contrary, but he replied to all my efforts, 'Already I have the taste of death on my tongue.' Also, 'If you don't stay, who will take care of my dearest Constanze?' 'Yes, dear Mozart, but first I must go and tell our mother that you would like me to stay with you, otherwise she will think that some misfortune has happened.' 'Yes, do that,' said Mozart, 'but come back soon.' Oh God, how terrible I felt! My poor sister came with me to the door and asked me for Heaven's sake to go to the priests of St Peter's and ask one of them to come, as if by chance. I did, but…I had a lot of difficulty in getting one of those inhuman priests to go. Then I hurried off to my mother who was waiting anxiously for me…Poor soul, how upset she was! I got her to go and spend the night with her eldest daughter…I ran back to my distraught sister as fast as I could. Süssmayer was there at Mozart's bedside; the famous Requiem was on the quilt and Mozart was explaining to him how he thought he ought to finish it after his death. He also told his wife to keep his death a secret until she had told Albrechtsberger, for the post [at St Stephen's], should be his. They searched for Dr Glosset, whom they found at the theatre, but who had to wait until the play was over. He came and prescribed cold poultices for Mozart's burning head, but they were such a shock to his system that he fell unconscious and remained in that state until he died. The last thing he did was to try and mouth the drum passages in the Requiem. *I can still hear that.*

Sophie, sister of Mozart's wife Constanze, writing in 1825. Mozart died at fifty-five minutes past midnight on 5 December 1791.

Joseph Lange's unfinished portrait of Mozart (below). Lange, a court actor, described himself as Mozart's brother-in-law, having married Aloisia Weber, the sister of Mozart's wife Constanze. For those who knew Mozart this was regarded as one of his best likenesses.

One of Haydn's tasks was to provide a Mass each year for the name day of Princess Marie Hermenegild Esterházy, and he composed six such works. This votive painting of the Bergkirche at Eisenstadt shows the church in which five of Haydn's late Masses were performed for the first time.

• **4 May** Haydn has a benefit concert in London at the King's Theatre. The programme includes the *Military* Symphony and the vocal piece the *Scena di Berenice*. The Royal Family invite him to remain in London, and he is offered a summer apartment at Windsor Castle.

• **19 May** Beethoven signs a contract with Artaria for the publication of his Trios for Piano, Violin and Cello, Op.1, against the advice of Haydn, who found the third of these almost too modern for its time.

• **15 August** Haydn leaves England for the last time. He arrives in Vienna five days later.

1796 The Esterházy musical establishment is revived. Between this year and 1802 Haydn will compose a mass each year for Princess Marie Hermenegild Esterházy's name day (above).

• Haydn composes his *Missa in tempore belli* (Mass in Time of War), notable for its use of trumpets and drums in the *Agnus Dei*.

• **8 January** Haydn conducts and Beethoven plays a piano concerto at a benefit concert for the singer Maria Bolla, held in the Kleiner Redoutensaal in Vienna (right).

• **February** Beethoven visits Prague, Dresden, Leipzig and Berlin.

1797 Cherubini composes his operatic masterpiece *Médée* (Medea), which receives its first performance in Paris.

• **31 January** Schubert is born in Vienna.

• **12 February** Haydn's *Emperor's Hymn*, 'Gott, erhalte Franz den Kaiser', modelled closely on the British 'God Save the King', is performed for the first time at the Burgtheater in Vienna, on the

A poster for the benefit concert at the Kleiner Redoutensaal in Vienna on 8 January 1796.

AVVISO. *1796*

Oggi Venerdì 8. del corrente Gennajo la Sigra. Maria Bolla, virtuosa di Musica, darà una Accademia nella piccola Sala del Ridotto. La Musica sarà di nuova composizione del Sigre. Haydn, il quale ne farà alla direzione.

Vi canteranno la Sigra. Bolla, la Sigra. Tomeoni, e il Sigre. Mombelli.

Il Sigre. Bethofen suonerà un Concerto sul Pianoforte.

Il prezzo dei biglietti d'ingresso sarà di uno zecchino. Questi potranno averfi o alla Cassa del Teatro Nazionale, o in casa della Sigra. Bolla, nella Parisergasse Nro. 444. al secondo piano.

Il principio sarà alle ore sei e mezza.

emperor's birthday. Haydn uses the song as a basis for his *Emperor* String Quartet, Op.76, No.3, which receives its first performance in September of this year.

> '*I was never so pious as when I wrote* The Creation. *Every morning I knelt and prayed to God to give me strength for my work.*'
> Haydn

- **Summer** The lack of documentation concerning Beethoven during this period suggests he may have been ill, possibly with a stomach ailment.

- **29 November** Donizetti is born in Bergamo.

1798 Haydn composes his ORATORIO *The Creation*, inspired by those he had heard in England, and his *Nelson Mass*. The Mass is remarkable for the starkness of its original orchestration of only trumpets, timpani and strings.

1799 Beethoven's First Symphony is probably completed this year. His piano SONATA known as the *Pathétique*, one of the composer's best loved, is published.

- Haydn's String Quartets Op.76, Nos.4 to 6, dedicated to Count Erdödy, are published by Artaria in Vienna.

- **19 March** Haydn's *The Creation* receives its first public performance at the Burgtheater in Vienna ★ (p.120).

◆ *Sonata and Sonata Form*

Sonata in its most basic application was simply descriptive of anything sounded, possibly as opposed to cantata, anything sung, and was sometimes applied to instrumental pieces of the late Renaissance. One of the longest surviving musical forms was the trio sonata, which many eighteenth-century composers published as their Opus One. Despite its name of trio, it was for four performers, two upper parts such as violins, with a foundation provided by a keyboard instrument such as harpsichord (or organ if intended for church use), and viola da gamba ◆ (p.39) or cello. Sonatas might also be for solo instrument such as violin, flute or oboe accompanied by harpsichord or piano. Another form of sonata was for solo keyboard, as in the harpsichord sonatas of Domenico Scarlatti, or the piano sonatas of Haydn and Mozart.

The term sonata is also used in a very different context, however, to describe how a composer develops musical material in, say, a symphony, and for this reason certain musicologists have tried, somewhat unsuccessfully, it must be admitted, to replace the term with 'first movement form', since

this is a more accurate description of its function. In essence, a theme is announced, and is then developed and expanded, before being restated in its original form and key, in the sequence: Exposition, Development, Recapitulation. There may also be an Introduction and a Coda (or tail piece). This method of composing was adopted towards the end of the eighteenth century, and became standard for composers of Classical music for many forms, including sonatas, concertos and symphonies.

Mozart dedicated his Sonatas for Violin and Piano Op.2, to Josepha von Auernhammer, a former piano pupil whose love for her teacher was unrequited.

1800-99

The Romantic Century

As the nineteenth century begins, Vienna is still the musical focus, although Paris will soon dispute supremacy, especially in opera. This is the Age of Romanticism when, for the first time in modern cultural history, one movement sweeps through all the arts, and the bonds between music and literature in particular become inextricably entwined. It is an age of giants among composers and virtuosi. Previously music had been written for the courts of Europe, but now it is being democratized. It it is no coincidence that musicians play a decisive role in the mid-century revolutions that shake the continent. As the century progresses, music also becomes the focal point for emerging national identities, especially in the north and east of Europe, and a new flavour enhances the rich repertoire of Classical music.

Wagner in reverie, detail of a painting by Franz von Lenbach.

1800-10
Beethoven Shocks the Public

The turn of the century sees a change in the career of Beethoven; the elegant virtuoso pianist of the Viennese salons becomes the serious composer. As his deafness curtails his social and performing life, he pours his musical soul into ever more important compositions, notably a symphony of enormous dimensions that profoundly influences the evolution of the form but confounds the greater part of his followers.

1800 Haydn composes his ORATORIO *The Seasons* (right), a work similar in scope to *The Creation* (p.127), completed two years earlier, and also inspired by Handel and the British choral tradition that he had encountered in England.

• **2 April** Beethoven's First Symphony is first performed in the Burgtheater, Vienna. It is well received despite being given an inferior rendition.

• **7 May** Death of Piccinni, aged seventy-two, in Passy, Paris.

• **24 November** The first performance takes place in Freiburg of Weber's second opera *Das Waldmädchen* (The Forest Maiden). Almost all the music of this work is now lost.

1801 11 January Cimarosa dies, aged fifty-one, in Venice.

• **24 April** Haydn's oratorio *The Seasons* is performed privately in the Schwarzenberg Palace in Vienna, repeated three days later, and then again on 1 May.

• **29 May** Haydn's *The Seasons* has its first public performance in the Redoutensaal, Vienna (below), with Beethoven present. Although the concert is badly attended, the work is is soon heard throughout Europe.

• **July–September** Haydn composes his *Schöpfungsmesse* (Creation Mass).

• **November** Weber returns to Salzburg and under the eye of Michael Haydn works on a Mass he has already begun, and composes his third opera, *Peter Schmoll*.

The title page of the first full score of Haydn's last oratorio, The Seasons, *as published by the firm of Breitkopf und Härtel in Leipzig in 1802.*

Haydn's The Seasons, *conceived as a sequel to The Creation (p.127), had three private performances in Vienna in the Schwarzenberg Palace, which may explain why its first public performance in the large Redoutensaal a month later was not well attended.*

• **3 November** Birth of Bellini in Sicily.

• **December** Beethoven publishes his Second Piano Concerto and First Symphony.

1802 Haydn writes his *Harmoniemesse* (Mass with Wind-band), in which he gives prominence to the orchestra's wind section.

• Weber completes the *Grosse Jugendmesse* (The Great Youth Mass), for soloists, choir, orchestra and organ.

OTHER EVENTS
1800 Discovery of ultraviolet rays
• Volta invents voltaic pile

1801 Act of Union of Great Britain and Ireland accords seats in British Parliament to Protestant Irishmen

1802 Napoleon is First Consul for life
• Goya: *The Two Majas*
• De Staël: *Delphine*

1803 Louisiana Purchase by US from France
• Britain declares war on France

1804 Napoleon crowned emperor in France
• Lewis and Clark start a two-year expedition across unexplored North America
• Schiller: *Wilhelm Tell*

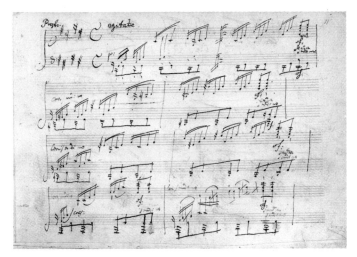

Beethoven's autograph of the opening of the last movement of his Moonlight *Sonata marked 'Presto – agitato' (Fast – agitated), in marked contrast to the slow, dreamy first movement. Composed in 1801, this sonata is probably the best known and most popular of his works for piano.*

• **3 March** Beethoven's *Moonlight* Piano Sonata, Op.27 (left), dedicated to his pupil Countess Guicciardi, is published.

• **Autumn** Beethoven completes his Second Symphony at Heiligenstadt, where, on 6 October, he writes the intensely personal document known as the 'Heiligenstadt Testament' in which he struggles to come to terms with his increasing deafness.

1803 Beethoven completes the Sonata for Violin and Piano Op.47, which he dedicates to the virtuoso violinist Kreutzer, though it is questionable whether the latter ever played it.

• **March** Weber's *Peter Schmoll* is probably first performed in Augsburg.

• **5 April** Beethoven's Second Symphony and Third Piano Concerto are first performed at a benefit concert at the Theater an der Wien.

• **June–October** Beethoven composes his Third Symphony, known as the *Eroica* ▲ (p.133), which he dedicates to Napoleon.

• **11 December** Berlioz is born in La-Côte-Saint-André, Isère.

• **26 December** Haydn makes his last active public appearance, when he conducts *The Seven Last Words* (p.116).

1804 Rossini, aged twelve, composes his set of six *sonate a quattro* (four-part string sonatas).

• **4 March** Johann Strauss the Elder is born in Vienna.

• **April–September** Beethoven composes his Triple Concerto for Violin, Cello and Piano.

• **20 May** Napoleon is proclaimed emperor of France. When the news reaches Vienna, Beethoven is bitterly disillusioned with his hero, and tears up the dedication page of the *Eroica*.

• **1 June** Glinka is born in Novospasskoye (now Glinka), near Smolensk.

• **11 June** Weber, aged seventeen, arrives in Breslau to take up his post as director of music, but alienates the staff of the city's theatre through his reforms. He mistakenly drinks from a wine bottle filled with engraving acid by his father. On his recovery, he resigns his post, since all his reforms have been negated.

• **November** Beethoven begins composing his *Waldstein* Piano Sonata, which he will dedicate to Count Waldstein, one of his earliest patrons.

★ *The dungeon scene from the 1814 production of Beethoven's opera* Fidelio, *where Leonore, sung by Anna Milder, prevents Pizarro, sung by Johann Michael Vogel, from murdering her husband. For this revival the composer provided a new overture, which was the fourth connected with the opera, and the one usually used today.*

1805 Beethoven completes the *Appassionata* Piano Sonata and his only opera, *Fidelio* ★ (p.131), in its first form, known as *Leonore*.

> *'If I write a symphony an hour long it will be found short enough!'*
>
> Beethoven on the reaction to *Eroica*

• **7 April** Beethoven conducts the first public performance of his *Eroica* Symphony at the violin virtuoso Franz Clement's benefit concert in Vienna. Its great length and startling novelty initially alienate the Viennese public ▲ (opposite).

• **28 May** Death of Boccherini in Madrid, aged sixty-two.

• **31 July** In the reorganization of the musical establishment at Lucca, Paganini becomes court violinist to Napoleon's sister, Elisa, Princess of Lucca and Piombino. His official appointment is effective from 1 January 1806.

1806 Beethoven finishes the three *Razumovsky* String Quartets, Op.59 (commissioned by Count Razumovsky), the Fourth Piano Concerto and the Fourth Symphony.

★ *Isabella Colbran, the Spanish soprano who became Rossini's first wife, painted in 1817 as Sappho in Mayr's early opera* Saffo. *Rossini and Isabella renewed their acquaintance in 1815, when the composer first arrived in Naples under contract to the impresario Barbaia, whose mistress Colbran had been.*

• **29 March** Beethoven's opera *Leonore* is given in its second version, with the overture known as *Leonore* No.3, and is well received.

• **April** Rossini becomes a student at the Liceo Musicale in Bologna.

• **Autumn** Weber is appointed director of music to Duke Eugen of Württemberg-Öls, though remains there less than a year, despite being very happy in his post.

• **23 December** Franz Clement, leader of the orchestra at the Theater an der Wien, gives the first performance of Beethoven's Violin Concerto in the course of a benefit concert held in the theatre for the violinist.

1807 11 April The soprano Isabella Colbran (left), future first wife of Rossini, makes a very favourable impression at her début in Bologna.

• **17 July** Weber becomes secretary to Ludwig, brother to Duke Friedrich of Württemberg, in Stuttgart. This year he consolidates his reputation as a VIRTUOSO pianist.

• **September** Beethoven conducts the first performance of his Mass in C at Eisenstadt, to celebrate the name day of Princess Maria Hermenegild Esterházy. Unfortunately, it fails to please Prince Nicolaus Esterházy, who is more used to Haydn's Masses on such occasions (p.126).

• **Autumn** Beethoven begins to write his Fifth Symphony, which contains the famous 'knocking motif' thought to represent Fate at the door. It has been suggested that this work is an expression of the composer's battle with his deafness – the hero's denial of his Fate. Significantly, the symphony begins in C Minor and moves to the more hopeful C Major, suggesting the hero triumphs, which is certainly true of the composer of this great work.

▲ *An Unfavourable Reception for Beethoven's 'Eroica'*

Some people, Beethoven's special friends, maintain that it is precisely this symphony that is his masterpiece, that this is the genuine style for first-rate music, and that if it fails to please now, it is because the public is not sufficiently cultured, from an artistic point of view, to appreciate all these ethereal beauties; when a few thousand years have elapsed it will not fail to make its effect. Another group denies that the composition has any artistic value and claims to see in it an unfettered quest for strangeness and effect. Through curious modulations and abrupt transitions, by joining together the most disparate elements, as for example when a pastoral in the grandest style is torn apart by the basses, by three horns, etc., a certain unwanted originality may result without much difficulty; but genius reveals itself not in the strange and the bizarre, but in the beautiful and the lofty. The third group, a very small one, stands halfway between the others – it concedes that the symphony has many beauties, but also grants that the continuity is often completely disrupted, and that the enormous length of this longest, and posssibly most difficult of all symphonies, exhausts even the connoisseur and for the mere music lover it is unbearable; it would like Beethoven to employ his undoubtedly enormous talents in offering us works like his early compositions which have put him eternally in the company of the greatest instrumental composers. It is afraid, however, that if Beethoven pursues his present

bent both he and the public will suffer. His music could soon reach the point where one would take no pleasure in it, unless well versed in the rules and problems of the art, but on the contrary would leave the concert hall with an unpleasant feeling of exhaustion from having been overwhelmed by a mass of disconnected and cumbersome ideas and a persistent noise from all the instruments. The public and Herr van Beethoven, who conducted, were not happy with each other on this evening; the public thought the symphony too weighty, too long, and himself too ill-mannered, because he did not incline his head to acknowledge the applause which came from a section of the audience. On the contrary, Beethoven felt that the applause was not sufficient.

From the Berlin *Der Freimüthige*, 26 April 1805

Beethoven painted in 1804 or 1805. This is the first of four portraits of the composer by Mähler, who was also a composer and singer, and therefore particularly well qualified to convey the sitter's inner personality. Certainly Beethoven kept this portrait until his death.

1808 Beethoven is offered an appointment at the court of King Jérôme Bonaparte, Napoleon's brother, in Kassel, but delays his acceptance of it. Negotiations are started to keep the composer in Vienna.

• Schubert, aged eleven, becomes a choirboy in the imperial court chapel, Vienna.

• **Summer** Beethoven is once again in Heiligenstadt (p.131), where he completes his Sixth Symphony, known as the *Pastoral* because the five movements have programmatic titles on a pastoral theme.

• **27 March** Haydn makes his last public appearance at a concert in Vienna, when Salieri conducts a performance of *The Creation* (p.127) in the hall of the old university.

• **22 December** Beethoven's Fifth and Sixth Symphonies, Choral Fantasy, Fourth Piano Concerto and several movements of the Mass in C are heard in public for the first time in Vienna in a marathon concert in the Theater an der Wien.

1809 Rossini has composed his first opera *Demetrio e Polibio* (Demetrius and Polybius), although it will not be performed for another three years.

• When it is known that Beethoven has agreed to go to Kassel, Archduke Rudolph (now a pupil of Beethoven), Prince Kinsky and Prince Lobkowitz, guarantee the composer a small income on the understanding that he will remain in Vienna.

• Beethoven composes his Fifth Piano Concerto, known as the *Emperor*, and his Piano Sonata Op.78, dedicated to Countess Therese von Brunsvik with whom he is deeply in love.

• **3 February** Mendelssohn is born in Hamburg.

• **4 May** In the face of the French invasion, Beethoven's pupil and patron Archduke Rudolph leaves Vienna with the Imperial family. The composer responds by writing his Piano Sonata *Das Lebewohl, Die Abwesenheit und Die Ankunft* (Farewell, Absence and Return).

• **31 May** Haydn dies in Vienna, aged seventy-seven.

• **15 June** Mozart's Requiem is given at a memorial service for Haydn in the Schottenkirche, Vienna.

1810 22 February Birth of Chopin at Zelazowa Wola, near Warsaw.

• **26 February** Weber is embroiled in a financial scandal in Stuttgart, arrested, and banished from the town.

• **May** Beethoven meets Bettina Brentano ▲ (opposite), who is to remain one of his most loyal and stimulating friends.

• **8 June** Birth of Schumann in Zwickau.

• **15 June** First performance of Beethoven's music to Goethe's *Egmont* at the Court Theatre, Vienna.

• **August** Beethoven goes to Baden for a cure. His hearing is now badly affected and his doctor has prescribed peace and a healthy diet.

• **October** Beethoven composes the String Quartet in F minor, Op.95.

• **3 November** *La cambiale di matrimonio* (The Matrimonial Exchange), Rossini's second opera, a one-act farce, is the first to be staged in public at the Teatro San Moisè in Venice.

'The entire art-loving world of Vienna was present, most of them in mourning. Everything was very dignified and worthy of Haydn.'
Account of Haydn's memorial service from the *Diaries of Joseph Carl Rosenbaum 1770–1829*

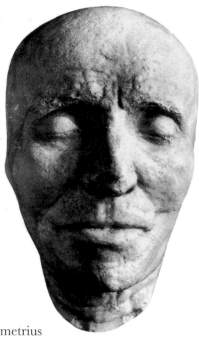

Haydn's death mask, preserved in the Haydn Museum, his former home. On his death the composer was buried outside Vienna, but Prince Nicolaus II Esterházy subsequently had his remains transferred to a tomb in the Bergkirche in Eisenstadt.

OTHER EVENTS
1809 The British under Arthur Wellesley (soon to be the Duke of Wellington) defeat the French at Talavera
• Napoleon annexes the Papal States and takes the pope prisoner
• Napoleon divorces Josephine

1810 Napoleon marries Archduchess Marie Louise of Austria. He annexes Holland, Hanover, Bremen and Lübeck
• Walter Scott: *The Lady of the Lake*

▲ Beethoven Opens his Heart

Beethoven's biographer Thayer relates that one day in May 1810 Beethoven was sitting at the piano in front of a song that he had just composed. Suddenly a pair of hands touched his shoulders. He looked up with a rather gloomy expression, but then his face lit up when he saw a beautiful young woman who put her mouth close to his ear and told him that her name was Brentano. The name alone was sufficient. He smiled and gave her his hand, and told her that he had just composed a beautiful song for her, which he offered to sing. The lack of beauty in his voice was more than compensated by the song itself.

On 28 May 1810 Bettina wrote to Goethe, telling him of her meeting with Beethoven. Her account then, and in almost everything else connected with the composer, was highly coloured, and is therefore to be treated with a certain amount of reserve. Even so, Beethoven obviously made an enormous impression on her, for which she seems to have been totally unprepared, and he, for his part, opened his heart to her in a way that he did to few others.

There are three letters from Beethoven to Bettina, dating from 1810–12, though her rather euphoric approach to editing means that only the autograph of 10 February 1811 may strictly be regarded as genuine:

Dear, dear Bettine,

I have already had two letters from you, and from your letters to Toni [Antonie Brentano, wife of Bettina's half-brother] see that you still think about me, and far too kindly. I carried your first letter around with me all summer, and it has frequently delighted me. Even though I do not write to you often, and you do not see me, I still write a thousand times to you a thousand letters in my mind....You are going to be married, dear Bettine, or are already so, and I have been unable to see you beforehand. May all the joy that matrimony brings to the married come to you and your husband [the poet Achim von Arnim]. What am I to tell you about myself? 'Pity my fate,' I cry with Johanna [Joan of Arc in Schiller's Die Jungfrau von Orleans*]. If I can withstand that and all other adversity for a few years, I will give thanks to Him the all-embracing and Highest. If you write to Goethe about me, choose all the words that express my great reverence and admiration for him. I am just about to write to him myself about* Egmont, *for which I have composed some music and, in fact, solely out of affection for his poems which make me happy. Who can give adequate thanks for a great poet who is the most precious jewel of a nation? And now no more, dear B. I did not get home until four o'clock this morning from a bacchanalian feast at which I laughed so much that I shall have to weep a corresponding amount today; uncontrolled joy often makes me turn back in on myself very strongly.... Now goodbye, dear, dear B, I kiss you sadly on your forehead and so set on you as with a seal all my thoughts of you. Write soon, soon, often to your friend Beethoven.*

★ *A portrait of Elisabeth (Bettina) Brentano, who on a visit to her half-brother in Vienna in 1810, made the acquaintance of Beethoven. It was probably Bettina who arranged the meeting between the composer and Goethe in Teplitz the following year.*

1811-1813
Enter Rossini

With no less than ten of his operas being mounted for the first time in the space of three years, it is clear that in the person of a young Italian called Rossini, a brilliant talent has arrived on the scene, destined to breathe new life into what is by now a moribund tradition, and to lay the foundations for another golden age of opera.

A set design for a production of Rossini's opera Tancredi *in Siracusa, which, in 1813, was the composer's first for the Teatro La Fenice in Venice. Based on a tragedy by Voltaire and Tasso's* Gerusalemme liberata, *the story is set at the time of the Crusades.*

1811 Schubert composes his first songs ◆ (p.139).

• **March** Beethoven writes the *Archduke* Piano Trio for Archduke Rudolph (p.134).

• **August** Having been ill for some time, Beethoven takes the advice of his doctor and visits the spa at Teplitz for the first time, for a cure.

• **22 October** Birth of Liszt at Raiding.

• **26 October** Rossini's two-act comic opera *L'equivoco stravagante* (The Dubious Eccentric) is first performed at the Teatro del Corso, Bologna.

1812 8 January Rossini's one-act comic opera *L'inganno felice* (The Happy Deception) is first given in the Teatro San Moisè, Venice.

• **11 February** Czerny gives the first Viennese performance of Beethoven's *Emperor* Piano Concerto (p.134).

• **March** Rossini's sacred opera *Ciro in Babilonia* (Cyrus in Babylon) is a failure when given at the Teatro Comunale, Ferrara.

• **May** Beethoven completes his Seventh Symphony, begun late the previous year, he then starts his Eighth Symphony, which he will finish in October.

• **9 May** Rossini's one-act farce *La scala di seta* (The Silken Ladder) is given for the first time at the Teatro San Moisè.

• **5 July** Beethoven returns to Teplitz, where he meets Goethe. The next day he writes the first of three letters to an unknown woman, 'The Immortal Beloved'. It is possibly to Antonie Brentano, sister-in-law to Bettine ▲ (p.135).

• **27 July** Beethoven goes to Carlsbad to meet the Brentanos. Twelve days later they all go to Franzensbrunn.

• **26 September** *La pietra del paragone* (The Touchstone), one of Rossini's happiest early operas, is first heard at La Scala, Milan.

• **October** Beethoven goes to Linz to try and end his brother Johann's relationship with Therese Obermayer, his 'housekeeper'. He has Therese thrown out of the house, but the couple defy him and marry in November.

OTHER EVENTS
1811 Goethe: *Dichtung und Wahrheit*
• Jane Austen: *Sense and Sensibility*

1812 Napoleon retreats from Moscow
• Lord Byron: *Childe Harold*
• Brothers Grimm: *Kinder-und Hausmärchen*

1813 The Cortes declare Mexico independent from Spain
• Jane Austen: *Pride and Prejudice*

'Tancredi in Siracusa *is the most beautiful musical composition of our time;* Aureliano in Palmyra, *as far as effect is concerned, is simply nothing like an opera by Rossini.'*
The music critic of *Il giornale Italiano*, 1813.

An annotated sketch showing Elvira's costume for the first Paris production of Rossini's opera L'Italiana in Algeri *in 1817. This was the composer's first opera to be heard in the city.*

1813 Founding of the Royal Philharmonic Society in London.

• Rossini's two-act opera *L'Italiana in Algeri* (The Italian Woman in Algiers, left), is first heard at the Teatro San Benedetto, Venice.

• **12 January** Weber arrives in Prague, where he becomes director of the opera.

• **8 February** Rossini's *Tancredi in Siracusa* (Tancredi in Syracuse, opposite) is first performed at the Teatro La Fenice, Venice.

• **22 May** Birth of Wagner in Leipzig.

• **Summer** Beethoven writes *Battle of Vittoria* for the inventor Mälzel's PANHARMONICON.

• **24 September** Death of Grétry ■ (p.115), aged seventy-two, in Paris.

• **9 October** Birth of Verdi at Le Roncole, near Busseto.

• **8 December** Beethoven's Seventh Symphony and *Battle of Vittoria* are performed in Vienna. The composer and Mälzel subsequently quarrel over the rights to the second work.

• **26 December** Rossini's serious opera *Aurelio in Palmira* (Aurelian in Palmyra) is first heard at La Scala, Milan.

◆ *The Expansion of Music in a New Century*

Beethoven is not the only composer who writes long works, whether piano sonatas or symphonies. Schubert, too, takes advantage of the new dimension in music, and indeed both composers seem to create the space in which they elaborate their musical designs. There is also an increase in the size of the instrumental forces needed, and a reciprocal process is at work, whereby instrument makers vie to meet the requirements of composers and performers, who in turn seize the opportunities offered for new effects of TIMBRE and improved technique and readily exploit them.

As Rossini evolves his operatic style and moves away from his childhood world of Italian opera, he is criticized for his use of effects – percussion especially – considered unsuitable for the opera house. Meanwhile, some members of Beethoven's audience cannot tolerate the great volume of noise ▲ (p.133).

Simultaneously, the impresario increases in importance, arranging concerts and transporting composers and performers from country to country on a much more extensive scale. We see the formation and foundation of permanent orchestras and the rise of the conductor. In short, we see the establishment of the international music community of performers and their public.

The soprano Giuditta Pasta, portrayed in 1830 in the midst of other artists who include the tenor Rubini, the bass Galli and the buffo *Frezzolini, as well as the librettist Romani. At either end of the bottom row are Donizetti and Bellini, for whom Romani supplied libretti.*

1814-15
Schubert's First Songs

Although only seventeen, Schubert now shows his ability to set words to music in a way that few have done, thus establishing a process that will continue throughout his life, and make German song one of the most highly esteemed forms of Western music.

1814 Schubert writes his first song to a text by Goethe, 'Gretchen am Spinnrad' (Gretchen at the Spinning Wheel, ◆ opposite).

- **15 January** Weber mounts Mozart's *Don Giovanni* at the Prague opera house, having totally reorganized the establishment (p.137).

- **27 February** Beethoven's Eighth Symphony is first given.

- **11 April** The pianist Ignaz Moscheles attends the first public performance of Beethoven's *Archduke* Piano Trio (p.136), with the composer at the piano. It is clearly becoming increasingly difficult for Beethoven to play in public any longer.

- **23 May** Beethoven's opera *Fidelio* (below), in revised form, is revived at the Kärntnertor Theatre in Vienna for the Congress, to great acclaim. The OVERTURE now known as *Fidelio* is added after the first peformance.

- **14 August** Rossini's comic opera *Il turco in Italia* (The Turk in Italy) is first performed at La Scala, Milan.

- **29 November** Beethoven conducts a concert in the Redoutensaal, Vienna, which includes his Seventh Symphony (p.136), his cantata *Der glorreiche Augenblick* (The Glorious Moment) and *Battle of Vittoria* (p.137). The last piece has become all the rage in Vienna.

> *'As soon as I have finished one song I begin on the next.'*
> Schubert

OTHER EVENTS

1814 Napoleon abdicates and is exiled to Elba
- Louis XVIII returns to France as king
- Congress of Vienna commences
- Stephenson's first steam locomotive
- Scott: *Waverley*

1815 Napoleon leaves Elba and returns to power
- Louis XVIII flees Paris
- Napoleon is defeated at the battle of Waterloo and imprisoned on St Helena
- Congress of Vienna ends
- Goya: *Witches' Sabbath*

The Congress of Vienna from 1814–15 was convened to restore the status quo in Europe after the Napoleonic wars. From a musical point of view it set the seal on Beethoven's international standing, since his opera Fidelio *was revived for the occasion, and he received various sums of money as gifts from visiting dignitaries.*

1815 Schubert composes his song 'Der Erlkönig' (The Erlking) to a poem by Goethe ◆ (below), and his Third Symphony.

• **March** Weber mounts a benefit production in Prague, Mozart's *Così fan tutte* (p.121), which is a financial success.

• **6 June** Weber, frustrated in his love for the singer Caroline Brandt, who refuses to marry him until he is financially secure, leaves Prague for Munich. He remains there until early September, working on his cantata *Kampf und Sieg* (Battle and Victory).

• **4 October** Rossini's arrival in Naples, under contract to the impresario Domenico Barbaia ◆ (p.137), is marked by the first performance of his opera *Elisabetta, regina d'Inghilterra* (Elizabeth, Queen of England), specially tailored to the taste of his new audience at the Teatro San Carlo.

• **14 November** Beethoven's brother, Casper Carl is dying. He makes a will, leaving his son Karl under the guardianship of his wife Johanna and the composer. Beethoven tries to have Johanna's name removed.

• **15 November** Caspar Carl dies of tuberculosis, leaving his wife and Beethoven as co-guardians of his son. The task will cause Beethoven mental and emotional torment, much of it of his own making.

• **15 December** Rossini signs a contract for *The Barber of Seville* ▲ (p.141), to be given in Rome early in the new year.

• **22 December** Weber's cantata *Kampf und Sieg* is well received by an appreciative though small audience in Prague.

• **26 December** *Torvaldo e Dorliska*, a semi-serious opera by Rossini, is first performed at the Teatro Valle, Rome.

Schubert at the piano with his friend Johann Michael Vogl standing behind him, singing, and Josephine Fröhlich sitting beside him at the keyboard.

◆ *The German 'Lied'*

Schubert did not invent the German solo song accompanied by piano, for there were certainly antecedents, for example, in the works of Haydn and Mozart, and in 1816 Beethoven was to compose one of the earliest SONG CYCLES in the genre with his An die ferne Geliebte (To the Absent Beloved). Nevertheless, from 1821 the songs that Schubert had started composing in the previous decade began to be performed and published, and he himself emerged as the composer who transformed German song into such a highly developed art form. Rather surprisingly, perhaps, his compositional technique for songs hardly developed at all, from his first song to his last, since his talent as a song writer was seemingly innate. He appeared to have a limitless supply of melodies, and a wide range of styles available to him, so that from the start he was able to respond sympathetically to texts, and find the means of expression best suited to enhance their meaning. His subtle HARMONIC changes to underline words and his changes of TONALITY for variations of mood, treated the text in a way that many opera composers aspired to but were unable to achieve.

Such subtleties had far reaching implications. New kinds of performers were required, both singers and accompanists, for Schubert's songs were no longer suitable for even gifted amateurs. They demanded a high degree of sophistication and technical ability, as well as a partnership of equals in order to bring the

music and words fully to life in the way Schubert had intended. Having developed and encouraged this new manner of performance, he initiated the blossoming of German song after his death, as many of his countrymen including Schumann, Wolf, Richard Strauss and Mahler readily followed where he had led the way.

1816-20
Rossini, King of Comic Opera

This year sees the first performance of Rossini's exuberant comic opera The Barber of Seville, *which confirms the youthful Italian as one of the most prolific and successful composers ever seen in Western music. Although many observers, including Beethoven, think that he is fit for nothing else but comic opera, Rossini will in fact lay the foundations for the new form of grand opera in Paris.*

Rossini as a young man (right), probably painted around 1816, the year of The Barber of Seville, *which was destined to become one of his greatest successes, and one of the most popular and enduring works in the entire operatic repertoire.*

Caricature of Rossini in Paris from 1819, the year The Barber of Seville *was first produced in that city. The composer is supporting, from left to right, the singers Manuel Garcia, Joséphine Fodor and Felice Pellegrini.*

1816 Schubert completes his Fourth and Fifth Symphonies and his Mass in C.

• **19 January** Beethoven is legally appointed the sole guardian of his nephew Karl (p.139), whom he sends to a boarding school.

• **13–14 February** The Teatro San Carlo, Naples, is burnt down.

• **20 February** After a shaky start, Rossini's *Barber of Seville* ▲ (opposite) triumphs at the Teatro Argentina, Rome.

• **Easter** Weber submits his resignation in Prague, which becomes effective this autumn.

• **April** Beethoven writes his SONG CYCLE *An die ferne Geliebte* ◆ (p.139).

• **4 December** Rossini's *Otello* (Othello) is first given at the Teatro del Fondo, Naples.

1817 Clementi publishes his tutor *Gradus ad Parnassum* (Steps to Parnassus).

• Schubert writes his songs 'An die Musik' (To Music), 'Die Forelle' (The Trout) and 'Der Tod und das Mädchen' (Death and the Maiden).

• **25 January** Rossini's comic opera in two acts *La Cenerentola* (Cinderella), based on the fairy tale, is performed for the first time at the Teatro Valle, Rome.

• **Autumn** Beethoven begins to compose his *Hammerklavier* Piano Sonata, Op.106.

• **11 November** *Armida*, Rossini's powerful 'magic' opera, is performed at the rebuilt Teatro San Carlo, Naples.

1818 Schubert composes his Sixth Symphony and the String Quartet in E Major.

• **February** Beethoven is so deaf he has to use conversation books, and has difficulty hearing the piano ▲ (p.145).

• **5 March** Rossini's three-act opera *Mosè in Egitto* (Moses in Egypt), termed an *azione tragico-sacra* (something approaching staged ORATORIO), is first given at Teatro San Carlo, Naples.

• **14 November** Donizetti makes his operatic début with *Enrico di Borgogna* (Henry of Burgundy) in Venice.

OTHER EVENTS
1816 Independence of Argentina
• Coleridge: *Kubla Khan*

1817 Independence of Venezuela under Bolívar
• Géricault: *The Raft of the 'Medusa'*

1818 Congress of Aix-la-Chapelle
• Independence of Chile
• First steamship crosses the Atlantic
• Mary Wollstonecraft Shelley: *Frankenstein*

1819 Florida purchased by US from Spain
• Victor Hugo: *Odes*

1820 Revolutions in Spain and Portugal
• Lamartine: *Méditations poétiques*

1819 Schubert writes the *Trout* Piano Quintet, after his song of the same name (opposite), which is the basis of the fourth MOVEMENT, a THEME and VARIATIONS. He also composes his Piano Sonata in A Major, Op.120.

• **11 January** Beethoven's nephew runs away and he loses his guardianship.

• **March** The composer and publisher Diabelli invites fifty Viennese composers, including Beethoven (p.144), Czerny, Liszt and Schubert, to write variations on a waltz of his.

• **11 April** Beethoven begins his *Missa solemnis* (right) for the consecration of his pupil Archduke Rudolph as Archbishop of Olmütz.

• **20 June** Birth of Offenbach in Cologne.

• **24 October** *La donna del lago*, Rossini's opera based on Sir Walter Scott's *The Lady of the Lake*, is first given at the Teatro San Carlo, Naples.

1820 Schubert composes his *Quartettsatz*, the first movement of a String Quartet in C Minor. Although the work is never finished, it heralds the composer's late string quartets.

• **8 April** Beethoven regains the guardianship of his nephew Karl through the Court of Appeal.

• **3 December** Rossini's serious opera *Maometto II* (Mahomet II) is first performed at Teatro San Carlo, Naples.

★ *Beethoven, as painted from life in 1819, holding the score of his* Missa solemnis, *which was originally intended for the enthronement of the Archbishop of Olmütz. It was not finished until late 1822, however, and the composer did not present the finished score to his patron until March 1823 (p.144).*

▲ *After the Second Night of 'The Barber of Seville'*

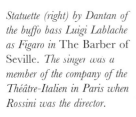

Statuette (right) by Dantan of the buffo bass Luigi Lablache as Figaro in The Barber of Seville. *The singer was a member of the company of the Théâtre-Italien in Paris when Rossini was the director.*

I was sleeping peacefully when I was suddenly awakened by a huge noise out in the street, together with a bright light from torches; as soon as I got up I saw that they were making for my hotel. Still half asleep, and bearing in mind the scene of the night before, I imagined that they were coming to set fire to the building, and I fled to a stable at the rear of the courtyard. However, after a few moments, I heard Garcia shouting for me at the top of his voice. Eventually he found me. 'Hurry up. Come on. Listen to those shouts of bravo, bravissimo, Figaro. An unprecedented success. The street is full of people. They want to see you.' 'Tell them,' I replied … 'that I f— them, their bravos and all the rest of it. I'm not coming out of here.' I don't know how Garcia put my refusal to that excited crowd – in fact he was hit in the eye by an orange, which gave him a black eye that didn't go away for several days. Meanwhile, the noise in the street continued to increase. Next the owner of the hotel arrived, panting. 'If you don't come, they'll set fire to the building. They're breaking the windows now.' 'That's your business,' I told him. 'All you have to do is keep away from the windows…I'm staying where I am.' Finally I heard some breaking panes. Then, weary with the fight, the crowd at last dispersed. I left my safe place and went back to bed. Unfortunately those brigands had put out two windows opposite my bed. It was January. I would be lying if I told you that the freezing air penetrating into my room gave me a charming night.

Rossini to Edmond Michotte, as told in the latter's *Une soirée chez Rossini à Beau-Séjour (Passy), 1858.*

1821-22
The Beginnings of Romanticism

A new spirit, previously only glimpsed in Italy, is now moving north of the Alps. Rossini's opera La donna del lago, *with its interest in Scott, has heralded a Romantic movement inspired by literature, but it is from an opera such as Weber's* Der Freischütz *that the movement will arise and embrace music and the visual arts.*

1821 March Berlioz (opposite) gains his bachelor's degree in Grenoble and, despite his inclination towards music, follows his father's wish that he should study medicine in Paris.

• **18 June** Weber's opera *Der Freischütz* (The Free Shooter) has its first triumphal performance in Berlin. The composer emerges as the champion of German opera, but he has developed tuberculosis.

• **August** Mendelssohn aged twelve, completes his Piano Sonata in G Minor, which will be pubished posthumously as his Opus 105.

• **November** Beethoven publishes his Piano Sonata Op.109.

• Mendelssohn's teacher Carl Friedrich Zelter takes him to meet Goethe in Weimar, and they establish a lasting and mutually influential friendship.

• **11 November** Weber is asked by Barbaia (p.139), now lessee of the Kärntnertor Theatre in Vienna, to compose an opera, *Euryanthe,* for the 1822–23 season.

• **25 December** Beethoven completes his Piano Sonata Op.110.

1822 Schubert (below) starts his *Unfinished* Symphony, and dedicates a set of VARIATIONS to Beethoven, which he delivers by hand. He has contracted syphilis and begins to show signs of his illness.

• **13 January** Beethoven completes his Piano Sonata Op.111.

• **16 February** *Zelmira*, Rossini's last opera for Naples, is first performed. He leaves the city and marries Isabella Colbran ★ (p.132) on 16 March.

Schubert and his friends, portrayed around 1821. In such gatherings as these, known as Schubertiade, much of the composer's vocal and piano music was heard for the first — and perhaps only — time, since public performances of his work were rare.

OTHER EVENTS
1821 Independence of Peru, Guatemala and Panama
• Faraday's electric motor and generator
• Constable: *The Hay Wain*
• Napoleon and Keats die

1822 Congress of Verona
• Turks invade Greece
• Independence of Brazil
• Pushkin: *Eugene Onegin*

• **13 April–8 July** A Rossini opera season in Vienna, put on by Barbaia, is a great success. In April Rossini visits Beethoven.

• **Summer** Beethoven visits Baden and writes the OVERTURE *The Consecration of the House* for the forthcoming opening of the Josephstadt Theatre in Vienna.

• **July–October** Mendelssohn travels with his family to Lake Maggiore in Italy. He composes the Piano Concerto in A Minor and the Violin Concerto in D Minor this year.

• **26 December** Rossini produces a revised version of *Mametto II* (p.141) for Venice.

◆ *Brass Instruments*

The brass was the last major group of instruments to be incorporated into the concert orchestra, largely because it could play in only a limited number of keys. Today the brass can play in virtually any key, being, in technical terminology, fully CHROMATIC, *whereas previously they only had certain notes available, known as the* HARMONIC *series. At the beginning of the nineteenth century, however, the only brass instruments able to play notes not in the harmonic series were the French horn, the trombone, those instruments with holes covered by the fingers or a key (such as the serpent), and the key trumpet, for which Haydn wrote his Trumpet Concerto in 1796. The key bugle was added to this group early in the century, but it was the invention of the valve, about 1815, that enabled all brass instruments to become chromatic.*

Not all developments went the same way, however, for as the century progressed and interest increased in earlier music – especially that of Bach, for example – certain techniques had to be revived. The practice of playing very high trumpet parts, known as CLARINO *technique, had virtually died out on the Continent, and its revival furthered the development of the trumpet.*

Although before the nineteenth centruy the brass were not considered orchestral instruments, they had filled other roles. The horn, for instance, had long been associated with hunting and the outdoors, and so easily complemented Weber's hunting choruses in Der Freischütz, *but it was now also seen as a romantic instrument, as used by Weber in* Oberon, *or Rossini at the beginning of his overture to* Semiramide. *Then there was the trombone, previously used in churches and in the opera*

house, which had to wait for Beethoven's Fifth Symphony for its début in the concert orchestra. For some the introduction of brass merely increased the sheer volume of sound, and at times that must have seemed the composer's sole intention, but when used with discrimination, it opened up an extremely wide range of orchestral colour and effect to the sympathetic orchestrator.

Berlioz's fascination with orchestration, and especially the brass section, often provoked satire, as in this Viennese caricature of 1846, in which members of the audience are overwhelmed by the sound.

1823-24
Beethoven's Late Works

As Beethoven retreats more and more into his inner world, forced upon him by his deafness and his increasing misanthropy, it seems as if he manages to distil into his music the very essence of his thoughts and feelings, which makes his late compositions some of the most intense in Western music.

1823 Beethoven completes the set of thirty-three Diabelli Variations for Piano, Op.120 (p.141), and is at work on his Ninth Symphony.

• Schubert composes his SONG CYCLE *Die schöne Müllerin* (The Beautiful Maid of the Mill) to poems by Wilhelm Müller.

• **3 February** *Semiramide* (Semiramis, ◆ p.143), Rossini's last opera composed for Italy, has its first performance at the Teatro La Fenice, Venice. He and his wife spend the summer in Bologna and then travel to Paris.

• **19 March** Beethoven presents a score of his *Missa solemnis* (left and ★ p.141) to Archduke Rudolph, Cardinal-Archbishop of Olmütz.

• **13 April** Liszt (below), aged twelve, plays at a concert in Vienna attended by Beethoven.

• **29 April** Weber conducts a performance of Beethovens's *Fidelio* in Dresden, though he is working hard to complete his own opera *Euryanthe* (p.142), which he does on 22 August, apart from the overture.

• **Late spring** Schubert who is very ill, returns to his father's house in Rossau to recuperate.

• **16 September** Weber leaves Dresden for Vienna.

• **5 October** Weber visits Beethoven at Baden.

• **25 October** Weber's opera *Euryanthe* is given in Vienna to a mixed reaction, and after twenty performances it is withdrawn from the repertoire.

• **16 November** A lavish banquet is given in Rossini's honour in Paris.

• **13 December** Rossini arrives in London.

• **20 December** Schubert's incidental music and OVERTURE to *Rosamunde* is performed for the first time at the Theater an der Wien.

• **29 December** Rossini travels to Brighton and is received by King George IV.

1824 Beethoven completes his Ninth Symphony, known as the *Choral* because the composer uses a chorus in the last movement for the first time.

• **2 March** Smetana in born in Litomysl.

• **7 March** Meyerbeer's opera *Il crociato in Egitto* (The Crusader in Egypt) is first given in Venice.

• **31 March** Weber, by now seriously ill (p.142), conducts his *Euryanthe* in Dresden.

The last manuscript page of the 'Kyrie' from Beethoven's Missa solemnis. *When visiting the composer in 1819, Schindler said Beethoven (opposite) looked as if he had been fighting a whole army of contrapuntalists during the process of composition.*

'Rossini is full of effects and epigrams in his music.'
Boïeldieu in a letter of 13 December 1823

OTHER EVENTS
1823 Monroe doctrine stops colonial settlements in America
• Mexico becomes a republic

1824 Accession of Charles X of France
• Byron joins the Greeks in their war against the Turks and dies at Missolonghi

Liszt aged twelve, playing at a concert in Paris in 1824.

A portrait of Beethoven (above) painted in 1823, commissioned by his Leipzig publishers, Breitkopf und Härtel, and now destroyed. Although Schindler, Beethoven's amanuensis and companion in the closing years of his life, deplored the likeness, the painting nevertheless conveys the composer's dogged determination.

• **April** The first performance of Beethoven's *Missa solemnis* takes place in St Petersburg, thanks to the efforts of Prince Galitzin, a gifted amateur cellist who also inspires Beethoven to compose the late string quartets.

• **7 May** Beethoven conducts part of the *Missa solemnis* and his Ninth Symphony in public in Vienna, though hears neither the music nor the applause ■ (below). Although the symphony is a great success with sections of the audience, the concert is a financial disaster for the composer.

• **18 August** Weber receives a letter from the management of Covent Garden, London, asking him to write an opera for the 1825 season, and to conduct it and *Der Freischütz* during the summer of that year. He agrees to compose *Oberon*.

• **4 September** Bruckner is born in Ansfelden, near Linz.

• **27 December** Despite the fiasco of the first rehearsal of his Mass for the Church of St Roch, Paris, Berlioz determines to become a composer.

▲ Beethoven's Affliction Affects his Playing

Beethoven's playing was doubtless much impaired by his cruel malady. Although, from experience and a knowledge of his instrument, a musician may imagine the effect of his performance, yet he cannot himself produce that effect when wholly deprived of the sense of hearing, more especially a sensitive man like Beethoven. His infirmity precluded his ascertaining the quantity or quality of tone produced by a certain pressure of his fingers on the pianoforte; hence his playing, latterly, became very imperfect. He possessed immense powers on the instrument; great velocity of finger, united with extreme delicacy of touch, and intense feeling; but his passages were indistinct and confused. Being painfully conscious, therefore, of his inability to produce any certain effect, he objected to perform before anyone, and latterly refused even his most intimate friends. These, however, would at times succeed in their desire to get him to the instrument, by ingeniously starting a question in counterpoint; when he would unconsciously proceed to illustrate his theory; and then branching out into a train of thought (forgetting his affliction), he would frequently pour out an extemporaneous effusion, of marvellous power and brilliancy. It is easy to imagine a purely mechanical performer, void of all feeling, previously to a stroke of deafness, who has conquered every difficulty of the instrument, playing a piece of music correctly, and to the satisfaction of those of a reciprocal feeling; but to a conformation like that of Beethoven, where light and shade, and delicacy of expression, were either all or nothing, the full achievement of his object amount to an almost impossibility.

Cipriani Potter, *Recollections of Beethoven*, from *The Musical World*, 1836

A selection of hearing aids (right) made for Beethoven by the inventor Mälzel (p.137). Today Beethoven's hearing might well have been restored by a simple operation to remove the growth or otosclerosis from his ear.

1825-30
Paris: A New Musical Metropolis

As stability returns to Europe in the decade following the close of the Napoleonic period, the focus of music inexorably moves away from Vienna to Paris, which now attracts composers to it in the way that the Austrian capital had done in the previous century, though with an even more international galaxy of composers and performers making their way to the city.

1825 February Beethoven finishes his String Quartet Op.127, the first of his late quartets, which are considered by many to be his finest work.

• **March** Mendelssohn visits Paris, and Cherubini's approval of his Piano Quartet in B minor, Op.3 (dedicated to Goethe), sets the seal on his future as a composer.

• **May** Beethoven, now almost completely deaf, goes to Baden and works on the String Quartet Op.132.

• **13 May** Chopin performs on a new keyboard instrument called the AEROMELODICON before the Tsar, who is in Warsaw to open the Polish Diet. The VIRTUOSO is presented with a diamond ring.

'If I could only live till I am a hundred and forty, my musical life would become decidedly interesting.'
Berlioz

• **June** Chopin publishes a Rondo for Piano as his Opus One.

• **19 June** Rossini's delightful comic opera *Il viaggio a Reims* (The Journey to Rheims) is staged in Paris to celebrate the coronation of Charles X, but the composer withdraws it and uses much of the music for a subsequent French opera, entitled *Le Comte Ory* (Count Ory).

• **10 July** Berlioz's Mass for the Church of St Roch (p.145) is well received when finally performed in Paris, strengthening him in his determination to become a composer ▲ (p.149).

• **August** Beethoven completes the String Quartet Op.132.

• **October** Mendelssohn, with astonishing facility, composes his effervescent Octet for Strings, inspired by Goethe's poems, the first work of the composer's maturity.

• **25 October** Johann Strauss the Younger is born in Vienna.

• **November** Beethoven completes the String Quartet Op.130.

• **1 December** Bellini makes his début as an operatic composer with *Adelson e Salvini* in Naples.

1826 Schubert (left) starts the SONG CYCLE for tenor or baritone and piano accompaniment *Die Winterreise* (The Winter Journey), one of the masterpieces of German song ◆ (p.139).

• Berlioz enrols as a student at the Paris Conservatoire.

• Mendelssohn writes his sparkling OVERTURE to *A Midsummer Night's Dream* (opposite).

• **16 February** Weber sets out from Dresden for London via Paris.

OTHER EVENTS
1825 Accession of Ludwig I of Bavaria
• Alexander I of Russia dies. The 'Decembrists' revolt but are crushed when Nicholas I succeeds as Tsar
• Manzoni: *I promessi sposi*
• Pushkin: *Boris Godunov*

1826 James Fenimore Cooper: *The Last of the Mohicans*

A watercolour of Schubert in 1825 (left), the year he began his Ninth Symphony, completed in 1828, but not performed until after his death, when Mendelssohn conducted a heavily cut version in 1829. Schubert's friends always felt that this was one of the best likenesses of the composer.

The autograph of the opening page of Mendelssohn's overture to A Midsummer Night's Dream, *composed in 1826. He was later to compose an accompanying set of incidental music for the play (p.158).*

• **8 March** Weber is given a rapturous reception by the public at his first London concert.

• **21 March** Beethoven's String Quartet Op.130, has its first performance. The original finale, the *Grosse Fuge* (The Great Fugue), is eventually published separately as Opus 133.

• **12 April** *Oberon*, Weber's last opera, completed this year, receives its first performance at Covent Garden, London. At the close of the work the composer receives the unprecedented honour of being called on to the stage to acknowledge the applause.

• **4 June** Weber dies in London, aged thirty-nine. He is buried initially in London, though eventually his successor in Dresden, Wagner, will arrange for his remains to be returned to Germany.

• **July** Beethoven completes the String Quartet Op.131.

• **30 July** Beethoven's nephew Karl attempts suicide, shooting himself in the head. He survives, but his act devastates Beethoven.

• **September–October** Beethoven takes Karl to his brother Johann at Gneixendorf, where he composes the String Quartet Op.135, and a new finale for his String Quartet Op.130.

• **2 October** Chopin's health is already beginning to cause concern to his family and friends.

• **9 October** Rossini's opera *Le siège de Corinthe* (The Siege of Corinth), a revised version of *Maometto II* (p.141), is performed for the first time at the Paris Opéra.

• **December** Beethoven catches cold and develops pneumonia on his return journey to Vienna. He recovers slightly, but then becomes dropsical and jaundiced. His abdomen swells massively and on 20 December he undergoes the first of four operations to relieve the pressure.

1827 February Mendelssohn's overture to *A Midsummer Night's Dream* (above) is first performed in public in Stettin.

• **26 March** Rossini's opera *Moïse et Pharaon* (Moses and Pharaoh), a revision of his *Mosè in Egitto* (p.140) is first given at the Paris Opéra.

• **26 March** Beethoven dies, aged fifty-six, in Vienna. His autopsy shows he suffered from cirrhosis of the liver.

• **29 March** Following a funeral service at St Stephen's cathedral, Beethoven is buried at Währing Cemetery (below).

Beethoven's funeral procession in Vienna on 29 March 1827. Some 20,000 people were said to have taken part in or attended the ceremony.

• **29 April** Mendelssohn's early opera *Die Hochzeit des Camacho* (Camacho's Wedding) has its first performance at the Berlin Schauspielhaus, but with only limited success.

1828 Paganini embarks on a series of tours throughout Europe lasting six years, which will take entire cities by storm; his virtuoso technique inspires performers and composers alike.

• In an amazing outpouring Schubert completes his Ninth Symphony known as the *Great* ★ (p.146), his last three piano sonatas and the String Quintet in C.

• **March** Berlioz hears Beethoven's Third and Fifth Symphonies played at the Paris Conservatoire under the direction of Habeneck, and is profoundly affected by the works ▲ (opposite).

• **29 March** Schumann matriculates as a law student at Leipzig University, though he has no wish to become a lawyer.

• **August** Schumann begins a course of piano study with the famous teacher Friedrich Wieck and meets his daughter Clara, then aged nine.

• **20 August** Rossini's opera *Le Comte Ory* is performed for the first time at the Paris Opéra.

• **31 October** Schubert's health seriously deteriorates. He becomes nauseous and can neither eat nor drink.

• **19 November** Death of Schubert, aged thirty-one, in Vienna.

1829 Berlioz begins his *Symphonie fantastique* (below), which sharply divides the critics at its first performance the following year.

• Mendelssohn's revival of Bach's *St Matthew Passion* (p.80) in Berlin, a century after its first performance, marks the re-birth of interest in Bach's music and that of the past in general.

• **3 August** The first performance of Rossini's masterpiece of Romantic opera, *William Tell*, proves to be his theatrical swan song, for afterwards he leaves Paris and composes little else for the rest of his life.

• **28 November** Birth of Anton Rubinstein at Vikhvatinets, in Russia.

Title page of the first edition of Berlioz's Symphonie fantastique, *which was first performed at the Paris Conservatoire on 5 December 1830. The score, which was published in 1845, is dedicated to Tsar Nicholas I, since Berlioz was planning to visit Russia at that time.*

A SA MAJESTÉ NICOLAS IER EMPEREUR DE TOUTES LES RUSSIES

SYMPHONIE FANTASTIQUE

PAR HECTOR BERLIOZ

Paris, G. BRANDUS & S. DUFOUR, rue Richelieu, 103.

1830 Auber establishes himself as one of the most successful composers of Parisian opera with *Fra Diavolo* (Brother Devil).

• Schumann writes his *Abegg* Variations for Piano, marking his emergence as a fully fledged composer. He has already begun to indulge in musical anagrams and the opening THEME of this work is derived from the letters of his friend Martha Abegg's surname, consisting as it does of the notes 'A,' 'B' (German for B-flat), 'E,' 'G' and 'G'.

• Mendelssohn composes the first of his *Songs without Words*, a new type of piano miniature in lyrical, Romantic style.

• **11 March** Bellini's opera *I Capuleti ed i Montecchi* (Capulets and Montagues), based on Shakespeare's *Romeo and Juliet* is first heard in Venice.

• **5 December** Berlioz's *Symphonie fantastique* (left) is first given in Paris, in the presence of Liszt.

• **26 December** Donizetti's opera *Anna Bolena* is first heard in Milan.

OTHER EVENTS
1827 Audubon: *Birds of North America*
• Heine: *Buch der Lieder*

1828 First performance of Goethe's *Faust* , part one

1829 Greek independence
• James Mill: *Analysis of the Mind*
• Balzac: *La comédie humaine*
• Hugo: *Les orientales*

1830 July Revolution in France
• Lamartine: *Harmonies poétiques et religieuses*
• Hugo: *Hernani*
• Stendhal: *Le rouge et le noir*

▲ *Berlioz's Paris*

The pursuit of grand dramatic music was a cult to which I dedicated myself, both body and soul. Instrumental music still had no meaning for me; the only concerts I had heard were at the Opéra, where the indifferent performances did not arouse my interest. The symphonies of Haydn and Mozart (usually more intimate works), when played by an inadequate orchestra in a building that was far too large and unsuitable from an acoustic point of view, had about as much effect as if they had been performed [in the open air].... As for the adoration of Rossini, which had recently become the latest thing for fashionable Parisians, it made me furious. My anger was increased by the entire manner of the new movement, which was totally in opposition to that of Gluck and Spontini. I could imagine nothing more exquisitely beautiful and genuine than the compositions of these great masters.

In contrast, Rossini's cynical approach to melody, his contempt for dramatic expression and good sense, his interminable repetition of one kind of cadence, his endless childish crescendo and crude bass drum, irritated me so much that I was blinded to the brilliant aspects of his genius, even in his exquisitely scored masterpiece, The Barber of Seville. I frequently agonized over the possibility of putting a mine under the Théâtre-Italien and blowing it up, together with its assembly of Rossinians... I entirely agree with Ingres when he describes certain of Rossini's works as 'the music of a charlatan'.

Berlioz, *Memoirs, 1864*

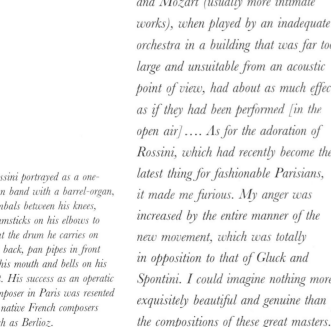

Rossini portrayed as a one-man band with a barrel-organ, cymbals between his knees, drumsticks on his elbows to beat the drum he carries on his back, pan pipes in front of his mouth and bells on his hat. His success as an operatic composer in Paris was resented by native French composers such as Berlioz.

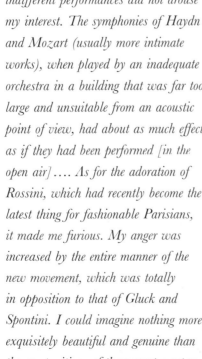

Rossini

Lith. Destouches.

1831-34
'Bel Canto': Bellini and Donizetti

With the retirement of Rossini from the theatre, the way is now open for Bellini and Donizetti to make their very different contributions to the development of Italian opera. Both composers elaborate a musical style which puts the human voice at the heart of their works, and requires the fine and beautiful vocal quality known as 'bel canto'.

1831 Schumann publishes the *Abegg* Variations (p.148) as his Opus One, and composes a piano suite entitled *Papillons* (Butterflies).

• Rossini, in Madrid, is asked by a Spanish priest to write a Stabat Mater.

• **4 April** Chopin gives the first of two concerts in Vienna, both of which fail with the public. He decides to go to Paris, arriving in September.

• **21 November** Meyerbeer's *Robert le diable* (Robert the Devil) realizes his ambitions for French grand opera when first given at the Paris Opéra.

• **26 December** Bellini's opera *Norma* opens in Milan.

1832 In an attempt to make the fourth finger of his right hand more flexible, Schumann restrains his third finger in a sling, which leaves the finger paralysed, shattering his hopes of a concert career.

• **26 February** Chopin's first Paris recital, although not a financial success, receives praise from Liszt and Mendelssohn. This year he writes his *Etudes* (Studies) Op.10, dedicated to Liszt, and publishes the Mazurkas Op.6, in Leipzig.

• **22 March** Death of Goethe ■ (opposite).

• **12 May** Donizetti's comic opera *L'elisir d'amore* (The Elixir of Love) is first performed in Milan.

• **14 May** Mendelssohn's *Fingal's Cave* or *Hebrides* Overture, is performed for the first time in London during a visit by the composer.

> *'I sit with ambassadors, princes, ministers, and don't even know how it happened...'*
> Chopin writing to a Polish friend in 1833

OTHER EVENTS
1831 Hugo: *Notre Dame de Paris*

1832 Goethe: *Faust* Part II (published posthumously)

1833 Slavery outlawed in British Empire
• Carlyle: *Sartor resartus*

1834 McCormick patents mechanical reaper
• Lytton: *The Last Days of Pompeii*

1833 Wagner writes his first complete opera *Die Feen* (The Fairies).

• **7 May** Brahms is born in Hamburg.

• **3 October** Berlioz marries the actress Harriet Smithson in Paris, with Liszt as one of the witnesses.

1834 Berlioz completes his symphony *Harold in Italy*, based on Byron's epic poem *Childe Harold*.

• **April** Bellini begins composing his opera *I Puritani* (The Puritans), in Paris.

• **3 April** Schumann founds the periodical *Neue Zeitschrift für Musik* (New Music Magazine) in Leipzig.

• **2 July** Schumann tells his mother that he wishes to marry Ernestine von Fricken, who has come to live with the Wieck family as a piano pupil.

Teatro La Scala in Milan, a shrine to Italian opera and the scene of so many memorable first nights. With its innovatory porte cochère, *to protect the audience, when alighting from coaches, this is the façade that would have been familiar to Rossini, Bellini and Donizetti.*

■ *Goethe and Romanticism*

Although Goethe himself roundly deplored Romanticism, as opposed to Classicism, it is almost impossible to consider the movement, especially in relation to music, without encountering him time and time again as a fount of inspiration for composers of many different temperaments. His drama *Faust* alone was the source of numerous operas and orchestral works, by composers such as Berlioz (p.160), Liszt (p.166) and Gounod (p.168). It occupied most of his working life, certainly from the early 1770s, and he only completed the second part in 1831, the year before his death. His *Egmont* (1787) subsequently drew incidental music from Beethoven, whose compositions Goethe much appreciated, although the two men never became friends, partly because of the composer's deafness, but also because his abrupt manner and rather bohemian style did not appeal to the somewhat fastidious and even aristocratic Goethe.

Goethe was himself a musician, and it is therefore not surprising that his lyric poems, many of which were written with the intention of their being set to music, inspired composers, including Mozart, Beethoven, Schubert and Wolf, to write countless songs. Indeed Schubert's admiration for the great man provoked him to send copies of his settings of Goethe's poems, but sadly these did not elicit a response.

During his earlier career Goethe had made his own attempts at theatre music with *singspiel* – a mixture of singing and spoken dialogue – although he abandoned this in 1782 when his *Die Fischerin* (The Fishermaiden) clearly could not stand up to comparison with Mozart's *Die Entführung aus dem Serail* (p.112) of the same year. Goethe had a boundless admiration for Mozart, which he was able to express in a very practical way after his appointment as director of the court theatre in Weimar in 1791. In 1796 he planned a production of *The Magic Flute* (to which he had written a sequel). He designed the costumes and the sets for it, demonstrating yet another of his talents.

Although Goethe's admiration for Mozart does point to the Classicism he prized so highly, there are elements in Mozart's music that were undoubtedly an inspiration to the Romantics. Both men can therefore be considered as the epitome of one style and the inspiration for the next.

The 'Walpurgisnacht' scene (Witches' Sabbath) to which Faust and Mephistopheles are led up the mountain by a will-o-the-wisp in Goethe's Faust.

1835-39
The flowering of Romanticism

Never has music been so in harmony with painting and literature.
Mutual influence between the arts is phenomenal: opera turns
to literature for its subjects, song writers to poetry, and composers
such as Chopin and Berlioz seek to express the extremes of human
emotion through their music.

1835 As a result of his love affair with Ernestine von Fricken (p.150), Schumann composes his piano works Symphonic Studies, based on a theme composed by Ernestine's father, and *Carnaval*, which contains a musical anagram of her birthplace, Asch.

• **24 January** Bellini captivates Paris with his opera *I Puritani* (p.150), at the Théâtre-Italien, but dies on 23 September before he is able to follow up his success. Rossini is one of the pall bearers at his funeral.

• **23 February** Halévy's opera *La Juive* (The Jewess) has its first performance in Paris.

• **12 March** Donizetti's opera *Marino Faliero* is first heard at the Théâtre-Italien, Paris.

OTHER EVENTS
1835 Constable: *The Valley Farm*

1836 Independence of Texas
• Barry designs Houses of Parliament, London
• Dickens: *Pickwick Papers*

1837 Morse telegraph
• Accession of Queen Victoria of Britain
• Carlyle: *The French Revolution*

The interior of Teatro San Carlo, Naples, in 1835, the year in which Donizetti's Lucia di Lammermoor *had its first performance on this stage.*

• **26 September** Donizetti's *Lucia di Lammermoor* has its first performance in Naples (left), and is destined to become one of the most influential Romantic operas.

• **September** Mendelssohn takes up his post as director of the Gewandhaus concerts in Leipzig and begins to revolutionize the musical life of the city.

• **9 October** Birth of Saint-Saëns in Paris.

• **9 November** Mendelssohn, Louis Rakemann and Clara Wieck cause a sensation at a concert in Leipzig when they perform Bach's Concerto in D Minor for Three Pianos.

• **18 December** Liszt has interrupted his concert career and is now living with Marie Countess d'Agoult, who gives birth to their first daughter, Blandine, in Geneva.

1836 Glinka composes his opera *A Life for the Tsar*, which shows the extent to which the Russian composer has to absorb Italian, French and German influences before evolving his own character as a composer.

• Chopin composes his first *Ballade* for piano, a form which he invents. He is thought possibly to have been inspired by a work by the Polish poet Mickiewicz on the theme of religious conflict when writing this piece.

★ *Glinka, seated at right, with three of his friends at Ketchanovka, a country estate near St Petersburg. It was here that he worked on his second opera,* Russlan and Ludmilla, *during the summer of 1838, though it was not completed until 1842 (p.157).*

• **1 January** Schumann deserts Ernestine von Fricken in favour of Clara Wieck, with whom he has now fallen in love. Her father is horrified and takes her to Dresden.

• **29 February** Meyerbeer's opera *Les Huguenots* is produced in Paris with overwhelming success.

• **22 May** Mendelssohn conducts the first performance of his ORATORIO *St Paul* in Düsseldorf.

• **24 November** Wagner weds the actress Minna Planer in Magdeburg.

1837 Berlioz is commissioned by the French government to compose his Requiem, also known as the *Grande Messe des Morts* (Great Mass of the Dead), which establishes his reputation as something of an orchestral megalomaniac ◆ (p.143).

• Liszt begins composition of his piano pieces *Années de pèlerinage* (Years of Pilgrimage), which capture all the emotional excitement of the young Romantic soul.

• Schumann composes most of the piano pieces entitled *Phantasiestücke* (Fantasy Pieces), Op.12, which he dedicates to the beautiful young Scottish pianist Robena Laidlaw.

• **2 January** Balakirev is born in Nijni Novgorod.

• **23 January** Field, pioneer of the piano study known as the NOCTURNE, dies in Moscow, aged fifty-four.

• **28 March** Mendelssohn marries Cécile Charlotte Jeanrenaud in Frankfurt, by whom he will have three sons and two daughters.

• **19–22 September** Mendelssohn directs his oratorio *St Paul* at the Birmingham Music Festival.

Liszt pictured in travelling attire in May 1838, when the composer was pursuing the restless existence that he subsequently termed his 'years of pilgrimage'.

• **17 October** Hummel dies in Weimar, aged fifty-nine.

• **5 December** Berlioz's *Requiem* is first performed in the church of Les Invalides, Paris.

• **24 December** Cosima, Liszt's second daughter by Marie d'Agoult and future wife of Wagner, is born in Como, Italy.

1838 Berlioz completes his opera *Benvenuto Cellini*, whose subsequent failure deeply affects him.

• Chopin's liaison with the French novelist George Sand (Madame Dudevant) begins (left).

• **6 January** Bruch is born in Cologne.

• **February–April** Schumann composes the piano SUITES *Scenes from Childhood* and *Kreisleriana*. Although his wife-to-be Clara eventually plays the first work, she never gives the second in full in public lest she weary her audience.

• **7 March** The Swedish soprano Jenny Lind makes her début in a performance of Weber's *Der Freischütz* (p.142).

• **June** Mendelssohn conducts a performance of Handel's oratorio *Joshua* in Cologne.

• **10 September** *Benvenuto Cellini*, Berlioz's opera, is first performed at the Paris Opéra, but is not a success, and has only two more performances on this occasion.

• **25 October** Bizet is born in Paris.

• **8 November** Chopin and George Sand arrive in Palma, Majorca (below).

Chopin as portrayed by Delacroix in 1838, when the composer embarked on his relationship with George Sand, who is shown in another fragment of the same painting listening to the composer playing the piano.

• **16 December** Berlioz conducts his *Symphonie fantastique* (p.148) and *Harold in Italy* (p.150) in Paris, in the presence of Paganini, who is deeply moved, and who two days later makes Berlioz a generous gift of money.

1839 The nucleus of the New York Philharmonic Orchestra is formed, an indication of a growing public interest in orchestral concerts.

• **1 January** Schumann discovers the manuscript of Schubert's Ninth *Great* Symphony (p.148) at the home of the composer's brother Ferdinand and sends it to Mendelssohn.

• **January** Chopin finishes his *Préludes* Op.28 for piano, with each piece being in a different MAJOR or MINOR KEY. He and George Sand will leave Majorca on 13 February, after their idyllic holiday turns sour – the weather and food are miserable, the people are hostile and Chopin becomes ill.

• **Late January** With the twenty thousand francs from Paganini, Berlioz begins to compose his *Romeo and Juliet* Symphony, which is central to his career as a composer.

A street scene in Palma, 1838, as depicted by George Sand's son Maurice, then aged fifteen, and a future pupil of Delacroix. Maurice and his sister Solange accompanied their mother to Majorca when she and Chopin spent the winter of 1838–39 there.

- **21 March** Birth of Mussorgsky in Karevo, in the Pskov district of Russia.

- **21 March** Mendelssohn conducts the first performance of Schubert's Ninth Symphony in Leipzig.

- **9 May** Daniel, Liszt's only son by Marie d'Agoult (p.152), is born, but the relationship is in difficulties.

- **19–21 May** Mendelssohn conducts Handel's *Messiah* ■ (p.89) and Beethoven's Mass in C in Düsseldorf.

- **6–8 September** Mendelssohn conducts his oratorio *St Paul*, his D minor Piano Concerto and Beethoven's Fifth and Seventh Symphonies in Brunswick.

- **17 November** Verdi makes his début as an operatic composer with *Oberto* in Milan.

- **24 November** Berlioz conducts the first performance of his dramatic symphony for solo voices, chorus and orchestra, *Romeo and Juliet*, in Paris. It is a great success, and is repeated on 1 and 15 December.

★ *A poster for the concert given in Vienna on 28 March 1842, which was effectively the first concert of the Vienna Philharmonic, though given by the Court Opera orchestra in the large Redoutensaal. A group of members from the opera orchestra had started giving orchestral concerts in 1833.*

★ *The actor Wilhelmine Schröder-Devrient as Romeo finds Juliet in her coffin in Bellini's* I Capuleti ed i Montecchi *(p.148).*

◆ *The Aesthetics of Romanticism*

*I*f Goethe ■ *(p.151) was a literary figure with deep musical leanings, then composers such as Berlioz and Schumann were musicians with deep literary leanings, and indeed both of them devoted a large amount of their energies to writing musical journalism and to publishing.*

Berlioz often resented having to write in order to live, but he was an extremely articulate person, and an interested oberserver of the times. It would have been surprising if he had not been able to commit his thoughts to paper, and at times much of the frustration that he felt at being unable to have his music performed or, when it achieved performance, failing to be accepted, was sublimated by being externalized in this way. The gods of his pantheon were Beethoven and Shakespeare, and the choice and juxtaposition are significant.

Schumann, too, was highly articulate, and responded to lyric texts as Schubert had done, though in nothing like so prolific a way. He did not have the same concerns as Berlioz who, as a Frenchman, saw the musical life of his country's capital city largely dominated by the works of foreigners, and meretricious ones at that. Schumann's response to other musicians, such as Brahms ■ (p.175), was often no less spontaneous; he was usually more circumspect than Berlioz in his choice of expression, though he could be incisive when necessary.

What both Berlioz and Schumann show in their writings that is new, however, is the fact that they are concerned with the overall development of music, and consider aesthetic theory to be parallel with the music itself. In the past, composers had only formulated aesthetic theories when challenged, by way of justification, or when dealing with what were basically the most practical elements of their art. To Vivaldi, Handel or even Bach such considerations would have seemed very strange indeed — they were too busy earning their living, fulfilling the wishes of their employers. Romanticism enabled, or indeed forced, the composer to stand back from the world and himself, in a totally new way.

1840-45
The Rebirth of Opera

Although opera was created in Italy, and was long regarded as the preserve of Italian composers and singers, by the end of the eighteenth century it had almost died out on its native soil. Even so it was an Italian, Rossini, who carried his art to Paris and there forged a new form of opera with his masterpiece William Tell, *only to retire from the stage at the height of his success. Nevertheless he had laid the foundations of the new Romantic opera.*

1840 Inspired by his love affair and eventual marriage to Clara Wieck (despite her father's determined opposition, p.153), Schumann composes no fewer than one hundred and twenty-eight songs this year.

• **11 February** Donizetti's comic opera *The Daughter of the Regiment* is produced for the first time at the Opéra-Comique in Paris and is given in Milan later this year.

• **7 May** Tchaikovsky is born in Kamsko-Votkinsk in the Vyatka district.

• **27 May** Death of Paganini, aged fifty-seven, in Nice.

• **12 September** Having been to court to establish his right to marry the woman of his choice, Schumann marries Clara Wieck at Schönefeld, near Leipzig, despite her father's continued disapproval.

1841 The invention of the saxophone, patented 1846, by Adolphe Sax gives composers a new range of INSTRUMENTAL TIMBRES.

• **23–26 January** In a burst of creative energy, Schumann sketches out his First or *Spring* Symphony, which he completes on 20 February.

• **31 March** Mendelssohn directs the first performance of Schumann's *Spring* Symphony at the Leipzig Gewandhaus.

• **26 April** Chopin gives one of his rare public concerts in Paris at this time, including the two Polonaises of Op.40, his second *Ballade* Op.38 (p.152), the Third Scherzo, and several of the *Préludes* (p.154).

• **28 June** Adam's *Giselle* is first given in Paris.

• **July** Mendelssohn leaves Leipzig for Berlin, at the invitation of the King of Prussia, but his hopes are destined to be disappointed, despite some initial success.

• **1 September** Clara Schumann gives birth to Marie, the first of eight children.

• **8 September** Birth of Dvořák in Nelahozeves, near Prague.

• **9 September** Schumann completes the symphony subsequently known as his Fourth in its original form.

• **26 December** Donizetti's *Maria Padilla* is first performed in Milan.

A portrait of Giuseppina Strepponi in her youth. She made her début in 1834, and played a decisive part in the staging of Verdi's first opera Oberto *(p.155) at La Scala in 1839. Three years later she created the role of Abigaille in Verdi's* Nabucco, *the score of which she is holding, the composer's first great success.*

OTHER EVENTS
1840 Louis Napoleon Bonaparte attempts to take the throne of France and is imprisoned
• First incandescent electric bulb

1841 *Punch* magazine founded
• Edgar Allan Poe: *Murders in the Rue Morgue*

1842 China concedes Hong Kong to Great Britain

1842 Meyerbeer becomes general music director of the Royal Opera House, Berlin.

• Glinka's second opera, *Russlan and Ludmilla*, is completed. The music still fails to find a truly Russian voice, however.

• **7 January** Rossini's Stabat Mater is heard for the first time in its completed form at the Théâtre-Italien, Paris and is an enormous artistic and commercial success.

• **February** Chopin gives a public concert in the Salle Pleyel, Paris, when he performs the Third *Ballade* and the Impromptu Op.51, together with three MAZURKAS and four NOCTURNES.

• **3 March** Mendelssohn conducts the first performance of his *Scottish* Symphony in Leipzig.

• **9 March** Verdi has his first great success with his opera *Nabucco* (opposite) in Milan.

• **15 March** Death of Cherubini (right), aged eighty-one, in Paris.

Cherubini and the Muse of Lyric Poetry, *painted by Ingres in 1842, the year of the composer's death. After a successful, though financially unrewarding early career in his native Italy, Cherubini settled in Paris in 1787 and survived the Revolution to become professor of composition at the newly founded Conservatoire, and director there in 1822.*

• **April** The Vienna Philharmonic Orchestra is founded, ★ (p.155).

• **12 May** Birth of Massenet in Montaud, near St Etienne.

• **19 May** Donizetti's opera *Linda di Chamounix* (Linda from Chamonix) is first performed in Vienna.

'Mendelssohn ... sees most clearly through the contradictions of this era, and reconciles them for the first time.'
Schumann

• **4 June** Schumann begins his first significant excercise in chamber music with his String Quartet in A Minor, Op.41, and before it is finished, starts work on a second one on 11 June.

• **8–22 July** Schumann composes the third quartet of Op.41.

• **September** Chopin and George Sand (p.154) settle in a Parisian apartment, which the composer will inhabit for the next seven years.

• **23 September** Schumann begins composing the Piano Quintet in E-flat Major, Op.44, which he completes in less than three weeks.

• **26 September** Berlioz conducts the first of two concerts in Brussels, the first time he conducts outside France.

• **20 October** Wagner's opera *Rienzi* ★ (p.158) takes Dresden by storm when first performed at the city's Opera House, and its magnificent cast and lavish production quickly ensures that the composer's fame spreads throughout Europe.

• **24 October** Schumann begins work on the Piano Quartet in E-flat Major, Op.47, which he completes a month later.

• **December** Heartened by his success in Brussels in September, Berlioz now ventures further, as far as Berlin, on a tour that will last until the following May.

★ *The finale of Act Two of Wagner's opera* Rienzi, *whose text the composer himself wrote, based on Bulwer Lytton's novel of the same name. The first performance, in Dresden in October 1842, lasted almost six hours, despite cuts, and Wagner even contemplated making two operas out of it.*

1843 2 January Wagner's *The Flying Dutchman* bewilders audiences at its first hearing in Dresden.

• **3 January** Donizetti ends his composing career with the first performance of his brilliantly witty *Don Pasquale* in Paris.

• **2–3 April** Opening of the Leipzig Conservatory, with Mendelssohn as director and Schumann one of the professors.

• **15 June** Grieg is born in Bergen.

• **16 June** Schumann completes his 'oratorio not for the oratory' *Das Paradies und die Peri* (Paradise and the Peri), which has its first performances in Leipzig on 4 and 11 December this year.

• **14 October** The first complete performance of Mendelssohn's incidental music to *A Midsummer Night's Dream* ★ (p.147) takes place in Berlin, and again four days later in public. It is a great success.

1844 Berlioz publishes his *Traité de l'instrumentation et d'orchestration modernes* (Treaty on Modern Instrumentation and Orchestration).

• **25 January** The Schumanns leave Leipzig for a five-month-long concert tour of Russia. Increasingly Schumann finds his career secondary to that of his wife.

• **9 March** Verdi's opera *Ernani*, based on a drama by Victor Hugo, is first performed at the Teatro la Fenice, Venice.

• **18 March** Birth of Rimsky-Korsakov at Tikhvin in the Novgorod district of Russia.

• **July** Mendelssohn completes his only Violin Concerto, one of his best loved works, and possibly the most popular violin concerto ever written.

• **1 August** Berlioz directs a concert as part of the Grand Festival de l'Industrie in Paris with more than one thousand performers.

• **Late August** Schumann has a nervous breakdown. After a visit to Dresden at the beginning of October he and his wife decide to leave Leipzig, which they do on 13 December.

1845 Glinka travels to Madrid and studies Spanish folk songs and dances.

• Liszt composes the choral pieces which he will eventually rewrite as the SYMPHONIC POEM *Les Préludes*, one of his most successful, if not one of his most distinguished, works.

• **13 March** After considerable revisions, Mendelssohn's Violin Concerto is performed in Leipzig for the first time.

• **12 May** Fauré is born in Pamiers, in the Ariège.

• **10 August** The Beethoven monument is unveiled in Bonn.

• **19 October** Wagner's opera *Tannhäuser* is received with only moderate acclaim at its first performance in Dresden.

◆ *The 'New' Subject Matter of Romantic Opera*

From its earliest days opera had used the plots from Classical mythology ◆ *(p.49)*, lifting musical drama on to the highest theatrical plane, and so carrying the minds and emotions of the audience to the point where they, too, experienced the feelings expressed by the characters on stage. Indeed, this remains today the aim of the serious opera composer, and, to the extent that human experience is neither all tragic nor all comic, the early operas reflected that fact in their inclusion of both serious and comic or buffo characters.

In time, however, it was felt that opera seria ◆ *(p.67)* should only include serious characters, and comedy was relegated to the realm of opera buffa. Moreover, serious characters tended to express their feelings in poetry, whereas comic characters spoke in dialect which, in Italy, for example, tended to be Neapolitan or Venetian. Needless to say, the court or state theatres tended to specialize in opera seria, and the smaller theatres were the home of opera buffa. France stood somewhat apart from Europe in its operatic practice, certainly during most of the eighteenth century ◆ *(p.109)*.

Ironically, as opera seria became less and less popular, and more and more remote from reality, it was opera buffa that provided a major source of inspiration to a composer such as Mozart, both in subject matter and in the way music was composed. Individual ARIAS for the singers became much less frequent, and the extended ensembles, where each voice might express a different emotion at the same time as the others, made the operas more true to life and more exciting.

The demise of opera seria did not mean that the old stories were completely abandoned by opera composers such as Verdi (left), but that for their plots or LIBRETTI many turned to other sources, such as Shakespeare (pp.146, 155, 161, 187), Sir Walter Scott (p.141), and Byron (p.150), Goethe ■ (p.151) and Schiller (p.172).

As the sources became increasingly contemporary, the links between literature and music in what we now call the Romantic period became closer than they had ever been before. This resulted in operas which, for the first time, reflected the spirit of the age both in their music and their libretti.

A lithograph of 1851, showing Verdi surrounded by scenes from his operas, with his most recent, Il trovatore, *in the bottom lefthand corner. One of Verdi's greatest achievements was to bring a much more accessible dimension of human emotion into opera.*

1846-49
Liszt: the Archetypal Romantic

*In a life and musical career spanning three-quarters of a century,
Liszt embodies what is to become the image of the Romantic artist.
At its worst it seems to represent self-indulgence, but at its best
it is the gathering up of human emotion on to its highest level.*

1846 Liszt composes the first of his *Hungarian Rhapsodies* for piano,
with gypsy melodies and dance rhythms ● (p.173).

• **1 January** Clara Schumann gives the first performance of her
husband's only Piano Concerto at the Leipzig Gewandhaus (below).

• **12 February** Schumann begins orchestrating his Second Symphony,
probably begun the previous December, but does not complete it until
19 October as he is attacked by nervous disorders.

• **15 February** Berlioz gives the first of three concerts in Pest, Hungary,
and includes an arrangement of the *Rákóczy March*, which is received with
rapture by the audience.

• **31 May–2 June** Mendelssohn directs the Aachen Music Festival,
conducting Haydn's *The Creation* (p.127), Handel's *Alexander's Feast*
(p.84) and Beethoven's Fifth Symphony (p.132).

• **11 June** Mendelssohn is in Liège for the sexcentenary celebrations
of the feast of Corpus Christi, for which he composes a CHORAL work.

• **14–16 June** Mendelssohn composes a festival song, a setting of
Schiller's *An die Künstler* (To the Artist), for a choral festival in Cologne.

• **26 August** Mendelssohn conducts the first performance of his ORATORIO
Elijah, composed this summer, in Birmingham.

• **5 November** Schumann's Second Symphony is first performed at the
Gewandhaus in Leipzig.

• **24 November** Schumann and Clara go to Vienna to give a series
of concerts.

• **6 December** Berlioz's oratorio-opera *La Damnation de Faust* (The
Damnation of Faust) is first performed at the Opéra-Comique, Paris,
but is an artistic and financial disaster.

*A drawing by Mendelssohn
dated 1 January 1847, of the
concert hall of the Gewandhaus
in Leipzig. The musical quote
beneath the lefthand picture
is the opening of Beethoven's
Fifth Symphony. On the right
is a domestic interior which,
from the text above, could be
intended as an ironic contrast
by the composer-artist.*

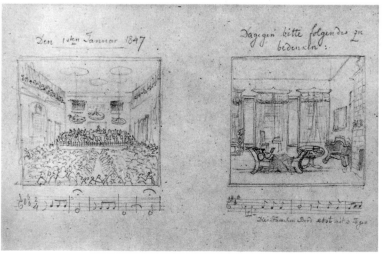

1847 1 January Schumann
conducts his *Spring* Symphony
(p.156) and his Piano Concerto,
with his wife as soloist, at one
of their concerts in Vienna, but
neither work produces much
enthusiasm.

• **21 January** Schumann
and Clara leave Vienna and
continue their concert tour
in Brno and Prague, before
returning to Dresden on
4 February.

• **11 February** Schumann
and Clara travel to Berlin.

★ *An almost indecipherable letter from Donizetti to his brother Giuseppe, written from the asylum at Ivry, near Paris, in late May 1846, where he was sent following a paralytic stroke in 1844. The composer was to remain at Ivry until six months before his death when he moved to Bergamo (p.162).*

• **14 February** Berlioz leaves Paris for Russia, arriving in St Petersburg a fortnight later.

• **17 February** Schumann conducts *Das Paradies und die Peri* (p.158) at the Singakademie in Berlin, but it is not a success.

• **1 March** Clara Schumann introduces her husband's Piano Quintet in E-flat Major (p.157) at a concert in Berlin.

• **14 March** Verdi's *Macbeth* is first performed at the Teatro della Pergola, Florence.

• **15 March** Berlioz's first Russian concert, which includes the first two parts of his *The Damnation of Faust*, is a resounding success, and earns him a great deal of money.

• **24 March** The Schumanns return to Dresden, but for a while they consider settling in Berlin.

• **2 April** Mendelssohn conducts his oratorio *St Paul* (p.153) in the Paulinerkirche, Leipzig, which is the last time he will appear as conductor in Germany.

• **5 April** Schumann drafts the OVERTURE to a new opera, *Genoveva*.

• **23 April** Berlioz conducts a performance of his *Romeo and Juliet* Symphony (p.154) in St Petersburg.

• **16–30 April** Mendelssohn conducts six performances of *Elijah* in London, Manchester and Birmingham. He returns to Frankfurt on 12 May, only to be faced with the death of his beloved sister Fanny two days later.

• **19 June** Berlioz directs a complete performance of *The Damnation of Faust* in Berlin on his return journey from Russia.

• **Mid-July** Mendelssohn, resting at Interlaken, composes his last great work, the String Quartet in F minor, Op.80, as a Requiem for his sister.

• **November** Berlioz leaves Paris for London, where he will stay for eight months until July 1848.

★ *The Paris Opéra in the 1840s during a performance of Meyerbeer's opera* Robert le diable *(p.150). The production was typical of the lavishly staged grand operas for which Paris was famous.*

• Flotow's opera *Martha,* incorporating the song 'The Last Rose of Summer', is first performed in Vienna.

• **4 November** Mendelssohn dies, aged thirty-eight, in Leipzig, and his remains are taken to Berlin.

• **26 December** Schumann finishes ORCHESTRATING the OVERTURE to *Genoveva,* and immediately starts work on the first act.

1848 Liszt ■ (p.163) becomes director of music at Weimar.

• **21 January** Birth of Duparc, the French song writer, in Paris.

• **16 February** Chopin gives his first public concert for six years at the Salle Pleyel, Paris, but with the outbreak of revolution he goes to Britain.

Chopin, dying, surrounded by his family and friends (from the left): Abbé Jelowicki, Chopin's sister Ludwika (Louise, who would take his heart back to Warsaw), Chopin, Princess Marcelina (Marcelline) Czartoryska, Gryzmala, and Kwiatkowski (the artist).

• **8 April** Death of Donizetti, aged fifty, in Bergamo ★ (p.161).

• **29 June** Berlioz gives a concert in London, which establishes his reputation in Britain, but he decides to return to France.

• **4 August** Schumann completes the SCORE of his opera *Genoveva.*

• **16 November** Chopin gives his last concert in London and leaves for Paris a week later.

1849 Meyerbeer's *Le Prophète* (The Prophet) is first given at the Paris Opéra ★ (p.161).

• Bruckner finishes his Requiem.

• Berlioz composes his Te Deum.

• Liszt's *Tasso: Lamento e Trionfo* (Tasso: Lament and Triumph) is first performed in Weimar.

• **9 March** Nicolai's comic opera *The Merry Wives of Windsor,* widely celebrated for its OVERTURE, is performed for the first time at the Royal Opera in Berlin.

• **April–May** Wagner actively supports the revolution, possibly by making hand-grenades. On 16 May a warrant for his arrest is issued in Dresden and, with Liszt's help, he flees to Switzerland ■ (p.171).

• **5 May** Schumann and Clara flee from Dresden as revolution breaks out.

• **July** Wagner writes his political treatise *Die Kunst und die Revolution* (Art and Revolution).

• **17 October** Chopin dies in Paris, probably of tuberculosis, aged thirty-nine (above and right).

• **30 October** Some 3000 people attend Chopin's funeral at the Madeleine in Paris. The singers Pauline Viardot and Luigi Lablache take part in a performance of Mozart's Requiem (p.122), and Chopin's own Funeral March is played in an orchestral version for the first time.

• **17 November** Ferdinand Hiller proposes to Schumann that he should succeed him as director of municipal music in Düsseldorf, though he still hopes for an improvement of the situation in Dresden.

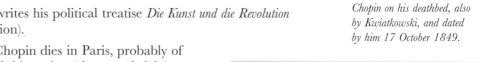

Chopin on his deathbed, also by Kwiatkowski, and dated by him 17 October 1849.

Liszt playing the piano, on which reposes a bust of Beethoven, with Marie d'Agoult at his feet. The seated figure immediately behind Liszt is George Sand in male attire. At left, also seated, is Alexandre Dumas, with Victor Hugo standing behind. The two figures in the centre are Paganini and Rossini, and behind them is a portrait of Byron.

■ Liszt's Legacy

Writing in December 1876 about the first performance in London of Liszt's *Mazeppa*, George Bernard Shaw entitled his article 'Liszt the Charlatan'. It is perhaps easy to condemn Liszt for doing so much in so many musical domains, some of it not particularly well. Such a view, however, ignores much that was positive about Liszt, and his reputation as a pianist has never been called into question. A writer for London's *The Musical World* in 1841 certainly found Liszt's playing inspiring:

'We walk through this world in the midst of so many wonders that our senses become indifferent to the most amazing things: light and life, the ocean, the forest, the voice and flight of the pigmy lark, are unheeded commonplaces; and it is only when some comet, some giant, some tiger-tamer…some winged being appears, that our obdurate fancies are roused into the consciousness that miracles do exist. Of the miracle genus is M. Liszt…the Aurora Borealis [Northern Lights] of musical effulgence, the Niagara of thundering harmonies!'

Reaction against such hyperbole was inevitable, though no one who had heard the music that Liszt composed for keyboard could accuse him of charlatanism. Critics of his orchestral and choral music, however, find patent weaknesses in its structure.

One of Liszt's major contributions was the immense amount of energy he poured into promoting and supporting the music and careers of others – usually younger composers – like Wagner, Berlioz and Schumann, especially during his Weimar years. In addition, through the force of his personality, he enhanced the status of music and musicians generally.

1850-55
Wagner and Verdi

Although Paris remains the home of grand opera, and is the goal of every aspiring opera composer, Wagner and Verdi – the two giants of the form – are the products of the German and Italian traditions respectively. Both will produce operas for Paris, but ultimately they will assert their independence and support their native traditions.

One of a series of photographs taken of Verdi in Paris in the early 1850s, when he was already an internationally recognized composer, and soon to embark on a new phase of his career with the first performance of his opera Rigoletto.

1850 Wagner publishes his anti-Semitic essay *Das Judentum in der Musik* (Jewishness in Music, ■ p.171).

• **19 February** Berlioz inaugurates the first concert of his Société Philharmonique in Paris, established to rival the Concerts du Conservatoire, but it lasts only until May next year.

• **31 March** Schumann accepts the post as director of municipal music in Düsseldorf.

• **1 June** The Bachgesellschaft, conceived to publish all Bach's known music, is inaugurated in Leipzig.

• **25 June** Schumann's opera *Genoveva* (p.161) is moderately successful when performed for the first time in the Stadttheater, Leipzig, conducted by the composer.

• **28 August** Liszt conducts the first performance of Wagner's *Lohengrin* in Weimar. This year Wagner makes sketches for *Siegfrieds Tod* (Siegfried's Death), which will become *Götterdämmerung* (The Twilight of the Gods), the fourth and final opera of *The Ring* cycle.

• **10–24 October** Schumann composes his Cello Concerto.

1851 6 February Schumann conducts the first performance of his Third or *Rhenish* Symphony in Düsseldorf.

• **11 March** First performance of Verdi's *Rigoletto* (left) at the Teatro La Fenice, Venice.

• **May** Wagner makes sketches for *Der junge Siegfried* (Young Siegfried), later to become *Siegfried*, the third opera of *The Ring* cycle.

• **3–19 December** Schumann revises his Fourth Symphony.

1852 13 June Liszt conducts the first performance of Schumann's incidental music to Byron's *Manfred* in Weimar.

• **26 June** Schumann goes to Godesberg to take a cure for a worsening illness that has been affecting him since the beginning of April.

• **1 July** Wagner completes the poem of *Die Walküre* (The Valkyrie), the second opera of *The Ring*.

• **3 November** Wagner completes the poem of *Das Rheingold* (The Gold of the Rhine), the first opera of *The Ring*.

• **21 November** Schumann shows signs of his incipient insanity.

1853 Liszt completes his Piano Sonata in B Minor.

• Brahms completes his Piano Sonata in C Major, Op.1.

• **19 January** First performance of Verdi's *Il trovatore* (opposite) at the Teatro Apollo, Rome.

A set for the dungeon scene, of Verdi's opera Il trovatore, *during which the 'Misere', one of the most famous passages in the whole of opera, is sung.*

• **6 March** First production of Verdi's *La traviata* at the Teatro La Fenice, Venice.

• **21 September** Schumann starts to compose a Violin Concerto for Joachim, aged twenty-two.

• **30 September** Brahms, aged twenty, is introduced to Schumann and Clara Schumann by the violinist Joachim. He remains in Düsseldorf until 3 November.

• **27 October** Schumann conducts what is to be his last concert in Düsseldorf.

1854 Liszt conducts the first performances of his SYMPHONIC POEMS *Orpheus, Les Préludes,* and *Mazeppa* in Weimar this year.

• **27 February** Schumann tries to commit suicide by throwing himself into the Rhine. He is taken to an asylum, where Clara cannot see him.

• **3 July** Birth of Janáček in Hukvaldy, Moravia.

• **10 December** *L'Enfance du Christ* (The Childhood of Christ), Berlioz's ORATORIO, is given complete for the first time in Paris.

1855 17 February First performance of Liszt's Piano Concerto in E-flat, with the composer as soloist and Berlioz conducting in Weimar.

• **March–June** Wagner is in London to conduct the Philharmonic season, but is savagely treated by the press. He makes closer acquaintance with Berlioz, who is also conducting in London at this time.

• **13 June** Verdi's *Les Vêpres siciliennes* (The Sicilian Vespers) is given for the first time at the Paris Opéra.

▲ *Opera in Weimar*

Poster for the first performance of Wagner's Lohengrin *at the court theatre in Weimar in August 1850, more than two years after its completion. The birth of Goethe was also celebrated on this occasion.*

About the middle of September the theatre opened, and we went to hear Verdi's Ernani *(p.158)*. Liszt looked splendid as he conducted the opera. The grand outline of his face and floating hair were seen to advantage as they were thrown into dark relief by the stage lamps. We were so fortunate as to hear all three of Wagner's most celebrated operas while we were at Weimar. G[eorge Henry Lewes], however, had not the patience to sit out more than two acts of Lohengrin *[left]*; and, indeed, I too was weary. The declamation appeared to me monotonous, and situations...were dwelt on fatiguingly. Without feeling competent to pass a judgment on this opera as music, one may venture to say it fails in one grand requisite of art, based on an unchangeable element in human nature – the need for contrast. With the Fliegender Holländer *[p.158]* I was delighted; the poem and the music were alike charming. The Tannhäuser *[p.158]*, too, created in me a great desire to hear it again. Many of the situations, and much of the music, struck me as remarkably fine. And I appreciated these operas all the better retrospectively when we saw Der Freischütz *[p.142]*, which I had never before heard and seen on the stage. The effect of the delicious music, with which one is so familiar, was completely spoiled by the absence of recitative, and the terrible lapsus from melody to ordinary speech. The bacchanalian song seemed simply ridiculous, sung at a little pot-house table at a party of two, one of whom was sunk in melancholy; and the absurdity reached a ne plus ultra, *when Caspar climbed a tree, apparently with the sole purpose of being shot.*

George Eliot, *Journal*, August–October 1854

1856-58
Offenbach: Opera's Lighter Side

Mining a seam of operatic richness that has more in common with Rossini than Wagner or Verdi, Offenbach brings delight to millions with his lighthearted approach to traditional themes — especially those from Classical mythology — that have inspired composers over the last two hundred years or more.

1856 3 January Liszt conducts at a festival in Vienna to celebrate the centenary of the birth of Mozart.

• **4 February** First performance of Verdi's *I vespri siciliani* (Les Vêpres siciliennes, p.165) at the Teatro La Scala, Milan.

• **23 March** Wagner finishes the score of his opera *Die Walküre* (p.164).

• **9 April** *Le Docteur Miracle* (Doctor Miracle), Bizet's one-act OPERETTA, is given at the Bouffes-Parisiens. This year he wins the Prix de Rome ● (p.181).

• **July** Liszt completes his *Dante* Symphony.

• **29 July** Schumann dies, aged forty-six, in Endenich.

• **31 August** Liszt's *Missa solennis* is first performed at Esztergom, Hungary.

• **September** Wagner begins composing *Siegfried*.

• **19 December** Wagner begins his sketches for *Tristan and Isolde*.

1857 7 January Liszt's Second Piano Concerto is first performed in Weimar by his pupil Hans von Bronsart, with the composer conducting.

• **22 January** Hans von Bülow gives the first performance of Liszt's Piano Sonata in B Minor in Berlin.

• **15 February** Death of Glinka, aged fifty-two, in Berlin.

• **12 March** First performance of Verdi's *Simone Boccanegra* at the Teatro La Fenice, Venice.

• **2 June** Elgar is born at Broadheath, near Worcester.

• **9 August** Wagner temporarily stops composing *Siegfried*.

'Love is like the Opéra: one is bored there, yet returns when Le Papillon *[The Butterfly], with music by Offenbach, is performed.'*
Flaubert, *L'Autographe*, December 1864

Wagner's 'Asyl' or refuge near the villa the Wesendoncks were building outside Zürich (opposite). Here he and his wife lived from April 1857 until August 1858, while he pursued his affair with Mathilde Wesendonck, the wife of his benefactor.

• **18 August** Liszt's daughter Cosima marries Hans von Bülow ★ (p.170). On their honeymoon the couple visit the Wagners.

• Wagner works on *Tristan and Isolde*, and sets to music five of the poems of Mathilde Wesendonck, with whom he is now in love (left).

• **5 September** Liszt's *Faust* Symphony receives its first performance in Weimar.

• **7 November** Liszt's Symphony to Dante's *Divine Comedy*, in reality two SYMPHONIC POEMS, is heard for the first time in Dresden.

OTHER EVENTS
1856 Buchanan wins US presidential election
• Death of Heine

1857 Baudelaire: *Les fleurs du mal*
• Flaubert: *Madame Bovary*

1858 Formation of Suez Canal Company
• The Ringstrasse begins to be built in Vienna

1858 Berlioz completes his opera *Les Troyens* (The Trojans) and reads it to Wagner, who is in Paris in January.

• **7 April** Wagner's wife, Minna, intercepts a letter of his to Mathilde Wesendonck, and so discovers the nature of their relationship. Wagner eventually leaves their home for good on 17 August and journeys to Venice, where he resumes work on *Tristan and Isolde*.

• **21 October** First performance of Offenbach's *Orpheus in the Underworld* at the Bouffes-Parisiens, Paris ■ (below).

• **15 December** First performance of Cornelius's opera *The Barber of Baghdad* in Weimar provokes hostility against Liszt, who resigns.

• **23 December** Puccini is born in Lucca.

The Wesendonck villa near Zürich, painted in 1857 (above). Wagner had met the silk merchant and his wife five years previously, and his infatuation for Mathilde provided the inspiration for Tristan and Isolde.

■ *The Offenbach Phenomenon*

Offenbach was sent to Paris at the age of fourteen by his father, a Jewish CANTOR in Cologne, because he felt that the French capital offered decidedly better prospects for a musical career than his native Germany at that time. He married in 1844 and in 1860 obtained French citizenship, by which time he had already firmly established his reputation in Paris and was on the verge of international fame.

In 1855 Offenbach had taken over a small theatre on the Champs-Elysées which he called the Bouffes-Parisiens, but within a year he had moved to the Passage Choiseul and took the name with him. His new style of OPERETTA reflected the move, for these were more sophisticated works in three acts, which

were given the name *opéra-bouffe*. Starting with *Orpheus in the Underworld*, he used more competent LIBRETTISTS, and an element of satire, directed against the comfortable world of the French Empire under Napoleon III. At this time the romantic content of the operas was lessened and Offenbach introduced a more unbridled type of music, which can be found in the can-can in *Orpheus*.

Offenbach yearned, however, to write a grand opera, and as the tide began to turn against *opéra-bouffe* in the last years of his life, he embarked on what was for him a totally new venture with *The Tales of Hoffmann* (p.182), which he virtually managed to complete before his death, though the first performance took place posthumously.

Offenbach's Orpheus in the Underworld, *the composer's first great success, which ran for two hundred and twenty-eight consecutive performances at the Bouffes-Parisiens – a record for its time.*

1859-64
International Romanticism

With the arrival of Wagner's opera Tannhäuser *in Paris (despite the scandal it causes), and the completion of Gounod's* Faust — *the setting of which become an almost obligatory exercise for any self-respecting Romantic composer — it is clear that the international language of music is now that of Romanticism.*

A caricature showing Verdi rehearsing his opera Un ballo in maschera (A Masked Ball) in Naples, where the work was originally to have been performed in the Carnival season of 1858. An attempted assassination of Napoleon III, however, caused the authorities to ban the opera, as the plot concerns the murder of Gustavus III of Sweden.

1859 February The French government committee, of which Rossini is the absentee president, establishes standard musical PITCH, giving it the weight of legal status.

• **17 February** Verdi's *Un ballo in maschera* (A Masked Ball) is first performed at the Teatro Apollo in Rome, despite problems with the censor over the LIBRETTO (left).

• **19 March** Gounod's *Faust* is first performed at the Théâtre-Lyrique, Paris, and is transferred to the Opéra, with RECITATIVES and ballet, setting the seal on the composer's success.

• **6 August** Wagner completes the composition of his opera *Tristan and Isolde* (p.166) in Lucerne.

• **2 October** *The Beatitudes*, part of Liszt's ORATORIO *Christus*, is performed in Weimar.

• **17 November** Wagner's wife joins him in Paris in an attempt to salvage their marriage, but their relationship is irreparably damaged.

• **13 December** The death of Liszt's son Daniel, aged twenty, in Berlin causes the composer great grief.

1860 March Wagner, who has publicly criticized Rossini's music, calls on the older composer in Paris, when they patch up their differences and discuss current musical trends.

• **13 March** Wolf is born in Windischgrätz, now Slovenjgradec.

• **7 July** Mahler is born in Kalište, Bohemia.

• **9 July** A new French version of Rossini's opera *Semiramide* (p.144) is a resounding success when first performed at the Paris Opéra.

• **6 November** Paderewski is born in Kurylówka, Poland.

1861 Verdi is commissioned to write an opera for the Imperial Theatre in St Petersburg. He begins writing *La forza del destino* (The Force of Destiny), and plans a trip to Russia (right).

• **13 March** After one hundred and sixty-four rehearsals, the revised staging of Wagner's *Tannhäuser* at the Paris Opéra is a fiasco and has only three performances, largely due to opposition from the Jockey Club. Its failure provides an opportunity for Berlioz's opera *Les Troyens* (The Trojans) to be accepted by the Paris Opéra.

OTHER EVENTS
1859 Millet: *The Angelus*
• Darwin: *Origin of Species*
• Tennyson: *Idylls of the King*

1860 Bohemia is granted political automony
• Degas: *Spartan Boys and Girls Excercising*
• Manet: *Spanish Guitar Player*
• George Elliot: *The Mill on the Floss*

1861 Emancipation of serfs in Russia
• Unification of Italy
• Civil war starts in America

1862 Bismarck becomes Chancellor of Prussia
• Hugo: *Les misérables*
• Turgenev: *Fathers and Sons*

1863 Gettysburg Address; emancipation proclamation
• Manet: *Olympia*

Verdi's passport (right) for his visit to Russia in 1861. He was in St Petersburg for the first performance of La forza del destino *at the Imperial Theatre in November 1862. Tsar Alexander II gave Verdi 20,000 roubles for the work.*

The cover of Bizet's piano score arrangement of his opera The Pearl Fishers, first performed when the composer was still only twenty-five. Its famous duet for tenor and baritone, early in the opera, is the only part generally still heard.

• **May** Liszt visits Paris, where he plays before Napoleon III and meets Wagner, Marie d'Agoult (p.152) and the twenty-two-year-old Bizet.

• **August** The first festival of the *Allgemeiner Deutscher Musikverein* takes place in Weimar.

• **Autumn** Princess Carolyne zu Sayne-Wittgenstein, who has been having an affair with Liszt, is granted a divorce, enabling her to marry the composer. The date is set for 22 October, Liszt's fiftieth birthday, but at the last minute the annulment is revoked.

• **November** Wagner begins the text of *Die Meistersinger von Nürnberg* (The Mastersingers of Nuremberg).

• **18 December** MacDowell is born in New York.

1862 Ludwig von Köchel begins his comprehensive catalogue of Mozart's compositions.

• **29 January** Birth of Delius in Bradford, Yorkshire.

• **22 August** Debussy is born in Saint-Germain-en-Laye.

• **September** Liszt's daughter Blandine dies at the age of twenty-six, having given birth to a son in July.

• **November** Wagner sees his wife in Dresden for the last time.

• **10 November** Verdi's opera *La forza del destino* (opposite) is first performed at the Imperial Theatre, St Petersburg.

• **23 November** The critic Eduard Hanslick ★ (p.175), caricatured in Wagner's *Die Meistersinger*, angrily leaves a reading of the text.

1863 The arrangement whereby Berlioz's opera *Les Troyens* is to be mounted at the Paris Opéra falls through, as the directors believe that the five hours necessary for a complete performance is too long.

• **11 July** The pope visits Liszt at his new residence, the monastery of the Madonna del Rosario, and hears him play the piano.

• **Summer** Rossini begins to compose his *Petite Messe solennelle* (right) his last composition of substance.

• **30 September** Bizet's opera *The Pearl Fishers* (above) is first performed at the Théâtre-Lyrique in Paris. Berlioz's encouraging review of the work, published on 8 October, is the latter's last piece of critical writing.

• **4 November** The second part of Berlioz's opera *Les Troyens*, entitled *Les Troyens à Carthage* (The Trojans at Carthage), is given at the Théâtre-Lyrique, Paris. It is a great success, and has twenty-one performances, though Berlioz deplores the liberties taken with his score.

★ *The annotation in Rossini's own hand, on the dedication page of his* Petite Messe solennelle. *He specifies twelve singers of three sexes, men, women and castrati, eight for the chorus and four for the solos. Since he always referred to his late works as the sins of his old age, he tells God that 'this little composition' is the last mortal sin of his old age.*

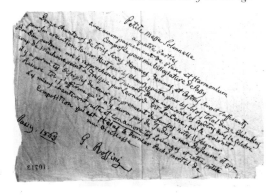

Liszt at the keyboard, with his daughter Cosima and her husband the conductor Hans von Bülow (right), photographed in Pest in August 1865.

1864 Brahms composes his *Lieder* (Songs) Op.33 and his Piano Quintet in F Minor, originally written as a string quintet, but rewritten, following the suggestions of Clara Schumann, for piano and strings.

• Grieg publishes a set of four Danish songs, *Heart Melodies*, written for his future wife, the singer Nina Hagerup.

• **March** Wagner is forced to leave Vienna, due to mounting debts. He is saved from embarrassment by King Ludwig II of Bavaria (opposite), who settles his arrears and houses him near Munich.

• **14 March** Rossini's *Petite Messe solennelle* ★ (p.169) is performed for the first time in Paris to mark the dedication of the private chapel at the home of Countess Pillet-Will.

• **19 March** Gounod's opera *Mireille*, based on a Provençal poem, is first performed at the Théâtre-Lyrique in Paris.

• **2 May** Meyerbeer dies, aged seventy-two, in Paris, having completed his final opera *L'Africaine* (The African Maid).

• **June** Liszt pays his first visit to the peaceful Villa d'Este at Tivoli ★ (p.180), where some of his best-loved piano music is to be written.

'I am in my sixty-first year; past hopes, past illusions, past lofty thoughts and high ideals.'
Berlioz, writing in 1864

• **June** Cosima von Bülow (above) visits Wagner near Munich, and they become lovers.

• **11 June** Richard Strauss is born in Munich.

• **August** Liszt visits Karslruhe with his daughter Cosima, and they go on to visit Wagner.

• **29 September** Bruckner's Mass in D Minor is completed and first performed in Linz on 20 November. He also finishes a symphony, which he later disparagingly designates as 'Number 0', this year.

• **October** Liszt visits Paris with his daughter Cosima.

• **17 December** Offenbach's *La Belle Hélène* (Beautiful Helen) is performed for the first time at the Théâtre des Variétés in Paris, which confirms that the composer has entered on the period of his greatest successes ■ (p.167).

OTHER EVENTS
1864 First International Workingmen's Association founded by Karl Marx
• First ascent of Matterhorn
• First successful transatlantic cable
• Lewis Carroll: *Alice in Wonderland*
• Tolstoy: *War and Peace*

■ *Wagner – God or Demon?*

Wagner is no doubt the most notorious example of the Romantic composer, a concept which he probably did more than anyone else to create and foster, though to which others such as Paganini, Berlioz and Wagner's father-in-law Liszt all contributed in various ways. There is much to deplore in Wagner's personality. By many acounts he was a rude, arrogant, selfish, greedy, bigoted, lascivious man. Certainly, he argued with many of his contemporaries, including Rossini (p.168), and could be disparaging about others'

A portrait of Wagner painted originally for his patron Ludwig II of Bavaria, whose bust is seen on the right of the picture. The king identified closely with the character of Lohengrin as portrayed in Wagner's opera.

work. He was outspokenly racist and published a notorious essay entitled *Das Judentum in der Musik* (p.164), accusing Jews of being cultural parasites. He also was criticized for his moral values – his first marriage was unhappy, and he had a series of relationships with married women, before living with Cosima (opposite).

That Wagner had genius, however, cannot be denied, and through sheer determination he realized his dream of opera as a unified artistic experience, and in so doing developed the form to unprecedented heights.

Wagner's relationship with Liszt was one of father and son, as can be seen from the very basic advice given by the older composer early in his career – Wagner was to be opportunistic, engineering his future success, while writing for the musical press. It was almost as if Liszt was his publicist, but then Liszt did know about promoting composers, and worked hard on behalf of others ■ (p.163).

Clearly Wagner's music is not accessible to all. Many agree with Rossini's words to the German composer Emil Naumann that Wagner has some good moments but some bad quarters of an hour. On the other hand, Rossini freely admitted that there were certain of Wagner's works that he wished he had written himself. Certainly music would never be the same again. At the very least Wagner opened up new dimensions, not only on the stage but also in orchestral sonority.

1865-67
The Music of Eastern Europe

The increase of interest in the music of Russia and the national idiom of the eastern extremities of the Austro-Hungarian empire, as seen in the works of Liszt and Brahms, helps to give stimulus to a rebirth of native music in countries such as Bohemia, long under foreign domination, but now finding their own voices.

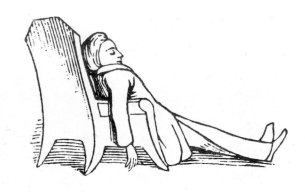

A caricature of the conductor Hans von Bülow during rehearsals of Tristan and Isolde *published in the Münchener Punsch in 1865.*

1865 Liszt surprises the world by taking minor orders in the church.

• **10 April** An illegitimate daughter, Isolde, is born to Wagner and Cosima ■ (p.171).

• **9 June** Nielsen is born on the Island of Funen, Denmark ● (opposite).

• **10 June** Wagner's *Tristan and Isolde* (p.166) is first given under Hans von Bülow in Munich (left).

• **17 July** Wagner begins to dictate *Mein Leben* (My Life).

• **10 August** Glazunov is born in St Petersburg ● (opposite).

• **December** Wagner is banished from Bavaria by King Ludwig II when his affair with Cosima causes a public scandal.

• **8 December** Sibelius is born at Hämeenlinna, Finland ● (opposite).

1866 Death of Wagner's first wife, Minna, in Dresden.

• **30 May** First performance of Smetana's second opera, *The Bartered Bride*, at the Provisional Theatre, Prague ● (opposite).

• **25 November** Bruckner completes his Mass in E minor.

1867 Berlioz is devastated by the death of his son.

• Johann Strauss (right) performs his *Blue Danube* waltz for the first time at the Paris Exhibition.

• **February** Berlioz conducts excerpts from his last opera, *Béatrice et Bénédict* in Cologne.

• **17 February** Birth of Wagner and Cosima's daughter Eva.

• **11 March** Verdi's *Don Carlos* is first performed at the Paris Opéra.

• **6 July** Liszt's *Christmas Oratorio*, from the now complete *Christus* (p.168), is given in Rome.

• **14 September** Bruckner begins his Mass in F Minor.

• **1 December** In Vienna, three movements from Brahms's *German Requiem* ★ (p.174) are performed.

OTHER EVENTS
1865 Assassination of Abraham Lincoln
• Thirteenth amendment (outlawing slavery) to US constitution ratified

1866 Christian Science founded
• Dostoyevsky: *Crime and Punishment*

1867 Alaska purchased from Russia for US
• Ibsen: *Peer Gynt*
• Marx: *Das Kapital*

Johann Strauss the Younger conducting at a court ball. In 1853 he had given the majority of the conducting work to his brother Joseph, though he would usually appear for the summer season.

The first edition of Smetana's From Bohemia's Woods and Meadows, *a movement of the symphonic suite that evolved over a period of some eight years and became known as* Má Vlast *(p.178).*

● *Eastern Europe Awakes*

The year 1848 was one of revolutions in Europe, a great explosion of nationalist feelings across the continent, especially in the east where Poland, Bohemia, Hungary and other nations had been absorbed by their larger neighbours. National languages had usually been suppressed in favour of those of the ruling power, but a growing awareness of the richness of the native culture and the potential strength of national identity was reflected in the rebirth of literature and music. Old traditions were explored, folk music and its idiom revived, which in turn fuelled nationalism.

Liszt, who did so much to support musicians generally ■ (p.163), made himself a champion of the cause of Hungary, especially through such works as his ORATORIO *The Legend of Saint Elizabeth* (below), though his right to be regarded as Hungarian was often questioned. Moreover the gypsy-style music, which he and Brahms introduced in works such as Liszt's *Hungarian Rhapsodies* (p.160), was decried as false. This may be true, but it awakened interest, people believed in it, and in turn others came to realise that there was more to music than the accepted international Romantic style that prevailed almost throughout Europe.

In Bohemia the situation was somewhat different, for that country was a distillation of European influences. In opera, it imitated the Italians, and in symphonies and chamber music it echoed the styles of German and Austrian masters. Then the wave of nationalism, which induced the Austrian leaders to grant Bohemia political automony in 1860, led native artists to develop a national art. In music, composers such as Smetana (above) turned to their folk lore. Meanwhile, the births of Nielsen, Glazunov and Sibelius, all in 1865, presaged a challenge to the supremacy of German music.

The title page of Liszt's oratorio The Legend of Saint Elizabeth, *completed in 1862 and first performed in Pest three years later, when the composer took minor orders in the Church.*

1868-70
Brahms: a New Bach or Beethoven?

A young man from Hamburg, a long established stronghold of musical excellence in northern Germany, combines Romanticism and Classicism in a way that for many music lovers recalls his great predecessors, Bach and Beethoven. For his cool and controlled intensity, combined with a deeply felt lyricism, Brahms will gain many devotees in the years ahead.

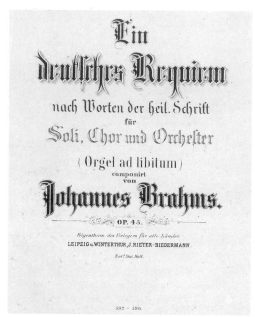

★ *The title page of Brahms's* German Requiem. *It took the composer nearly eleven years to complete this, his greatest choral work. There were incomplete performances in 1867 (p.172) and 1868.*

1868 Grieg, aged twenty-five, completes his Piano Concerto, which he will play to Liszt, in Rome.

• **February** Tchaikovsky writes his First Symphony.

• **10 February** Rossini's opera *William Tell* (p.148) has its five hundredth performance at the Paris Opéra.

• **10 April** The first four movements of Brahms's *German Requiem* (left) are performed in Bremen Cathedral to a rapturous reception.

• **21 June** Wagner's *Die Meistersinger* (p.169) receives its first performance in the Court Theatre, Munich, conducted by Von Bülow.

• **26 September** Rossini holds the last of his Saturday musical evenings in his Paris apartment.

• **1 October** Bruckner begins teaching as a professor at the Vienna Conservatory.

• **November** Cosima goes to live with Wagner.

• **13 November** Rossini dies in Paris, aged seventy-six. Over four thousand people attend his funeral.

1869 Brahms publishes the first two volumes of his *Hungarian Dances*, written for piano DUET, in which he refers strongly to Hungarian folk and gypsy music ● (p.173).

• Wagner resumes composing *Siegfried* (p.166), the third drama of his opera cycle *The Ring* (p.164).

• **Spring** Wagner publishes a reprint of his essay *Das Judentum in der Musik* ■ (p.171), against the advice of his friends.

• **8 March** Berlioz dies, aged sixty-five, in Paris. He is buried three days later in Montmartre cemetery.

• **5 April** Birth of Roussel in Tourcoing.

• **6 June** Wagner and Cosima have a son, Siegfried.

• **August** Liszt is in Munich and attends rehearsals of Wagner's opera *Das Rheingold* (p.164).

• **22 September** Wagner's *Das Rheingold* is first performed in Munich under the direction of a local conductor, Franz Wüllner, despite the composer's strenuous efforts to prevent it.

• **Christmas** Wagner reads his sketch for *Parsifal* to Nietzsche, who has become a frequent visitor.

OTHER EVENTS
1868 Browning: *The Ring and the Book*
• Dostoyevsky: *The Idiot*

1869 Opening of Suez Canal
• First US transcontinental railway
• First Vatican Council
• Verne: *20,000 Leagues under the Sea*

1870 Schliemann excavates site of Troy
• Rome becomes capital of Italy
• Franco-Prussian War
• Papal infallibility proclaimed at Vatican Council

'The German Requiem *is a work of exceptional significance and high craftsmanship.*' The anti-Wagnerian critic Eduard Hanslick.

1870 25 May First performance of the ballet *Coppélia*, with music by Delibes, at the Paris Opéra.

• 26 June Wagner's opera *Die Walküre* (p.164) is first performed in Munich, again without the composer's participation, though Liszt subsequently attends.

• July Mussorgsky submits his opera *Boris Godunov*, completed the year before, to the direction of the Imperial Theatres for performance.

• 18 July Hans von Bülow's marriage to Cosima is officially dissolved.

• 25 August Wagner marries Cosima in a Protestant church in Lucerne.

• Summer Tchaikovsky extensively revises his fantasy OVERTURE *Romeo and Juliet*, composed the previous October–November, in response to Balakirev's comments.

★ *A portrait of Brahms made about the time that he first arrived in Vienna in 1862 and met Eduard Hanslick, then visiting professor in music history at the university. By engaging Brahms as a pianist to illustrate his lectures, Hanslick introduced him to intellectual society.*

★ *Eduard Hanslick with quill pen, as doyen of musical criticism, tells Wagner how to compose.*

■ *Welcome, Brahms!*

In October 1853 Schumann had written a piece in the music review *Neue Zeitschrift für Musik* which described Brahms in terms that he might well have found embarrassing: 'He has arrived, this chosen youth, over whose cradle the Graces and Heroes seem to have watched. His name is Johannes Brahms; he comes from Hamburg, where he has been working in quiet obscurity…. His outward appearance alone assures us that he is one of the chosen. Seated at the piano, he opened up miraculous regions. We were drawn into an enchanted circle.'

Schumann continued in the same spirit at great length, but what follows, when one looks beneath the words, is an interesting assessment of Brahms's achievement up to this point. First was his ability to conjure almost orchestral INSTRUMENTAL TIMBRES from the piano, then the lyrical quality of his SONATAS, which Schumann compares with symphonies, and lastly the variety of his output, both in form and content, which could be tempestuous, but all within one unified and unifying stream of creativity. He ends: 'His comrades greet him on his first step in the world, where possibly wounds await him, but the bay and laurel also; we welcome this brave warrior.'

1871-73
Bizet Enlivens French Music

Although he is near the end of his brief career, Bizet brings a welcome freshness and lightness to French music. He devotes himself to composing opéra comique, *though his harmony is too advanced for the average opera lover. This, and an unsatisfactory libretto, causes the failure of his next opera,* Djamileh, *but he will soon write one of the world's most popular operas,* Carmen.

1871 Wagner completes the SCORE of *Siegfried* (p.174).

• Brahms writes his *Schicksalslied* (Song of Fate) for chorus and orchestra.

• Johann Strauss the Younger composes his OPERETTA *Indigo, or The Forty Thieves* ● (p.183).

• **April** Having determined to produce *The Ring* (p.164) at a festival in Bayreuth, the Wagners visit the town, but decide a new opera house will have to be built for the purpose.

• **November** The Bayreuth municipal council offer Wagner a free site for the new opera house.

• **December** Amidst a storm of publicity Wagner's *Lohengrin* is staged in Bologna, the first time any Wagner opera has been mounted in Italy.

• **24 December** Verdi's opera *Aida* (below), commissioned to celebrate the opening of the new opera house in Cairo, has its first performance.

1872 6 January Birth of Scriabin in Moscow.

• **22 May** The foundation stone of the Bayreuth opera house is laid.

• **11 September** Bruckner completes his Second Symphony, but it is rejected by the Vienna Philharmonic Orchestra.

• **October** Liszt makes a visit to Bayreuth, marking an improvement in relations with the Wagners.

• **12 October** Vaughan Williams is born at Down Ampney, Gloucestershire.

• **November** Wagner looks for singers for Bayreuth.

• **10 November** Bizet's newly-orchestrated SUITE, based on his music for Daudet's play *L'Arlésienne* (The Maid of Arles) is received with enthusiasm in Paris.

1873 Brahms writes his first String Quartets Op.51.

• **7 February** Tchaikovsky's Second Symphony, known as the *Little Russian*, is first given in Moscow.

• **1 April** Birth of Rachmaninov in Semyonovo.

• **May** The death of Alessandro Manzoni prompts Verdi to start work on a Requiem Mass for his friend, to be performed a year after the writer's death.

• **29 May** Liszt conducts the first complete hearing of his ORATORIO *Christus* (p.168) in Weimar.

• **31 December** Bruckner completes his Third Symphony, which he dedicates to Wagner.

OTHER EVENTS
1871 Bismarck becomes Chancellor of Germany
• Paris Commune; Third Republic
• Darwin: *The Descent of Man*

1872 Civil War in Spain
• Whistler: *The Artist's Mother*
• Daudet: *Tartarin de Tarascon*
• Nietzsche: *The Birth of Tragedy*

1873 Republic proclaimed in Spain
• Tolstoy begins *Anna Karenina*

A poster for Verdi's Aida *for a production at Teatro La Fenice, Venice, in 1881, ten years after its first performance in Cairo. Although commissioned to celebrate the opening of the Cairo opera house, it was not given there until two years later.*

The setting for Act One of the original production of Bizet's opera Carmen *at the Opéra-Comique in 1875. Bizet died during one of the early performances and it is said that the same evening Célestine Galli-Marie, who sang the title role, almost collapsed during the fortune-telling card scene on stage, and then did so in the wings, although no news of Bizet's death had reached the theatre.*

■ *Bizet Challenges Wagner and Liszt*

Bizet may not have been very perceptive when he declared that Berlioz had genius but lacked talent, but on Wagner he was more accurate. He saw all too clearly that French opera was now in thrall, and as he wrote to his mother-in-law, Madame Halévy in May 1871, he was no friend of Wagner's, whom he saw as the voice of nineteenth-century Germany. He also believed Wagner to be so thick-skinned that he was impervious to criticism ■ (p.171). Indeed, he wondered whether he had a heart. And yet, Bizet was unable to deny his immense enjoyment of Wagner's music, its fascination, tenderness and luxuriousness. The last thing he would do, however, would be to imitate him, and if he thought that he was doing so, he would abandon composition. As he expressed it in another letter to Madame Halévy three days later, 'the more beautiful the model is, the more ridiculous the imitation becomes'.

Bizet had much more individuality than being simply an anti-Wagnerite, as his opera *Carmen* (above) clearly demonstrates. For all his admiration of Wagner's musical achievement, Bizet found his treatment of love unreal, by implication, whereas *Carmen* is about passion, and as such almost anti-romantic, though not necessarily anti-Romantic. Tchaikovsky, who had been sent the score in 1875, though he did not see the opera until 1876, was so deeply moved by it, that his brother Modest declared that he had an almost unwholesome passion for it. As unlike anything by Tchaikovsky as one might imagine, apart from *The Queen of Spades* ★ (p.188), Bizet's opera impressed itself on the Russian by its sincerity, although he was uncomfortable with the reality that he saw as decadence. It was, however, precisely the reality that was to renew opera as the century drew towards its close.

1874-76
Mussorgsky: the Voice of Russia

Although only one of his operas, Boris Godunov, *is staged during his lifetime, and he writes very little for the orchestra, Mussorgsky makes an enormous contribution to Western music in general and Russian music in particular. His realism, and his ability to penetrate and portray character in music are unique.*

1874 Mussorgksy (right) completes two major works this year, his *Pictures at an Exhibition* (opposite), and the SONG CYCLE *Sunless*.

• **8 February** Mussorgsky's complete *Boris Godunov* (below) is performed in St Petersburg and is received with enthusiasm.

> *'Wagner ... at the moment does not receive anyone.'*
> Tchaikovsky to his brother Modest, August 1876

• **27 March** *The Two Widows*, Smetana's new opera, is received with great enthusiasm, but its popularity is short-lived. The composer begins work on the large SYMPHONIC CYCLE *Má Vlast* ★ (p.173).

• **5 April** J. Strauss's operetta *Die Fledermaus* (The Bat) is given in Vienna.

• **22 May** Verdi's Requiem (p.176), conducted by the composer, has its first performance in the Church of San Marco, Milan. Although condemned by Wagnerites and those who find it too operatic, it is destined to become one of Verdi's most esteemed works.

• **13 September** Schoenberg is born in Vienna.

• **20 October** Ives is born in Danbury, Connecticut.

• **21 November** Wagner completes the SCORE of *The Ring* (p.164).

• **22 November** Bruckner completes his Fourth Symphony.

Portrait of Mussorgsky painted after he had been admitted to hospital suffering from alcoholic epilepsy in March 1881. Three weeks later he was dead.

1875 5 January A new Paris Opéra, rebuilt to a design by Charles Garnier after a fire, is officially opened by President Mac-Mahon.

• **14 February** Bruckner begins his Fifth Symphony.

• **3 March** Bizet's *Carmen* ■ (p.177) is first performed at the Opéra-Comique in Paris, but is condemned for its indecency, its dramatic weaknesses and its paucity of melody.

• **7 March** Birth of Ravel in Ciboure, near Saint-Jean-de-Luz.

• **14 March** *Vyšehrad*, the first section of Smetana's *Má Vlast*, has its first performance and is enthusiastically received.

• **4 April** *Vltava*, the second part of *Má Vlast*, is also received well, but Smetana is now deaf, and cannot hear the music or applause.

• **3 June** Bizet dies, aged thirty-six, in Paris.

1876 22 April Tchaikovsky completes his ballet *Swan Lake*.

• **16 May** Bruckner finishes the first draft of his Fifth Symphony.

• **13 August** First complete performance of Wagner's *The Ring*, in Bayreuth (opposite). Liszt, who is present, meets Tchaikovsky.

• **4 November** First performance of Brahms's First Symphony, conducted by Otto Dessoff, in Karlsruhe.

Title page of the first edition of Mussorgsky's opera Boris Godunov, *which was dismissed by the critics at its first performance, but warmly applauded by the public.*

OTHER EVENTS

1874 First Impressionist Exhibition in Paris

1875 Mary Baker Eddy: *Science and Health*
• Tolstoy completes *Anna Karenina*

1876 Telephone invented by Bell
• Renoir: *Le bal du Moulin de la Galette*
• Mallarmé: *L'après-midi d'un faune*
• Twain: *Tom Sawyer*

Hartmann's design for the main façade of the Great Gate of Kiev, which is thought to reflect the female and male elements of Russian headwear. Mussorgsky saw this work in a memorial exhibition of the artist's work and was inspired to compose his suite Pictures at an Exhibition.

● *Musical life in Russia*

Tchaikovsky was sent to attend the first complete cycle of *The Ring* in Bayreuth in 1876 as an official Russian representative. This shows that the significance of the event had been appreciated in Russian musical circles, and that if any Russian composer was of sufficient stature to represent the country, it was Tchaikovsky. When seen in its historical context, this underlines how rapidly musical events had progressed in Russia.

Apart from the theatres in Moscow and St Petersburg, there was little professional public music-making in Russia, and most of that was provided by foreign visitors until the Russian Musical Society was inaugurated in 1859, which in turn gave rise to the founding of the conservatories of Moscow and St Petersburg. When the latter opened in 1862, Tchaikovsky was one of the first students. In less than fifteen years, therefore, Russia had a native composer who was the product of its own system. There had been other Russian composers previously, notably Glinka, but only now was a recognizable national school emerging. In fact Tchaikovsky drew adverse criticism upon himself because he was not sufficiently Russian, unlike composers such as Borodin, Balakirev, Mussorgsky, Rimsky-Korsakov and Cui, known as the *kuchka*, or 'mighty handful'. For them, based in St Petersburg, Tchaikovsky was far too Western in his music. Ironically, as he discovered when he visited Prague, outside Russia Tchaikovsky was admired as the representative of nascent Slav music, especially in those countries striving to assert their cultural independence.

1877-79
The New French Spirit

As the general standard of musical life in France wanes, and loses the talent of Bizet, Saint-Saëns brings a new spirit. He is not destined to win recognition as an opera composer, but among his many talents and abilities, his skill as a pianist – and the legacy of his piano concertos in particular – assure him of a place in the history of music.

Saint-Saëns's Samson et Dalila *was conceived as an oratorio in the late 1860s, but the form did not enjoy the interest in France that it had in England and Germany.*

1877 Saint-Saëns's opera *Samson et Dalila* (Samson and Delilah, left) is first performed in Weimar, thanks to Liszt.

• **4 March** Tchaikovsky's *Swan Lake* (p.178) has its first performance at the Bolshoi Theatre in Moscow.

• **28 April** Bruckner completes the revision of his Third Symphony (p.176) in its second version.

• **August** Bruckner completes his Fifth Symphony.

• **August** Liszt, in Italy, composes the piano pieces inspired by the gardens of the Villa d'Este (below) in the third book of *Années de pèlerinage* (p.153).

• **September** Wagner begins composition of what is to be his last opera, *Parsifal*.

• **16 December** Bruckner conducts the first performance of his Third Symphony, but the result is a disaster. The publisher Theodor Rättig, however, proposes to issue the symphony in parts the following year, and a piano DUET version is made.

• **30 December** Brahms's Second Symphony is first performed by the Vienna Philharmonic Orchestra under Hans Richter and is a triumph.

1878 Summer Brahms completes his Violin Concerto, which he dedicates to the violinist Joachim.

• Dvořák composes his *Three Slavonic Rhapsodies*, Op.45. Much more successful are his *Slavonic Dances*, originally conceived as a set of eight piano duets and published this year by Simrock in Berlin. The composer orchestrates them, and his fame and fortune are made almost overnight.

1879 George Grove begins to publish his *Dictionary of Music and Musicians* in four volumes. The task will take ten years, and new and enlarged editions will follow.

• **1 January** Joachim gives the first performance of Brahms's Violin Concerto, conducted by the composer, at a concert in the Leipzig Gewandhaus. The critics are not impressed, but the work will become one of the most popular violin concertos in the repertoire.

• **29 March** Tchaikovsky's opera *Eugene Onegin* is given for the first time at the Maly Theatre in Moscow.

OTHER EVENTS
1877 Edison invents phonograph
• Monet: *La gare Saint-Lazare*

1878 Microphone invented by David Hughes
• Hardy: *The Return of the Native*

1879 Edison invents improved incandescent electric light
• Ibsen: *The Doll's House*
• Dostoyevsky: *The Brothers Karamazov*

★ *The gardens of the Villa d'Este at Tivoli, where rooms were put at Liszt's disposal over several years, and which inspired three pieces from the final volume of his* Années de pèlerinage.

● *The Paris Conservatoire and the Prix de Rome*

An audition at the Paris Conservatoire. Among the jury members are Thomas, Gounod, Massenet and Delibes. It was against such sterile formality that Berlioz, Debussy and Ravel all protested in their time.

Throughout the nineteenth century the foundations of French musical life were laid at the Paris Conservatoire, an institution which provided an excellent grounding in general musicianship and training, but which became ossified and seemingly unable to embrace new ideas or recognize talent that did not fall within its predetermined conceptions.

The institution of the Prix de Rome at the Conservatoire is a vivid example of this, for in theory its aims were excellent. Deserving students were sent to live in Rome at the Villa Medici and enjoy a period of study and recreation free from the worries of earning a living or finding a situation. In reality the prize was less highly thought of, and French composers from Berlioz to Debussy were eloquent in expressing their views. More often than not the prize was seen more as an imposition, since it was awarded to the winner of a competition in the course of which students had to compose a cantata. As Debussy wrote in the collection published as *Monsieur Croche, antidilettante:*

'I do not deny that it is fairly good music, but does anyone imagine that I am so lacking in taste that I will stand on the rostrum, violin in hand, to listen to the oboe playing the only melody in the adagio?'
The violinist Sarasate on Brahms's Violin Concerto.

' "Among the institutions on which France prides herself, do you know any more ridiculous than the institution of the Prix de Rome? I am aware that this has often been said and still more often written, but apparently without any effect, since it continues to exist with that deplorable obstinacy which distinguishes absurd ideas."

'I ventured to answer that possibly the institution derived its strength from the fact that it had attained in certain circles the position of a superstition. To have won or not to have won the Prix de Rome settled the question of whether one did or did not possess talent. If it was not absolutely certain, it was at least convenient and provided public opinion with a sort of ready-reckoner.'

1880-82
The Golden Age of Light Music

There is a thriving tradition of light music in Vienna that Mozart, Haydn and even Beethoven had not disdained in their time. In the eyes of Wagner and his followers, however, the serious composer has nothing to do with such a tradition. In their view, the function of music – and, by implication, all art – is to elevate the mind.

1880 Paine's Second Symphony, entitled *In Spring*, is first performed in Cambridge, Massachusetts, and is the first native symphony to be published in America.

• Johann Strauss writes one of his best loved waltzes, *Roses from the South*.

• **17 January** César Franck's Piano Quintet is first performed in Paris, with a disapproving Saint-Saëns as the pianist. The emotional tone of the music is regarded as erotic, and therefore inappropriate, even by Liszt.

• **21 January** Rimsky-Korsakov's opera *May Night* is first performed at the Maryinsky Theatre in St Petersburg.

• **5 June** Bruckner completes the third version of his Fourth Symphony (p.178).

• **5 October** Offenbach dies in Paris, aged sixty-one.

1881 The Boston Symphony Orchestra is founded.

• Paine composes the incidental music for *Oedipus tyrannus*.

• **10 February** Offenbach's *The Tales of Hoffmann* ■ (p.167) is first performed, posthumously, at the Opéra-Comique, Paris.

• **20 February** Richter conducts the first performance of Bruckner's Fourth Symphony, which is a triumphal vindication for the composer.

• **24 March** A revised version of Verdi's *Simone Boccanegra* (p.166) is first given at La Scala, Milan.

• **25 March** Bartók is born in Sînnicolaul Mare, Romania.

• **28 March** Mussorgsky dies, aged forty-two, in St Petersburg ★ (p.178).

• **3 September** Bruckner completes his Sixth Symphony.

• **23 September** Bruckner begins work on his Seventh Symphony.

• **22 October** Accompanied by his granddaughter Daniela, Liszt celebrates his seventieth birthday in Rome.

1882 The Berlin Philharmonic Orchestra is founded.

• **13 January** Wagner completes *Parsifal* (left), the culmination of almost five years of work.

• **17 June** Birth of Stravinsky in Oranienbaum, near St Petersburg.

• **26 July** First of sixteen performances of *Parsifal* at Bayreuth conducted by Hermann Levi, except the last which Wagner himself conducts, despite extreme exhaustion.

• **September** Wagner leaves for Venice.

• **16 December** Kodály is born in Kecskemét, Hungary.

OTHER EVENTS

1880 Pavlov experiments on conditioned reflexes
• Zola: *Nana*

1881 Tsar Alexander II assassinated
• President Garfield shot
• Panama Canal begun

1882 Koch discovers tuberculosis germs
• Triple Alliance
• Manet: *The Bar at the Folies Bergère*

'I knelt before him and… said: "Oh Master, I worship you!" Then he said: "Be calm, Bruckner. Goodnight!"'
Bruckner to Wagner during the first performances of *Parsifal*.

Poster for Wagner's last opera Parsifal. *In fact he described it as a 'Bühnenweihfestspiel' – a stage dedication festival play. The work was not enacted again until it was produced at the Metropolitan Opera House in New York in 1903.*

● *Vienna*

Interior of the old Burgtheater in Vienna, as portrayed by Klimt, shortly before it closed for the last time in 1888. Beethoven made his Viennese début here as a concert pianist in March 1795 (p.124), and it was often the venue for charity concerts for the Musicians' Benevolent Fund.

Although Vienna retained its attraction for serious musicians, compared with the heady days when Mozart, Haydn, Beethoven and Schubert were alive, it was in many respects living on past glory. True, Brahms and Bruckner were working there, and the institutions that had been in place throughout the century were still in operation, yet the most flourishing aspect of music-making in Vienna was the lighter creations of Johann Strauss the Younger, who was by now an international celebrity. Indeed, for many people his music was the very essence of Vienna. He had already taken Paris and London by storm with his waltzes, when Offenbach, on a visit to Vienna, told him that he should write OPERETTAS. Strauss's *Indigo, or The Forty Thieves* (p.176) in 1871 may be regarded as the beginning of the Viennese school of operetta. The following year he was invited to America to take part in the opening celebrations in Boston of the centenary of American Independence. In five weeks he conducted more than forty concerts and received 100,000 dollars. He never really liked travel, however, his heart was in Vienna, and he returned with some of his greatest successes still to come. Although forbidden to compose by his doctor in 1885, he went on to complete *The Gypsy Baron* (right) that year, and in 1894 celebrated the fiftieth anniversary of his début as a conductor in Vienna with festivities that lasted for a week. He had come to epitomize one aspect of the city's character.

The original poster (right) for Johann Strauss the Younger's operetta The Gypsy Baron, *which was first performed on the eve of his sixtieth birthday and made Hungarian subjects extremely popular in Vienna.*

1883-84
Bruckner, the Last of the Romantics

Often disregarded in his own lifetime, and relegated by many of his contemporaries to the role of a poor shadow of Wagner, Bruckner eventually emerges as one of the most dedicated and sincere of all Romantic composers, and one destined to be held in high regard by future generations.

Wagner's death mask, made on the day after his death.

1883 Paine's CANTATA *The Nativity* is published in Boston.

• The Metropolitan Opera is founded in New York.

• The Amsterdam Concertgebouw Orchestra is founded.

• Richard Strauss, aged nineteen, completes his First Concerto for French Horn, the instrument on which his father is a virtuoso. It will be almost sixty years before Strauss writes his Second Horn Concerto.

• **11 February** The second and third movements of Bruckner's Sixth Symphony (p.182) are performed in Vienna. Brahms joins in the huge ovation that the music receives.

• **13 February** After a bitter argument with Cosima, Wagner (left) suffers a fatal heart attack in Venice. He is buried five days later in Bayreuth.

• **22 May** Liszt conducts a memorial concert for Wagner in Bayreuth.

• **Summer** Brahms virtually completes his Third Symphony.

• **5 September** Bruckner completes his Seventh Symphony.

• **28 September** Bruckner works on the final version of his Te Deum.

• **3 December** Webern is born in Vienna.

• **22 December** Varèse is born in Paris.

1884 Massenet's opera *Manon*, based on Prévost's romance about the courtesan, *Manon Lescaut*, is first performed at the Opéra-Comique, Paris.

• *Le Villi*, Puccini's first operatic success, is performed in Milan and Turin.

• **10 January** The Italian version of Verdi's *Don Carlos* (p.172) is first heard at La Scala, Milan.

• **March** Dvořák arrives in London, at the invitation of the Philharmonic Society, to conduct his Stabat Mater at the Albert Hall. His Sixth Symphony is also introduced with considerable success.

• **7 March** Bruckner completes his Te Deum, and then begins work on his Eighth Symphony.

• **12 May** Death of Smetana, aged sixty, in Prague.

• **Summer** Brahms works on the composition of his Fourth Symphony at the resort of Mürzzuschlag.

• **30 December** Bruckner's Seventh Symphony is first performed in Leipzig by the Gewandhaus Orchestra under the direction of Arthur Nikisch, and is a great success.

'He composes nothing but high treason, revolution and murder.'

A critic on Bruckner's String Quintet, published in 1884.

OTHER EVENTS
1883 Daimler patents automobile motor
• Nietzsche: *Also sprach Zarathustra*
• Robert Louis Stevenson: *Treasure Island*

1884 Pasteur inoculates against rabies
• Mean solar day adopted as unit of universal time
• Rodin: *The Burghers of Calais*
• Seurat: *Sunday Afternoon on the Grande Jatte*
• Twain: *Huckleberry Finn*

Bruckner piously kept a daily list of his prayers (opposite):
A = Ave Maria;
C = Credo;
S = Salve Regina;
V = Vater unser.
The underlinings refer to the number of times he said each prayer.

Alberto Franchetti, Mascagni and Puccini during their days at the Milan Conservatory, from which the latter graduated in 1883. Puccini was one of a succession of generations of musicians from the ancient town of Lucca, to the north of Pisa.

◆ The Symphony Orchestra

In the nineteenth century the inclusion of the percussion section, and individual instruments such as the harp, finally saw the symphony orchestra reach the form in which we know it today, with its complement of around a hundred instruments, which may be augmented for certain works. Inevitably the process may be seen as increasing the potential for volume, and certain composers were only too happy to take advantage of this.

At the beginning of the century Beethoven had been criticized for the sheer volume he required in certain passages ▲ (p.131), Rossini too, but today we appreciate their ORCHESTRATION more

readily. There seems to be pure joy at times in the way Beethoven throws musical phrases from one group of instruments to another, and Rossini explores the basic nature of instruments in such a way that we almost feel we are hearing them for the first time. His Messa di Gloria, written for Naples in 1820, glitters with such effects.

By way of contrast, Rossini can weave a sinuous coil of sound as in the opening passage of the overture to William Tell (p.148), with its five cellos, that Berlioz likened to 'the silence of nature when the elements and the human passions are at rest'. Despite his frequent strictures on Rossini's music, Berlioz usually praised his orchestration, for he too was concerned not just to create sound, as he was popularly portrayed, but unusual effects. The orchestration and instrumental TIMBRE of the symphony orchestra now offered an astonishing array of possibilities to the composer, and this before the invention of more exotic instruments such as the CELESTA, which so caught Tchaikovsky's imagination for the dance of the Sugar Plum Fairy in The Nutcracker (p.191). In fact the gifted ORCHESTRATORS, of whom Tchaikovsky was certainly one, have never relied on additional effects such as the celesta. The art of orchestration required that a composer should know thoroughly the technical capabilites of the basic groups of instruments as they evolved and were developed by makers in response to the new opportunities offered. As orchestral music became increasingly exciting, the concert-going public demanded to hear more, resulting in a number of new orchestras being founded and concert halls opened.

1885-90
Tchaikovsky in Florence

Russia had by no means been bereft of music prior to the nineteenth century, but most of it had either been church music or the product of foreigners working there. Now, however, Tchaikovsky, following in the steps of such composers as Glinka and Mussorgsky, gives to Slav music generally its first internationally recognized composer.

1885 Tchaikovsky completes his *Manfred* Symphony, which is well received the following year, though he suspects that the audience does not really understand it.

• Bruckner's Seventh Symphony (p.184) has its first performance in New York, and is also heard this year in Dresden, Frankfurt, Utrecht and The Hague – though not yet in Vienna. He completes his Eighth Symphony.

• Johann Strauss the Younger storms Vienna with his OPERETTA *The Gypsy Baron* ● (p.183), though at the dress rehearsal critics predicted a fiasco.

• Franck composes his Symphonic Variations for piano and orchestra, for the pianist Louis Diémer.

• Gilbert and Sullivan complete *The Mikado*, marking one of the highpoints of their particular brand of comic opera.

• Dvořák introduces his Sixth Symphony to the London public, and he becomes known as 'The Bohemian Brahms'.

• **9 February** Berg is born in Vienna.

• **Summer** Brahms completes his Fourth Symphony (p.184).

• **25 October** Brahms conducts the first performance of his Fourth Symphony. He has had grave reservations about the work until Hans von Bülow compliments it highly when directing the rehearsal.

1886 Franck composes his Sonata for Violin and Piano in A Minor for Eugène Ysaÿe, whose performances help to make it one of Franck's most popular pieces.

• Dvořák's ORATORIO *Saint Ludmila* is performed at the Leeds Music Festival (left).

• Charles Mustel invents the CELESTA ◆ (p.185).

• **10 January** Richter conducts the first performance of Bruckner's Te Deum with orchestra (p.184), in Vienna.

• **March** The first Viennese performance of Bruckner's Seventh Symphony, conducted by Richter, is a great success. The work is becoming his most universally admired and frequently played composition.

• **31 July** Liszt dies in Bayreuth, aged seventy-five. Bruckner, invited by Cosima Wagner, plays a magnificent organ improvisation on themes from *Parsifal* ★ (p.182) at his funeral on 3 August.

Dvořák occupies pride of place in the centre of this sketch from the 1886 Leeds Music Festival.

OTHER EVENTS
1885 First American street railway
• Brooklyn Bridge built
• Cézanne: *Mont Sainte Victoire*
• Maupassant: *Contes et nouvelles*

1886 Statue of Liberty unveiled
• American Federation of Labor organized
• Loti: *Le pêcheur d'Islande*

1887 Strindberg: *Der Vater*

1888 Accession of Kaiser Wilhelm II
• Van Gogh: *Sunflowers*

1889 Paris World Fair
• Brazil made a republic
• Eiffel Tower completed
• Rodin: *The Thinker*

1890 Ibsen: *Hedda Gabler*

1887 Richard Strauss writes his symphonic fantasy *Aus Italien* (From Italy), which disturbed many listeners with its discords at its first performance.

• Fauré writes his Requiem in memory of his father.

• The virtuoso pianist Paderewski gives his first recital in Vienna

• **5 February** Verdi's *Otello*, his first entirely new opera for sixteen years, has its first triumphant performance at La Scala, Milan.

• **28 February** Death of Borodin, aged fifty-three, in St Petersburg.

• **4 September** Bruckner completes his Eighth Symphony, though almost immediately begins revising it.

1888 Franck completes his Symphony in D Minor, which splits the critics into two opposing factions at its first hearing the following year.

• Birth of Irving Berlin.

• Rimsky-Korsakov completes *Sheherazade* (below), one of his most famous orchestral compositions.

• Satie composes his *Gymnopédies* (Nude Gymnasts) for piano, pieces which almost certainly influence Debussy.

Painting of an imaginary scene showing (from the left): Verdi, Puccini, Arrigo Boïto, Mascagni, Umberto Giordano and Leoncavallo.

• Wolf, in his first creative burst of energy of songwriting, sets forty-three of Eduard Mörike's poems in less than three months.

• **13 February** Mahler becomes musical director of the Budapest opera.

• **May–26 August** Tchaikovsky composes his Fifth Symphony, which does not please the Russian critics, though it is greeted with enthusiasm in Hamburg the following year.

• **19 October** Tchaikovsky completes the fantasy OVERTURE *Hamlet*.

• **17 November** Tchaikovsky's Fifth Symphony, conducted by the composer, is first performed in St Petersburg.

1889 Richard Strauss conducts the first performance of his SYMPHONIC POEM *Don Juan* in Weimar, to great acclaim.

• Wolf begins his *Spanisches Liederbuch* (Spanish Song Book), forty-four settings of Spanish religious and secular songs.

• Mahler brings a new and unique creative vision to his First Symphony, completed the year before, and now heard for the first time in Budapest.

• The fourth and final version of Bruckner's Fourth Symphony is published.

• Dvořák completes his Eighth Symphony.

A painting dating from 1892. The exoticism of the subject echoes the interest shown at this time by composers such as Rimsky-Korsakov in Asiatic and oriental themes, which in his case led to Sheherazade.

• **17 February** Despite an initial reluctance by the orchestra to perform the work, Franck's Symphony in D minor is first given in Paris by the Société des Concerts du Conservatoire, to mixed reactions.

1890 Encouraged by the success of his *Don Juan,* Strauss composes the SYMPHONIC POEM *Death and Transfiguration.*

• Bruckner's Third Symphony, revised the year before in its third and final version, is published at the expense of the Emperor of Austria.

• Dvořák's Eighth Symphony is performed for the first time in Prague and in London to enthusiastic applause in both cities.

• Wolf completes his *Spanisches Liederbuch* (p.187).

• **15 January** First public performance of Tchaikovsky's ballet *The Sleeping Beauty* at the Maryinksy Theatre in St Petersburg.

• **10 March** Bruckner completes his revision of his Eighth Symphony, and begins revising his First Symphony.

• **May** Mascagni has a resounding success with his opera *Cavalleria rusticana* (Rustic Chivalry, ✳ p.191), at the Teatro Costanzi in Rome.

• **3 October** The first performance of Borodin's opera, *Prince Igor,* takes place three years after the composer's death (p.187). The work has been completed and orchestrated from sketches by Rimsky-Korsakov, assisted by his pupil Glazunov.

• **8 November** Franck dies, aged sixty-eight, in Paris.

• **19 December** To the composer's disgust, Tchaikovsky's new opera *The Queen of Spades* (below) receives only twelve performances at the Maryinsky Theatre in St Petersburg, despite its warm reception the first time it is heard, but it is revived the following year.

• **21 December** Bruckner's Third Symphony, in its final version, is now performed in Vienna under Richter and is received with enthusiasm.

Maria Slavina as the countess in Tchaikovsky's The Queen of Spades, *in the 1890 production at the Maryinsky Theatre in St Petersburg. In the opera, Hermann literally frightens the countess to death in his determination to discover the secret of the card game.*

▲ *Tchaikovsky in Florence*

In January 1890 Tchaikovsky travelled to Florence, taking with him the LIBRETTO of Pushkin's *The Queen of Spades*, prepared by his brother Modest. The following extract from Tchaikovsky's diary shows the composer enjoying his work and leading a busy social life in this, one of his favourite cities, but also reveals a host of burdens and anxieties:

Tchaikovsky portrayed in the last year of his life, when he looked much older than his fifty-three years.

18 JANUARY THURSDAY.

Arrival in Florence. Weather damp but warm. Room bad. Looked at an apartment in the hotel, rented it and agreed terms. With Nazar [his acting valet] to the church of San Miniato. Lunch at Gilli e Letta café. Home. We arranged our effects. First dinner. Separate table. Good.

19 JANUARY FRIDAY.

Began work and not bad. (Lifted the start from Napravnik.) The day went very well. After lunch wandered about. A cold wind was blowing, but in our rooms we have the sun.

20 JANUARY SATURDAY.

Worked well. Not so homesick. All as it ought to be. In the evening at the Pagliano Theatre. Fat singer [Amneris in Aida]. A rogue of a conductor. Dreadful choruses. By and large it is all provincial. Left after the second act.

21 JANUARY SUNDAY.

Worked well in the morning, but badly after lunch. Strolled, went to the Cascine Park – right to the end. Dined badly because of tiredness and exertion at work. Wandered in and out of cafés. A letter at home. The fireplace. Conversation with Nazar.

22 JANUARY MONDAY.

Weather still cold but clear. Got up, read the newspapers, drank tea with honey as usual. Worked well…. Became rather emotional. Dined excellently…. Beautiful, but cold, moonlit night.

27 JANUARY SATURDAY.

Work proving slightly difficult [the finale of the first scene]. After lunch, at Nazar's request, went to look for the Russian church – had a difficult time finding it. After dinner the Pagliano Theatre; the first two acts of Aida again. (The ridiculously fat singer with a voice like a street-seller's.) This time the orchestration of Aida seemed dreadfully coarse to me in places. As always, was delighted with the beginning of the scene between Aida and Amneris.

28 JANUARY SUNDAY.

Work. Dinner. Sitting in various cafés. A chat with Nazar on returning home. Read the score of Grétry's Richard Coeur de Lion [■ p.115]. There is terrible boredom and a feeling of desolation in my core.

1891-94
Realism and Symbolism

Verismo — as the new realism becomes known — is not entirely new, but in Italy it dates from the appearance of Mascagni's Cavalleria rusticana *and Leoncavallo's* I pagliacci. *Meanwhile Debussy's interpretation of Mallarmé's Symbolist poem* L'Après-midi d'un faune *changes the course of music.*

1891 Brahms composes his Clarinet Trio in A Minor, Op.114 and Clarinet Quintet in B Minor, Op.115 for Richard Muehlfeld, clarinettist of the Meiningen Orchestra.

• Dvořák's Requiem has its first performance at the Birmingham Music Festival to a tumultuous reception. The composer receives an honorary doctorate from the University of Cambridge.

> '*His tale of love is just the same as the love of real people.*'
>
> From the prologue to Leoncavallo's
> *I pagliacci*

• Rachmaninov, who is studying at the Moscow Conservatory, completes his First Piano Concerto.

• Wolf composes the first volume of his *Italienisches Liederbuch* (Italian Song Book).

• **April** Bruckner completes the revision of his First Symphony.

• **23 April** Prokofiev is born in Sontsovka in the Ukraine.

• **13 December** Bruckner's First Symphony in its revised form is first performed in Vienna under Richter.

1892 Leoncavallo's opera *I pagliacci* (The Clowns or Strolling Players) is given at the Teatro dal Verme in Milan, conducted by Arturo Toscanini.

• Dvořák pays his first visit to America. He is commissioned to compose a Te Deum for the Columbus anniversary this year, and is made director of New York National Conservatory of Music.

OTHER EVENTS
1891 Conan Doyle: *The Adventures of Sherlock Holmes*

1892 Cézanne: *The Card Players*
• Maeterlinck: *Pelléas et Mélisande*
• Toulouse-Lautrec: *At The Moulin Rouge*

1893 Oscar Wilde: *Salome*

1894 Accession of Tsar Nicholas II
• Dreyfus Affair in France
• Kipling: *Jungle Book*
• Shaw: *Candida*

An assembly of the Vienna Wagner-Verein, during a recital of Wolf's songs. The composer is at the piano and standing is the singer Ferdinand Jäger.

- **10 March** Honegger is born in Le Havre.
- **22 April** Lalo dies, aged sixty-nine, in Paris.
- **Summer** Fauré (left) begins to compose his SONG CYCLE *La Bonne Chanson* (The Good Song), inspired by, and eventually dedicated to, the singer Emma Bardac, who subsequently becomes Debussy's second wife.
- **August** Bruckner pays his last visit to Bayreuth, where he prays daily at Wagner's grave.
- **4 September** Milhaud is born in Aix-en-Provence.
- **18 December** Bruckner's revised Eighth Symphony, dedicated to the emperor, is first performed in Vienna under Richter's baton.
- **18 December** The first public performance of Tchaikovsky's ballet *The Nutcracker*, in St Petersburg, is greeted with little enthusiasm.

A rather cruel caricature of Fauré as the composer of the song cycle La Bonne Chanson. *The artist contrasts the ideal of beautiful women with the elderly rodent-like man.*

★ *Final scene of* Cavalleria rusticana *from the original production at the Teatro Costanzi, Rome (p.188). Mascagni wrote the opera for a competition and won first prize.*

◆ *A New Mood of Verismo*

Verismo is often taken to mean that from about 1890 onwards opera plots suddenly began to deal with real-life situations whereas before, by implication, they had not; but Verdi's La traviata *(p.165), for example, deals with the world of courtesans, and the heroine (though admittedly by now 'redeemed') dies of consumption on stage at the end of the opera. Indeed, there is an interesting letter from Verdi to the* LIBRETTIST *Cammarano, written five years before* La traviata, *when the composer heard who was going to sing the role of Lady Macbeth in a production of his opera:*

'[Tadolini] looks good and beautiful, and I want Lady Macbeth to look evil and ugly. Tadolini sings impeccably, and I should prefer Lady Macbeth not to sing. Tadolini has a wonderful voice, clear, pure and strong; and I want Lady Macbeth to have a hard, hoarse, mournful voice. Tadolini's voice suggests an angel; I want a voice that suggests a devil…

'There are two very important moments in the opera: the duet between Lady Macbeth and her husband and the sleep-walking scene. If these fail, the whole opera collapses. These two pieces must on no account be sung. They are to be acted and declaimed in a very dark, veiled tone. Unless this can be achieved, the entire effect will be lost.'

What Verdi was presaging was the fact that eventually it was not content alone that would achieve verismo in opera, for no matter what the subject matter, it is not 'real' for ordinary people to express themselves in song. What changed was presentation – passion in Bizet's Carmen *as opposed to Wagner's romantic love – and style of singing. Of course there is always a need for beautiful singing, but the call for only* bel canto *disappears.*

The cover of a special issue of L'illustrazione italiana, published in 1893, devoted to Verdi and his opera Falstaff, which had its first performance that year at La Scala Milan.

1893 Puccini has his second great operatic success with *Manon Lescaut* at the Teatro Regio in Turin.

• **9 February** Verdi's last opera, *Falstaff* (above), has its first performance at La Scala, Milan.

• **Summer** Dvořák is again in America, where he composes his String Quartet in F major, his *Spilville* String Quintet in E flat major and his Ninth Symphony *From the New World*.

• **6 November** Tchaikovsky dies in St Petersburg, aged fifty-three, after completing his Sixth Symphony.

• **16 December** Dvořák's New World Symphony is first given at Carnegie Hall, played by the New York Philharmonic Orchestra.

1894 Debussy composes his *Prélude à l'après-midi d'un faune* (Prelude to the Afternoon of a Faun, ■ opposite).

• **12 February** Von Bülow dies, aged sixty-four, in Cairo.

• **23 December** Debussy's *Prélude à l'après-midi d'un faune* is first performed at a Société Nationale concert in Paris, and is received with such enthusiasm by the audience that it is given an encore.

Poster for the fifty-second season of the Philharmonic Society of New York.

PHILHARMONIC SOCIETY OF NEW YORK

FIFTY-SECOND SEASON, 1893-1894.

Synopsis of Compositions

TO BE PERFORMED AT THE

Second Public Rehearsal and Concert

ON DECEMBER 15th and 16th, 1893, AT

✳ MUSIC HALL ✳

ANTONIN DVORAK :
Symphony No. 5, E minor, op. 95 (Manuscript.)
"FROM THE NEW WORLD."

■ *Debussy and Mallarmé*

A sketch of the Symbolist poet Stéphane Mallarmé by Whistler, used as the frontispiece to a book of his poems published in 1893.

Stéphane Mallarmé (left), regarded as the leader of the French Symbolist movement, was born in Paris in 1842. All his life he taught English in *lycées,* struggling against poverty and discomfort to write his poetry. He worked in Tournon and Avignon before being given a post in Paris, and during the last fifteen years of his life (he died in 1898) kept a *salon,* frequented by young writers, on Tuesdays at his home in the Rue de Rome.

He began his long poem *L'Après-midi d'un faune* in 1865, when he was still at Tournon, but did not complete it until 1876. Its subtle and sensuous language plays on the musicality of the words, which are thereby endowed with more than their basic meaning. Not surprisingly, perhaps, Debussy responded to this text as he responded to other Mallarmé texts, and in fact his last set of three songs, dating from 1913, was on poems by the poet.

Debussy began composing his response to the poem in 1892, and completed it two years later. His *Prélude à l'après-midi d'un faune* was destined to become a key work in Western Classical music. Through its form – or apparent lack of it – it broke new ground in a startling way, and influenced a great deal of music that came after it. It is, however, essentially a reaction to the poem in general terms, and not an attempt to 'interpret' it, line by line, in music, although Debussy's composition was originally intended as incidental music to accompany a recitation or dramatic presentation of the poem. By the time he had finished it, however, it had taken

The cover, designed by Bakst, for the programme for the première in 1912 of the Diaghilev ballet L'Après-midi d'un faune *with Nijinsky as the Faun. The overt sexuality of the dancer's performance caused a scandal.*

on a life of its own. The first performance in the concert hall on 23 December 1894 was so successful that it was repeated there and then by popular demand. Diaghilev's subsequent ballet, with designs by Bakst (below), dates from 1912.

Debussy's music has often been defined as impressionistic, and there are certain similarities between, say, its technique and feeling and the painting of Monet. The two share to some extent a lack of thematic definition, a delight in glowing tones, and a preference for the effect of splashes of colour (orchestral in the case of Debussy). To say no more than that, however, as far as Debussy is concerned, is rather to undervalue his significance in musical terms, for the effect of impressionism was only achieved by a basic coherence of structure and a masterly control of the means.

1895-97
The End of Romanticism

With the magnificent trio of Bruckner, Mahler and Strauss, the mainstream of Romanticism seems to come to a glorious close, though Strauss survives well into the next century, and in various forms and with other composers elsewhere in the world, Romanticism never seems totally to disappear.

1895 Strauss completes his symphonic TONE POEM *Till Eulenspiegels lustige Streiche* (Till Eulenspiegel's Merry Pranks).

• Dvořák composes his Cello Concerto, one of the most important in the repertoire, in America.

• **July** Bruckner (right) retires to a lodge at Schloss Belvedere in Vienna, lent to him by the Austrian emperor.

• **10 July** Birth of Orff in Munich.

• **16 November** Hindemith is born in Hanau.

'I will present to Him the score of my Te Deum, and He will judge me mercifully.'
Bruckner

1896 Brahms composes his *Four Serious Songs*, closely connected with the death of Clara Schumann in May this year.

• MacDowell completes his *Indian Suite*, based on Native American melodies and rhythms.

• Wolf's opera *Der Corregidor* (The Magistrate) is first performed in Mannheim.

• **12 January** Bruckner, now so ill that he has to be carried into the hall, attends his last concert, a performance of his Te Deum. Also on the programme is Strauss's *Till Eulenspiegel*.

• **1 February** Puccini's opera *La Bohème* is first performed at the Teatro Regio in Turin, conducted by Toscanini. Initially the audiences are puzzled, but the work soon gains in popularity.

A postcard with scenes from Puccini's La Bohème, *one of his most popular and musically cohesive works.*

• **11 October** Death of Bruckner, aged seventy-two, in Vienna. His funeral takes place three days later. Wolf is not admitted because he has no ticket, and Brahms because he arrives too late.

In the last few years of his life, Bruckner suffered from heart disease, and was often short of breath. He became unable to climb the stairs at the lodge at Schloss Belvedere, and so lived on the ground floor.

1897 Strauss composes his tone poem *Don Quixote*.

• Mahler is made conductor of the Vienna Opera.

• Sousa composes the march *Stars and Stripes Forever*.

• **12 March** D'Indy's 'musical action' or opera *Fervaal* is given at the Théâtre de la Monnaie in Brussels, and in Paris the following year.

• **3 April** Death of Brahms, aged sixty-three, in Vienna.

OTHER EVENTS
1895 Roentgen discovers X-rays
• First public film show

1896 First public radio demonstration by Marconi
• Gauguin: *Maternity*
• Chekhov: *The Seagull*

1897 J. J. Thomson discovers electrons
• Edmond Rostand: *Cyrano de Bergerac*

Verdi conducting a performance of Aïda *in Paris. After this opera he wrote no others for sixteen years, and concentrated on his conducting engagements in Paris, Vienna and London.*

◆ *The Ever-Increasing Role of the Conductor*

Throughout the history of music there had been occasions when one person gave a lead as to when a piece was to begin and end, how fast or slow it should be played, how loud or soft. The greater the number of performers involved, the greater the need for such a leader. However, the concept of a conductor as we know it today would have been almost inconceivable until the advent of Romanticism. Before that time, such considerations as tempo (speed) and dynamics (loudness or softness) in the music tended to vary from section to section or movement to movement, but not from bar to bar. Even when the composer was present, and in charge, he was usually seated at a harpsichord or piano and directed the ensemble from the keyboard, but only at crucial points in the work.

Romanticism in music brought infinitely more changes of TEMPO, DYNAMIC, TONAL COLOUR and ORCHESTRATION, which in turn implied interpretation. No matter how carefully a composer might mark his music with indications as to performance, no two performances could be exactly the same.

The larger the orchestra, the greater the need for one person in charge to control the relative balance not only between the groups of instruments but also within the groups of instruments when divided into several parts.

Some composers were capable conductors, and therefore established what they envisaged for the performance of their music, but others – such as Bruckner – were not, and had therefore to entrust their music to the care of the new breed. Inevitably charges of showmanship were levelled against certain conductors, and at times it seemed as if they became more important than the composer – a feeling which has not diminished in the twentieth century.

1898-99
The Romantic Legacy

As Germany has long been the source of so much of the inspiration and impetus given to music during the century, aspiring composers have been drawn to it, and to Leipzig in particular, to complete their education. As the native traditions become more established, however, the national schools of music begin to flourish on the margins of Europe, and also across the Atlantic.

1898 MacDowell, professor of music at Columbia University since 1896, completes his *Sea Pieces*, destined to become one of his best known works.

• **7 January** Rimsky-Korsakov's opera *Sadko*, the story of an eleventh-century minstrel, is first performed in Moscow after being refused for the Imperial Theatres (below).

• **8 March** Richard Strauss's *Don Quixote* (p.194) is first given in Cologne.

• **26 September** George Gershwin is born in Brooklyn.

• **27 December** Richard Strauss completes his TONE POEM *Ein Heldenleben* (A Hero's Life) in Berlin.

OTHER EVENTS
1898 Spanish-American War
• Paris Métro opens
• H.G. Wells: *The War of the Worlds*
• Mallarmé dies

1899 Boer War begins
• First tape recordings made
• Commonwealth of Australia inaugurated

Rimsky-Korsakov in 1898, the year his opera Sadko *was performed in Moscow following a donation by a private sponsor.*

1899 Ravel composes his *Pavane pour une infante défunte* (Pavane for a Dead Infanta), written for the Princesse Edmond de Polignac.

• Schoenberg writes his string sextet *Verklärte Nacht* (Transfigured Night), which is rejected for performance by the Vienna Tonkünstler-Sozietät on the grounds that it has an unorthodox chord in it.

• Sibelius (below) composes *Finlandia* for a Press Pension Fund pageant. Its melody will become a focus in the cause of Finnish independence.

• Scott Joplin composes his *Maple Leaf Rag*.

• Elgar completes his *Enigma Variations*.

Sibelius in 1894, five years before he composed his tone poem Finlandia, *which helped to raise international awareness of the Russian threat to Finland.*

◆ *New Directions in Music*

As the century drew to a close, centres of gravity were shifting, and had in fact almost imperceptibly been doing so for some time. Leipzig had long been a focal point for students from all over the world, but, as national conservatories began to form their own musicians and musical traditions, its attraction began to fade.

Italy's operatic tradition persisted, but its conservatories had long ceased to maintain the prestige that they had enjoyed in the eighteenth century. The Paris Conservatoire continued to form musicians who were excellently equipped from a technical point of view, but the chief role of Paris was to act as a catalyst and draw talent to it, though with such composers as Fauré, Debussy and Ravel it was to enjoy a final blossoming of native talent. Vienna was in a similar situation, though it would foster the most exciting developments in music in the new century.

In Russia the national tradition was by now well established and flourishing. Most striking, however, was the rise of new, usually nationalist, schools in Scandinavia, Britain, Spain, Hungary and the Americas, though in the case of the United States it would take rather longer for its composers to find their own identities.

For better or for worse, the basic unity of nineteenth-century musical language, inherited from previous centuries, was destined to be fragmented irrevocably in the very near future, as composers sought new ways in which to articulate the anxiety, confusion and bewilderment of contemporary life and the human place in it. For many the new reality was almost too much to bear.

1900-Today

The Century of Modernism

In the twentieth century music plays an even greater part in the day-to-day lives of people through the advent of recording and broadcasting in sound and vision. The ability to hear live music is now within the grasp of many more people, and the international concert and opera repertoire continues to expand. Within the composers' world, however, the prospect is not so heart-warming. In common with other art forms in the new century, music undergoes a crisis, and a deep split develops between the traditional and the avant-garde, which the passage of time will do nothing to bridge. On the contrary, it seems as if there can be little hope of reconciling the two, and many music lovers are bewildered by the difficulties they encounter in trying to learn a new musical language. In the broadest context, however, music continues to enhance and enrich the lives of human beings.

Set for Maxwell Davies's opera Taverner *at the Royal Opera House, Covent Garden, 1983.*

1900-02
The Old and New Worlds Unite

The dawn of a new century sees strong native traditions established across virtually the whole of Europe – including Britain, which is no longer a land without music – and the birth of a new generation of composers in both North and South America who will eventually give the New World a voice of its own.

A poster for Puccini's Tosca. *The melodramatic twists of the plot have a tendency to mask the underlying tautness of the work's harmonic structure, which, in this opera, includes Puccini's first experiments with a whole-tone scale.*

1900 14 January Puccini's opera *Tosca* (left) is performed for the first time at the Teatro Costanzi in Rome to a less than enthusiastic audience, but gradually achieves popularity.

• **2 March** Weill is born in Dessau.

• **July** Ravel is dismissed from Fauré's class at the Paris Conservatoire, having failed to win the Prix de Rome ▲ (p.203) on two consecutive occasions. His tutor is dismayed.

• **2 July** Sibelius's *Finlandia* is first given in Helsinki (p.196).

• **3 October** Elgar's ORATORIO *The Dream of Gerontius* receives its first performance in Birmingham.

• **14 November** Aaron Copland is born in Brooklyn.

1901 Rachmaninov composes his Sonata for Cello and Piano and Second Piano Concerto.

• **January** Ravel returns to Fauré's class as an observer.

• **27 January** Verdi dies, aged eighty-eight, in Milan.

• **27 October** Debussy's symphonic SUITE *Nocturnes* is performed in full for the first time in Paris.

• **11 November** Ravel composes the piano piece *Jeux d'eau* (Fountains), inspired by Liszt ■ (p.163).

• **21 November** Richard Strauss's opera *Feuersnot* (Fire Famine) is first given in Dresden, but in Berlin it is taken off after seven performances at the request of the empress, and the composer is asked to resign.

• **25 November** Mahler's Fourth Symphony receives its first performance in Munich.

1902 Schoenberg begins work on a SYMPHONIC POEM, *Pelleas und Melisande* (Pelleas and Melisande), seemingly unaware that Debussy has composed an opera on the same subject.

• Mahler completes his Fifth Symphony and in March marries Alma Schindler, also a composer.

• **2 March** Sibelius conducts the first performance of his newly completed Second Symphony in Helsinki.

• **18 March** Schoenberg's *Verklärte Nacht* (p.197) is first given in Vienna.

• **29 March** Walton is born in Oldham, Lancashire.

• **30 April** Debussy's opera *Pelléas et Mélisande* is first performed at the Opéra-Comique in Paris.

• **9 June** Mahler conducts the first performance of his Third Symphony in Krefeld.

OTHER EVENTS
1900 Boxer Rebellion in China ends
• Zeppelin constructs the first dirigible
• Hopkins's first studies of vitamins
• Freud: *The Interpretation of Dreams*
• Conrad: *Lord Jim*

1901 Marconi sends first wireless trans-Atlantic telegraphic signals
• Planck elaborates quantum theory
• Mann: *Buddenbrooks*

1902 US buy control over the Panama Canal
• Chekhov: *Three Sisters*

Strauss 'is a master-composer just as Mozart was.'
A. Johnstone in the *Manchester Guardian*, 17 October 1902

● *Russian Piano Music*

The excellence of Russian piano music, and indeed the standard of music teaching in general, at the turn of the century owed a great deal to the efforts of the two brothers Anton and Nikolai Rubinstein.

The Russian Musical Society was launched in 1859, then in September 1862 Anton set up the St Petersburg Conservatory, and in 1866 Nikolai set up the Moscow Conservatory with Tchaikovsky as one of its teachers of music theory. Nikolai remained in charge in Moscow until his death in 1881, but Anton resigned from St Petersburg in 1867 and spent the next twenty years giving a series of concert tours throughout Europe and America.

Anton Rubinstein, who did so much to develop classical music in Russia through his compositions, his conducting and his piano playing.

In 1887 Anton returned once more to direct the St Petersburg Conservatory, and it was just before he resumed the appointment that he inaugurated his famous Historical Concerts. These seven-week series traced the development of keyboard music from its earliest days. Starting in January 1886, Rubinstein would give a recital in the Hall of the Nobility in Moscow, repeat it in the German Club the next day for students, and then go to St Petersburg with the same programme.

In this way Rachmaninov, who began studying at the Conservatory in Moscow in the autumn of 1885, became familiar with a much wider range of piano repertoire than might otherwise have been the case, and also developed a deep admiration for Rubinstein's playing. Rachmaninov's teacher Nikolai Zverev was in the habit of inviting many of Moscow's musical celebrities to his home for a musical evening on a Sunday. Often he would ask his pupils to play for his guests, and in this way the young composer made the acquaintance of, among others, Rubinstein and Tchaikovsky, both of whom profoundly influenced Rachmaninov.

1903-05
The Lure of Paris

With Fauré, Debussy and Ravel, French music enjoys one of its greatest periods of brilliance, and Paris continues to attract artistic talent of all kinds. At the heart of official musical life all is not well, however, for the Conservatoire is in crisis and institutions such as the Opéra are in decline.

A page from Janáček's piano sketches for his opera Jenůfa, *on which he worked for some ten years, beginning it in late 1893 or early 1894, but not completing it until 1904. Even after its première that year, he carried out revisions on no less than three occasions.*

1903 Ravel completes his String Quartet and the SONG CYCLE *Shéhérazade*, and begins his *Sonatine* for piano.

• **1 January** Debussy is awarded the Cross of Chevalier of the Légion d'Honneur.

• **11 February** Bruckner's unfinished Ninth Symphony receives its first performance in Vienna.

• **22 February** Wolf dies in an lunatic asylum in Vienna.

• **June–July** While staying on the Isle of Wight, Richard Strauss begins his *Sinfonia domestica* (Domestic Symphony).

• **Summer** Mahler begins work on his Sixth Symphony.

1904 London Symphony Orchestra founded.

• Ives completes his Third Symphony, begun in 1901.

• Debussy abandons his first wife, Lily (who attempts suicide), for the singer Emma Bardac, wife of a banker, and dedicatee of Fauré's song cycle *La Bonne Chanson* (p.191).

• **21 January** Janáček's opera *Jenůfa* (left) is first performed in Brno.

• **8 February** Sibelius's Violin Concerto is first given in Helsinki.

• **17 February** First performance of Puccini's *Madama Butterfly* at La Scala, Milan, which is a fiasco, though it is repeated in Brescia in a slightly revised form in May with more success.

• **5 March** Première of Ravel's String Quartet in Paris.

• **21 March** Richard Strauss conducts the first performance of his *Sinfonia domestica* in New York.

• **1 May** Dvořák dies, aged sixty-three, in Prague.

• **17 May** Ravel's *Shéhérazade* is first given in Paris.

• **Summer** Mahler completes his Sixth Symphony and starts his Seventh.

• **September** Sibelius begins work on his Third Symphony.

• **18 October** Mahler's Fifth Symphony is performed for the first time in Cologne.

1905 As a result of the refusal of the authorities at the Paris Conservatoire to allow Ravel to compete again for the Prix de Rome, the director, Dubois, resigns, and Fauré is appointed in his place.

• Schoenberg completes his First String Quartet.

• De Falla composes his first opera *La Vida breve* (Life is Short), while still a student at the Madrid Conservatory.

OTHER EVENTS
1903 Wright Brothers' first successful aeroplane flight

1904 Russo-Japanese War begins
• Panama Canal is begun
• Chekhov: *The Cherry Orchard*

1905 Norway separates from Sweden
• First Russian Revolution – establishment of Soviets
• Edison's first moving picture

The original cover for Debussy's La Mer, *which was published in 1905. The design is based on a print by Hokusai entitled* The Great Wave.

- **2 January** Tippett is born in London.

- **26 January** Schoenberg's *Pelleas und Melisande* (p.200) is performed in Vienna for the first time.

- **Spring** Janáček completes his opera, *Osud* (Fate, or Destiny).

- **Summer** Mahler completes his Seventh Symphony.

- **July** Debussy is in Eastbourne, Sussex, where he finishes the first set of his *Images* for piano. This year he has a daughter by Emma Bardac, whom he marries after divorcing his wife Lily.

- **15 October** Debussy's SYMPHONIC POEM *La Mer* ('The Sea, opposite), completed in March this year, is performed in Paris.

- **9 December** Richard Strauss's opera *Salome* is first performed in Dresden. It is both a critical and financial success, and he is subsequently able to build himself a villa at Garmisch.

- **30 December** Lehár's most successful work, the OPERETTA *The Merry Widow* is performed in Vienna for the first time, bringing the composer worldwide fame.

This portrait of Debussy was painted around 1902 at the time of the first performances of Pelléas et Mélisande.

▲ *Debussy Satirizes the Opéra…*

Everybody knows, at least by repute, the national Opera House. I can assure you from painful experience that it has not changed. An unprepared stranger would take it for a railway station and, once inside, would mistake it for a Turkish bath.

They keep making curious noises which the people who pay call music…you must not believe them.

By special order and a State subsidy this theatre may produce anything it chooses; it matters so little what, that luxurious loges à salons [drawing-room boxes] have been installed, so called because they are the most convenient places for no longer hearing a single note of music: they are the last salons where conversation still takes place.

In all this I am by no means attacking the genius of the directors, since I am convinced that the best wills are broken there against a solid and deadly wall created by headstrong bureaucracy…. Moreover, it will never change, short of a revolution, although revolutionaries do not always turn their attention to that kind of monument. One might wish for a fire, if that did not affect too indiscriminately people who are assuredly innocent.

… and the Prix de Rome

Suddenly someone tapped me on the shoulder and said breathlessly: 'You've won!' Whether you believe me or not, I can nevertheless assure you that my happiness evaporated. I saw clearly the problems, the worries that the most insignificant official accolade entails. Above all, I felt that I was no longer free.

I can see the dining room at the Villa [Médicis in Rome] where all the portraits of the prizewinners of the past and yesterday are lined up. They go right to the ceiling; you can no longer even make them out very clearly. It's true that people do not even talk about them any more. In all these faces one finds the same slightly sad expression. They seem uprooted. After a few months the proliferation of these frames, all the same dimensions, gives the onlooker the impression that it is the same Prix de Rome winner repeated to infinity.

Debussy, *M. Croche antidilettante*, 1921.

1906-10
The European Symphonic Tradition

In Austria and Germany, and eastwards to Russia, the symphonic tradition is brought to a magnificent climax through the music of Mahler and Strauss, Scriabin and Rachmaninov; in Britain, too, a symphonist of stature emerges with Elgar. Even as it reaches its peak, however, there is a movement away from such splendour.

1906 Schoenberg composes his First Chamber Symphony.

• **6 January** First performance of Ravel's piano SUITE *Miroirs* at the Société Nationale in Paris.

• **10 March** First performance of Ravel's *Sonatine* in Lyons.

Mahler photographed in 1907, the year he discovered that he was suffering from a heart condition and left Vienna for New York. There he was a visiting conductor at the Metropolitan Opera and then the New York Philharmonic Society. He returned to Austria every summer, however.

• **18 April** The Grand Opera House, San Francisco is destroyed by fire, following a massive earthquake.

• **27 May** Mahler (left) conducts the première of his Sixth Symphony in Essen.

• **17 August** Strauss conducts the Vienna Philharmonic Orchestra in a programme including works by Mozart and Bruckner at this, the first Mozart Festival, held in Salzburg.

• **23 August** Vaughan Williams's *Norfolk Rhapsody No.1*, based on English folk tunes ◆ (p.207) is given for the first time at a Promenade Concert in London.

• **25 September** Shostakovich is born in St Petersburg.

• **Autumn** Rachmaninov and his family move to Dresden, where he begins his Second Symphony.

1907 Rachmaninov writes his First Piano Sonata and completes his Second Symphony.

• Scriabin completes his *Poem of Ecstasy* for orchestra.

• Ravel completes the vocal SCORE of his opera *L'Heure espagnole* (Spanish Time), and begins his orchestral piece *Rapsodie espagnole* (Spanish Rhapsody).

• **5 February** Schoenberg's First String Quartet (p.202) receives its first performance in Vienna.

• **5 March** The first music to be broadcast on radio, Rossini's *William Tell* (p.148), is transmitted from New York.

• **27 April** Stravinsky's First Symphony is first given in St Petersburg.

• **5 July** Mahler's elder daughter, Maria Anna, dies of diphtheria, and he himself is found to have a heart ailment. He retires from the Hofoper in Vienna and leaves for New York (left).

• **September** Rimsky-Korsakov completes his opera *The Golden Cockerel* (opposite), though it will not be performed until 1909.

• **4 September** Death of Grieg, aged sixty-four, in Bergen.

• **25 September** Sibelius conducts the first performance of his Third Symphony in Helsinki.

OTHER EVENTS
1906 Deaths of Ibsen and Cézanne

1907 Triple Entente (Britain, Russia and France)
• Picasso: *Les Demoiselles d'Avignon*

1908 First model 'T' Ford produced

1909 Robert Peary reaches North Pole
• Frank Lloyd Wright: Robie House, Chicago

1910 Mexican revolution
• Union of South Africa created
• Discovery of protons and electrons
• Russell and Whitehead: *Principia Mathematica*

1908 Bartók completes his First String Quartet.

• Berg completes his Piano Sonata Op.1.

• Debussy completes his piano suite *Children's Corner*, dedicated to his daughter Claude-Emma (Chou-Chou), who will survive him by only one year.

• Schoenberg completes his Second String Quartet. It is the last work that the composer writes with a KEY SIGNATURE ◆ (p.225).

• Janáček begins his opera *Mr Brouček's Excursion to the Moon*, which he will not complete until 1917.

• **January** Vaughan Williams goes to Paris and takes lessons from Ravel for the next three months.

• **8 February** Rachmaninov's Second Symphony, which he finished in January in Dresden, is first heard in Moscow.

• **15 March** Ravel's *Rapsodie espagnole* receives its first performance in Paris.

• **5 April** Herbert von Karajan is born in Salzburg.

• **17 June** Stravinsky's TONE POEM *Fireworks* receives its first performance in St Petersburg ■ (p.209).

• **21 June** Rimsky-Korsakov dies, aged sixty-four, near St Petersburg.

• **19 September** Mahler conducts the first performance of his Seventh Symphony in Prague.

The title page, designed by Ivan Bilibin and dated 1908, for the score of Rimsky-Korsakov's last opera The Golden Cockerel, *which he completed in 1907. There were censorship problems, however, and it was not performed until after his death.*

★ *In 1906 Richard Strauss's* Salome *was first given at La Scala, Milan, with Toscanini conducting. This somewhat unlikely collaboration between the conductor and a composer who was an accomplished conductor in his own right, prompted this cartoon in the Milanese press.*

◆ *The Conductor-Composer*

The twentieth century saw a new member in the group of travelling virtuosi; the internationally famous conductor now took his place alongside the singers, pianists, violinists and other solo instrumentalists who went on world tours almost as a matter of course, and earned large amounts of money for doing so.

Rachmaninov composed music in which he would feature as solo pianist, in the tradition of Chopin and Liszt before him, but he also appeared as composer-conductor, as did Mahler, Strauss and many others. Indeed, it is almost impossible to imagine some of the scores of these composers without the parallel function of their creators as conductors. The sheer number of performers involved, and the lushness of the scoring, epitomizes late-Romantic symphonic writing. At the same time, however, it is clear that the wonder of the symphony orchestra is the astonishing variety of TIMBRES and textures that it can offer the composer, and that those are best exploited, and appreciated by the listener, by thinning out the orchestral texture rather than simply adding to it. The whole ensemble is best reserved for moments of climax, the possibilities of which had now been increased by the larger auditoria in which such music tended to be performed.

• **22 September** Strauss completes his opera *Elektra*.

• **4 November** Webern's Opus One, a *passacaglia* for orchestra, is performed for the first time in Vienna.

• **3 December** Elgar's First Symphony is first performed in Manchester (right).

• **10 December** Birth of Messiaen in Avignon.

• **11 December** Carter is born in New York.

1909 Schoenberg completes his SONG CYCLE *Das Buch der hängenden Gärten* (Book of the Hanging Gardens) and Five Orchestral Pieces, Op.16.

• Webern composes his Five Movements for String Quartet, Op.5.

• Rachmaninov composes the SYMPHONIC POEM *The Isle of the Dead* and the Third Piano Concerto.

• Kodály writes his First String Quartet.

• Bartók marries the sixteen-year-old Marta Ziegler, a piano student of his.

• **9 January** Ravel's piano SUITE *Gaspard de la nuit* is first performed in Paris. He ORCHESTRATES his opera *L'Heure espagnole* (p.204) this year and begins his ballet *Daphnis et Chloé*.

• **25 January** Strauss's opera *Elektra* has its first performance in Dresden.

• **May** Strauss begins to compose his opera *Der Rosenkavalier*.

• **Summer** Mahler sketches out his Ninth Symphony.

• **7 August** Schoenberg completes his Three Piano Pieces, Op.11.

• **28 November** Rachmaninov gives the first performance of his Third Piano Concerto in New York.

1910 Berg composes his String Quartet, Op.3.

• Webern completes his Six Orchestral Pieces, Op.6.

• Kodály marries Emma Sándor.

• Rachmaninov sets the Liturgy of St John Chrysostom for mixed choir.

• Elgar composes his Violin Concerto and begins his Second Symphony.

• Scriabin composes his *Prometheus, the Poem of Fire*, for a huge orchestra with enlarged PERCUSSION section, chorus and a light or colour organ.

• **5 January** Debussy completes the first book of his *Préludes* for piano.

• **9 March** Barber is born in West Chester, Pennsylvania.

• **20 April** Ravel's *Mother Goose* suite for piano duet, completed this year, is first performed in Paris. The programe also includes Fauré's song cycle *La Chanson d'Eve* (The Song of Eve) and Debussy's *D'un cahier d'esquisses* (From a Sketchbook), with Ravel as solo pianist.

• **29 May** Balakirev dies, aged seventy-three, in St Petersburg.

A portrait of Elgar by Philip Burne-Jones painted in 1913. Although Elgar had effectively made his farewell with his Second Symphony in 1911, and the 1914–18 war was to destroy the fabric of his world, he had two more works to leave to posterity, the elegiac tone poem Falstaff *(p.210) and the Cello Concerto ★ (p.215).*

• **25 June** First performance of Stravinsky's ballet *The Firebird* ■ (p.209) at the Paris Opéra by the Ballets Russes.

• **September** Vaughan Williams conducts the first performance of his *Fantasia on a Theme of Thomas Tallis* for string orchestra in Gloucester.

• **12 September** Mahler conducts the first performance of his Eighth Symphony, the *Symphony of a Thousand*, in Munich.

• **26 September** Strauss completes his opera *Der Rosenkavalier*.

• **12 October** Vaughan Williams conducts the first performance of his *Sea Symphony* in Leeds.

• **10 November** Elgar's Violin Concerto is given its first performance by Fritz Kreisler in London.

• **10 December** Puccini's opera *La fanciulla del West* (The Girl of the Golden West) is first given at the Metropolitan Opera House, New York.

Bartók using a two-way Edison wax cylinder sound-recorder in 1908 to record folksongs in a rural district of Czechoslovakia. His dedication, in partnership with Kodály, ensured that thousands of songs that might otherwise have been lost were preserved for posterity .

◆ *Folk Music*

The rise of nationalistic schools in the nineteenth century had often been stimulated by folk lore and the folk idiom of its music, so that a recognizable national character was imparted to the music of, for example, Hungary, Bohemia, Russia, Finland and Norway ◆ *(p.197). Very often, however, this did not depend on folk tunes as such, but rather a particular melodic inflection or rhythm. The Hungarian element in Liszt and Brahms, for example, falls into this category.*

Yet the real folk music still survived in rural areas, where it was rarely written down but passed on from generation to generation. Under the impact of improved communications and the drift from the countryside to cities, there was a great danger of that music being lost. Fortunately some composers realized this, and in Hungary, for example, Kodály and Bartók (right) worked to record as much as they could before it was too late. By 1912 they had collected three thousand songs. In England, Vaughan Williams and Holst collected some eight hundred songs between 1903 and 1913. Other countries fared less well, though in France D'Indy managed to collect many songs from the regions of the Vivarais, Vercors and Cévennes, and as early as 1886 he used a tune in his Symphonie sur un chant montagnard français *or* Symphonie cévenole *(Symphony on a French Mountain Song or Symphony from the Cévennes).*

It was right that this music should be preserved for posterity, though for some composers it took up time that they might be devoting to their own music, and did not necessarily provide

them with direct inspiration or thematic material for that music. Folk song may be used as the theme for sets of variations, but by its very nature it rarely lends itself to extended treatment. Indeed, in the case of Vaughan Williams with **Linden Lea**, *he was able to write a song so like a folk song that many people still*

imagine it to be one. In general terms, folk music and concert repertoire music remain separate entities, though without folk music the concert repertoire would be much the poorer. At best, nationalistic composers such as Smetana and Dvořák, Sibelius ★ *(p.197) and Grieg, Albéniz and Granados, have distilled the national personality through their music which embraces the folk element and to a degree synthesizes it, but leaves it intact.*

1911-15
Russian Ballet Conquers the West

The long established aristocratic tradition of Russian ballet is now brought to the West and is a revelation. It either enthrals or appals, but rarely leaves the spectator unmoved, and draws to it many of the best contemporary creative artists who are happy to collaborate in the development of this new medium.

1911 Schoenberg writes his Six Little Piano Pieces, Op.19.

• Webern composes his Five Pieces, Op.10.

• Bartók composes his only opera, *Duke Bluebeard's Castle*, which he submits for a competition, but it is rejected. He also composes his *Allegro barbaro* (Barbaric Allegro) for piano, in response to criticism of Kodály and himself as 'young barbarians'.

• Nielsen (right) completes his *Sinfonia espansiva*.

Photograph of Nielsen, whose late Romanticism was planted firmly in the twentieth century. His six symphonies, however, have an astringent quality due to his use of polytonality and dissonance.

• **26 January** Strauss's opera *Der Rosenkavalier* is first performed in Dresden.

• **3 April** Sibelius conducts the première of his Fourth Symphony in Helsinki.

• **18 May** Mahler dies in Vienna, aged fifty.

• **19 May** Ravel's opera *L'Heure espagnole* (p.204) has its first performance at the Opéra-Comique in Paris.

• **22 May** Debussy's incidental music to *The Martyrdom of St Sebastian* (left), written for the dancer Ida Rubinstein, has its first performance at the Théâtre du Châtelet, Paris.

• **24 May** Elgar's Second Symphony has a muted reception at its first performance in London.

• **13 June** Stravinsky's ballet *Petrushka* is first given in Paris.

• **7 July** Menotti is born in Cadegliano, Italy.

• **20 November** The posthumous first performance of Mahler's *Das Lied von der Erde* (The Song of the Earth) is given in Munich.

1912 Berg completes his Five Orchestral *Altenberg* Songs, Op.4.

• Prokofiev completes his First Piano Concerto.

• **8 June** Ravel's ballet *Daphnis et Chloé* is performed by the Ballets Russes at the Théâtre du Châtelet, Paris.

Bakst's costume design for Ida Rubinstein as St Sebastian, in The Martyrdom of St Sebastian, *with music by Debussy. Before having even seen the text, the church forbade Catholics to attend the work, and there were demonstrations outside the theatre.*

• **26 June** Bruno Walter conducts the posthumous first performance of Mahler's Ninth Symphony in Vienna.

• **5 September** Cage is born in Los Angeles.

• **16 October** First performance in Berlin of Schoenberg's *Pierrot lunaire* ★ (p.210), a SONG CYCLE with small orchestra.

• **25 October** Richard Strauss's opera *Ariadne auf Naxos* (Ariadne on Naxos) is given in Stuttgart as a double bill with his incidental music to Molière's *Le Bourgeois Gentilhomme*. Strauss will revise the opera considerably.

■ *Stravinsky*

Stravinsky was truly one of the giants of twentieth-century music. His father was a renowned bass singer at the Maryinsky Theatre in St Petersburg, but did not want his son to follow a musical career, and made him study law. Once he had gained his diploma in 1905, however, Stravinsky went to study with Rimsky-Korsakov (p.196), at that time director of the St Petersburg Conservatory, for three years. By 1908, with his brilliant score for *Fireworks* (p.205), Stravinsky had established his own musical personality. Diaghilev heard a performance of the work and commissioned Stravinsky to compose for his Ballets Russes.

The result was *The Firebird* (p.207), which at its première in 1910 immediately made Stravinsky famous. Even greater fame – or notoriety – came with the first performance of *The Rite of Spring* ▲ (p.211) in 1913, one of the key works in twentieth-century music.

Subsequently Stravinsky went through a long phase of NEO-CLASSICISM (a return to the earlier Classical style of music), beginning with the Pergolesi music that he arranged for the ballet *Pulcinella* (p.216) in 1920, and lasting until his opera *The Rake's Progress* (p.238). Within this Neo-Classicism, however, there were excursions into such diverse areas as Baroque music, which can be seen in his Octet of 1923 (p.218), and jazz, as in his *Ebony* Concerto of 1945 (p.235).

When Stravinsky adopted SERIALISM ◆ (p.225) however, the establishment was taken by surprise. Some thought the move a speculative venture on the composer's part, coming as it did so close after Schoenberg's death (p.238), but in so doing they wilfully ignored the subtlety of Stravinsky's intellect and his totally personal musical language, built on a highly refined sense of the balance between notes, phrases, CHORDS, and rhythm. His ear for ORCHESTRATION was also part of this delicate balance. Nadia Boulanger, his lifelong champion, would always point to the closing chord of his *Symphony of Psalms* (p.224) where, in her analysis, the whole effect turned on the disposition of the one note from the oboe without which, in her opinion, the whole would fail to exist.

Stravinsky in 1930, at a time when he was increasingly composing music for the concert hall rather than the stage.

A poster for the première of Schoenberg's Pierrot Lunaire in which Albertine Zehme was billed as the reciter, though the soloist in fact hovers between singing and speaking, observing the pitch of the notes as notated, but then abandoning them, thus producing a disoriented and hitherto unexplored world for the listener.

1913 Berg composes his Four Pieces for clarinet and piano, Op.5.

• Rachmaninov composes his Second Piano Sonata ● (p.201) and his CANTATA *The Bells*.

• Prokofiev completes his Second Piano Concerto and his opera *Maddalena* begun in 1911.

• Satie composes his *Descriptions automatiques* for piano.

• **25 January** Lutoslawski is born in Warsaw.

• **23 February** Schoenberg's cantata *Gurrelieder* (Songs of Gurre, a castle in Denmark) is first given in Vienna.

• **March–April** Ravel collaborates with Stravinsky in orchestrating Mussorgsky's *Khovanschina* for Diaghilev.

• **1 April** De Falla's first opera *La Vida breve* (Life is Short) is given in Nice.

• **10 May** Fauré's *Pénélope* has its first performance in Paris at the Théâtre des Champs-Elysées and is a success.

• **29 May** The first performance of Stravinsky's ballet *The Rite of Spring* at the Théâtre des Champs-Elysées, Paris, is a scandal ▲ (opposite).

• **1 October** Elgar's TONE POEM *Falstaff* is first performed in Leeds.

• **22 November** Britten is born in Lowestoft, Suffolk.

1914 Stranded in Switzerland by the outbreak of war, Stravinsky settles there until the armistice. He writes his Three Pieces for String Quartet.

• **27 March** Vaughan Williams's *London* Symphony is first performed. The composer writes little for the next five years.

• **May** Sibelius visits America, where he receives an honorary degree at Yale. He composes *The Oceanides* and begins sketching the Fifth Symphony.

OTHER EVENTS
1911 Revolution in China
• Amundsen reaches the South Pole

1912 Balkan wars
• *The Titanic* sinks
• Kandinsky: *Improvisation*

1913 DH Lawrence: *Sons and Lovers*
• Mann: *Death in Venice*
• Proust: *Remembrance of Things Past*

1914 World War I begins
• Panama Canal opened

1915 First U-boat attacks; sinking of the *Lusitania*
• Bragg's *X-rays and Crystal Structure*
• Morgan: *Mechanism of Mendelian Heredity*

A scene from Prokofiev's ballet Chout, designed by Larionov. Commisioned by Diaghilev, and completed in 1915, the work was first performed in Monte Carlo. The composer revised it in 1920, and when it was given in Paris in 1921, Prokofiev conducted.

• **August** Stimulated by the entry of France into the war on 2 August, Ravel completes his Piano Trio.

• **4 August** Richard Strauss begins to compose the opera *Die Frau ohne Schatten* (The Woman without a Shadow).

1915 Stravinsky begins work on *Renard* (The Fox) for four singers and chamber orchestra.

• Rachmaninov composes his Vespers or All-night Vigil.

• Prokofiev completes his *Scythian* Suite and *Chout* (Buffoon, opposite).

• Bartók composes his Sonatina for piano and begins his Second String Quartet, which he will take two years to complete.

• Berg completes his Three Orchestral Pieces, Op.6.

• Ives completes his 'Concord' Sonata for piano, begun in 1911.

• **January** Ravel's Piano Trio has its first performance.

• **27 April** Death of Scriabin, aged forty-three, in Moscow.

• **July–August** Debussy composes his Sonata for Cello and Piano.

• **September** Debussy completes his last masterpieces for his own instrument, the Twelve Studies for piano.

• **September** Debussy composes his Sonata for Flute, Viola and Harp.

• **28 October** Richard Strauss's *Alpen* Symphony is first heard in Berlin.

• **8 December** Sibelius conducts the first performance of his Fifth Symphony in Helsinki.

▲ *The Impact of Stravinsky's 'The Rite of Spring'*

The performance began. No sooner had it commenced when the excitement began. The scene now so well known with its brilliantly coloured background now not at all extraordinary, outraged the Paris audience. No sooner did the music begin and the dancing than they began to hiss. The defenders began to applaud. We could hear nothing, as a matter of fact I never did hear any of the music of The Rite of Spring *because it was the only time I ever saw it and one literally could not, throughout the whole performance, hear the sound of music. The dancing was very fine and that we could see although our attention was constantly distracted by a man in the box next to us flourishing his cane, and finally in a violent altercation with an enthusiast in the box next to him, his cane came down and smashed the opera hat the other had just put on in defiance.*

Gertrude Stein from *The Autobiography of Alice B. Toklas*, (1933)

The general impression of this choreography I had then, and have kept until today, is the irresponsibility with which it was devised by Nijinsky. It clearly revealed his incapacity to assimilate and appropriate to himself the revolutionary idea that constituted Diaghilev's creed.... How far all this was from what I had desired!

Stravinsky *Chroniques de ma vie* (1935)

A scene from the 1913 Ballets Russes production of The Rite of Spring *(right). Both Nijinsky's choreography and Stravinsky's music caused outrage at its first performance.*

1916-17

The Softer Voice of Spain

Spain has often inspired composers from elsewhere in Europe to bring a touch of the exotic into their music, and the French in particular have carried on a long love affair with their neighbour across the Pyrenees. Now, however, it is the turn of the Spanish to make their own music, and show what they can do.

1916 Bartók composes his Suite for Piano.

• Ives completes his Fourth Symphony.

• Holst (below) composes his suite *The Planets* for orchestra.

• Nielsen completes his Fourth Symphony, the 'Inextinguishable'.

• Schoenberg completes his Four Orchestral Songs, Op.22.

• **28 January** Granados's opera *Goyescas* is first heard at the Metropolitan Opera House ● (opposite). On their return home from the première on 24 March, the composer and his wife die in the English Channel, when a German submarine torpedoes their ship.

• **26 May** Janáček conducts the first performance of his opera *Jenůfa* at the Prague National Opera.

• **4 October** The revised version of Richard Strauss's *Ariadne* (p.208) is given in Vienna, with Lotte Lehmann in the role of the Composer.

1917 Schoenberg begins writing his ORATORIO *Die Jakobsleiter* (Jacob's Ladder).

• Berg begins work on his opera *Wozzeck*.

• Rachmaninov revises his First Piano Concerto and gives what is to be his last concert in Russia ● (p.201).

• Prokofiev completes his First Violin Concerto and his opera *The Gambler*.

• Janáček completes his opera *Mr Brouček's Excursion to the Moon* (p.205) and adds *Mr Brouček's Excursion to the Fifteenth Century*, making one work, *Mr Brouček's Excursions*.

• Holst composes his choral masterpiece *The Hymn of Jesus*.

• **28 March** Puccini's opera *La Rondine* (The Swallow) is first performed in Monte Carlo.

• **7 April** De Falla's ballet *The Three-cornered Hat* has its first performance in Madrid.

• **18 May** Satie's ballet *Parade* has a scandalous première, with a lighting failure causing the audience to riot. The work, commissioned by Diaghilev, is

> '*Spain is my second musical homeland.*' Ravel

Holst at his work table, a painting of 1914. Holst had to rely on teaching for a living, and from 1905 until he died he was music director of a girls' school in London.

Satie's first orchestral score, with Picasso's first stage designs, Cocteau's first scenario and Massine's first choreography. This year Satie also writes his 'symphonic drama' *Socrate*.

• **6 June** Satie gives a concert of his music and that of Durey, Auric and Honegger. These last three, together with Tailleferre, Poulenc and Milhaud, will comprise the group known as *Les Six* (The Six, left). Satie becomes the spiritual mentor of the group and Cocteau their publicist.

• **November** Ravel completes his piano suite *Le Tombeau de Couperin* (Couperin's Monument), which he will subsequently ORCHESTRATE.

• **10 November** Fauré's Second Sonata for Violin and Piano is first performed in Paris. He begins his First Sonata for Cello and Piano this winter.

• **December** Rachmaninov leaves Russia with his family for good.

• **13 December** Richard Strauss conducts the one hundredth performance of *Der Rosenkavalier* (p.207) in Dresden.

Cocteau surrounded by five of the members of the group of French composers known as Les Six: Poulenc, Germaine Tailleferre, Durey, Milhaud and Honegger. Cocteau's caricature portrait of the sixth member, Auric, hangs on the wall behind them.

The front cover of an early piano work by Ravel entitled Habanera, *which conveys both the exoticism of Spain and his love for the country and its music, which he inherited from his mother. His approach to the Spanish element was not to indulge in pastiche, however, but to produce his own personal expression.*

● *The Spanish Element in Music*

Of all the composers who wrote with a Spanish accent, it was perhaps Ravel who came closest to producing an authentic style, as De Falla described in an article written after the Frenchman's death: 'Ravel's Spain was an ideal of Spain, conveyed to him through his mother, whose exquisite conversation, always in excellent Spanish, enchanted me, when she conjured up for me her youth spent in Madrid. I understood then how much fascination these captivating nostalgic evocations had held for her son since childhood, enlivened no doubt by the power given to all memories by the theme of song or dance inseparably bound up there.'

The two founders of the modern Spanish piano school were Albéniz and Granados, both of whom introduced a geniune Spanish element into their music, drawn from native traditions. Both men composed operas, and Granados turned for his to the *zarzuela*, a kind of popular opera. De Falla went to his native Andalusia for inspiration, and his *El amor brujo* (Love the Magician) started out as a *gitanería* or gypsy-inspired mixture of songs, dances and spoken material, which he subsequently reworked as a ballet with songs. Of his keyboard music, his *Nights in the Gardens of Spain* for piano and orchestra represents one of the highpoints of Spanish Romanticism.

1918-19
The Twilight of Romantic Opera

Although Strauss will continue to compose operas for another twenty years or more, and Puccini has still one more opera which he will almost complete before he dies, glamour and verismo *alone are not enough, and the trend is inexorably away from grand opera to works that reflect more closely the concerns of contemporary society.*

1918 Bartók composes his ballet *The Wooden Prince*.

• Webern completes his Four Songs Op.13.

• Stravinsky completes the ballet *Les Noces* (The Wedding) and *L'Histoire du soldat* (The Soldier's Tale) for speaker and seven instruments, as well as *Ragtime* for CIMBALON, PERCUSSION and nine instruments.

• **25 March** Death of Debussy, aged fifty-five, in Paris.

• **26 March** Death of Cui, aged eighty-three, in St Petersburg.

• **21 April** First performance of Prokofiev's *Classical* (First) Symphony in St Petersburg.

• **25 August** Birth of Bernstein in Lawrence, Massachusetts.

• **December** Rachmaninov gives his first concert in America.

• **14 December** Première of Puccini's *Il trittico* (The Triptych) at the Metropolitan Opera House, New York. The three operas are *Il tabarro* (The Cloak), *Suor Angelica* (Sister Angelica) and *Gianni Schicchi*.

OTHER EVENTS
1918 End of World War I
• Female suffrage in Britain
• Civil War in Russia

1919 Treaty of Versailles
• League of Nations, World Court and International Labour Organization set up
• First trans-Atlantic aeroplane crossing

The cover of Rag-Time Parade, *a suite of pieces made up from the music of Satie's 'realist ballet'* Parade *(p.212), though jazz as such was not actually performed in Paris until the following year.*

1919 Bartók completes his ballet or 'grotesque pantomime' *The Miraculous Mandarin* ★ (p.222), but because of the violence and sexuality of its scenario it is not performed in Budapest.

• Janáček composes his SONG CYCLE *The Diary of One who Disappeared*.

• Stravinsky composes *Piano Rag Music* and Three Pieces for Clarinet, both works influenced by jazz, as well as the Neo-Classical ballet *Pulcinella*, using music by Pergolesi.

• Hindemith composes the one-act opera *Mörder, Hoffnung der Frauen* (Murderer, Hope of Women), his First Solo Viola Sonata, and his First String Quartet.

• **10 April** Fauré says goodbye to the theatre with the choreographic *divertissement Masques et bergamasques* (Masks and Bergamasques) at the Monte Carlo Theatre. Two days later his *Fantaisie* for piano and orchestra, composed in 1918, is given its first performance in the same theatre.

• **Autumn** Sibelius completes the definitive version of his Fifth Symphony (p.210).

• **10 October** The first performance in Vienna of Strauss's opera *Die Frau ohne Schatten* (p.211) is not a success.

• **26 October** Elgar's Cello Concerto (opposite) is first given in London.

• **1 December** Richard Strauss becomes joint director, with Franz Schalk, of the Vienna State Opera ■ (opposite).

★ *Elgar conducting at a recording of his Cello Concerto in 1920, the year after its composition, with Beatrice Harrison as soloist. Through its thinned-out textures, the concerto is a masterly balance between orchestra and solo cello.*

■ *Richard Strauss – Opera at the Crossroads*

Strauss's tenure at the Vienna State Opera may be seen, in retrospect, as a golden age. He mounted what were virtually his own productions of *Der Freischütz, Carmen, Tannhäuser, Fidelio, Don Giovanni* and *The Flying Dutchman*. He and Schalk brought back Puccini's operas, and in the Redoutensaal put on *The Marriage of Figaro, The Barber of Seville, Don Pasquale* and, in an imaginative triple bill, Mozart's *Bastien and Bastienne*, Pergolesi's *La serva padrona* and Weber's *Abu Hassan*. Strauss conducted *Così fan tutte*, both in Vienna and in Salzburg, where the performances may be regarded as having fixed the opera once and for all in the international repertoire. Then there were Strauss's own works, as well as those by his contemporaries such as Pfitzner's *Palestrina* and Korngold's *Die tote Stadt*.

A caricature showing Richard Strauss conducting under the watchful eye of Franz Schalk, his co-director at the Vienna State Opera, with whom he had an uneasy and morally exhausting relationship, which could never have lasted.

Nevertheless it was in many ways a twilight time, for the co-direction with Schalk, and the precarious situation of the Vienna Opera House's finances, meant that the arrangement was unlikely to have been of long duration. More significant in musical terms, however, was the fact that Strauss showed not the slightest interest in the music of Bartók, Berg, Hindemith, Prokofiev, Schoenberg or Stravinsky. In fact he is said to have asked Hindemith, 'Why do you compose like that? You don't need to. You have talent.'

Ineluctably, Strauss's world was vanishing, and there is a close parallel between his situation and that of Elgar in England. This same year, 1919, saw the completion of Elgar's last masterpiece, his Cello Concerto (above), after which he fell into almost total silence, unable to come to terms with what he saw around him. Strauss was not so easily silenced, but his sentiments were much the same.

1920-24
The Turbulent Twenties

In the years immediately after World War I it is not only political and social orders that are undergoing profound changes, for with the passing of such composers as Bruch, Saint-Saëns, Fauré and Puccini and the arrival of Schoenberg, Webern and Bartók, the very nature of music is clearly changing also.

1920 Kodály completes his Serenade for two violins and viola.

• Stravinsky composes his *Symphonies of Wind Instruments* and completes his ballet *Pulcinella* ■ (p.209).

• Hindemith composes his one-act opera *Das Nusch-Nuschi* (a mythical creature half giant rat, half alligator).

• **January** Ravel refuses to accept the Légion d'Honneur, already reported in the press. He begins work on the Sonata for Violin and Cello and the opera *L'Enfant et les sortilèges* (The Child and the Spells).

• **28 February** Ravel's SUITE *Le Tombeau de Couperin* (p.213) is performed as a ballet in Paris.

• **14 May** The revised version of Vaughan Williams's *London Symphony* (p.210) is performed in London.

• **22 August** The first Salzburg Festival opens ◆ (p.237).

• **August–November** Richard Strauss ■ (p.215) visits South America, conducting his operas and giving concerts with the Vienna Philharmonic.

• **2 October** Bruch dies, aged eighty-two, in Berlin.

• **4 December** Korngold's opera *Die tote Stadt* (The Dead City) is given in Hamburg and creates his international reputation.

• **12 December** Ravel's *La Valse*, rejected by Diaghilev as being unsuitable music for a ballet, is first performed in Paris.

1921 Fauré completes his last SONG CYCLE, *L'Horizon chimérique* (The Vanishing Horizon), Second Cello Sonata and Second Piano Quintet.

• Varèse completes *Amériques* (Americas) for large orchestra.

• Webern completes his Six Songs, Op.14, begun in 1917.

• Hindemith composes his one-act opera *Sancta Susanna*.

• Prokofiev completes his Third Piano Concerto, begun in 1917.

• **January** Sibelius pays his last visit to London and meets Busoni.

• **11 June** Honegger's opera *King David* is first given in Mézières in Switzerland; it is subsequently adapted for performance as an ORATORIO.

• **16 December** Saint-Saëns dies, aged eighty-six, in Algiers.

• **30 December** Prokofiev's opera *The Love for Three Oranges* (above) receives its first performance at the Chicago Opera House.

'...marvellous ideas, which were unfortunately baulked by the...singers'

Stravinsky on Bronislava Nijinska's production of *Mavra*

Two grotesque Russian figures for Prokofiev's The Love for Three Oranges, *which was was first heard in Chicago in 1921, though these designs were probably intended for the first Russian performances in St Petersburg in 1926.*

1922 Copland goes to Paris to study with Nadia Boulanger, and composes his *Passacaglia* for piano, which he dedicates to his teacher.

• Hindemith completes his *Kammermusik Nr.1* (Chamber Music No.1) for twelve players, his *Suite 1922* for piano, Second Solo Viola Sonata and Third String Quartet.

• Nielsen completes his Fifth Symphony.

• Webern completes his Five Sacred Songs for voice and mixed quintet, Op.15, begun in 1917.

• **26 January** Vaughan Williams's Third *(Pastoral)* Symphony is first given in London. The final movement contains a soprano solo.

• **26 February** Saint-Saëns's *Carnival of the Animals* is first performed posthumously in Paris – the composer did not consider the work serious enough to allow it to be given during his lifetime.

• **29 May** Birth of Xenakis in Braila, Romania.

• **2 June** Stravinsky's opera *Mavra* is first performed in Paris, directed by Nijinsky's sister, Bronislava Nijinska.

• **11 November** The BBC begin radio broadcasting of music in England.

Bartók and Kodály with Ivan Busitia in Romania in 1917 (below), at a time when the two composers had done much of their collecting of folk songs ◆ (p.207), though the turmoil created by war had in any case dislocated their researches.

◆ *New Horizons*

In the years immediately following World War I it became apparent that considerable changes had already occurred in the musical domain, and that the picture would continue to evolve considerably in the immediate future. In the first place, Western music was no longer dominated to anything like the same extent that it had been previously by the Paris-Vienna axis, even if those two cities still played an extremely important part in introducing the new and sensational.

The fact that there were now flourishing native traditions of music in eastern Europe was abundantly clear from the activities of Janáček, Kodály, Bartók, Prokofiev and, of course, Stravinsky, though he rapidly became such an international figure that he could hardly be regarded as solely Russian, even at this time. Nevertheless he was a direct product of the Russian tradition. In Scandinavia, Sibelius and Nielsen carried on a process, which although greatly indebted to the nineteenth-century international –

largely German – influence at the outset, now had a strongly nationalist character that inspired others to value their native talents. America would eventually find its own voice, too, though by a somewhat different process, absorbing first many different cultures and influences, including many from Europe.

In Europe itself some composers reacted against received tradition by turning to contemporary elements such as jazz and cabaret music for inspiration, but the most profound changes would be much more intellectually rigorous. By establishing meeting places like the Donaueschingen Festival and the International Society for Contemporary Music, composers indicated the extent to which they now needed to express solidarity with each other and assert their identity, in contrast to the music of the past and those composers of the present who upheld that past. This conscious break was but a foretaste of the much more profound divisions that were soon to fragment Western music irreparably.

1923 Schoenberg completes his Five Piano Pieces, Op.23, together with the Serenade for septet, Op.24, composed this year, and the Piano Suite, Op.25, begun in 1921. These three works mark the development of the composer's serial technique ◆ (p.225).

• Bartók completes his Dance Suite for orchestra. This year he divorces his first wife and marries Ditta Pásztory.

• Prokofiev completes his opera *The Fiery Angel*.

• Stravinsky composes his Octet for wind instruments ■ (p.209).

• Hindemith completes his SONG CYCLE *Das Marienleben* (The Life of the Virgin Mary), which he will revise between 1936 and 1948.

• Poulenc composes his ballet *Les Biches* (The Does).

• **February** Fauré completes his Trio for Piano and Strings and then begins work on his only string quartet.

• **19 February** Sibelius conducts the first performance of his Sixth Symphony in Helsinki.

• **28 May** Birth of Ligeti in Tîrnâveni, Transylvania.

• **12 June** Walton's *Façade* (right) for speaker and small chamber ensemble, to texts by Edith Sitwell, is first performed publicly in London.

• **5 July** Walton's String Quartet is performed in London, and in Salzburg on 4 August during the course of the first festival of the International Society for Contemporary Music known as ISCM ◆ (p.217).

• **19 November** First performance of Kodály's *Psalmus Hungaricus* takes place in Budapest to celebrate the fiftieth anniversary of the creation of the city.

1924 12 February First performance in New York of Gershwin's *Rhapsody in Blue*, with the composer as soloist.

• **24 March** The first performance of Sibelius's Seventh Symphony is given in Stockholm.

• **8 May** Honegger's TONE POEM for orchestra, *Pacific 231*, has a highly successful first performance.

• **6 June** The first performance of Schoenberg's MONODRAMA *Erwartung* (Expectation) is given in Prague.

• **October** Milhaud's ballet *La Création du Monde* (The Creation of the World) is given at the Théâtre des Champs-Elysées in Paris, where its jazz rhythms take the audience by surprise.

• **14 October** The first performance of Schoenberg's music drama *Die glückliche Hand* (The Lucky Hand) takes place at the Volksoper in Vienna.

• **6 November** First performance of Janáček's opera *The Cunning Little Vixen* in Brno, considered one of the most important Czech operas of the century.

• **4 November** Death of Fauré, aged seventy-nine, in Paris. His pupil Roger-Ducasse completes his String Quartet.

• **4 November** Richard Strauss's opera *Intermezzo* is first given in Dresden, conducted by the composer.

• **29 November** Death of Puccini, aged sixty-five, in Brussels (left). His opera *Turandot* is left incomplete.

Detail from a design by John Armstrong for one of the backdrops of Walton's Façade *at its London première in 1931.*

Poster for the fifth performance of Boïto's posthumous opera Nerone, *which Toscanini was to have conducted on 29 November 1924 at La Scala, Milan, but which was abandoned when it was learnt that Puccini had just died.*

Opposite: Arnold Dolmetsch, centre, with his son Carl, left, in his workshop at his home in Haslemere after his return from America. In 1925 a festival of early music was established there, and the following year he completed a replica set of a full family of recorders.

◆ *The Early Music Revival and the Search for Authenticity*

An interest in early music has not been solely a twentieth-century phenomenon. Mendelssohn's performance of Bach's St Matthew Passion *in 1829 (p.148), followed by his three-piano concerto in 1835 (p.152) and a series of Handel and Haydn* ORATORIOS *helped to keep alive interest in major composers. Of course certain Beethoven and Mozart*

works never fell out of favour, which helps to explain Tchaikovsky's admiration for the latter, but as far as lesser-rank composers were concerned, there was considerable ignorance. This was not wilful neglect, for until virtually the end of the eighteenth century music had always been contemporary music, and, as fashions changed, composers were forgotten and new names came to the fore. It was not only the names that were forgotten, however, for performance practice changed, old instruments were forgotten, and would-be performers had sometimes no idea for what instruments or forces works were originally intended.

The more determinedly scholarly approach to early music began roughly in the last quarter of the nineteenth century, when composers such as D'Indy, whom we have already encountered as a collector of folk song ◆ (p.207), also showed interest in

PLAINSONG *and Baroque music, and set up the Schola Cantorum in Paris to further this interest. There were several others, amongst whom one might name Dolmetsch, Busoni, Casadesus, Respighi and Casella, who not only examined the music, but the instruments on which it was played and, as far as they could determine, the way in which it was played. The Polish pianist Wanda Landowska, who virtually reinvented harpsichord playing, taught at the Schola Cantorum between 1900 and 1913, where D'Indy mounted performances of Monteverdi's operas after World War I.*

The Authenticity Controversy

When in 1937 Nadia Boulanger made her recordings of Monteverdi's MADRIGALS *the 'fond sonore' or accompaniment was provided by a piano. Purists might well throw up their hands in dismay, but what is clearly manifest is her instinctive feel for style and interpretation that makes one forget the anachronism.*

The quest for authenticity is not an end in itself. Of course it is very instructive to hear music performed as it might have been heard, and this may bring us to a fundamental reappraisal of the music itself in certain cases, but it is ultimately a road to nowhere. Indeed, at the present time listeners to certain radio stations are deprived of the opportunity of hearing a major part of the symphonic repertoire largely because it cannot be broadcast on 'authentic' instruments, despite the fact that there are many instruments still in use today – especially stringed instruments – that could hardly be more authentic, having been made by the greatest makers of their day. It is, of course, dangerous to apply such an argument across the board, but authenticity as an end in itself is a sterile pursuit, unless it is backed up with a knowledge of style and the composer's intentions. That requires more than the seal of authenticity.

1925-30
Breaking the Mould

At the heart of Europe a search for new forms of expression in music, painting and literature, precipitates a break with the forms and conventions of the past. Not all composers feel able to follow the new discipline, and in some countries it is regarded with suspicion or greeted with hostility, as the twentieth century is characterized by the collapse of a recognized international style in Western music.

1925 Bax composes his Second Symphony.

• Berg completes his Chamber Concerto for piano, violin and thirteen wind instruments, both as a fiftieth-birthday present to Schoenberg and, with Webern, as a celebration of the three composers who now make up the Second Viennese School ◆ (p.225).

Set designs for the first performance of Berg's first opera Wozzeck *at the Unter den Linden opera house in Berlin in December 1925.*

• **8 January** Stravinsky conducts a concert of his own music at Carnegie Hall – his first American appearance as a conductor.

• **11 January** Nadia Boulanger plays the organ in the première of Copland's *Symphony for Organ and Orchestra*, which she commissioned. Damrosch conducts the Boston Symphony Orchestra in New York on this occasion.

• **21 March** First performance of Ravel's one-act opera *L'Enfant et les sortilèges* (The Child and the Spells, right) in Monte Carlo.

• **26 March** Birth of Boulez in Montbrison.

• **21 May** Busoni's opera *Doktor Faustus* is first produced in Dresden.

• **June** First performance of Fauré's String Quartet in Paris.

• **1 June** Bloch conducts the première of his NEO-BAROQUE *Concerto Grosso No.1* for piano and strings.

• **6 June** The first performance of Prokofiev's Second Symphony, in two movements, takes place in Paris.

• **1 July** Death of Satie, aged fifty-nine, in Paris.

• **25 July** The first performance of Hindemith's *Concerto* for orchestra is given in Duisburg.

• **7 October** Holst's *Choral* Symphony, based on the poetry of John Keats, is heard for the first time at the Leeds Festival.

• **24 October** Berio is born at Oneglia, Italy.

• **20 November** Copland's *Music for the Theater*, for small orchestra and piano, is given for the first time in Boston.

• **11 December** Nielsen conducts the première of his Sixth Symphony, completed on 5 December, in Copenhagen.

• **14 December** Berg's opera *Wozzeck* (above) has its first performance in Berlin after one hundred and thirty-seven rehearsals, and the composer's international reputation is established.

L'enfant et les Sortilèges

Maurice Ravel Colette

The title page for the first edition of the score of Ravel's opera L'Enfant et les sortilèges, *to a text by Colette. In view of Ravel's obsession with childhood, it was a subject admirably suited to his talents.*

1926 Berg completes his *Lyric Suite* for string quartet, the composer's first work using the twelve-note method ◆ (p.225).

• Rachmaninov completes his Fourth Piano Concerto.

• **10 January** Strauss conducts the first film version of *Der Rosenkavalier* (p.208) in Dresden. On 12 April he repeats the performance in London and makes a recording of extracts from it the next day ◆ (p.233).

• **25 April** The première of Puccini's opera *Turandot*, conducted by Toscanini, is given at La Scala, Milan. Although the work has been completed after the composer's death by Franco Alfano, only Puccini's music is performed on this occasion.

• **12 May** Shostakovich's First Symphony is first given in St Petersburg.

• **22 June** Webern's Five Pieces for Orchestra, Op.10 are performed for the first time in Zurich, thirteen years after their completion (p.208), establishing his international reputation.

■ *Schoenberg: The Future and the Past*

Schoenberg introduced the most original and probably most influential innovation not only into twentieth-century music, but the whole of Western Classical music. He was also a great composition teacher. In the discarding of the system of tonality that had hitherto been fundamental to music, he achieved what no one else had done before, a complete break with the past. He was the first composer to feel the need for such a shift in direction. His predecessors had followed their dictates within a broad convention, rather than consciously setting out to forge new techniques, though naturally there had always been composers who were regarded as modern, and even avant-garde, in their day. One sees with Beethoven and Wagner, for instance, a feeling that existing means were inadequate to convey their creative thoughts.

Composers who followed Schoenberg, such as Boulez ■ (p.251), for example, in his famous article entitled 'Schoenberg is dead', written after his death in 1951, have demoted him and pointed to his pupil Webern as a more significant pioneer of twentieth-century music. In Boulez's estimation, Schoenberg persisted in clinging on to forms that his own serial method had rendered meaningless.

He had virtually gone back to Brahms. For the same reason Boulez also dismissed Stravinsky. As the twentieth century draws to its close, however, Schoenberg's strength has proved to be that he showed a way forward while not annihilating the past. With Boulez and his followers it remains to be seen whether they will speak a language that is comprehensible to the musical world at large.

Schoenberg photographed in the twenties, and already showing the determination and uncompromising intellectual stance, which brought about one of the most fundamental changes not only in the construction of twentieth-century music, but also in society's perception of the very nature and function of music.

- **29 June** *Sinfonietta* by Janáček (below) is first performed in Prague.

- **1 July** Birth of Henze in Gütersloh, Westphalia.

- **Summer** In a burst of activity, Bartók composes his First Piano Concerto, Piano Sonata, *Nine Little Pieces*, and the SUITE *Out of Doors*.

- **16 October** Kodály's SINGSPIEL *Háry János* is given for the first time in Budapest.

- **9 November** Première of Hindemith's opera *Cardillac* in Dresden.

- **28 November** Bartók's ballet *The Miraculous Mandarin* (right) is first given in Cologne. The work is censored by the mayor of Cologne because of its salacious subject matter.

- **18 December** First performance in Brno of Janáček's eighth opera, *The Makropoulos Affair* (opposite).

- **26 December** First performance of Sibelius's SYMPHONIC POEM *Tapiola* in New York.

1927 Bartók composes his String Quartet No.3.

- Hindemith writes a comic opera *Hin und Zuruck* (There and Back Again).

- Webern completes his String Trio.

- **8 January** First performance of Berg's *Lyric Suite* in Vienna (p.221).

- **15 January** Strauss's opera *Intermezzo* is first produced in Vienna.

- **28 January** Copland's Piano Concerto recieves its first performance with the Boston Symphony Orchestra conducted by Koussevitzky.

- **29 January** Goossens conducts a performance of the second movement of Ives's Fourth Symphony, though it will not have a complete performance for thirty-eight years (p.246).

- **10 February** First performance of Ernst Křenek's opera *Jonny spielt auf* (Johnny Strikes up) in Leipzig.

- **18 March** Rachmaninov's Fourth Piano Concerto fails to please the audience when he is soloist at its first performance in Philadelphia.

- **24 March** The orchestral suite from Kodály's *Háry János* is first performed in Barcelona.

- **20 March** Berg's Chamber Concerto is first performed in Berlin.

- **27 March** Strauss conducts Beethoven's Ninth Symphony in Dresden on the centenary of Beethoven's death (p.147).

- **8 April** Première of Varèse's symphonic poem *Arcana* in Philadelphia.

- **30 May** Ravel's Sonata for Violin and Piano is first given by Georges Enesco and the composer.

- **30 May** Stravinsky's opera-oratorio *Oedipus Rex* (Oedipus the King), an early example of his NEO-CLASSICISM, is first performed in Paris.

★ *Two costume sketches for Bartók's ballet* The Miraculous Mandarin, *which caused discomfort to the theatre direction in Budapest because of the violence and sexuality of its scenario, rather than a rejection of the music.*

Janáček's sketch for the 'Fanfare' in his Sinfonietta, *composed in 1926. Note the absence of ruled lines for the staves on which the music is written; the composer preferred to draw his own.*

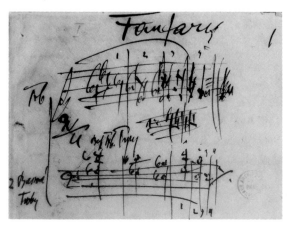

OTHER EVENTS
1925 Beginning of molecular biology
- Scott Fitzgerald: *The Great Gatsby*

1926 General strike in Britain
- First all-sound films
- Hemingway: *The Sun also Rises*

1927 Lindbergh's solo trans-Atlantic flight
- Chinese civil war
- First TV transmission
- Heisenberg and others - uncertainty principle in quantum physics
- Virginia Woolf: *To the Lighthouse*

Čapek's design for the office of the lawyer in Janáček's opera The Makropoulos Affair. *The play on which the opera was based was by Karel Čapek, the artist's brother, who felt that his work was hardly a subject for an opera, but the composer was convinced that it would be suitable as a vehicle for his music.*

- **1 July** First performance of Bartók's First Piano Concerto in Frankfurt.

- **19 September** Schoenberg's String Quartet No.3 is first given in Vienna.

- **30 September** The International Musicological Society is founded.

- **6 November** Shostakovich's Second Symphony, *To October*, is first performed in St Petersburg.

- **5 December** Janáček's *Glagolitic Mass* is first heard in Brno.

1928 Bartók composes his String Quartet No.4.

- Webern completes his Symphony.

- **5 January** Walton's *Sinfonia concertante* is first performed in London.

- **16 January** Webern's String Trio is first performed in Vienna.

- **30 March** Toscanini is appointed conductor of the newly formed Philharmonic-Symphony Society of New York.

- **27 April** Stravinsky's ballet *Apollon Musagetes* (Apollo Father of the Muses) is first given in Washington.

A scene from Brecht and Weill's The Threepenny Opera, *derived from Gay's* The Beggar's Opera *(p.78). Whereas Gay had simply wanted to counterbalance the abundance of Italian opera in London during the eighteenth century, two hundred years later in Germany, this work took on a much heavier political significance.*

• **6 June** Richard Strauss's opera *Die ägyptische Helena* (The Egyptian Helen) is first performed in Dresden.

• **3 August** Weill's *The Threepenny Opera* is given in Berlin (left).

• **12 August** Janáček dies, aged seventy-four, in Ostrava, Czechoslovakia.

• **22 August** Stockhausen is born in Burg Mödrath, near Cologne.

• **11 September** Janáček's String Quartet No.2, *Intimate Letters*, is first given in Brno.

• **22 November** Ravel's *Boléro* is performed at the Paris Opéra (below).

• **2 December** Schoenberg's *Variations for Orchestra*, his first orchestral work to use his twelve-note method ◆ (opposite) is first performed in Berlin.

• **13 December** The Philharmonic-Symphony Society of New York gives the first performance of Gershwin's *An American in Paris* at Carnegie Hall.

1929 Schoenberg completes his comic opera *Von Heute auf Morgen* (From One Day to the Next).

• **17 May** Prokofiev's Third Symphony, based on material from the opera *The Fiery Angel* (p.218), is first performed in Paris.

• **8 June** Hindemith's comic opera *Neues vom Tage* (News of the Day) is first performed in Berlin.

• **19 August** Diaghilev dies, aged fifty-seven, in Venice.

• **3 October** Walton's Viola Concerto is first performed in London, with Hindemith as the soloist.

• **6 December** Stravinsky performs the piano solo in the première of his *Capriccio* for piano and small orchestra.

• **18 December** Première of Webern's Symphony in New York.

1930 The BBC Symphony Orchestra is formed.

• Prokofiev completes his Fourth Symphony.

• **18 January** Shostakovich's opera *The Nose* is first performed in St Petersburg, and his Third Symphony nine days later.

• **12 April** Janáček's opera *From the House of the Dead* is given posthumously in Brno.

• **5 May** Milhaud's opera *Christoph Colomb* has a triumphant first hearing in Berlin.

• **4 July** Berg's concert ARIA *Der Wein* (Wine) is first performed in Königsberg.

• **August** Ravel writes his Piano Concerto for the Left Hand, for Paul Wittgenstein.

• **13 December** Stravinsky's *Symphony of Psalms*, dedicated to the Boston Symphony Orchestra, is first performed in Brussels.

> '*Here's a piece that they won't ever have the effrontery to include in their Sunday afternoon concert programmes.*'
> Ravel on his *Boléro*

Ravel composed Boléro *in response to a request from Ida Rubenstein, though what he produced bore little resemblance to the Spanish original. It was a huge success, nevertheless, and in 1941 Serge Lifar made a new version with costumes – one of which is shown here – designed by Léon Leyritz.*

◆ *Atonality and Twelve-Note Serialism*

Atonality, or the rejection of the conventional keys such a C major or B minor, was not suddenly introduced into Western music at this time. One may detect a movement away from tonality in some of the late piano pieces of Liszt, for example, and the process had been a gradual one. Nevertheless the appearance of serialism may be said to have made the traditional key system redundant for those composers who decided to embrace it.

The new technique developed by Schoenberg that was to have such far-reaching implications for the development of Western music was not elaborated in a short space of time, but emerged gradually. Some commentators detect moves in that direction as early as Berg's Altenberg songs (p.208), written in 1912, and in Schoenberg's own Die Jakobsleiter (p.212), begun in 1917, but the composer himself only seems to have become aware of the direction in which he was moving from 1920 onwards, when he was going through what might be termed a NEO-CLASSIC phase. His first three works in the new style are the Five Piano Pieces Op.23, the Serenade Op.24, and the Piano Suite Op.25 (below). Only the last of the three is a fully twelve-note serial piece, since the other works include non-serial movements, and movements that have more or fewer than twelve notes.

In the chromatic scale used in Western music there are twelve notes – i.e. all the black and white notes on a piano keyboard from middle C to the B natural above it. Hence the term dodecaphony which is sometimes used, meaning 'twelve sounds or notes' in Greek. These twelve notes are arranged by the composer in a fixed order, known as a series, hence the other term 'serialism'. The series may then be used to generate melodies and harmonies, and may be used in the compositional process in a number of ways. For example, the way in which the notes are arranged may be taken to provide the melody, or as a sequence of chords, or as a melody with accompaniment. Serialism thus establishes a framework within which the composer may work, and so help to create extended compositions, which had been a problem for Schoenberg in the decade leading up to his elaboration of the practice, though it does not itself dictate a particular style of composition. But crucially it can completely free the composer from tonality, as the series, as opposed to the key, is the fundamental feature of a work.

Opening page of Schoenberg's autograph score of his Piano Suite Op.25. The precision of the copy leaves no doubt as to the clarity of the composer's inner vision.

1931-35
Novelty and Diversity

If the twenties were turbulent, the thirties are restless. As the shadows lengthen in Europe, several composers choose to emigrate to America, though throughout the inter-war years Paris continues to act as a catalyst for those of other national traditions and disciplines who need to find their own voice through contact with, and the stimulus of, this focus of talent and innovation.

Prokofiev was a consummate pianist, as well as being a composer, and it is easy to forget that he had considerable skill as a conductor.

1931 Stravinsky composes his Violin Concerto for the violinist Samuel Dushkin.

• Prokofiev (right) writes his Fourth Piano Concerto, for the left hand, for Paul Wittgenstein (p.224).

• Bartók completes his Second Piano Concerto.

• Varèse completes *Ionisation* for thirty-five percussion instruments and two sirens, the first work from a Western composer solely for such forces.

• **8 April** Shostakovich's ballet *Bolt* is first performed in St Petersburg.

• **13 April** Webern's String Quartet Op.22 is badly received when first performed in Vienna.

• **16 April** Richard Strauss conducts Mozart's opera *Idomeneo* (p.110) at the Vienna Opera.

• **25 April** Prokofiev's First String Quartet is performed in Washington.

• **3 October** Death of Nielsen, aged sixty-six, in Copenhagen.

• **10 October** Walton's ORATORIO *Belshazzar's Feast* is first performed in Leeds.

'*Music is, by its very nature, essentially powerless to express anything at all...*'
Stravinsky,
Chronicle

• **2 December** Death of D'Indy, aged eighty, in Paris.

• **26 December** After a try-out in Boston on 8 December, George and Ira Gershwin's *Of Thee I Sing* opens in New York. It runs for over four hundred performances, and becomes the first musical to win the Pulitzer Prize.

1932 Sir Thomas Beecham founds the London Philharmonic Orchestra, and conducts their inaugural concert on 7 October.

• Stravinsky composes his *Duo concertant* for violin and piano with the violin part conceived for Samuel Dushkin.

• Poulenc composes his Concerto for Two Pianos.

• **5 and 14 January** Ravel's piano concertos are first performed, respectively, the one for left hand by Paul Wittgenstein as soloist in Vienna and the one for two hands by Marguerite Long as soloist in Paris.

• **24 March** Randall Thompson's first significant work, his Second Symphony, is first performed in New York.

• **31 October** Prokofiev is the soloist in the first performance of his Fifth Piano Concerto in Berlin.

OTHER EVENTS
1931 Japan invades Manchuria
• O'Neill: *Mourning Becomes Electra*

1932 Neutron discovered
• Huxley: *Brave New World*

1933 Hitler appointed Chancellor of Germany – burning of the Reichstag
• Toynbee: *A Study of History*

1934 Nazi putsch in Austria
• Joliot discovers induced radioactivity

1935 Italy invades Ethiopia
• T.S. Eliot: *Murder in the Cathedral*

1933 FM radio is invented.

• Kodály writes *The Dances from Galánta*, one of his best known orchestral works, to celebrate the eightieth anniversary of the Budapest Philharmonic Society.

• Prokofiev is commissioned to write the music for the film *Lieutenant Kijé* ◆ (p.233).

• Stravinsky collaborates with André Gide on his opera *Perséphone*, which includes mime, spoken dialogue and dance.

• **23 January** First performance of Bartók's Second Piano Concerto in Frankfurt.

• **1 February** Vaughan Williams's Piano Concerto in C Major has its first performance.

• **6 March** First performance in New York of Varèse's *Ionisation*.

• **30 May** Schoenberg is dismissed from the Prussian Academy of Arts in Berlin. On 24 July he reconverts to Judaism and on 31 October arrives in America, having fled from Nazi persecution ◆ (p.229).

An accomplished viola player, Hindemith is shown here in the early thirties rehearsing with the members of a piano quartet: the violinist Bronislaw Huberman, the cellist Pau Casals and the pianist Artur Schnabel.

★ The Temptation of St Anthony, *one of the three panels of the Isenheim altarpiece by Mathias Grünewald (c.1455–1528), a German artist whose life and work inspired Hindemith to compose both an opera and a symphony entitled* Mathis der Maler.

• **1 July** Richard Strauss's opera *Arabella* is first performed in Dresden.

• **15 October** Première of Shostakovich's Piano Concerto No.1, written for piano, strings and solo trumpet, in St Petersburg.

1934 Hindemith (above) completes his opera and symphony both entitled *Mathis der Maler* (Mathias the Painter, left).

• Messiaen arranges the organ piece *L'Ascension* (The Ascension), from an orchestral composition of the year before.

• Virgil Thomson completes his opera *Four Saints in Three Acts,* begun in 1928, to a libretto by Gertrude Stein.

• Webern composes his Concerto for Nine Instruments.

• **22 January** Shostakovich's opera *Lady Macbeth of the Mzensk District* (opposite) is first performed in St Petersburg.

• **23 February** Death of Elgar, aged seventy-six, in London.

• **23 February** The first performance of Britten's choral work *A Boy Was Born* is broadcast live.

• **12 March** Hindemith's *Mathis der Maler* symphony is first performed in Berlin.

• **30 April** Stravinsky's *Perséphone* is given for the first time in Paris.

• **May** The first Glyndebourne Festival begins this month ◆ (p.237).

Shostakovich's second opera was Lady Macbeth of the Mzensk District, *which he intended as the first of a trilogy of operas examining the position of women at different points in Russian history. He worked on it from 1930 to 1932, and the first performance took place in St Petersburg in 1934, with designs by Dmitriev.*

- **25 May** Death of Holst, aged fifty-nine, in London.

- **3 June** The American Musicological Society is founded in New York.

- **10 June** Death of Delius, aged seventy-two, at Grez-sur-Loing.

- **15 July** Birth of Birtwistle in Accrington, Lancashire.

- **8 September** Birth of Maxwell Davies in Manchester.

- **20 October** Richard Strauss completes his opera *Die schweigsame Frau* (The Silent Woman).

- **7 November** Rachmaninov gives the first performance of his *Rhapsody on a Theme of Paganini* in Baltimore.

- **30 November** Berg's Symphonic Suite (a set of five pieces drawn from his opera *Lulu*) is first performed in Berlin, conducted by Kleiber, who resigns as director of the Opera four days later because he can no longer tolerate the Nazi régime.

- **3 December** Walton's Symphony No.1, without its finale, is first performed in London.

- **25 December** Shostakovich's Cello Sonata is given in St Petersburg.

1935 Berg completes his Violin Concerto, commissioned by the American violinist Louis Krasner.

- Honegger composes his oratorio *Joan of Arc at the Stake*.

- Messiaen composes his rhythmically exuberant organ piece *La Nativité du Seigneur* (The Birth of the Lord).

- Rachmaninov begins to compose his Third Symphony.

- Shostakovich composes his First String Quartet.

Bartók on board the S.S. Escalibur, which took him from Europe to settle in America in October 1940. Although he travelled with his wife, this photograph symbolizes the artistic and cultural isolation to which he had committed himself.

- **8 April** Bartók's Fifth String Quartet is first performed in Washington.

- **10 April** Vaughan Williams's Fourth Symphony is well received when performed for the first time in London.

- **17 May** Death of Dukas, aged sixty-nine, in Paris.

- **24 June** Richard Strauss's opera *Die schweigsame Frau* is produced in Dresden, but is banned after the fourth performance because the librettist, Stefan Zweig, is a Jew. Strauss resigns his position as president of the Reichsmusikkammer on 13 July, giving old age as his reason.

- **30 September** Gershwin's opera *Porgy and Bess* is performed in Boston, and is at once a landmark in American musical history.

- **12 October** The tenor Luciano Pavarotti is born in Modena.

- **6 November** Walton's entire Symphony No.1 is performed in London.

- **1 December** Prokofiev's Violin Concerto No.2 is first given in Madrid.

- **24 December** Berg dies as a result of an infected insect bite, aged fifty, in Vienna.

◆ *An International Dimension*

The twenties and thirties saw increased contact between Europe and America in both directions. Although there was far less opportunity for opera performances in America, there were plenty of receptive audiences for other kinds of music, and Bartók, Rachmaninov, Schoenberg, Stravinsky and Varèse chose to go there.

Prokofiev left Russia as early as 1918, and although he had an initial success, both as a virtuoso pianist in America and as an avant-garde composer in Paris, after 1925 he found himself estranged from those who had lionized him in the French capital and alienated in any case from the traditionalists who had never accepted him. In 1933 he decided to return to Russia, with all that that would imply for his artistic freedom.

From America had come composers such as Copland and Thomson, both of whom studied with Nadia Boulanger in Paris. Gershwin came to see what Europe had to offer, including lessons from Ravel perhaps, though the latter – no doubt wisely – declined to take him on. The old continent of Europe, and Paris in particular, continued to exercise a fascination which Gertrude Stein described when she wrote of what made Paris and France the natural background of the art and literature of the twentieth century. 'Their tradition kept them from changing and yet they naturally saw things as they were, and accepted life as it is, and mixed things up without any reason at the same time. Foreigners were not romantic to them, they were just facts, nothing was sentimental they were just there, and strangely enough it did not make them make the art and literature of the twentieth century but it made them be the inevitable background for it.'

1936-38
Music in America

In the cultural melting pot that is America in the early part of the century it is almost inevitable that Classical musicians should look to Europe for training, but once a generation or two have studied there and returned, America begins to find its own idiom.

1936 Copland finishes his orchestral piece *El Salón México* ◆ (opposite).

• Rachmaninov completes his Third Symphony.

• Shostakovich finishes his Fourth Symphony.

• Varèse composes his *Densité 21.5* for solo platinum flute (platinum has a density of 21.5).

• **19 April** First performance of Berg's Violin Concerto is posthumously given in Barcelona, though Webern is unable to conduct as intended.

• **2 May** Première of Prokofiev's *Peter and the Wolf*, based on a children's fairy story and written for orchestra and narrator, in Moscow.

1937 21 January Bartók's *Music for Strings, Percussion and Celesta* is first performed in Basle.

• **2 June** Berg's unfinished *Lulu* (p.228) is first performed in Zürich.

• **8 June** Première of Orff's ORATORIO *Carmina Burana* in Frankfurt.

• **11 July** Gershwin dies, aged thirty-eight, in Hollywood.

• **21 November** Shostakovich's Fifth Symphony is first performed in St Petersburg. The work shows an acceptance of the official Soviet criticisms.

OTHER EVENTS
1936 Rome-Berlin Axis
• Spanish Civil War

1937 Picasso: *Guernica*

1938 Hitler annexes Austria
• Munich Agreement
• Nuclear fission discovered – Hahn and Strassmann split uranium atom
• Penicillin developed

A design by Oliver Smith for Copland's ballet Rodeo *(p.234). In 1938 Copland had treated a similar theme with the ballet* Billy the Kid, *and the two works added to the composer's journey towards a truly American dimension in his music* ◆ *(opposite).*

1938 Messiaen writes a SONG CYCLE for soprano and piano *Chants de terre et de ciel* (Songs of Earth and Sky) on the birth of his son.

• Copland writes his ballet *Billy the Kid* ◆ (below).

• **16 January** Bartók's Sonata for Two Pianos and Percussion is first performed in Basle, with the composer and his wife as soloists.

• **8 May** Stravinsky's *Dumbarton Oaks* Concerto is first performed in Washington, conducted by Nadia Boulanger.

• **28 May** Hindemith's opera *Mathis der Maler* ★ (p.227) is first performed in Zürich.

• **24 July** First performance of Richard Strauss's one-act opera *Friedenstag* (Peace Day) in Munich.

• **18 August** Britten is the soloist in the first performance of his Piano Concerto at a Promenade Concert in London.

• **22 September** Webern's String Quartet, the last of the composer's CHAMBER works, is first performed in Pittsburgh.

• **15 October** Richard Strauss's opera *Daphne* is first given in Dresden.

• **5 November** Barber's *Adagio for Strings* ◆ (below) is given in New York.

• **28 December** Death of Ravel, aged sixty-two, in Paris.

> 'True music...must repeat the thoughts and aspirations of the people and the time. My people are Americans. My time is today.'
> Gershwin

The front cover, designed by Carl Ruggles, for Ives's composition for choir and orchestra entitled: Lincoln, the Great Commoner.

◆ The Search for Identity

When Copland and other Americans studied in Europe they did not necessarily return home with a complete musical personality. In the case of Copland his acquired compositional skill was only a point of departure. He needed something more, and with Music for the Theater in 1925 *(p.220)*

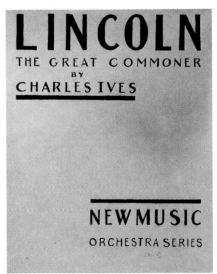

he turned to jazz for inspiration, as Gershwin had done the year before with Rhapsody in Blue *(p.218). In 1932 Gershwin used Latin American influences in his* Cuban Overture, *and in 1933 Copland, following his visit to South America, began* El Salón México, *which he completed in 1936. Meanwhile, in 1935, Gershwin had found the music of black America for* Porgy and Bess *(p.229), whereas Copland looked to cowboy folklore for his ballets* Billy the Kid, *and* Rodeo *(opposite), and the hymns of the Shaker sect for* Appalachian Spring

(p.235). Eventually Copland did find his own voice, for his music transcends any one idiom, and, as Ives had done before him, expresses something about America that is at once both the wide open spaces and the long city streets and avenues. The same feeling was to be achieved by Barber with his Adagio for Strings, *arranged from the* ADAGIO *of his only String Quartet (1936), and his* Knoxville Summer of 1915 *(p.236).*

As these examples show, genuine folk music alone cannot provide sufficient substance to sustain a musical tradition. In Europe it was the remarkable achievement of composers such as Bartók, Kodály and Vaughan Williams to preserve folk music before it disappeared, but that music was only of limited use in art music. A tune such as 'The Peacock' might be used for a set of VARIATIONS *by Kodály (p.232) or 'Greensleeves' for a* FANTASIA *by Vaughan Williams, but the tune remains itself. If, on the other hand, a composer merely adopts certain inflections of rhythm or harmonic effects that suggest a particular folk music, then the danger is that he or she will be accused of pastiche.*

Ultimately, the true national voice is found beneath and beyond such effects. Composers must discover this, as Ravel was able to do with Spanish music ● (p.213), and Vaughan Williams with his Fantasia on a Theme of Thomas Tallis *(p.207).*

1939-45
In Time of War

Europe and much of the rest of the world is plunged into another conflict, this time – despite the slaughter of World War I – much more devastating in its impact on the lives of ordinary people and in the endurance of its effects. Music manages to survive, however, even in some of the darkest places.

1939 The Amsterdam Concertgebouw Orchestra commissions Kodály to write a work – *Variations on a Hungarian Folksong*, or *The Peacock Variations* – to celebrate its fiftieth anniversary ◆ (p.231).

• Messiaen writes the organ piece *Les Corps glorieux* (The Glorious Bodies) and a SONG CYCLE for soprano and piano, *Poèmes pour Mi* (Poems for Mi), dedicated to his first wife.

• Prokofiev composes the CANTATA *Alexander Nevsky*, based on his film score ◆ (opposite).

• Rachmaninov leaves Europe for the last time. In America he records the First and Third Piano Concertos and Third Symphony (left).

• 440 vibrations per second for 'A' is adopted as standard international PITCH.

• **20 January** Ives's 'Concord' Sonata for piano receives its first performance in New York, and establishes the composer's reputation.

• **23 March** Bartók's Second Violin Concerto is first performed in Amsterdam.

• **May** Britten leaves England for America.

• **5 November** Shostakovich's Sixth Symphony is first performed in St Petersburg.

• **7 December** Walton's Violin Concerto is first performed in Cleveland.

1940 Britten composes his *Sinfonia da Requiem*.

• Messiaen, who is serving his military service, is captured and interned in a prisoner-of-war camp. While there he composes his *Quatuor pour la fin du temps* (Quartet for the End of Time) .

Portrait of Rachmaninov at the keyboard. Although he wrote symphonies and vocal music, the piano was supremely this composer's instrument. The advent of improved recording technology enables us to know how he envisaged his piano music in performance.

• Shostakovich edits Mussorgsky's opera *Boris Godunov* (p.178).

• **28 March** Britten's Violin Concerto is first performed in New York.

• **21 April** Tippett's Double String Concerto is first given in London.

• **11 June** Bartók's *Divertimento* is first performed in Basle.

• **July** Strauss begins to compose his opera *Capriccio*.

• **7 November** Stravinsky's Symphony in C has its first performance in Chicago.

• **23 November** Shostakovich's Piano Quintet is first given in Moscow.

• **6 December** Schoenberg's Violin Concerto has its first performance in Philadelphia.

A recording session (right) for Walton's soundtrack to Laurence Olivier's film Hamlet, *released in 1948. The task imposed on the composer was not simply one of synchronization, for Olivier expected the score to be an organic part of the film, and not just background music.*

◆ *Film Music*

The possibilities opened up to composers by moving films were enormous. One of the first to grasp them was Saint-Saëns, already in his early seventies, who in 1907 provided a musical SCORE for a film on the assassination of the Duc de Guise. Once synchronized sound was developed, then the idea of a score being an organic and artistic part of a film became apparent, and offered composers new opportunities for their work to be made known, as well as considerable financial reward.

Britten, Copland, Honegger, Milhaud, Prokofiev, Shostakovich, Vaughan Williams and Walton are only a few of the long list of composers who were happy to work for the cinema.

Schoenberg declined to write a score for Pearl Buck's The Good Earth, *even though he was said to have been offered $50,000, but one can well understand why he might have found the experience unpalatable.*

At one level film music is little more than programme music, without the composer having the freedom to choose his or her own programme. This is not to deny that considerable skill is required in writing for film, and Britten, for one, gained useful experience through writing for the British GPO film unit in the 1930s. The need to produce appropriate soundtrack effects with extremely limited means stood him in very good stead later,

and helped him to develop his already sensitive ear for SONORITIES. His music for Instruments of the Orchestra *(1946) was able to stand perfectly well in its own right as the concert programme piece* The Young Person's Guide to the Orchestra, *as could Prokofiev's score for Eisenstein's* Alexander Nevsky *(1938), which he subsequently turned into a CANTATA of the same title.*

Several films have been made of the lives of great composers and musicians, where their music is introduced at appropriate points. These have helped enormously to popularize particular works or parts of them, and individual MOVEMENTS are often used as theme music or background music. As a result certain works have been reintroduced to the non concert-going public, although how much this extends to and enhances a general appreciation of a particular composer's works in the longer term remains open to question.

1941 Copland composes his Piano Sonata.

• Honegger composes his Second Symphony.

• Shostakovich composes his Seventh Symphony, which he dedicates to Leningrad (now St Petersburg).

• **3 January** Première of Rachmaninov's *Symphonic Dances* in Philadelphia.

• **20 January** Bartók's Sixth String Quartet is first heard in New York.

• **3 April** Walton's *Scapino* OVERTURE has its first performance in Chicago.

• **July** Britten writes his First String Quartet and is awarded the Library of Congress Medal for services to chamber music.

• **December** Rachmaninov records the Fourth Piano Concerto, which he has revised this year.

1942 Bernstein ■ (p.245) composes his *Jeremiah* Symphony.

• Hindemith completes his theoretical piano work *Ludus tonalis* (The Tonal School), or *Studies in Counterpoint, Tonal Organization and Piano Playing*.

• **8 February** Stravinsky's *Danses Concertantes* is first heard in Los Angeles.

• **5 March** Shostakovich's Seventh Symphony receives its first performance in Kuibishev (left).

• **17 April** Britten returns to England.

• **16 October** Copland's ballet *Rodeo* ★ (p.230) is first performed at the Metropolitan Opera House, New York.

1943 Messiaen writes his piano duet *Visions de l'Amen* (Visions of the Amen).

• **18 January** Prokofiev's Seventh Piano Sonata is first given in Moscow.

• **27 March** Tippett's Second String Quartet is first performed in London.

• **28 March** Rachmaninov dies, aged sixty-nine, in Los Angeles.

• **6 June** Shostakovich's Second Piano Sonata is first heard in Moscow.

• **24 June** Vaughan Williams's Fifth Symphony is first heard in London.

Poster for a performance of Shostakovich's Seventh Symphony in Moscow in 1942, which he composed in St Petersburg during the siege of 1941 by the Germans. In this work, supremely, the composer proclaimed his willingness to put his music at the service of the nation.

• **11 August** Richard Strauss's Second Horn Concerto is performed for the first time in Salzburg.

• **4 November** Shostakovich's Eighth Symphony is given in Moscow.

1944 Messiaen composes his *Trois petites liturgies de la Présence Divine* (Three Little Liturgies of the Divine Presence) for women's voices, piano, Martenot Waves ◆ (p.239), strings and percussion, and *Vingt regards sur L'Enfant-Jésus* (Twenty Glances at the Child Jesus) for piano solo.

• Prokofiev composes his Fifth Symphony.

• **6 February** Première of Schoenberg's Piano Concerto in New York.

• **19 March** Tippett's ORATORIO *A Child of Our Time* is given in London.

• **14 November** Shostakovich's Second String Quartet is first performed in St Petersburg.

• **1 December** Bartók's *Concerto for Orchestra* is first heard in Boston.

• **30 December** Prokofiev's Eighth Piano Sonata is given in Moscow.

OTHER EVENTS
1942 United Nations Alliance
• Battle of El Alamein

1943 Germans halted at Stalingrad
• Italy surrenders

1944 International Monetary Fund set up
• President Roosevelt elected to fourth term
• Allied armies invade Europe

1945 Germany surrenders – Yalta Conference
• Atomic bombs dropped on Japan
• United Nations Assembly in New York
• Radio astronomy
• Jet planes and rockets further developed

1945 Boulez ■ (p.251) writes his *Trois psalmodies* (Three Psalmodies), though subsequently he will withdraw all works composed prior to 1946.

• Messiaen composes *Harawi*, for soprano and piano, the first of three works on love and death and the Tristan and Yseult story.

• Stravinsky composes his *Ebony* Concerto ■ (p.209).

• **13 January** Prokofiev conducts the first performance of his Fifth Symphony in Moscow. After the concert he has a bad fall.

• **12 April** Richard Strauss finishes his *Metamorphosen* ◆ (below).

• **7 June** Britten's opera *Peter Grimes* is first performed in London, marking the rebirth of British opera.

• **15 September** Webern is accidentally shot by an American soldier and dies, aged sixty-one, near Salzburg.

• **26 September** Bartók dies, aged sixty-four, in New York, having ORCHESTRATED all but a few bars of his Third Piano Concerto.

• **4 October** Copland's symphonic suite from his ballet *Appalachian Spring* ◆ (p.231) is first performed in Washington.

• **3 November** Shostakovich's Ninth Symphony is performed for the first time in St Petersburg.

> *'…Plain, singing, comparatively uncomplicated and slightly folksy. Direct and approachable.'*
> Copland on his *Appalachian Spring*.

◆ The Effects of War

The Vienna State Opera House (below) in flames in 1945.

The relative ease with which musicians were able to communicate with foreign colleagues prior to the war was seriously affected, as were their individual lives, especially in Europe. In 1940 Messiaen found himself in a prisoner-of-war camp, Stalag VIIIA at Görlitz, where he was inspired to compose his Quator pour la fin du temps *(p.232)*.

In Russia Prokofiev's contrasting Fifth and Sixth were war symphonies, whilst Shostakovich's Seventh *(opposite)*, dedicated to the city of Leningrad, was supremely so. There is, however, a quality in Shostakovich's music that transcends the contemporary context, and the work becomes a symphony about all human life and tragedy, and mankind's resilience and ability to survive.

On 2 October 1943 bombs destroyed the Munich National Theatre where, seventy-three years previously, Richard Strauss had first heard Der Freischütz *(p.142)* and where his father had sat in the pit as first horn player for forty-nine years. At the time Strauss felt that this was the greatest catastrophe of his life, but more was to come. On 12 February 1945 Dresden was destroyed, with its theatre, and the following month the Vienna State Opera House suffered the same fate *(right)*. That winter Strauss re-read all Goethe's works, which prompted him to write Metamorphosen; *music for the passing of an age.*

Musicians also suffered deeply from the war. Webern, by one of those cruel acts of fate, survived until the liberation and then, on a visit to Salzburg to see his daughters, was shot in error by an American soldier.

The month before, Menuhin and Britten had visited Belsen to play to the survivors. The effect this had on Britten, according to Peter Pears, influenced everything that he subsequently wrote, especially the Holy Sonnets of John Donne *completed that year and his* War Requiem *(p.245)*.

1946-49
The Post-War Years

As life begins to return to normal, composers are able to travel once more, to meet colleagues, exchange ideas and experience new works. The music festival now becomes a forum for such encounters for composers, performers and audiences.

1946 The Darmstadt meetings are established ◆ (opposite).

• Ives's Third Symphony is given its first public performance, and is awarded the Pulitzer Prize the following year.

• Tippett finishes his Third String Quartet and *Little Music for Strings*.

• **24 January** The first performance of Stravinsky's Symphony in Three Movements takes place in New York.

• **25 January** Richard Strauss's *Metamorphosen* ◆ (p.235) is performed for the first time in Zürich.

• **8 February** The first performance of Bartók's Third Piano Concerto is given in Philadelphia.

• **12 June** Prokofiev's opera *War and Peace* has its first performance, in its first version, in St Petersburg.

• **12 July** Britten's opera *The Rape of Lucretia* is first performed at Glyndebourne ◆ (opposite).

• **August** Schoenberg suffers a heart attack that leaves him an invalid, but on recovery he composes his last CHAMBER work, the String Trio.

1947 Barber composes *Knoxville Summer of 1915*, an evocative piece for soprano and orchestra.

• Boulez completes his CANTATA *Le Visage nuptial* (The Nuptial Face).

• The BBC commissions the opera *Troilus and Cressida* from Walton (below).

• The Edinburgh International Festival is opened ◆ (opposite).

• **11 October** Prokofiev's Sixth Symphony is performed for the first time in St Petersburg ◆ (p.235).

1948 Cage composes his *Sonatas and Interludes* for PREPARED PIANO.

• Shostakovich completes his First Violin Concerto and his SONG CYCLE *From Jewish Folk Poetry*, but witholds them both because of official Stalinist attitudes towards music ● (p.241).

• Stravinsky begins work on his opera *The Rake's Progress*.

• Messiaen completes his *Turangalîla-symphonie*, for large orchestra, piano and Martenot Waves ◆ (p.239).

• **5 June** The first Aldeburgh Festival opens ◆ (opposite).

OTHER EVENTS
1946 Nuremberg war trials
• First session of United Nations
• Le Corbusier: Unité d'habitation, Marseilles

1947 Marshall Plan
• Indian Independence
• Greek civil war

1948 State of Israel founded
• Assassination of Mahatma Gandhi

1949 North Atlantic Defence Pact
• Communist government in China
• Orwell: *1984*

Walton portrayed by the English artist Michael Ayrton in 1948, the year in which he married and settled permanently on the Italian island of Ischia in the Bay of Naples. It was at this time that he began work on his opera Troilus and Cressida.

- **20 September** Richard Strauss completes his *Four Last Songs*.
- **October** Schaeffer broadcasts five studies in MUSIQUE CONCRETE .
- **27 October** Stravinsky's Mass is first performed in Milan.

1949 Boulez completes his *Livre pour quatuor* (Book for Quartet), a work he subsequently withdraws (p.235).

- Messaien writes his experimental piano pieces *Cantéjodayâ* at Tanglewood
◆ (below), and *Quatre études de rythme* (Four Studies of Rhythm).
- Shostakovich composes his Fourth String Quartet, but witholds it.
- Schoenberg composes his *Phantasy* for violin and piano, and the unaccompanied choral work *Dreimal tausend Jahre* (Three Thousand Years).
- **9 July** Britten's Spring Symphony is first performed in Amsterdam.
- **8 September** Richard Strauss dies, aged eighty-five, in Garmisch.
- **2 December** Bartók's Viola Concerto is first given in Minneapolis.
- **15 December** Shostakovich's ORATORIO *Song of the Forests* – an 'official' work – is first performed in St Petersburg.

A scene from Britten's opera A Midsummer Night's Dream *(p.244), as performed at Glyndebourne in 1984, although originally written for the composer's own festival at Aldeburgh.*

◆ *Music Festivals*

The ending of the war in Europe inspired a celebrating of restored artistic freedom by the resumption of established festivals – such as those at Salzburg and Donaueschingen, and of the International Society for Contemporary Music – and the setting up of new ones, such as Darmstadt, both national and international. Edinburgh, beginning in 1947, was one of the first and most significant international festivals, and was an inspiration to many others such as Aldeburgh.

Several well established German and British festivals had survived from the nineteenth century into the twentieth, very often with a strong bias to choral music, and these were often appropriate occasions to introduce new works, usually of a more conservative nature, into the repertoire.

Although not festivals in the generally accepted meaning of the term, the Bayreuth Wagner seasons, the British Henry Wood Promenade Concerts and the Glyndebourne Festival Opera are nevertheless annual events that operate only on a seasonal basis.

The French never took to regular festivals, apart from Aix-en-Provence, though more recently several smaller festivals have been organized, and there is a similar situation in Italy where one or two festivals, notably the Maggio Musicale in Florence, remain well established, while others such as Spoleto and Montepulciano often depend very much on the presence and activities of individual personalities, namely Menotti and Henze.

Music festivals have been established in America since the nineteenth century, and this century the Library of Congress Chamber Music Festival, Tanglewood and Aspen have all helped foster the advancement of music.

Inevitably financial considerations play a large part in the organization of festivals, and some rely heavily on the standard concert repertoire, but the best bring together internationally recognized musicians to perform new works, or revive neglected ones. In this way the commemoration of composers' births and deaths, which can have the nature of a festival or be part of one, provide an opportunity to re-evaluate their works.

1950-52
The Electronic Age

Advances in sound technology accelerate the progress of electroacoustic music after World War II, presenting composers, performers and audiences alike with the most challenging development in serious music since dodecaphony, and threatening an even greater division.

1950 Copland composes his SONG CYCLE for voice and piano, *Twelve Poems of Emily Dickinson,* and his Piano Quartet.

• Menotti composes his opera *The Consul* (below).

• Messiaen composes his *Messe de la Pentecôte* (Mass of Pentecost) for organ.

• Poulenc writes his Stabat Mater for soprano, mixed choir and orchestra.

• Schoenberg composes *De profundis* (Psalm 130) for unaccompanied choir.

• **22 May** Richard Strauss's *Four Last Songs* (p.237) are given in London.

• **23 June** Webern's Second Cantata is first performed in Brussels.

1951 RTF French Radio and Television establishes the first studio designed specifically for electroacoustic composition under Schaeffer ◆ (opposite).

• Boulez composes *Polyphonie X* for eighteen solo instruments, which he subsequently withdraws (p.235).

• Bernstein conducts the first public performance of Ives's Second Symphony.

• **May** Britten and Pears give the first performance of Tippett's song cycle *The Heart's Assurance,* one of his most impassioned compositions.

• **13 July** Schoenberg dies, aged seventy eight, in Los Angeles, leaving unfinished the first of a projected sequence of psalms, *Modern Psalm,* to his own text, for speaker, chorus and orchestra.

• **11 September** Première of Stravinsky's opera *The Rake's Progress* at Teatro La Fenice, Venice ■ (p.209).

• **1 December** Britten conducts the first performance of his opera *Billy Budd* at Covent Garden.

Menotti's first full-length opera The Consul, with the composer's own text, was first given in Philadelphia in 1950. Seen here is the soprano Patricia Neway, who sang the leading role of Magda at the world première, as well as in the first performances in New York and London the following year.

1952 Shostakovich composes an 'officially approved' choral work *The Sun Shines on our Motherland.*

• Messiaen writes his *Livre d'orgue* (Organ Book).

• Boulez completes his *Structures 1* for two pianos.

• Cage produces his electronic work *Imaginary Landscapes No.5,* created from splicing tapes ◆ (opposite) and his *Water Music* (right).

• **28 October** Stokowski organizes a concert of contemporary music in the Museum of Modern Art, New York, incorporating tape-recorded works by Ussachevsky and Otto Luening ◆ (opposite).

• **23 December** Shostakovich's *24 Preludes and Fugues* are first performed in St Petersburg.

Schaeffer (opposite) in 1951, the year in which he was put in charge of the first studio designed solely for electroacoustic work at the French national radio station in Paris. Others followed in Germany, Italy and America.

Cage's score for his Water Music, *which demands water to be poured from one receptacle to another at very precise moments, as well as sounding a siren whistle and switching off a radio.*

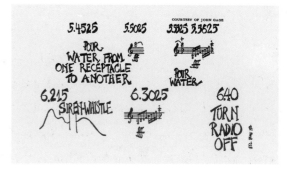

◆ *Electroacoustic Music and its Instruments*

Although electroacoustic instruments existed before World War II, notably the Hammond organ and the Ondes Martenot or MARTENOT WAVES, it was the general availability of the tape recorder after the war that gave the impetus to the speedy development and expansion of electroacoustic music.

In France Pierre Schaeffer made his first broadcast of MUSIQUE CONCRETE in 1948 (though using disk recordings), and three years later RTF, the national radio, set up the first studio dedicated entirely to electroacoustics with Schaeffer in charge. At about the same time in Germany, Radio Cologne was organizing a studio for electronic music which began operating in 1953, and John Cage in New York had begun to work with three other composers interested in the possibilities of Music for Magnetic Tape. At Colombia University Vladimir Ussachevsky and Otto Luening were pursuing a separate development. There were naturally other pioneers, including a Milan studio of RAI, Italian national radio. As further technological developments were made, composers embraced them and explored their potential.

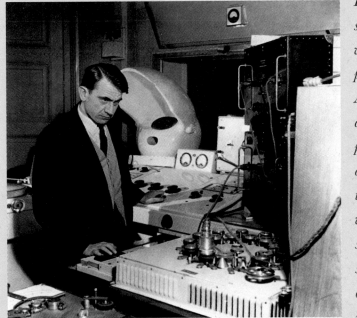

In the 1960s the voltage-control synthesizer was developed, which meant that the electronic devices could be connected to each other much more readily, and in many more ways than had been possible before. The immediate effect of this innovation was a huge expansion of electronic music studios.

The operation of most audio devices that produce electronic sound is controlled by knobs, dials or switches. An oscillator may be provided with a dial that enables the operator to select the frequency (which effects the PITCH), a knob to control amplitude (whether its loud or soft), and a number of switches for varying the waveform (which affects the nature of the sound).

If these manual controls are operated from voltage control, then many more devices can be activated from a single source. It is also possible to cascade devices, for example arrange a series of oscillators, the first controlled by the second, which is in turn is controlled by a third.

In the early 1960s a comprehensive instrument was assembled for the origination and development of electronic sound. Robert Moog and Donald Buchla, in America , almost simultaneously developed modular synthesizers in various sizes, with the largest offering an enormous potential range of sound and control.

In order to regulate manually sources of voltage control, a keyboard similar to that use on a piano was introduced, which for many observers seemed recognizable as a musical instrument.

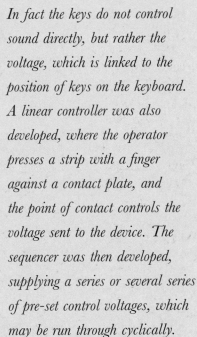

In fact the keys do not control sound directly, but rather the voltage, which is linked to the position of keys on the keyboard. A linear controller was also developed, where the operator presses a strip with a finger against a contact plate, and the point of contact controls the voltage sent to the device. The sequencer was then developed, supplying a series or several series of pre-set control voltages, which may be run through cyclically.

The development of contact microphones to amplify vibrations in solid objects, the application of filters and potentiometers to sounds, and the use of ring modulators to distort and transform sounds – a process used by Stockhausen – all helped to give impetus to the expansion of electronic music in the 1960s. Almost at the same time, computers were being applied to the composition of music. Computers may be used to generate the pitch of notes and their duration, and so provide a highly accurate SCORE for performers, making computer-generated music an area where more developments will undoubtedly take place.

1953-56
Freedom and Restraint

Although there no longer seem to be any limits to the expansion of music in its many manifestations in the West, under the Communist regimes of Eastern Europe composers still find their work controlled by generally unsympathetic authorities.

1953 Boulez writes *Le Marteau sans maître* (The Masterless Hammer), for contralto, alto flute, XYLORIMBA, VIBRAPHONE, percussion, guitar and viola.

• Messiaen completes his *Réveil des oiseaux* (Awakening of the Birds) for piano and orchestra.

• Prokofiev completes his ballet *The Tale of the Stone Flower*.

• In the post-Stalin era, Shostakovich (left) begins work on his Tenth Symphony, his first for eight years ● (opposite).

• Radio Cologne sets up an electronic music studio under Eimert ◆ (p.239).

• **14 January** Vaughan Williams's *Sinfonia Antarctica*, based on music for the film *Scott of the Antarctic* ◆ (p. 233), is first given in Manchester.

• **5 March** Prokofiev dies, aged sixty-one, near Moscow, on the same day as Stalin.

• **29 August** Tippett's *Fantasia Concertante on a Theme of Corelli* is first performed in Edinburgh.

• **7 December** Première of Shostakovich's Tenth Symphony in St Petersburg.

1954 Stockhausen publishes *Studie II*, the first electronic score.

• Varèse completes *Déserts* (Deserts), with four sections for woodwind, piano and percussion, interspersed with three taped sections.

A portrait of Shostakovich which conveys something of the inner frustration that he experienced, and the spirit of resignation he cultivated, as he endured the often hostile attitude of state officials to his music, which they were in a position to criticize or even suppress.

• **12 March** First (concert) performance of Schoenberg's *Moses and Aaron* in Hamburg.

• **19 May** Ives dies, aged seventy-nine, in New York.

• **14 September** Britten conducts the première of his opera *The Turn of the Screw* at Teatro La Fenice, Venice.

• **3 December** Walton's opera *Troilus and Cressida* ★ (p.236) is not a success at Covent Garden.

1955 27 January First performance of Tippett's opera *The Midsummer Marriage* (opposite).

• **3–4 May** Enesco dies, aged seventy-three, in Paris.

• **11 May** First performance of Bliss's Violin Concerto in London.

• **29 October** First performance of Shostakovich's First Violin Concerto in St Petersburg.

• **27 November** Honegger dies, aged sixty-three, in Paris.

OTHER EVENTS
1953 Korean War ends
• Watson-Crick model of DNA molecule
• Mount Everest climbed
• Beckett: *Waiting for Godot*

1954 MASER (Molecular amplification by stimulated emission of radiation)

1955 Warsaw Pact set up

1956 Hungarian uprising crushed by Russia
• Suez crisis

'Z [hdanov] ...has been the arch-enemy of liberal artistic musical thought for twenty years... immensely dislikeable.'
Peter Pears,
2 December
1966

A ballet scene from the first performance of Tippett's opera The Midsummer Marriage, *composed to his own libretto, with stage design by the sculptor Barbara Hepworth.*

1956 Stockhausen completes *Gesang der Jünglinge* (Song of the Three Holy Children), for a combination of synthetic and recorded vocal sounds; *Klavierstück XI* (Piano Piece XI), and *Zeitmasse* (Tempos) for five wind instruments.

• Messiaen composes his *Oiseaux exotiques* (Exotic Birds) for piano, two clarinets, xylophone, percussion and wind and orchestra.

• **21 April** Carter's *Variations for Orchestra* is first performed in Louisville, Kentucky.

• **14 May** Vaughan Williams's Eighth Symphony is first performed in London.

• **13 September** First performance of Stravinsky's *Canticum sacrum* in Venice.

• **7 October** First performance of Shostakovich's Sixth String Quartet in St Petersburg.

• **24 October** Nono's *Il canto sospeso* (The Interrupted Song), for soloists, choir and orchestra, is first performed in Cologne, bringing him international recognition.

● *Music under Communist Regimes*

The death of Stalin in 1953 did not mean that the official state attitude towards composers and their music altered overnight. As late as 1980, Schnittke was prevented by the Russian authorities from going to London for the first performance of his Second Symphony, commissioned by the BBC, and a certain amount of subterfuge was involved in sending the material out of the country prior to its performance because it incorporated words from the Christian Mass.

The careers of both Prokofiev and Shostakovich must therefore be seen in this context. No matter how much composers intend their music to be of use to the community, they still have their own artistic, creative vision, which is compromised by being told how and what to write. In the then satellite states of Poland, East Germany, Czechoslovakia and Hungary conditions were much less difficult, as shown by the establishment of a festival for contemporary music in Warsaw in 1956 – an event which it would have been inconceivable to hold on Russian territory.

A cartoon (right) which appeared in the official Soviet musical journal, Sovetskaya muzyka, *in 1948, during the height of the persecution and humiliation of composers such as Prokofiev and Shostakovich, who are shown worshipping the god of modernism.*

1957-59
The Middle Way

The impact of dodecaphony, serialism and electroacoustics creates a dilemma for those who stand in the mainstream of serious music, since they seem to be obliged to choose one or the other, but some composers show that there are areas of common ground.

1957 Bernstein's OPERETTA *Candide* is first performed, and he completes *West Side Story*.

• Boulez composes his Third Piano Sonata, though initially only publishes two MOVEMENTS.

• Hindemith's five-act opera *Die Harmonie der Welt* (The Harmony of the World) is first performed in Munich.

• Stockhausen completes *Gruppen* (Groups) for three orchestras.

• Tippett completes his Second Symphony.

• **1 January** Britten conducts the first performance of his ballet *The Prince of the Pagodas* at Covent Garden.

• **25 January** The first performance of Walton's Cello Concerto is given in Boston.

• **26 January** Poulenc's opera *The Carmelites* is given its first triumphant performance at Teatro La Scala, Milan.

• **10 May** Shostakovich's Second Piano Concerto is performed for the first time in Moscow.

• **6 June** Schoenberg's *Moses and Aaron* has its first stage performance in Zürich.

• **17 June** Stravinsky's ballet *Agon* is first performed in Los Angeles.

• **20 September** Death of Sibelius, aged ninety-one, at Järvenpää, Finland.

• **30 October** Shostakovich's Eleventh Symphony is performed for the first time in Moscow.

1958 Boulez begins *Pli selon pli* (Fold by Fold), for soprano, harp, VIBRAPHONE, CELESTA, piano, percussion and orchestra. The piece has a subtitle *Portrait of Mallarmé*. The composer will modify it over the next decade.

• Messaien (left) completes his *Catalogue d'oiseaux* (Catalogue of Birds), thirteen pieces for piano based on birdsong transcribed by the composer.

• Lutoslawski composes his *Funeral Music* for orchestra, in memory of Bartók.

• Varèse completes his *Poème électronique* (Electronic Poem) to be played over four hundred loudspeakers in the Philips Pavilion, designed by Le Corbusier and Xenakis, at the World Fair in Brussels.

Messiaen photographed in the process of notating birdsong, which provided the inspiration for several of his compositions, especially the Catalogue d'oiseaux. *He had the ability to capture the rapid sounds, which he would then sometimes slow down in order to extract individual phrases.*

• **5 February** Tippett's Second Symphony is first performed in London.

• **2 April** Vaughan Williams's Ninth Symphony is first heard in London.

• **2 May** Varèse's *Poème électronique* is first played in Brussels.

• **26 August** Vaughan Williams dies, aged eighty-six, in London.

• **23 September** Stravinsky's *Threni*, based on the Biblical *Lamentations of Jeremiah*, is first performed in Venice.

1959 Messiaen completes *Chronochromie* (Time-colour) for orchestra.

• Orff composes his 'funeral game' *Oedipus der Tyrann*.

• Poulenc composes his opera *La Voix humaine* (The Human Voice).

• Shostakovich completes an edition of Mussorgsky's opera *Khovanshchina*.

• Stockhausen composes *Refrain* for piano, celesta and vibraphone.

• **15 July** Death of Bloch, aged seventy-eight, in Portland, Oregon.

• **28 August** Death of Martinu, aged sixty-eight, in Liestal, Switzerland.

• **4 October** Première of Shostakovich's First Cello Concerto.

A photograph of Hindemith in a teaching session (below), probably taken after he was appointed to a post at Yale University, where he remained until 1953.

◆ *The Persistence of Tonality*

Until Stravinsky embraced serial technique ■ (p.209) in 1951, many composers and musicians such as his devoted friend Nadia Boulanger felt able to ignore it or deplore it. This apparent volte face on Stravinsky's part threw them into a considerable dilemma, though when one looks at his career with the benefit of hindsight, and the way in which it had evolved and changed direction on several occasions, one is rather more surprised that he did not turn to serialism sooner.

Nevertheless the defection or adherence, depending on which side of the divide one stood, only served to highlight the extent to which music was now split into two opposing parties. A few composers tried to occupy a middle ground, of whom Hindemith (right) was one of the more articulate. In the introduction to his Elementary Training for Musicians *(1946) he deplored the traditional kind of basic instruction for students that made it difficult for them to become truly independent creative composers. As he went on, 'They either cannot take the step out of their narrow concept of tonality (which by the uniform nomenclature for a tone and all its derivations is distorted almost to the point where reason turns into nonsense!), or they plunge more easily than others into what is assumed to be a new freedom of tonal disorder and incoherence.'*

In practice such a stance commanded little support from either side, least of all the serial school. The works of both Britten and

Copland provide us with examples of the use of serial technique and twelve-note composition, and one would hardly brand either of them as notoriously avant-garde composers in their day.

They illustrate the fact that it is possible to combine the two traditions up to a point, and Schoenberg himself wrote tonal music after he had embarked on his journey into serialism.

By its very nature avant-garde music usually has to make its statement and wait for the listener to arrive at the same point. What Hindemith, Britten, Copland and many others did was to insist that ultimately tonality remained relevant and valid for the twentieth century.

1960-63
New Forms of Patronage

Although there are still private patrons sufficiently wealthy and informed to commission compositions, it is increasingly the state and civic institutions who ensure that contemporary works are written, either as direct commissions or through festivals and competitions.

1960 Stockhausen finishes *Carré* for four ensembles of voices and instruments, and *Kontakte,* mixing taped and live sound.

• **10 January** First performance of Stravinsky's *Movements* for piano and orchestra in New York (below).

• **15 May** Shostakovich's Seventh String Quartet is performed for the first time in St Petersburg, as is his Eighth String Quartet on 2 October.

• **11 June** Britten conducts the première of his opera *A Midsummer Night's Dream* at Aldeburgh ◆ (p.237).

1961 Poulenc composes his *Sept répons des ténèbres* (Seven Responsaries for Tenebrae) for choir and orchestra.

• Boulez completes the second set of his *Structures* (p.238) for two pianos.

• Penderecki composes his *Threnody*, a lament for the victims of Hiroshima, for fifty-two strings.

• **20 May** First performance of Henze's opera *Elegy for Young Lovers* in Schwetzingen.

• **15 October** First performance of Shostakovich's Twelfth Symphony in Moscow.

1962 Copland composes his twelve-tone ◆ (p.225) orchestral *Connotations* for the opening season of the New York Philharmonic Orchestra in the Lincoln Center, New York, conducted by Bernstein ■ (opposite).

• Messaien composes *Sept Haï-Kaï* (Seven Haiku) for piano, after a visit to Japan.

• **29 May** Tippett's opera *King Priam* is first performed at the consecration of the new Coventry Cathedral.

• **30 May** First performance of Britten's *War Requiem* in Coventry (opposite).

• **18 December** Shostakovich's Thirteenth Symphony causes a scandal when first performed in Moscow.

1963 Stockhausen publishes *Plus-Minus*, diagrams and instructions without any specified instruments or musical NOTATION.

• Tippett completes his *Concerto for Orchestra*, dedicated to Britten.

• **30 January** Death of Poulenc, aged sixty-four, in Paris.

• **8 March** The first performance of Walton's *Variations on a Theme of Hindemith*, with the composer conducting, takes place in London.

• **10 December** Bernstein's Third Symphony is first given in Tel Aviv.

• **28 December** Death of Hindemith, aged sixty-eight, in Frankfurt.

OTHER EVENTS

1961 Berlin Wall erected
• First manned space flights

1962 Cuban missiles crisis
• Second Vatican Council convenes

1963 Assassination of President Kennedy

A photograph of a rehearsal for the first performance of Britten's War Requiem. *In order to make the work an act of post-war reconciliation, Britten chose an international team of soloists in Galina Vishnevskaya, Dietrich Fischer-Dieskau and Peter Pears, though Heather Harper eventually sang the soprano part because Vishnevskaya was not available.*

■ *The New Musical Director*

Bernstein, conducting in 1976, caught in characteristic gesture. Towards the end of his life he conducted a cycle of major Romantic symphonies into which he poured enormous energy and commitment.

The rise of a figure such as Leonard Bernstein would not necessarily have been out of place in the nineteenth century, but was unusual in the second half of the twentieth century. There were several other conductors who were able to compose, and who managed to bridge the divide between classical and popular music, but now it was less readily accepted that a person should play several roles – those of conductor, pianist and composer of both popular and serious music.

As a young man Bernstein intended becoming a pianist, though he also studied composition, and then sprang to fame instantly when he was called upon at short notice to take over from Bruno Walter to conduct a concert with the New York Philharmonic in November 1943. By 1949 Bernstein had been appointed conductor of the New York Symphony Orchestra, and in 1958 of the New York Philharmonic. He had already shown his bridging of two traditions long before this, however, for 1944 saw the first performance of his symphony, *Jeremiah* (p.234), the same year he composed the ballet music for his Broadway success *Fancy Free*.

Bernstein himself was aware of the strands that made up his musical personality – jazz, Jewish liturgy, a New England childhood – to which one might add the excitement of New York and, latterly, Christian liturgy. Indeed the *Chichester Psalms* (p.246) provide an inspired synthesis of Jewish and Christian experience. His musical *Candide* (p.242) was perhaps too clever to be popular and too popular to be serious, but with *West Side Story* (p.242), first as a musical and then as a film, he captured a vast middle ground between popular and classical music. At the very least he stands as one who brought music in all its diversity to the widest possible audiences.

1964-73
The Resurgence of Opera

Once seen as an entertainment largely for the wealthy, intellectuals and aesthetes, opera now becomes an increasingly popular form of music. The standard international repertoire remains for the most part intact, but Monteverdi and Cavalli enjoy a revival, and new, socially relevant works are staged.

1964 Messiaen composes *Et exspecto resurrectionem mortuorum* (And I Look for the Resurrection of the Dead) for brass and percussion (chimes), and *Couleurs de la cité céleste* (Colours of the Celestial City), for piano, three clarinets, xylophone, xylorimba, marimba, percussion and brass.

• Stockhausen writes *Momente*, for soprano, four choruses, eight brass, two electronic organs and three percussion and *Mikrophonie I*, for six performers using a variety of implements and electronic equipment to make sound from a rimless gong.

• **12 March** Britten conducts the first performance of his Cello Symphony in Moscow.

• **12 June** Britten conducts the première of his 'Church Parable' *Curlew River* (below) during the Aldeburgh Festival ◆ (p.237).

• **13 August** Mahler's reconstructed Tenth Symphony is performed for the first time in London.

• **20 November** Shostakovich's Ninth and Tenth String Quartets are first performed in Moscow.

1965 Bernstein writes *Chichester Psalms*.

• Ligeti completes his Requiem for soloists, two choirs and orchestra.

• Penderecki completes his *St Luke Passion*.

• Stockhausen composes *Mikrophonie II*, using electronic modulation of the sound produced by a small choir.

• **26 April** Stokowski conducts the first public performance of Ives's Fourth Symphony (p.222).

• **6 November** Varèse dies, aged eighty-one, in New York (opposite).

1966 19 January Première of Tippett's CANTATA *The Vision of St Augustine* in London with the composer conducting.

• **5 April** Britten completes the second of his 'Church Parables', *The Burning Fiery Furnace*.

• **28 May** First performance in St Petersburg of Shostakovich's Eleventh String Quartet.

• **6 August** Henze's opera *The Bassarids*, is first produced in Salzburg.

• **25 September** Shostakovich's Second Cello Concerto is first performed in Moscow.

• **8 October** Stravinsky's *Requiem Canticles* is first performed in Princeton.

> *'... the unlimited space of the newly discovered electronic sound world.'*
> Stockhausen on *Kontakte*

OTHER EVENTS

1964 Mandela jailed

1965 Gemini space flights

1966 Chinese Cultural Revolution

1967 Six-day War between Arab and Israel

1968 Czechoslovakia invaded by Russia

1969 First men on moon

1970 US enter Cambodia

1971 Indo-Pakistani war

1972 British impose direct rule on Northern Ireland

1973 Watergate begins

Peter Pears as the Mad Woman in Curlew River, *the first of Britten's 'Church Parables' in which he transposed the setting of a Japanese Noh play to a mediaeval English church.*

1967 Stockhausen completes *Hymnen* (below), a taped work lasting two hours, and composes *Prozession*, using a new system of NOTATION.

• The Beatles make their record *Sergeant Pepper's Lonely Hearts Club Band*, a landmark in rock recording history.

• **6 March** Death of Kodály, aged eighty-four, in Budapest.

• **26 September** First performance of Shostakovich's Second Violin Concerto in Moscow.

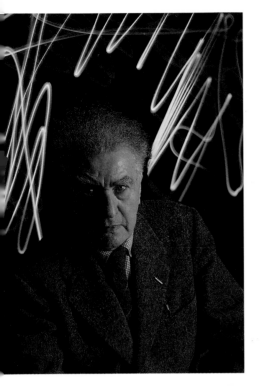

A portrait of Varèse in front of a light sculpture. The French composer moved to the USA where he took up citizenship in 1927, though he never entirely forgot his European origins.

1968 Berio composes his *Sinfonia*, for eight voices and orchestra, which catapults him to international attention.

• Stockhausen completes *Aus den sieben Tagen* (From the Seven Days), which has no musical notation and does not specify voices or instruments required for performance.

• **22 April** Britten completes the third of his 'Church Parables' entitled *The Prodigal Son*.

• **14 September** First performance of Shostakovich's Twelfth String Quartet in St Petersburg.

1969 Messiaen composes his ORATORIO *La Transfiguration de Notre Seigneur Jésus-Christ* (The Transfiguration of Our Lord Jesus Christ), solo instruments, orchestra and choir, and *Méditations sur le mystère de la Sainte Trinité* (Meditations on the Mystery of the Holy Trinity) for organ.

• **22 April** Maxwell Davies composes his *Eight Songs for a Mad King*, based on the life of George III of England.

• **20 June** Penderecki's opera *The Devils of Loudun* is first performed in Hamburg.

• **29 September** First performance of Shostakovich's Fourteenth Symphony in St Petersburg.

1970 Lutoslawski composes his Cello Concerto.

• Reich composes his *Four Organs* for live performance.

• Stockhausen returns to conventional notation for *Mantra*, for two pianos.

• **5 February** Carter's *Concerto for Orchestra* is first given in New York.

• **13 September** First performance of Shostakovich's Thirteenth String Quartet in St Petersburg.

• **2 December** Tippett's third opera *The Knot Garden* is first produced at Covent Garden, London.

An extract (below) from what Stockhausen called his 'reading score' of Hymnen, a work for tape completed in 1967, which incorporates snatches of music from the national anthems of Italy, German, France, Japan, Great Britain, Israel, Canada and 'The Battle Hymn of the Republic'.

1971 Ginastera writes his opera *Beatrix Cenci*, based on the story of the Italian beauty, which uses atonal ◆ (p.225) and ALEATORIC principles.

• Nono composes *Ein Gespenst geht um in der Welt* (A Ghost Goes about in the World) for soprano, chorus and orchestra.

• Stockhausen completes *Trans*, the transcription of one of the composer's dreams of orchestral strings in magenta light, and *Sternklang* (Starsound) for five electronic groups spaced around a public park at night.

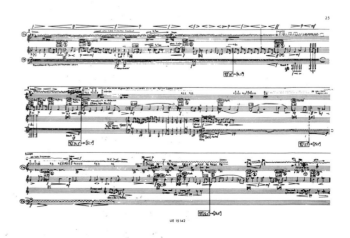

A set design by John Piper for Britten's last opera, Death in Venice, *which represents the interior of St Mark's Basilica.*

• **6 April** Death of Stravinsky, aged eighty-eight, in New York.

• **16 May** Britten's opera *Owen Wingrave*, written specially for the medium, is shown on BBC television.

• **8 September** Bernstein's *Mass, A Theatre Piece for Singers, Players and Dancers*, based on the Roman Mass, with additions by Stephan Schwartz and the composer is performed for the first time in Washington.

1972 Ligeti completes his *Double Concerto* for flute and oboe.

• Lutoslawski composes his *Preludes and Fugue* for string orchestra.

• Pendercki composes his Violin Concerto.

• Stockhausen produces a definitive version of *Momente* (p.246).

The Sydney Opera House (below) was designed by the Danish architect Jørn Utzon in 1956, and was built between 1959 and 1973, by which time the architect had resigned from the project. Initially, it was ill-suited for its purpose and underwent major internal modifications, but there is no doubt that it is a spectacular building in a magnificent setting.

• **8 January** Shostakovich's Fifteenth Symphony is first heard in Moscow.

• **3 March** First performance of Boulez's *...Explosante/fixe...* in Stuttgart ■ (p.251), in which computers determine musical entrances ◆ (p.239).

• **1 June** First performance of Birtwistle's *The Triumph of Time* in London.

• **22 June** First performance of Tippett's Third Symphony in London.

• **12 July** First performance of Maxwell Davies's opera *Taverner* at Covent Garden, London.

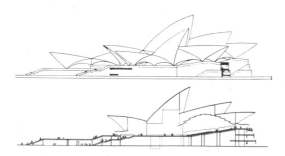

1973 Reich composes his Music for Mallet Instruments, Voices and Organ.

• The Sydney Opera House is completed (left).

• **26 May** First performance of Tippett's Third Piano Sonata in Bath.

• **16 June** Britten's last opera, *Death in Venice*, based on the novella by Thomas Mann, is first performed at Snape, Aldeburgh (above).

• **12 November** Shostakovich's Fourteenth String Quartet is first heard in St Petersburg.

Opposite: A scene from Birtwistle's opera Punch and Judy, *which was first performed at the Aldeburgh Festival in 1968. The composer drew on an earlier work, a suite of rather dissonant movements entitled* Tragoedia, *dating from 1965, for material for the opera. The title hints at the extent to which an interest in Greek Classical drama has inspired much of Birtwistle's work.*

◆ A New Role for Opera

One of the most interesting developments in the second half of the twentieth century has been the enormous growth in the popularity of opera. The old repertoire remains intact, and the star system prevails, but opera now enjoys a much wider audience than at any time since its creation. There are more permanent opera companies than ever before, so that in theory live opera is easily available to the public.

In practice, however, the seat prices at the national opera houses of some countries are far beyond the reach of average people, at least to permit their attendance on a regular basis. Fortunately, new opportunities to hear works have been created through broadcasting. The concept of filmed opera is not a particularly novel one – Strauss directed Der Rosenkavalier and recorded extracts from it as early as 1926 (p.221) – but until well into the second half of the century, opera was thought of as primarily a live experience, and this will always remain the case. Nothing can replace the effect of the contact between performers and audience in the theatre. In this context it is interesting to note that, despite Britten's efforts to compose his opera Owen Wingrave especially for television, he subsequently revised it for the opera house. Nevertheless, with so much opera now broadcast on television and available on video, people may see and hear the works much more readily, and then attend live performances if they choose to do so.

Such a potentially enormous audience has stimulated composers and directors to think far beyond the traditional opera-going public, and use the medium for putting strong political and social content into their works (left). At the same time opera production itself has evolved – not always for the best, it must be admitted – towards a greater emphasis on the perceived 'message' of the works. Other benefits from this new-found popularity include the revival of unjustly neglected works, as funds permit, and the increasingly common practice of sharing productions with other opera houses in order to help offset originating costs. Where national funding is limited, sponsorship is often provided by commercial companies, who have become major patrons in the provision of opera in a way that could hardly have been envisaged in the earlier part of the century.

In another development, opera stars themselves have done much to popularize individual ARIAS, or have crossed over into the domain of popular music ◆ (p.253), thus reaching listeners who would not traditionally have thought of themselves as opera-lovers, via the record companies.

In conclusion it would seem that the new generation of opera-lovers will ensure that there is little danger of opera disappearing as a living form in Western music.

1974-84
A New Discipline

Boulez and Stockhausen pursue their paths with new determination, but the future of traditional musical language is in question with the deaths of Britten and Shostakovich. The minimalism of Glass, and Schnittke's voice from Russia, however, ensures its survival.

1974 Messiaen completes *Des Canyons aux étoiles* (From the Canyons to the Stars), for piano and orchestra.

• **18 January** Monteverdi's opera *Il ritorno d'Ulisse in patria* (p.38) receives its first American performance in Washington.

• **20 October** Henze's *Tristan* – preludes for piano, orchestra and electric sound – is first performed in London.

• **15 November** First performance of Shostakovich's Fifteenth String Quartet in St Petersburg.

1975 Boulez inaugurates IRCAM, the Institute for Acoustic/Music Research and Co-ordination in Paris ■ (opposite).

• Stockhausen composes *Musik im Bauch* (Music in the Belly), a 'ceremony' for six percussionists.

• **23 January** Shostakovich's SONG CYCLE for voice and piano *Suite on Verses of Michelangelo Buonarotti* is first performed in St Petersburg.

• **9 August** Shostakovich dies, aged sixty-eight, in Moscow.

1976 Glass composes his minimalist opera *Einstein on the Beach*.

• **24 February** Carter's *A Mirror on which to Dwell* for soprano and nine players is first performed in New York.

• **18 July** Stockhausen's music drama *Sirius* ★ (p.252), a tribute to American astronauts, receives its first performance in Washington.

A scene from Glass's opera with an Eyptian theme, Akhenaten, as produced at the English National Opera in London in 1985.

• **4 December** Death of Britten, aged sixty-three, at Aldeburgh.

1977 Xenakis composes *Jonchaies*.

• Carter completes his *Symphony of Three Orchestras*.

1978 Stockhausen embarks on his new music drama project entitled *Licht* (Light).

• **10 February** Carter's *Syringa* for two voices and orchestra, based on ancient Greek texts, is first given in New York.

• **17 March** Ligeti's opera *Le grand macabre* is first performed in Stockholm.

1979 24 February The first complete performance of Berg's *Lulu* (p.228) is given in Paris.

• **22 October** Nadia Boulanger dies, aged ninety-two, in Paris.

OTHER EVENTS
1974 President Nixon resigns

1975 Vietnam war ends

1976 Mao Tse-tung dies

1977 'Boat people' flee Vietnam

1978 Camp David Middle East peace talks

1979 Shah of Iran ousted by Ayatollah Khomeini

1980 Vietnam war ends

1981 President Sadat assassinated

1982 Iran-Iraq War starts

1983 AIDS virus identified

1984 Indira Gandhi assassinated

1980 Lutoslawski composes his Concerto for Oboe, Harp and Strings.

• Tippett completes his Triple Concerto for Violin, Viola and Cello.

1981 Babbitt composes his *Ars combinatoria* for classical instruments.

• **23 January** Barber dies, aged seventy, in New York.

1982 Michael Nyman writes the soundtrack to Peter Greenaway's film *The Draughtsman's Contract*.

1983 Messiaen completes his only opera, *St François d'Assise* (St Francis of Assisi), requiring an orchestra of one hundred and twenty players and a chorus of one hundred and fifty singers, in addition to the soloists.

• **8 May** Walton dies, aged eighty-one.

1984 Glass composes another minimalist opera *Akhenaten* (opposite).

• Tippett completes his huge choral work *The Mask of Time*.

■ *Boulez – Contemporary Colossus*

Boulez, photographed here in 1968, is not only a gifted composer and theorist, but a talented conductor of the works of certain composers, bringing to their scores a deep understanding of their creators' intentions and a faithful and highly sensitive interpretation, with particular attention to balance in orchestration.

Pierre Boulez began his musical studies at the Paris Conservatoire in 1942, and studied HARMONY with Messiaen for a year in 1944. It was René Leibowitz's direction of a performance of Schoenberg's Wind Quintet in 1945, however, that drew Boulez away to study serial technique ◆ (p.225) with Leibowitz, and persuaded him that Webern was in fact more significant than his teacher Schoenberg, therefore Boulez took up what he saw as the most valuable lessons to be learnt

from him. At the same time, Boulez absorbed much from the music of Debussy and Stravinsky, and despite his movement away from traditional compositional techniques, he has always found time to conduct works by composers for whom he has respect.

In 1954 Boulez founded the Domaine Musical to promote contemporary music in France, but became disenchanted with the French attitude to that music, and five years later went to Germany to work. In 1975, he returned to Paris to set up IRCAM in the Pompidou Centre.

As far as his own music is concerned, Boulez withdrew everything he had written prior to 1946, as he subsequently withdrew *Livre pour quatuor*, dating from 1948–49, and *Polyphonie X* of 1951. He introduced aleatory (controlled chance) into his composition some time after this, but since he tends to revise his work constantly, it is hard to date this precisely.

In general terms, however, his music remains concerned above all with clarity of texture and extremely refined ORCHESTRAL COLOUR, as one might expect from one with such a delicate ear for orchestral TIMBRES and his sensitivity to the human voice.

1985-2000

Continuing improvements in the quality of sound recording and reproduction techniques, the proliferation of outlets through radio channels and television, the added ease of access through tape and compact disc mean that never before have there been such opportunities to enjoy Classical music.

★ *A scene from Stockhausen's music drama* Sirius, *taken at a performance in 1990.* Sirius *is a star, from which visitors have come to earth, in order to celebrate the cycles concerned with the seasons, the stars and life itself here. From a musical point of view the work marked a new phase for the composer, in which he explored ways of creating, combining and tranforming melodies.*

1985 Compact discs arrive on the market.

• Maxwell Davies completes his Third Symphony.

• Stockhausen completes *Samstag* (Saturday).

• **16 March** Death of Sessions, aged eighty-eight, in Princeton.

1986 Birtwistle completes *Earth Dances* and his opera *The Mask of Orpheus,* on which he has worked since 1974.

1987 Adams completes his opera *Nixon in China.*

• Reich composes *The Four Sections.*

• Berio composes *Formazioni* (Formations).

1988 Stockhausen completes *Montag* (Monday).

• Reich composes *Different Trains.*

• Berio composes *Ofanim.*

1989 **16 July** Death of Von Karajan.

• **November** The Berlin Wall is demolished to the strains of Beethoven's 'Ode to Joy' from the Ninth Symphony (p.144).

1990 Pavarotti (opposite) sings at the World Cup football match.

• Berio composes his *Renderings* for orchestra.

• **2 December** Death of Copland, aged ninety, in New York.

1991 Mozart bicentennial celebrations end with a performance of his Requiem (p.124) timed to finish at the moment the composer died.

1992 Rossini bicentennial celebrations bring performances of his operas around the world.

• Glass composes *Voyage.*

• **28 April** Death of Messiaen.

1993 Michael Nyman composes the film soundtrack for Jane Campion's *The Piano.*

1994 **9 February** Death of Lutoslawski.

OTHER EVENTS

1985 Gorbachev is made leader of the USSR

1986 Chernobyl nuclear reactor explodes

1987 *Glastnost* and *perestroika* in USSR

1988 End of Iran-Iraq War
• George Bush elected president of USA

1989 Tiananmen Square massacre

1990 Germany reunified
• Iraq invades Kuwait

1991 Break-up of USSR, CIS formed
• Gulf War
• Civil War starts in former Yugoslavia
• Maastricht summit

1992 Bill Clinton elected president of USA

1993 Israel-Palestine peace talks

1994 Democratic elections in South Africa

1995 Opening of the Channel Tunnel
• *What's the Story Morning Glory* (Oasis) becomes the biggest-selling CD album in the world

1996 8 January, death of former French president François Mitterand

1997 Guggenheim Museum, Bilbao, completed

1998 Fiftieth anniversary of Israeli Declaration of Independence

1999 Launch of Euro currency
• New Reichstag building opened in Berlin

2000 The start of the third millennium is celebrated worldwide

Opposite: Luciano Pavarotti photographed in 1984 during the course of a gala performance on the stage of the Royal Opera House, Covent Garden, London.

1995 Centennial season of the Henry Wood Promenade Concerts in London.

1996 **29 January** Teatro La Fenice, Venice, one of the world's most famous opera houses, is gutted by fire.

1997 Thomas Ades completes *Asyla*, his major work for orchestra.

• James Horner writes the love theme for the film *Titanic*.

1998 Sir Simon Rattle is appointed Chief Conductor of the Berlin Philharmonic Orchestra with effect from 2002.

1999 **12 March** Death of Yehudi Menuhin, aged eighty-three.

• **1 December** London's Royal Opera House, Covent Garden, re-opens with a gala programme of opera and ballet after a major renovation.

2000 **28 July** Celebrations for the 250th anniversary of the death of J.S. Bach reach their climax on this day.

◆ *Twentieth-Century Audiences*

*I*n the second half of the twentieth century the ability to listen to almost any kind of music at virtually any time and in any place has increased the size of potential audiences to a degree that composers in previous centuries can never have imagined, even in their idlest daydreams. Now Classical music belongs to everyone and anyone who chooses to enter into its world. There are, of course, still those who are drawn to it, yet feel that it is in some way beyond their understanding, and at the the same time there are professional musicians who, for various reasons, are anxious about the side-effects of the broadcasting explosion.

Apart from the continuing need for musicians and listeners to be involved in live performance on the grounds that nothing can replace such an experience, those whose livelihood depends on audiences attending their concerts and performances in theatres and opera houses often find it hard to strike a balance between presenting star performers in standard repertoire, which is likely to fill the house, and fresh but less well known talent in more adventurous programmes. Furthermore, a minority of composers fear that if music becomes too accessible, the incentive to go out and seek new or unfamiliar works is diminished.

The ability of the record companies and broadcasters to promote individual performers and composers means that certain works receive exposure that in previous generations would have required decades to achieve in the concert hall or on the stage, whilst others receive none at all. Despite the illusion of listeners never having had so much choice in the past, it is often difficult to avoid accepting the taste of presenters, commentators and publicists so as to form our own opinions. The task of separating the enduring from the ephemeral is never an easy one, and even the experts have been proved sadly wrong on occasion.

At least the present situation enables listeners to sample, and to consolidate the known and trusted, but one hopes that they will also be encouraged and stimulated to branch out into new paths and venture into less well known territory. This has happened in a remarkable way for early music over the last fifty years or so ◆ (p.219), but without a similar phenomenon for more recent music, the outlook is much less encouraging.

REFERENCE DATA

A group of bowed and plucked stringed instruments, lute, guitar and cello, rest on a musical score this seventeenth-century painting.

Biographical Index of Composers

Abbatini, Antonio Maria
Tiferno, modern Città di Castello c.1595; †Tiferno 1679. Italian church musician who wrote one of the earliest comic operas.

Adam, Adolphe Charles
Paris 24 July 1803; †Paris 3 May 1856. French composer of opera and ballet, of which *Giselle* (p.156) is the best known.

Adam de la Halle
Arras c.1237; †Naples c.1288, or England, after 1306. French composer, *trouvère*, worked in Naples where his pastoral comic opera *Le Jeu de Robin et de Marion* (p.14) was performed.

Agazzari, Agostino
Siena 2 December 1578; †Siena 10 April 1640. Italian church musician and composer of pastoral opera *Eumelio* (p.26).

Ahle, Johann Georg
bapt. Mühlhausen 12 June 1651; †Mühlhausen 2 December 1706. J.S. Bach's predecessor as organist at Mühlhausen.

Albéniz, Isaac
Camprodón, Catalonia 29 May 1860; †Cambo-les-Bains 18 May 1909. Spanish composer and pianist, and creator of the modern Spanish nationalist school of music.

Albert, Heinrich
Lobenstein, Thuringia 8 July 1604; †Königsberg 6 October 1651. German composer, pupil of his cousin Schütz, famous for his songs, *Arien oder Melodien* (p.36).

Albinoni, Tomaso Giovanni
Venice 14 June 1671; †Venice 17 January 1751. Italian composer (of independent means) of operas and instrumental works admired by J.S. Bach.

Albrechtsberger, Johann Georg

Klosterneuburg 3 February 1736; †Vienna 7 March 1809. Austrian composer, director of music at St Stephen's Cathedral, Vienna and teacher of Beethoven 1794–95.

Allegri, Gregorio
Rome 1582; †Rome 17 February 1652. Italian church musician, most famous for his Miserere (p.104), sung during Holy Week in St Peter's, Rome.

Amadei, Filippo
fl.1690–1730. Italian cellist and composer of oratorio and opera, who once worked with Handel.

Anerio, Giovanni Francesco
Rome c.1567; †Graz 11 June 1630. Italian composer who played an important part in the process leading to the development of oratorio.

Anglebert, Jean Henri d' *see* **D'Anglebert**

Arensky, Anton Stepanovich
Novgorod 12 July 1861; †Terioki, Finland 25 February 1906. Russian composer, pianist and conductor.

Auber, Daniel François Esprit
Caen 29 January 1782; †Paris 12 May 1871. French composer of almost seventy operas, of which *La Muette de Portici* is the most famous. He inaugurated the style of French grand opera, thereby influencing Meyerbeer, Halévy and Rossini.

Auric, Georges
Lodève 15 February 1899; †Paris 23 July 1983. French composer, one of Les Six.

Babitt, Milton
Philadelphia 10 May 1916. American composer and mathematician.

Bach, Carl Philipp Emanuel
Weimar 8 March 1714; †Hamburg 14 December 1788. German composer, the fifth son of J.S. Bach, known as the Bach of Berlin and Hamburg.

Bach, Johann Christian
Leipzig 5 September 1735; †London 1 January 1782 German composer, the youngest son of J.S. Bach, known as the English or London Bach.

Bach, Johann Sebastian
Eisenach 21 March 1685; †Leipzig 28 July 1750 German composer, organist and church musician, widely regarded as one of the world's greatest composers by virtue of the depth and sincerity, clarity and intellectual honesty of his best music ■ (p.65) and ■ (p. 77).

Bach, Wilhelm Friedemann
Weimar 22 November 1710; †Berlin 1 July 1784. German composer, the eldest son of J.S. Bach, known as the Bach of Halle.

Bacilly, Bénigne de *see* **De Bacilly, Bénigne**

Balakirev, Mily Alexeyevich

Nizhni-Novgorod 2 January 1837; †St Petersburg 29 May 1910. Russian composer, one of the 'mighty handful'.

Barber, Samuel
West Chester, Pa. 9 March 1910; †New York 23 January 1981. American composer.

Barraqué, Jean
Paris 17 January 1928; †Paris 17 August 1973. French composer.

Bartók, Béla
Nagyszentmiklós, Romania 25 March 1881; †New York 26 September 1945. Hungarian composer, whose technical grasp of Western music and intuitive perception of folk traditions made him one of the most significant forces in twentieth-century music.

Bataille, Gabriel
c.1575; †Paris 17 December 1630. French composer and lutenist who played an important role in the development of court ballet and solo song.

Bax, Arnold
London 8 November 1883; †Cork 3 October 1953. British composer of Romantic tone poems and symphonies.

Beethoven, Ludwig van
* *Bonn 16 December 1770;*
† *Vienna 26 March 1827.* German
composer, probably the greatest
figure in Classical music through
the stature of his works.

Belli, Domenico
fl.1610–20. Italian composer
of lute songs and opera who
worked in Florence.

Bellini, Vincenzo
* *Catania, Sicily 3 November 1801;*
† *Puteaux, Paris 23 September 1835.*
Italian composer of opera in a
lyrical style, who formed a bridge,
with Donizetti, between Rossini
and Verdi.

Benevoli, Orazio
* *Rome 19 April 1605;* † *Rome
17 June 1672.* Italian composer of
church music, once credited with
the Salzburg Festival Mass (p.54).

Bennett, Richard Rodney
* *Broadstairs, Kent 29 March 1936.*
English composer and pianist.

Berg, Alban
* *Vienna 9 February 1885;* † *Vienna
24 December 1935.* Austrian
composer, student of Schoenberg.
Together with Webern the three
constitute the Second Viennese
School ◆ (p.225).

Berio, Luciano
* *Oneglia, Imperia 24 October 1925.*
Italian composer.

Berlioz, Hector Louis

* *La Côte-Saint-André, Isère
11 December 1803;* † *Paris
8 March 1869.* The first, and
possibly the greatest, French
Romantic composer.

Bernhard, Christoph
* *Danzig c.1627;* † *Dresden
14 November 1692.* German
composer, pupil of Schütz and
Carissimi, important in the
pre-Bach era.

Bernstein, Leonard
* *Lawrence, Mass. 25 August 1918;*
† *New York 14 October 1990.*
American composer, pianist
and conductor ■ (p.245).

Berti, Giovanni Pietro
fl.1620–30 Venetian church
musician, singer and organist.

Berwald, Franz Adolf
* *Stockholm 23 July 1796;* † *Stockholm
3 April 1868.* Swedish Romantic
composer, who wrote a number of
symphonies as well as an opera.

Biber, Heinrich Ignaz Franz von
*bapt. Wartenberg, Bohemia 12 August
1644;* † *Salzburg 3 May 1704.*
Austrian violinist and composer,
most famous for his works for
solo violin and his trio sonatas.

Birtwistle, Harrison
* *Accrington, Lancashire 15 July 1934.*
English composer, who drew
inspiration from the verse-refrain
form of Classical Greek drama.

Bizet, Georges
* *Paris 25 October 1838;* † *Bougival
3 June 1875.* French composer,
renowned for his opera *Carmen*
■ (p.177).

Bliss, Arthur
* *London 2 August 1891;* † *London
27 March 1975.* British composer,
pupil of Vaughan Williams and
Holst, but also influenced by
Stravinsky and Les Six.

Bloch, Ernest
* *Geneva 24 July 1880;* † *Portland,
Oregon 15 July 1959.* American
composer and teacher of Swiss-
Jewish origin, whose works often
have a Jewish theme and a
rhapsodic quality.

Blow, John
* *Newark, Nottinghamshire February
1649;* † *London 1 October 1708.*
English composer especially for the
voice and harpsichord, church
musician and teacher of Purcell.

Boccherini, Luigi

* *Lucca 19 February 1743;* † *Madrid
28 May 1805.* Italian cellist and
composer, especially of string
chamber music.

Böhm, Georg
* *Hohenkirchen, near Orhdruf
2 September 1661;* † *Lüneburg
18 May 1733.* German organist
and composer with whom Bach
probably worked.

Bononcini, Giovanni Battista
* *Modena 18 July 1670;* † *Vienna
9 July 1747.* Italian ecclesiastical
and operatic composer who
worked in Rome, Vienna and
London.

Borodin, Alexander Porfiryevich
* *St Petersburg 12 November 1833;*
† *St Petersburg 27 February 1887.*
Russian composer and chemist,
one of the 'mighty handful'.

Boulanger, Nadia
* *Paris 16 September 1887;*
† *Paris 22 October 1979.* French
composition teacher, perhaps
the greatest this century. Her
sister Lili (1893–1918) was a
gifted composer.

Boulez, Pierre
* *Montbrison, Loire 26 March 1925*
French composer, conductor
and teacher.

Brahms, Johannes
* *Hamburg 7 May 1833;* † *Vienna
3 April 1897.* German Romantic
composer, regarded by many as
the successor to Beethoven.

Britten, (Edward) Benjamin
* *Lowestoft 22 November 1913;*
† *Aldeburgh, Suffolk 4 December 1976.*
Probably the most important
English composer of the twentieth
century.

Bruch, Max
* *Cologne 6 January 1838;* † *Berlin 20
October 1920.* German Romantic
composer, most famous for his
First Violin Concerto.

Bruckner, Anton
* *Ansfelden 4 September 1824;* † *Vienna
11 October 1896.* Austrian organist
and composer of some important
Romantic symphonies.

Bull, John

* *c.1563;* † *Antwerp 12 March 1628.*
English organist and keyboard
composer.

Busoni, Ferruccio Benvenuto
* *Empoli, near Florence 1 April 1866;*
† *Berlin 27 July 1924.* Italian
pianist, composer and theorist.

Buxtehude, Dietrich
* *Bad Oldesloe, Holstein c.1637;*
† *Lübeck 9 May 1707.* German
organist and composer.

Byrd, William
* *Lincoln 1543;* † *Stondon Massey,
Essex 4 July 1623.* Foremost
English composer of keyboard
and vocal music.

Caccini, Francesca
* *Florence 18 September 1587;*
† *Lucca c.1640.* Italian
composer, daughter of Giulio.

Caccini, Giulio
* *Tivoli c.1550; buried Florence
10 December 1618.* Italian
composer, singer and teacher.

Cage, John
* *Los Angeles 5 September 1912.*
† *New York 12 August 1992*
American composer.

Caldara, Antonio
Venice c.1670; †Vienna 28 December 1736. Italian composer of cantatas, oratorios and operas.

Cambert, Robert
Paris c.1628; †London 1677. French composer, organist and keyboard player.

Campra, André
bapt. Aix-en-Provence 4 December 1660; †Versailles 14 June 1744. French composer of Italian origin, creator of *opéra-ballet*.

Caproli, Carlo
Rome c.1615; †Rome c.1673. Italian violinist and composer.

Carissimi, Giacomo
bapt. Marino, near Rome 18 April 1605; †Rome 12 January 1674. Italian composer ■ (p.33).

Carter, Elliott
New York 11 December 1908. American composer.

Carver, Robert
1487; †c.1546. Scottish composer.

Casella, Alfredo
Turin 15 July 1883; †Rome 5 March 1947. Italian composer, pianist and conductor.

Castelnuovo-Tedesco, Mario
Florence 3 April 1895; †Los Angeles 17 March 1968. Italian composer and pianist.

Cavalieri, Emilio de'
Rome c.1550; †Rome 11 March 1602. Italian composer of one of the earliest operas.

Cavalli, Pier Francesco
Crema 14 February 1602; †Venice 17 January 1676. Italian composer of opera and church music.

Cerone, Domenico Pietro
Bergamo 1566; †Naples 1625. Italian singer and theorist, author of the treatise *El melopeo y maestro*.

Cesti, Marc'Antonio
bapt. Arezzo 5 August 1623; †Florence 14 October 1669. Italian composer of cantatas and operas, especially *Il pomo d'oro* (p.48).

Chabrier, (Alexis) Emmanuel

Ambert, Puy-de-Dôme 18 January 1841; †Paris 13 September 1894. French composer who strongly influenced modern French music.

Chambonnières, Jacques Champion de
Paris or Chambonnières c.1601; †Paris 1672. French composer and harpsichordist.

Charpentier, Gustave
Dieuze, Moselle 25 June 1860; †Paris 18 February 1956. French opera composer.

Charpentier, Marc-Antoine
Paris c.1645; †Paris 24 February 1704. French composer, especially of church music.

Chausson, Ernest
Paris 20 January 1855; †Limay, near Mantes, Yvelines 10 June 1899. French composer.

Chávez, Carlos
Mexico City 13 June 1899; †Mexico City 2 August 1978. Mexican composer.

Cherubini, Luigi
Florence 14 September 1760; †Paris 15 March 1842. Italian composer and teacher of religious music.

Chopin, Frédéric
Zelazowa Wola, near Warsaw 22 Febraury 1810; †Paris 17 October 1849. Polish Romantic composer and virtuoso pianist.

Cimarosa, Domenico
Aversa, near Naples 17 December 1749; †Venice 11 January 1801. Italian composer of opera.

Coelho, Manuel Rodrigues
Elvas c.1555; †Lisbon c.1635. Portuguese organist and composer of the first printed Portuguese instrumental music.

Copland, Aaron
Brooklyn 14 November 1900; †North Tarrytown, New York 2 December 1990. American composer.

Corelli, Arcangelo
Fusignano, near Ravenna 17 February 1653; †Rome 8 January 1713. Italian composer ■ (p.55).

Cornelius, Peter
Mainz 24 December 1824; †Mainz 26 October 1874. German composer of songs and opera.

Corsi, Jacopo
c.1550; †Florence 1604. Italian nobleman responsible for the first opera *Dafne* ◆ (p.25).

Couperin, François 'Le Grand'

Paris 10 November 1668; †Paris 11 September 1733. French harpsichordist and composer.

Crüger, Johann
Grossbreesen 9 April 1598; †Berlin 23 February 1662. German organist, composer and theorist.

Cui, César Antonovich
Vilnius, Lithuania 18 January 1835; †St Petersburg 26 March 1918. Russian composer and critic. One of the 'mighty handful.'

Czerny, Carl
Vienna 20 February 1791; †Vienna 15 July 1857. Austrian composer and virtuoso pianist.

Dallapiccola, Luigi
Pisino d'Istria 3 February 1904; †Florence 19 February 1975. Italian serialist composer.

D'Anglebert, Jean Henri
Paris 1628; †Paris 23 April 1691. French composer, organist and harpsichordist.

Dargomyzhsky, Alexander Sergeyevich
Troitskoye, Tula district 14 February 1813; †St Petersburg 17 January 1869. Russian pianist and composer.

Davies, Peter Maxwell
Manchester 8 September 1934. English composer.

De Bacilly, Bénigne
Lower Normandy c.1625; †Paris 1690. French composer and vocal theorist.

Debussy, Claude
Saint-Germain-en-Laye 22 August 1862; †Paris 25 March 1918. French composer and important innovator in twentieth-century music ■ (p.193).

Delibes, Léo
St Germain-du-Val, Sarthe 21 February 1836; †Paris 16 January 1891. French composer, known for his ballet *Coppélia* (p.175).

Delius, Frederick
Bradford, Yorkshire 29 January 1862; †Grez-sur-Loing 10 June 1934. English composer of German origin.

Desprez or Des Prés, *see* **Josquin Desprez**

Destouches, André Cardinal
bapt. Paris 6 April 1672; †Paris 7 February 1749. French composer at the court of Louis XV.

D'Indy, (Paul Marie Théodore) Vincent
Paris 27 March 1851; †Paris 2 December 1931. French composer and teacher.

Dittersdorf, Carl Ditters von
Vienna 2 November 1739; †Castle of Rothlhotta, Bohemia 24 October 1799. Austrian composer and violinist.

Dohnányi, Ernö (Ernst von)

Bratislava 27 July 1877; †New York 9 February 1960. Hungarian composer, pianist and conductor.

Donizetti, Gaetano

Bergamo 29 November 1797; †Bergamo 8 April 1848. Italian opera composer; contemporary and rival of Bellini.

Dowland, John

London or Dublin December 1562; buried London 20 February 1626. English composer and lutenist, famed for his melancholy songs.

Dowland, Robert

London c.1591; †London 28 November 1641. English lutenist, son of John.

Drese, Adam

Thuringia December 1620; †Arnstadt 15 February 1701. German composer, associate of Schütz and members of the Bach family.

Dufay, Guillaume

near Cambrai c.1400; †Cambrai 27 November 1474. Franco-Flemish composer during the period of transition from mediaeval to Renaissance styles.

Dukas, Paul

Paris 1 October 1865; †Paris 17 May 1935. French composer; teacher of Messiaen.

Duni, Egidio Romualdo

Matera 9 February 1709; †Paris 11 June 1775. Italian composer influential in founding French *opéra-comique.*

Dunstable, John

c.1380; †London 24 December 1453. English composer whose influence spread to the continent, where he may have lived for twelve or more years.

Duparc, Henri

Paris 21 January 1848; †Mont-de-Marsan 12 February 1933. French song writer who studied under Franck. His output was intense but restricted.

Durey, Louis

Paris 27 May 1888; †3 July 1979. French composer, one of Les Six, until he broke with them in 1921.

Dvořák, Antonin

Nelahozeves, Bohemia 8 September 1841; †Prague 1 May 1904. Czech nationalist composer.

Eimert, Herbert

Bad Kreuznach 8 April 1897; †Cologne 15 December 1972. German composer and theorist.

Elgar, Edward

Broadheath, near Worcester 2 June 1857; †Worcester 23 February 1934. English composer.

Enesco, Georges

Liveni 19 August 1881; †Paris 4 May 1955. Romanian composer and violinist.

Falla, Manuel de

Cadiz 23 November 1876; †Alta Gracia, Argentina 14 November 1946. Spanish composer ● (p.213).

Fauré, Gabriel Urbain

Pamiers, Ariège 12 May 1845; †Paris 4 November 1924. French post-Romantic composer.

Feo, Francesco

Naples 1691; †Naples 28 January 1761. Italian composer.

Ferrabosco, Domenico Maria

Bologna 14 February 1513; †Bologna February 1574. Italian composer.

Ferrari, Benedetto

Reggio Emilia 1597; †Modena 22 October 1681. Italian composer who worked with Manelli on the first public opera in Venice (p.36).

Field, John

Dublin 26 July 1782; †Moscow 11 January 1837. Irish composer and pianist.

Flotow, Friedrich von

Teutendorf, Mecklenburg 26 April 1812; †Darmstadt 24 January 1883. German composer remembered for his opera *Martha* (p.162).

Franck, César Auguste Jean Guillaume Hubert

Liège 10 December 1822; †Paris 8 November 1890. French organist and composer.

Franck, Melchior

Zittau, Saxony c.1580; †Coburg 1 June 1639. German composer.

Frescobaldi, Girolamo

Ferrara 15 September 1583; †Rome 1 March 1643. Italian composer, especially for the organ.

Froberger, Johann Jacob

bapt. Stuttgart 19 May 1616; †Héricourt 6/7 May 1667. German organist and keyboard composer.

Fux, Johann Joseph

Hirtenfeld, Styria 1660; †Vienna 13 February 1741. Austrian composer and theorist.

Gabrieli, Andrea

Venice c.1515; †Venice 1586. Italian composer.

Gabrieli, Giovanni

Venice c.1556; †Venice 12 August 1612. Nephew of Andrea, who composed for St Mark's, Venice.

Gagliano, Marco da

Gagliano, Tuscany 1 May 1582; †Florence 25 February 1642. Italian composer of early opera.

Galilei, Vincenzo

Santa Maria in Monte, near Florence c.1520; buried Florence 2 July 1591. Italian composer and theorist.

Galuppi, Baldassare

Burano, Venice 18 October 1706; †Venice 3 January 1785. Italian composer.

Gasparini, Francesco

Camaiore, near Lucca 5 March 1668; †Rome 22 March 1727. Italian composer of church music and opera.

Gay, John

Barnstaple, Devonshire 30 June 1685; †London 4 December 1732. English writer and composer of the ballad opera *The Beggar's Opera* (p.78).

Gershwin, George

Brooklyn 26 September 1898; †Beverley Hills, California 11 July 1937. American composer of the opera *Porgy and Bess* (p.229).

Gesualdo, Carlo, Prince of Venosa

Naples 1560; †Gesualdo 8 September 1613. Italian composer.

Gibbons, Orlando

bapt. Oxford 25 December 1583; †Canterbury 5 June 1625. English composer of madrigals, church music, and music for consort and keyboard.

Ginastera, Alberto

Buenos Aires 11 April 1916; †Geneva 25 June 1983. Argentinian composer.

BIOGRAPHICAL INDEX

Glass, Philip
*Baltimore 31 January 1937.
American composer.

Glazunov, Alexander Konstantinovich
*St Petersburg 10 August 1865;
†Neuilly-sur-Seine 21 March 1936.
Russian composer, conductor
and teacher.

Glière, Reinhold
*Kiev 11 January 1875; †Moscow
23 June 1956. Russian composer.

Glinka, Mikhail Ivanovich
*Novospasskoye [now Glinka], near
Smolensk 1 June 1804; †Berlin 15
February 1857. Russian nationalist
lyric composer.

Gluck, Christoph Willibald
*Erasbach 2 July 1714; †Vienna 15
November 1787. German composer
and important reformer of opera.

Goldmark, Karl
*Keszthely 18 May 1830; †Vienna
2 January 1915. Hungarian
composer.

Gounod, Charles François

*Paris 18 June 1818; †Paris 18
October 1893. French composer,
chiefly of vocal music and opera.

Grainger, Percy Aldridge
*Brighton, Melbourne 8 July 1882;
†White Plains, New York 20 February
1961. Australian-American
composer, pianist and collector
of folk songs.

Granados, Enrique
*Lérida 27 July 1867; †English
Channel 24 March 1916. Spanish
composer and pianist.

Grandi, Alessandro
*c.1575; †Bergamo 1630. Italian
composer renowned for his church
music.

Graun, Carl Heinrich
*Wahrenbrück c.1703; †Berlin
8 August 1757. German composer
of operas, who was director of
music to Frederick the Great.

Graupner, Johann Christoph
*Kirchberg 13 January 1683;
†Darmstadt 10 May 1760.
German composer, competitor
with Bach for the post of Leipzig
cantor ■ (p.77).

Grétry, André Modeste
*Liège 8 February 1741;
†Montmorency 24 September 1813.
French opera composer of
Flemish origin, most famous for
Richard Coeur-de-Lion ■ (p.115).

Grieg, Edvard Hagerup
*Bergen 15 June 1843; †Bergen
4 September 1907. Norwegian
nationalist composer, pianist
and conductor. He is most
famous for his piano music and
his songs, which draw strongly
on Norwegian folk tunes.

Guédron, Pierre
*Beauce, Normandy 1565; †?Paris
c.1620. French court composer,
a precursor of Lully.

Guglielmi, Pietro Alessandro
*Massa 9 December 1728; †Rome
18 November 1804. Prolific Italian
composer, especially of opera.

Guido of Arezzo
*c.995; †Avellana 1050. Italian
Benedictine monk, theorist and
teacher, who lived for a time in
Arrezo ★ (p.13).

Halévy, Jacques Fromental
*Paris 27 May 1799; †Nice
17 March 1862. French composer
of Romantic opera, teacher and
father-in-law to Bizet.

Hammerschmidt, Andreas
*Brüx, Bohemia 1611; †Zittau,
Saxony 29 October 1675. German
organist and composer of mainly
church music in the new style,
which originated in Italy with
Peri, Caccini and Monteverdi.

Halle, Adam de la *see* **Adam
de la Halle**

Handel, George Frideric
*Halle 23 February 1685; †London
14 April 1759. German composer,
naturalized British, mainly of
opera and oratorio, which he
largely created in Great Britain
■ (p.65) and ■ (p.89).

Hasse, Johann Adolf
bapt. Bergedorf, near Hamburg 25
March 1699; †Venice 16 December
1783. Amazingly prolific German
opera composer known in Italy as
'Il caro Sassone', the dear Saxon.
He married the prima donna
Faustina Bordoni ★ (p.78)

Hassler, Hans Leo
bapt. Nuremberg 26 October 1564;
†Frankfurt 8 June 1612. German
composer, the first to receive an
Italian training.

Haydn, Franz Joseph
*Rohrau 31 March 1732; †Vienna
31 May 1809. Austrian composer
who, with Mozart and Beethoven,
formed the great trio of Classical
Viennese composers ■ (p.99)
and ■ (p.103).

Haydn, Michael
bapt. Rohrau 14 September 1737;
†Salzburg 10 August 1806. Austrian
composer, younger brother of
Franz Joseph.

Henze, Hans Werner

*Gütersloh 1 July 1926. German
composer in all main media,
especially of opera and ballet.

Hidalgo, Juan
*Madrid c.1612; †Madrid 30 March
1685. Spanish composer.

Hiller, Ferdinand

*Frankfurt 24 October 1811; †Cologne
12 May 1885. German composer,
pianist and conductor. He was
friends with Berlioz, Chopin,
Liszt, Mendelssohn, Meyerbeer
and Schumann, and wrote much
on this Romantic circle.

Hindemith, Paul
*Hanau 16 November 1895;
†Frankfurt 28 December 1863.
German composer, viola player
and theorist.

Hoger of Laon,
Presumed French author of tenth-
century musical treatise Musica
enchiriadis (p.12).

Holst, Gustav
*Cheltenham 21 September 1874;
†London 25 May 1934. English
composer of Swedish origin, best
known for his orchestral suite
The Planets (p.212).

Honegger, Arthur
*Le Havre 10 March 1892;
†Paris 27 November 1955.
French composer of Swiss origin.
A member of 'Les Six', he is
known for his chamber and
orchestral music.

Hucbald
*In or near Tournai c.840;
†St Amand 20 June 930. Monk
of St Amand who wrote one
of the first treatises on music
De harmonica institutione (p.12).

Hummel, Johann Nepomuk
*Bratislava 14 November 1778;
†Weimar 17 October 1837. Austrian
composer and pianist, and a pupil
of, among others, Mozart. He
was influential in the development
of the piano virtuoso.

Humperdinck, Engelbert

*Siegburg 1 September 1854;
†Neustrelitz 27 September 1921.
German composer, particularly of
opera, and teacher.

Indy, Vincent d' *see* **D'Indy,
Vincent**

Isaac, Heinrich or **Henricus**
*Flanders c.1450; †Florence 26 March
1517. Flemish composer at the
court of Emperor Maximilian I.

Ives, Charles
*Danbury, Connecticut 20 October
1874; †New York 19 May 1954.
American composer.

Janáček, Leos
*Hukvaldy, Moravia 3 July 1854;
†Ostrava, Moravia 12 August 1928.
Czech nationalist composer and
innovator in harmony, rhythm
and instrumentation.

Joachim, Joseph
*Kittsee, near Bratislava, 28 June
1831; †Berlin 15 August 1907.
Austro-Hungarian composer,
conductor, violinist, and teacher.

Jolivet, André
*Paris 8 August 1905; †Paris
20 December 1974.
French composer.

Jommelli, Niccolò
*Aversa, near Naples 10 September
1714; †Naples 25 August 1774.
Italian composer of operas.

Joplin, Scott
*Texas 24 November 1868; †New York
1 April 1917. American composer,
especially of ragtime.

Josquin Desprez or des Prés
*St Quentin c.1440; †Condé
27 August 1521. Franco-Flemish
Renaissance composer.

Kabalevsky, Dmitri Borisovich
*St Petersburg 30 December 1904;
†Moscow February 1987. Russian
composer.

Kagel, Mauricio Raúl
*Buenos Aires 24 December 1931.
Argentinian composer.

Keiser, Reinhard
bapt. Teuchern, near Weissenfels
12 January 1674; †Hamburg
12 September 1739. German
composer of vocal music.

Kerle, Jacobus de
*Ypres c.1532; †Prague 7 January
1591. Franco-Flemish composer.

Kerll, Johann Kaspar
*Adorf, Vogtland 9 April 1627;
†Munich 13 February 1693.
German composer.

Khachaturian, Aram Ilyich
*Tbilisi 6 June 1903; †Moscow
1 May 1978. Russian composer.

Kittel, Kaspar
*Lauenstein 1603; †Dresden 9 October
1639. German composer.

Kodály, Zoltán

*Kesckemét, Hungary 16 December
1882; †Budapest 6 March 1967.
Hungarian composer, teacher
and collector of folk music.

Korngold, Erich Wolfgang
*Brünn 29 May 1897; †Hollywood
29 November 1957. Austrian
composer.

Krieger, Adam
*Driesen 7 January 1634; †Dresden
30 June 1666. German composer.

Kuhnau, Johann
*Geising 6 April 1660; †Leipzig
5 June 1722. German composer.

La Guerre, Michel de
*Paris c.1605; buried Paris 13
November 1679. French composer.

Lalo, Edouard Victor Antoine
*Lille 27 January 1823; †Paris
22 April 1892. French composer.

Landi, Stefano
*Rome c.1590; †Rome 28 October
1639. Italian composer.

Landini, Francesco

*Fiesole or Florence c.1325; †Florence
2 September 1397. Blind Florentine
organist and prolific composer.

**Lassus, Roland de (Orlando
di Lasso)**
*Mons 1532; †Munich 14 June 1594.
Franco-Flemish composer.

Lawes, Henry
*Dinton, Wiltshire 5 January 1596,
†London 21 October 1662. English
composer.

Lecocq, Alexandre Charles
*Paris 3 June 1832; †Paris 24 October
1918. French composer.

Legrenzi, Giovanni
bapt. Clusone, near Bergamo 12 August
1626; †Venice 27 May 1690.
Italian composer.

Lehár, Franz
*Komárom, Hungary 30 April 1870;
†Bad Ischl 24 October 1948.
Austrian composer of light opera.

Leoncavallo, Ruggero
*Naples 8 March 1857; †Montecatini,
Tuscany 9 August 1919. Italian
composer, famous for his opera
I pagliacci (p.190).

Leoninus (Léonin),
Late twelfth-century French
composer attached to Notre
Dame Cathedral, Paris.

Ligeti, György
*Dicsöszentmárton [Tirnaveni],
Transylvania 28 May 1923.
Hungarian composer and
musicographer.

Liszt, Franz
*Doborján, Hungary, now Raiding,
Austria 22 October 1811; †Bayreuth
31 July 1886. Hungarian
composer, pianist and conductor
■ (p.163).

Locke, Matthew
*Exeter 1622; †London, August 1677.
English composer and organist.

Lotti, Antonio
*?Venice c.1667; †Venice 5 January
1740. Italian composer of opera
and oratorio.

Lully, Jean-Baptiste
[Giovanni Battista Lulli]
*Florence 28 November 1632; †Paris
22 March 1687. French violinist
and composer ■ (p.53).

Lutoslawski, Witold
*Warsaw 25 January 1913;
†Warsaw 9 February 1994.
Polish composer.

Luzzaschi, Luzzasco
*Ferrara c.1545; †Ferrara 11
September 1607. Italian organist
and composer.

MacDowell, Edward Alexander
*New York 18 December 1861; †New
York 23 January 1908. American
pianist and composer.

Machaut, Guillaume de
*?Machaut, Ardennes c.1300;
†Rheims 13 April 1377. French
composer and poet.

Maderna, Bruno
*Venice 21 April 1920; †Darmstadt
13 November 1973. Italian
composer and conductor.

Mahler, Gustav
Kaliste, Bohemia 7 July 1860; †Vienna 18 May 1911. Austrian composer and conductor.

Malipiero, Gian Francesco
Venice 18 March 1882; †Treviso 1 August 1973. Italian composer.

Manelli, Francesco
Tivoli 1595; †Parma September 1667. Italian composer whose opera *L'Andromeda* (p.36) opened the first public opera house in Venice.

Marazzoli, Marco
Parma 1619; †Rome 26 January 1662. Italian composer of the first comic opera, with Mazzocchi.

Marcello, Alessandro
Venice 1684; †Venice 1750. Italian composer, brother of Benedetto.

Marcello, Benedetto
Venice 24 July 1686; †Brescia 25 July 1739. Italian composer of aristocratic birth.

Marenzio, Luca
Coccaglio, Brescia c.1553; †Rome 22 August 1599. Italian composer.

Marini, Biagio
Brescia c.1597; †Venice 20 March 1665. One of the earliest Italian violinist-composers.

Martin, Frank
Geneva 15 September 1890; †Naarden 21 November 1974. Swiss composer.

Martini, Padre Giovanni Battista
Bologna 24 April 1706; †Bologna 3 August 1784. Italian composer, teacher and musicologist.

Martinů, Bohuslav
Polička, Bohemia 8 December 1890; †Liestal, Switzerland 28 August 1959. Czech composer.

Mascagni, Pietro
Livorno 7 December 1863; †Rome 2 August 1945. Italian composer.

Massenet, Jules Emile Frédéric
Montaud, Loire 12 May 1842; †Paris 13 August 1912. French operatic composer.

Mattheson, Johann
Hamburg 28 September 1681; †Hamburg 17 April 1764. German composer and theorist, one of the founders of musicology.

Mazzocchi, Domenico
bapt. Veja, near Città Castellana 8 November 1592; †Rome 20 January 1665. Italian composer, brother of Virgilio.

Mazzocchi, Virgilio
bapt. Veja, near Città Castellana 22 July 1597; †Veja 3 October 1646. A pupil of his brother, he and Marazzoli worked together on the first comic opera.

Mendelssohn Bartholdy, Felix (Jakob Ludwig)
Hamburg 3 February 1809; †Leipzig 4 November 1847. German Romantic composer.

Menotti, Gian Carlo
Cadegliano 7 July 1911. Italo-American composer.

Mersenne, Marin
La Soultière, Maine 8 September 1588; †Paris 1 September 1648. French music theorist.

Merulo, Claudio
Correggio, Reggio Emilia 8 April 1533; †Parma 5 May 1604. Italian composer and organist.

Messiaen, Olivier
Avignon 10 December 1908; †Paris 28 April 1992. French composer.

Meyerbeer, Giacomo

[Jakob Liebmann Meyer Beer]
Berlin 5 September 1791; †Paris 2 May 1864. German composer.

Milhaud, Darius
Aix-en-Provence 4 September 1892; †Geneva 22 June 1974. French composer.

Monferrato, Natale
Venice c.1603; †Venice 23 April 1685. Italian composer.

Monteverdi, Claudio
bapt. Cremona 15 May 1567; †Venice 29 November 1643. One of the greatest Italian composers of opera and church music.

Morales, Cristóbal de
Seville c.1500; †Málaga between 4 September and 7 October 1553. Spanish composer.

Morley, Thomas
Norwich c.1557; †London October 1602. English composer and music publisher.

Mozart, Leopold
Augsburg 14 November 1719; †Salzburg 28 May 1787. Austrian composer and violinist, father of Wolfgang Amadeus.

Mozart, Wolfgang Amadeus
Salzburg 27 January 1756; †Vienna 5 December 1791. Austrian composer of some of the greatest and best loved music in the Classical repertoire ▲ (pp.101, 105, 111, 121 and 125).

Mussorgsky, Modest Petrovich
Karevo, Pskov district 21 March 1839; †St Petersburg 28 March 1881. Russian composer.

Neefe, Christian Gottlob
Chemnitz 5 February 1748; †Dessau 26 January 1798. German composer, early teacher of Beethoven.

Nicolai, Otto
Königsberg 9 June 1810; †Berlin 11 May 1849. German composer and conductor.

Nielsen, Carl August
Island of Funen, Denmark 9 June 1865; †Copenhagen 3 October 1931. Danish composer.

Nono, Luigi
Venice 29 January 1924; †8 May 1990. Italian composer.

Ockeghem, Johannes
?Dendermonde c.1410; †Tours 6 February 1497. Franco-Flemish composer.

Offenbach, Jacques
Cologne 20 June 1819; †Paris 5 October 1880. French composer of mostly light opera ■ (p.167).

Orff, Carl
Munich 10 July 1895; †Munich 29 March 1982. German composer.

Pachelbel, Johann
bapt. Nuremberg 1 September 1653; buried Nuremberg 9 March 1706. German organist and composer.

Paderewski, Ignaz Jan

Kurylówka, Podolia 6 November 1860; †New York 29 June 1941. Polish pianist and statesman.

Paganini, Niccolò
Genoa 27 October 1782; †Nice 27 May 1840. Italian virtuoso violinist and composer.

Paine, John Knowles
Portland, Maine 9 January 1839; †Cambridge Mass. 25 April 1906. American composer and teacher.

Paisiello, Giovanni
Taranto 9 May 1740; †Naples 5 June 1816. Italian composer of some one hundred operas.

Palestrina, Giovanni Pierluigi
Palestrina 9 May 1525; †Rome 2 February 1594. Italian composer.

Pallavicino, Carlo
Salò c.1630; †Dresden 29 January 1688. Italian composer.

Panufnik, Andrzej
**Warsaw 24 September 1914;
†Twickenham 23 September 1991.*
Polish composer.

Pasquini, Bernardo
**Massa di Valdinievole 7 December
1637; †Rome 21 November 1710.*
Italian composer and keyboard
virtuoso.

Pendercki, Krzysztof
**Debica, near Cracow 25 November
1933.* Polish composer.

Pergolesi, Giovanni Battista

**Jesi 4 January 1710; †Pozzuoli, near
Naples 16 March 1736.* Italian
composer of sacred and secular
vocal music.

Peri, Jacopo
**Rome 20 August 1561; †Florence
12 August 1633.* Italian composer
of early opera.

Perotinus (Pérotin)
*c.1160; †between 1200 and 1220.
French composer attached to
Notre Dame Cathedral, Paris,
influential in the development
of the motet.

Perti, Giacomo Antonio
**Crevalcore, near Bologna 6 June 1661;
†Bologna 10 April 1756.* Italian
composer of the later Bologna
school.

Petrassi, Goffredo
**Zagarolo, near Palestrina 16 July
1904.* Italian composer.

Pfitzner, Hans
**Moscow 5 May 1869; †Salzburg
22 May 1949.* German composer
and conductor, who modelled his
work on the German Romantics.

Philippe de Vitry
**Vitry, Champagne 31 October 1291;
†Meaux or Paris 9 June 1361.*
French composer and poet.

Philips, Peter
*?London c.1560; †Brussels 1628.
English composer.

Piccinni, Niccolò
**Bari 16 January 1728; †Passy,
Paris 7 May 1800.* Italian
composer of opera.

Piston, Walter
**Rockland, Maine 20 January 1894;
†Belmont, Mass. 12 November 1976.*
American composer.

Playford, John
**Norwich 1623; †London November
1686.* English music publisher.
His son Henry succeeded him.

Pollarolo, Carlo Francesco
*Brescia c.1653; †Venice 1722.
Italian church musician and
opera composer.

**Porpora, Nicola Antonio
Giacinto**
**Naples 17 August 1686; †Naples
3 March 1768.* Italian opera
composer and singing teacher.

Porta, Giovanni
**Venice c.1690; †Munich 21 June
1755.* Italian opera composer.

Poulenc, Francis
**Paris 7 January 1899; †Paris 30
January 1963.* French composer.

Praetorius, Michael
**Creuzburg 15 February 1571;
†Wolfenbüttel 15 February 1621.*
German composer.

Prokofiev, Sergei Sergeyevich
**Sontsovka, Ukraine 23 April 1891;
†Moscow 5 March 1953.* Russian
composer, pianist and conductor.

Puccini, Giacomo
**Lucca 23 December 1858;
†Brussels 29 November 1924.*
Italian composer of opera.

Purcell, Henry
**London 1659; †London 21 November
1695.* English court composer.
His brother Daniel was also a
composer.

Quantz, Johann Joachim
**Oberscheden, near Göttingen 30
January 1697; †Potsdam 12 July
1773.* German composer, flautist
and theorist ▲ (p.93).

**Rachmaninov, Sergei
Vassilyevich**
**Semyonovo 1 April 1873; †Los
Angeles 28 March 1943.* Russian
composer and virtuoso pianist.

Rameau, Jean-Philippe
*bapt. Dijon 25 September 1683;
†Paris 12 September 1764.* French
composer, keyboard player and
theorist.

Ravel, (Joseph) Maurice
**Ciboure, near St-Jean-de-Luz
7 March 1875; †Paris 28 December
1937.* French composer.

Reger, Max
**Brand, Oberpfalz 19 March 1837;
†Leipzig 11 May 1916.* German
composer.

Reich, Steve
*New York 3 October 1936.
American composer.

Reincken, Johann Adam

**Wildeshausen 27 April 1623;
†Hamburg 24 November 1722.*
German composer and organist.

Respighi, Ottorino
**Bologna 9 July 1879; †Rome 18
April 1936.* Italian composer.

**Rimsky-Korsakov, Nikolai
Andreyevich**
**Tikhvin, Novgorod district 18 March
1844; †St Petersburg 21 June 1908.*
Russian composer, conductor
and teacher.

Rore, Cipriano de
**Malines 1516; †Parma between
11 and 20 September 1565.* Franco-
Flemish composer.

Rosenmüller, Johann
**Ölsnitz, Vogtland c.1619; buried
Wolfenbüttel 12 September 1684.*
German composer.

Rossi, Luigi
**Torremaggiore near Foggia 1598;
†Rome 18 February 1653.* Italian
composer, organist and singer.

Rossi, Michelangelo
**Genoa c.1601; buried Rome 7 July
1656.* Italian composer of opera.

Rossini, Gioacchino Antonio
**Pesaro 29 February 1792; †Paris
13 November 1868.* Italian opera
composer, whose works include
The Barber of Seville ▲ (p.141).

Rousseau, Jean-Jacques
**Geneva 28 June 1712; †Ermenonville
2 July 1778.* French philosopher,
writer and composer. One of the
encyclopaedists ♦ (p.95).

**Roussel, Albert (Charles
Paul Marie)**
**Tourcoing 5 April 1869; †Royan
23 August 1937.* French composer.

Rovetta, Giovanni
**Venice c.1596; †Venice 23 October
1668.* Italian composer and
church musician.

Rubinstein, Anton Grigoryevich
**Vikhvatinets, Podolsk district
28 November 1829; †Peterhof, near
St Petersburg 20 November 1894.*
Russian pianist, composer,
teacher and conductor. His
brother Nikolai pursued a
similar career ● (p.201).

Sacrati, Francesco Paolo
*Parma; †Modena 20 May 1650.
Composer of the first Italian
opera given in France.

Saint-Saëns,(Charles) Camille
**Paris 9 October 1835; †Algiers
16 December 1921.* French
composer and virtuoso pianist.

Salieri, Antonio
**Legnano Veneto, near Verona 18
August 1750; †Vienna 7 May 1825.*
Italian composer, contemporary
of Mozart in Vienna, teacher
of (among others) Beethoven,
Liszt, Meyerbeer, Moscheles,
Schubert and Süssmayr.

Sweelinck, Jan Pieterszoon
Deventer May 1562; †Amsterdam 16 October 1621. Dutch composer, organist and teacher.

Szymanowski, Karol

Tymoszówka, Ukraine 6 October 1882; †Lausanne 29 March 1937. Polish composer.

Tailleferre, Germaine
Paris 19 April 1892; †Paris 6 November 1983. French composer, one of the group Les Six.

Tartini, Giuseppe
Pirano, Istria 8 April 1692; †Padua 26 February 1770. Italian violinist composer and teacher.

Taverner, John
Tattershall, Lincolnshire c.1490; †Boston c.1545. English composer.

Tchaikovsky, Piotr Ilyich
Kamsko-Votkinsk, Vyatka district 7 May 1840; †St Petersburg 6 November 1893. Russia's first international composer ▲ (p.189).

Telemann, Georg Philipp
Magdeburg 14 March 1681; †Hamburg 25 June 1767. German composer.

Thomson, Virgil
Kansas City 25 November 1896; †New York 1989. American composer.

Tippett, Michael (Kemp)
London 2 January 1905; †London 8 January 1998. English composer.

Titelouze, Jehan
St Omer c.1563; †Rouen 24 October 1633. French composer.

Tomkins, Thomas
St Davids, Pembrokeshire 1572; buried Martin Hussingtree, 9 June 1656. English composer.

Torelli, Giuseppe
Verona 22 April 1658; †Bologna 8 February 1709. Italian composer.

Tregian, Francis
Cornwall 1574; †London 1619. English composer, compiler of the *Fitzwilliam Virginal Book* ★ (p.29).

Tunder, Franz
Burg, Fehmarn Island 1614; Lübeck 5 November 1667. German composer, who founded the Abendmusiken recitals in Lübeck.

Turina, Joaquín
Seville 9 December 1882; †Madrid 14 January 1949. Spanish composer.

Ussachevsky, Vladimir
Hailar, Manchuria 21 October 1911; †1990. Russo-American composer.

Varèse, Edgar
Paris 22 December 1883; †New York 6 November 1965. American composer of French origin.

Vaughan Williams, Ralph

Down Ampney, Gloucestershire 12 October 1872; †London 26 August 1958. English composer.

Veracini, Francesco Maria
Florence 1 February 1690; †Florence 31 October 1768. Italian opera composer.

Verdi, Giuseppe
Le Roncole, Busseto, Parma 9 October 1813; †Milan 27 January 1901. Italian composer who raised nineteenth-century Italian opera to new heights.

Viadana, Lodovico da
[Lodovico Grossi]
Viadana, near Mantua c.1560; †Gualtieri, near Mantua 2 May 1627. Italian composer, important in the development of *basso continuo*.

Victoria, Tomás Luis de
Avila 1548; †Madrid 27 August 1611. Spanish composer of sacred music.

Villa-Lobos, Heitor
Rio de Janiero 5 March 1887; †Rio de Janiero 17 November 1959. Brazilian composer.

Vinci, Leonardo
Strongoli c.1690; †Naples 27 May 1730. Italian opera composer.

Vitali, Giovanni Battista
Bologna 18 February 1632; †Modena 12 October 1692. Italian composer, especially of string music.

Vitry, Philippe de, *see* **Philippe de Vitry**

Vittori, Loreto
bapt. Spoleto 16 January 1604; †Rome 23 April 1760. Italian composer and castrato singer.

Vivaldi, Antonio Lucio
Venice 4 March 1678; †Vienna 28 July 1741. Italian violinist and composer, famed for his instrumental music ■ (p.71).

Wagner, (Wilhelm) Richard
Leipzig 22 May 1813; †Venice 13 February 1883. German composer ■ (p.171), who developed a new method of through-composition for opera.

Walton, William
Oldham, Lancashire 29 March 1902; †Ischia 8 May 1983. English composer.

Weber, Carl Maria (Friedrich Ernst) von
Eutin, Holstein 18 December 1786; †London 4 June 1826. German Romantic composer.

Weber, Fridolin von
1761; †1833 Half-brother of Carl Maria and also his teacher.

Webern, Anton von
Vienna 3 December 1883; †Mittersill, Salzkammergut 15 September 1945. Austrian composer.

Weill, Kurt

Dessau 2 March 1900; †New York 3 April 1950. German composer.

Wellesz, Egon Joseph
Vienna 21 October 1885; †Oxford 9 November 1974. Austrian composer, teacher and musicologist.

Widmann, Erasmus
bapt. Schwäbisch-Hall 15 September 1572; †Rothenburg 31 October 1634. German composer.

Widor, Charles-Marie
Lyons 21 February 1844; †Paris 12 March 1937. French composer, organist and teacher.

Wolf, Hugo
[Philipp Jakob] *Windischgrätz, now Slovenjgradec 13 March 1860; †Vienna 22 February 1903.* Austrian composer, especially of songs.

Wolf-Ferrari, Ermanno
Venice 12 January 1876; †Venice 21 January 1948. Italian composer.

Xenakis, Iannis
Braila, Romania 29 May 1922. French composer, born in Romania to Greek parents.

Zemlinsky, Alexander von
Vienna 14 October 1871; †Larchmont, New York 15 March 1942. Austrian composer and conductor.

STRINGS	
2	small violins
10	viole da braccio
2	contrabass viols
2	bass lutes
2	?bass citterns
3	bass gambas
WOODWIND	
2	recorders
2	cornetts
BRASS	
4	trumpets
5	trombones
OTHER	
1	harp
2	harpsichords
3	small organs

The Development of the Orchestra

The Early Orchestra

Although we know what instrumental forces were available to Monteverdi in Mantua for performance of his opera *Orfeo* in 1607 (left), there was no orchestra as such in existence, and the large body of some forty musicians at the composer's disposal simply represented all the instrumentalists in the employ of the Duke of Mantua at that time. With such a wide range of choice, however, the composer's musical instinct made him decide to use certain instruments for particular passages and effects during the course of the work, and we see an early example of ORCHESTRATION at work. Throughout the rest of the century, however, instruments tended to be chosen for their application and function in church or chamber, indoors or out-of-doors, and the practice was to develop and extend families and groups of related instruments, rather than to bring together a range of instruments, such as we find in the present-day orchestra.

The Classical Orchestra

By 1700 it was widely accepted that the core of any orchestral group was the string family of first and second violins, violas, cellos and contrabasses, who provided the four-part HARMONY. They were accompanied by and usually directed from either a harpsichord or organ, depending on the nature of the performance. Oboes, flutes and bassoons were now added, but sometimes the oboists doubled on the flutes so that both could not be played simultaneously. This was not seen as a disadvantage, since musical COLOUR and contrast at this time varied from MOVEMENT to movement, rather than within a movement. For much the same reason trumpets and drums were seen as a body apart, and, because in addition they could only play in certain KEYS, they were only used in particular movements. By 1753 Dresden (right) had one of the largest orchestras in Europe.

STRINGS	
8	first violins
7	second violins
4	violas
3	cellos
3	double basses
WOODWIND	
2	flutes
5	oboes
5	bassoons
BRASS	
2	horns
2	trumpets
OTHER	
2	pairs of kettledrums
2	harpsichords

STRINGS	
21	first violins
20	second violins
18	violas
8	first cellos
7	second cellos
10	double basses
WOODWIND	
2	piccolos
2	flutes
2	oboes
1	cor anglais
2	clarinets
1	bass clarinet
4	bassoons
BRASS	
4	valve horns
2	valve trumpets
2	cornets
3	trombones
1	bass trombone
1	bass tuba
OTHER	
4	harps
2	pairs of timpani
1	bass drum
1	pair of cymbals

The Romantic Orchestra

Possibly the greatest difference between the Classical and Romantic orchestras was the departure of the CONTINUO instruments as orchestras expanded and composers ceased to write music for them. All the basic instruments were now on hand, and might be used from one moment to the next rather than from one movement to another. Berlioz much admired the orchestra of the Berlin Opera which, for special occasions in the 1840s, could provide 14 first violins, 14 second violins, 8 violas, 10 cellos, 8 double basses, 4 flutes, 4 oboes, 4 clarinets, 4 bassoons, 4 horns, 4 trumpets, 4 trombones, timpani, bass drum, cymbals and 2 harps. The balance between strings, woodwind and brass had altered radically. Berlioz in his 1844 treatise on instrumentation outlined an even larger orchestra (left) for the effects that he introduced into his own compositions. The orchestra was becoming a vast palette, from which the composer might choose almost any combination of colours.

A distinction must be made, however, between the extended range of orchestral sound and sheer volume. In practice composers did not often become the orchestral megalomaniacs of the caricatures. Both Rossini and Berlioz were ridiculed and condemned for the increase in volume, for which they were only partly responsible. Newer, larger theatres (often used for orchestral concerts before special halls were built) made traditional forces seem inadequate. Berlioz attributed his early lack of enthusiasm for Mozart, Haydn and even Beethoven to the infrequency and poor quality of performances of their works, played in buildings that were too large and acoustically unsuitable.

The Modern Orchestra

Wagner developed the orchestra to even greater proportions than those
achieved by Berlioz, and contributed to its standardization, since the
SCORES of his operas required a minimum complement of instruments,
without which they could not be performed. He was not alone in this,
of course, for the emergence of an international operatic and concert
repertoire virtually imposed uniform conditions, though standards still
varied enormously from place to place. Fixed seating plans for orchestras
tended to become more common as experience taught composers and
the new breed of conductor how to achieve the best effect for the listener.
Even today, however, some conductors prefer variations; for example,
instead of first and second violins being placed together on the conductor's
left, the seconds are on the right, at the front of the orchestra, although
these are relatively small differences in terms of the overall pattern.
One significant development of the modern period, however, has been
the emergence of the smaller chamber orchestra for the performance
of more intimate music, and a return to the forces and instruments
used by composers in their own day.

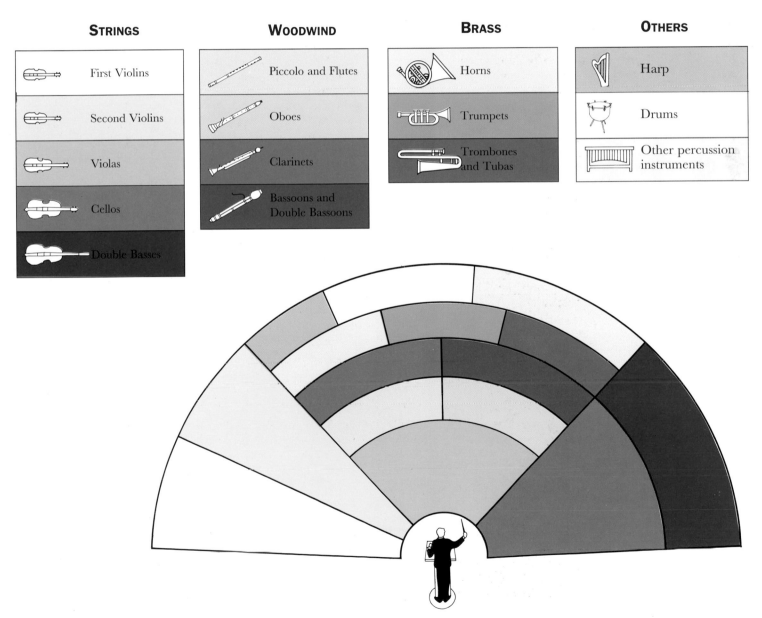

STRINGS

First Violins

Second Violins

Violas

Cellos

Double Basses

WOODWIND

Piccolo and Flutes

Oboes

Clarinets

Bassoons and
Double Bassoons

BRASS

Horns

Trumpets

Trombones
and Tubas

OTHERS

Harp

Drums

Other percussion
instruments

Timeline of Musical Events

———| LIVES OF THE COMPOSERS   ● DEVELOPMENT OF THE ORCHESTRA   ● DEVELOPMENT OF MUSICAL INSTRUMENTS

| 1600 | 1605 | 1610 | 1615 | 1620 | 1625 | 1630 | 1635 | 1640 | 1645 | 1650 | 1655 | 1660 | 1665 | 1670 | 1675 | 1680 | 1685 | 1690 | 1695 |

CARISSIMI

VICTORIA

G. GABRIELI

GESUALDO

SWEELINCK

PRAETORIUS

BYRD

LULLY

GIBBONS

BUXTEHUDE

DOWLAND

FRESCOBALDI

MONTEVERDI

CHARPENTIER

CORELLI

PURCELL

A. SCARLATTI

COUPERIN

ALBINONI

SCHÜTZ

VIVALDI

RAMEAU

J.S. BACH

D. SCARLATTI

HANDEL

● Monteverdi details the orchestral forces for his opera *Orfeo*.

●———● The violin ensemble known as *Les Vingt-quatre violons du roi* and the wind ensemble *Les douze grands hautbois* are established under Louis XIII of France.

● Giovanni Gabrieli's posthumously published *Canzoni e sonate* specify individual instruments.

● Lully forms the violin ensemble known as *Les petits violons*.

● The Compenius organ is installed in Frederiksborg Castle, Denmark.

●———● Praetorius works on his *Teatrum instrumentorum*, detailing current musical instruments, published in Wolfenbüttel as part of vol.II of *Syntagma Musicum*.

● Death of the violin maker Girolamo Amati, teacher of Stradivari and Guarneri.

● Kircher's *Musurgia universalis*, detailing musical instruments, is published in Rome.

● One of the earliest recorded uses of the oboe, by Lully in Paris.

Stradivari labels/makes his first cello. ●

18th

1700　1705　1710　1715　1720　1725　1730　1735　1740　1745　1750　1755　1760　1765　1770　1775　1780　1785　1790　1795

PERGOLESI

GLUCK

HAYDN

SALIERI

MOZART

CHERUBINI

BEETHOVEN

PAGANINI

WEBER

ROSSINI

SCHUBERT

DONIZETTI

BUXTEHUDE

CHARPENTIER

CORELLI

A. SCARLATTI

COUPERIN

ALBINONI

VIVALDI

RAMEAU

J.S. BACH

D. SCARLATTI

HANDEL

● Keiser uses French horns for the first time in an opera, his *Octavia*, in Hamburg.

● Clarinets are detailed for the first time in a musical score.

● Johann Stamitz goes to Mannheim and becomes leader of the orchestra in 1748.

● Subscription concerts begin in Hamburg.

Mozart composes his last three symphonies, deploying all the orchestral forces then in use. ●

● Denner of Nuremberg develops the clarinet from the chalumeau.

● Cristofori pioneers the first pianofortes.

● The contrabassoon is first introduced.

● Hampel develops the technique of handstopping,
which revolutionizes French horn playing.

Erard invents the *fourchette* (fork) mechanism for the harp. ●

Haydn writes his Trumpet Concerto for key trumpet. ●

19th

| 1800 | 1805 | 1810 | 1815 | 1820 | 1825 | 1830 | 1835 | 1840 | 1845 | 1850 | 1855 | 1860 | 1865 | 1870 | 1875 | 1880 | 1885 | 1890 | 1895 |

DVOŘÁK

SCHOENBERG

JANÁČEK

DEBUSSY

MAHLER

R. STRAUSS

RACHMANINOV

RAVEL

BARTÓK

STRAVINSKY

WEBERN

BERG

HAYDN

SALIERI

CHERUBINI

BEETHOVEN

PAGANINI

WEBER

ROSSINI

SCHUBERT

DONIZETTI

PUCCINI

BERLIOZ

CHOPIN

SCHUMANN

LISZT

WAGNER

VERDI

OFFENBACH

BRAHMS

BRUCKNER

BIZET

MUSSORGSKY

TCHAIKOVSKY

• Beethoven writes for trombones as symphonic instruments, and considerably extends the use of timpani and French horns in the orchestra. His treatment of the piano is also new.

• Mendelssohn uses a baton to conduct.

• Wagner uses sixteen horns in *Tannhäuser*.

Berlin Philharmonic Orchestra founded. •

Metropolitan Opera House opens in New York •

• A valve is introduced for the trumpet.

• Spohr invents the chin rest for the violin.

• Boehm devises the cylinder-bore flute.

• The bass tuba is invented.

• Sax produces the family of saxhorns.

The Celesta is patented. •

20th

| 1900 | 1905 | 1910 | 1915 | 1920 | 1925 | 1930 | 1935 | 1940 | 1945 | 1950 | 1955 | 1960 | 1965 | 1970 | 1975 | 1980 | 1985 | 1990 | 1995 | 2000 |

DVOŘÁK

SCHOENBERG

JANÁČEK

DEBUSSY

MAHLER

R. STRAUSS

RACHMANINOV

RAVEL

BARTÓK

STRAVINSKY

WEBERN

BERG

PUCCINI

COPLAND

WALTON

TIPPETT

SHOSTAKOVICH

MESSIAEN

BRITTEN

LUTOSLAWSKI

BERNSTEIN

BOULEZ

HENZE

STOCKHAUSEN

GLASS

- The Symphony Hall, Boston becomes the new home of the Boston Symphony Orchestra.

- Odeon release the first full orchestral recording.

- Orchestral size reaches an extreme with the first performance of Schoenberg's *Gurrelieder* for an enormous ensemble.

- In the first performance of Xenakis's *Terretektorh* players sit in and among the audience.

- The Sydney Opera House opens.

- Maurice Martenot first demonstrates his electronic melody instrument the Martenot Waves.

- Laurens Hammond develops the Hammond organ.

- Electric guitars are first manufactured.

- Cage writes his first music for prepared piano.

- The RCA electronic music synthesizer is demonstrated for the first time.

- Hiller and Isaacson produce their computer-generated *Illiac Suite*.

Glossary of Musical Terms

adagio (Ital. 'at ease', or 'slowly') Indication of the **tempo** at which a piece is to be played or sung. Also the name given to the slow **movement** of a composition.

aeromelodicon A patented keyboard instrument of the sort frequently invented in the nineteenth century, but which never established itself.

air or **ayre** Essentially a song-like tune for instrument or voice, when it is synonymous with the French *air de cour* and the Italian **aria**, though with the rise of opera the latter came to mean a much more formal vocal composition.

aleatory (Lat. 'dice') A type of contemporary music in which the composer allows an element of chance to occur either in its composition or performance.

allegro (Ital. 'happy') Indication of a fast **tempo** and also the name of a **movement**.

alto (Ital. 'high') A high male voice. The term in vocal music for the second highest voice, whether sung by men or women. Instruments of this approximate range also take the name.

anthem A sacred vocal work of the English-speaking church, the equivalent of the Latin **motet**.

antiphon (Grk. 'sound across') A short passage, usually from the psalms, often sung as responses between groups of singers or between a soloist and choir, hence the adjective antiphonal for any music thus performed.

aria (Ital.) Air or song, though chiefly for the extended form found in opera and **oratorio**, often in three sections, and subsequently applied to major individual vocal passages in opera. The **da capo** aria, in the form A-B-A was one of the conventions of eighteenth-century opera.

atonality *see* **tonality.**

ballade An extended dramatic piano piece, probably first used in this sense by Chopin.

ballad opera English dramatic form where spoken dialogue alternates with songs.

baritone Man's voice, between **bass** and **tenor.**

basso continuo (Ital. 'continuous bass') The common **harmonic** accompaniment supplied by a **keyboard** instrument or lute, indicated in the music by the bass notes with figures and or accidentals (sharps or flats) above them, indicating the **chords** to be played. In practice the term is almost the same as **figured bass.**

bitonal *see* **tonality.**

bolero A Spanish dance in triple time.

brass General term used for all the members of the trumpet, horn and related families when constituting a section of an orchestra or wind band.

canon The difficult practice of repeating a **melody** either vocally or instrumentally, at a delayed passage of time, and overlapping the first use of the melody. Also a composition using this technique, to which not all melodies lend themselves.

cantata (Ital. 'sung') An extended vocal composition for one or more voices, accompanied by any number of instruments.

cantor In the Christian and Jewish religions a **solo** singer responsible for performing passages of the **liturgy** which are usually unaccompanied.

cantus firmus (Lat. 'fixed song') The term often used for the **tenor** in fifteenth-century **polyphonic** music.

canzona or **canzone**, pl. **canzoni** (Ital. 'song') Originally a type of poem, it was first applied to the musical setting of the poem and then to a short instrumental piece often employing elements of the **fugue.**

canzonetta (Ital. 'little song') Diminutive of **canzona** though reserved for vocal compositions.

caprice or **capriccio** Essentially a free style of vocal or instrumental composition not falling into any specific category, akin to the **fantasia.**

carol A lyric form consisting of verses with refrain, now almost exclusively reserved for songs at Christmas.

castrato pl. **castrati** A castrated male singer who underwent surgery to preserve his youth's treble voice, which in the adult became powerful, and enjoyed great popularity during the eighteenth century.

catch Originally a **round** for voices, the term came to be associated specifically with humorous, and sometimes indecent versions.

celesta A keyboard percussion instrument in which suspended metal plates with wooden resonators are struck, invented by Mustel of Paris about 1880. Tchaikovsky was one of the first composers to use it.

chamber music Originally vocal or instrumental music for the chamber, as opposed to the church or theatre. Later used for almost any intimate work less suited to the concert hall.

chorale or **choral** Usually designates a hymn tune of the German Proestant tradition, used by Bach, for example, for many of his organ and sacred vocal compositions.

chord Two or more notes played or sung simultaneously, usually according to strict rules. A basic distinction exists between a **concord,** a pleasant-sounding chord, and a **discord,** which is the opposite.

chorus A group of singers, a composition for such a group, or simply the refrain sung by everyone.

chromatic (Grk.) A term applied to **harmony**, a **melody** or an instrument that employs all the twelve semitones that occur in the octave that is the basic **scale** or succession of notes in Western music.

cimbalon A keyboard percussion instrument of folk origins found in Eastern Europe, especially Hungary.

clarino A term used chiefly to describe the florid, high trumpet parts in Baroque music.

colour, tonal colour and **orchestral colour** an idea borrowed from painting whereby the possibilities for contrast provided by the different instruments, and the same instruments playing in different parts of their overall range, is likened to applying different touches of colour to the orchestral texture. Some composers have made deliberate attempts to link such sounds directly to specific colours.

coloratura An elaborate, highly ornamented part for **soprano** voice, usually high in **pitch.** The term is also applied to those performers who specialize in singing such parts.

comédie-ballet A combination of singing and ballet for the stage used particularly by Lully in his collaboration with Molière, and the forerunner of French serious opera.

concerto A composition for instruments in which the element of contrast, either between a **solo** instrument or a small group of instruments and the main body, is essential.

concerto grosso A **concerto** in which the contrast is between a small group of instruments and the main body.

concitato style (Ital. 'roused' or 'stirred') A vigorous character given by the composer to a piece of music.

concord *see* **chord.**

conductor The director of a large musical performance.

consort A group of voices or instruments, either of the same family (**woodwind**, **brass**, etc.) or mixed, in which case in England the term broken consort was applied.

continuo The accompanying instrument or instruments that play continuously throughout a composition.

contralto A low-**pitched** woman's voice.

counterpoint and **contrapuntal** The practice of combining **melodies**, or adding a second **melody** to a first.

cycle A composition consisting of a succession of related sections. In a **song cycle** the sections are the individual poems which may follow a narrative, or simply be on a related theme. In a **symphonic cycle** the term usually implies a succession of **movements** of symphonic proportion, though not observing the traditional form of a symphony. When a musical **theme** or themes are used in common to movements, then the term cyclic or cyclical form is used.

da capo (Ital. 'from the beginning') *see* **aria.**

discord *see* **chord.**

dissonance Essentially an unpleasant sound created by the effect of two or more notes simultaneously, as in a **chord** though what were once technically dissonances have become perfectly acceptable with the passage of time.

divertissement A short passage of instrumental music, often informal in nature, inserted into a longer composition, or a short entertainment in its own right.

dodecaphony *see* **twelve-note music.**

duet or **duo** A composition for two singers or instrumentalists.

duple time The rhythm of a piece of music where the beat is in two, rather than three (**triple**) or four (quadruple).

duplum The upper voice in early **polyphonic** music.

dynamic The degree of softness or loudness with which a part of music is to be performed.

electroacoustic Sounds caused by electricity.

elegy A vocal or instrumental composition of lament.

ensemble (Fr.'together') A group of voices or instruments performing together.

entrée (Fr. 'entry') In French ballet an instrumental introduction, and also an act of an **opéra-ballet**. Subsequently used for any introductory passage in music, often march-like in character.

extemporize or **improvize** To perform vocally or instrumentally without music, often using a given **theme** as a point of departure. Especially associated with organ music.

fantasia, fantaisie and **fantasy** A form of vocal or instrumental music that does not conform to any of the accepted forms such as **sonata**, **concerto** or **symphony**, though Beethoven, for example, composed a sonata in the form of a fantasia.

figured bass *see* **basso continuo**

fugue A vocal or instrumental composition marked by the repetition of a phrase or **melody**, and its development using a variety of technical devices such as **counterpoint.**

Gradual Part of the Proper of the **Mass.**

Gregorian chant *see* **plainsong.**

harmony or **harmonic structure** The process of combining sounds in music in the broadest sense, though often restricted to the process of providing accompaniment to a **melody**, traditionally according to strict rules, which have been relaxed with the passage of time. In more extended compositions the harmonic structure is a fundamental ingredient of the overall result.

harmonic series Overtones which are produced by instruments when any given note is sounded. **brass** instruments use harmonics as part of their normal playing technique, whereas stringed instruments tend to reserve them for special effects only.

hexachord The group of six notes in the scale used by Giudo of Arezzo (p.13).

improvize *see* **extemporize**

incidental music Instrumental and or vocal music composed to accompany a play or film where music is not an integral part of the work.

inflection or **intonation** In **plainsong** all the sections or groups of notes other than one repeated note. By extension, **melodic inflection** refers to a group of notes that create a particular effect or impart an individual character to a **melody.**

intermezzo (It.) Originally a short composition played or sung between sections of a longer work such as a play, and a short comic opera played between the acts of a tragedy. It was subsequently used for purely orchestral passages in operas, **movements** of **chamber** and orchestral works that did not adhere to standard forms, and also to piano works. The unifying concept is that of a certain independence of form.

interval A description of the difference in **pitch** between two notes.

intonation In **plainsong** the same as **inflection**. In general terms used to identify whether music is being played or sung in tune, according to the **key.**

jongleurs Mediaeval travelling musicians and entertainers (p.14).

key and key signature In Western Classical music a piece of music composed between the seventeenth century and the greater part of the twentieth century usually has its **harmonic** and **melodic** centre on a **scale** in which all the notes are related to a key note, indicated by the key signature, which can be any one of the twelve semitones available to a composer, in either the **major** or **minor**, according to choice.

keyboard instruments The members of the piano and harpsichord families ❈ (p.51).

key trumpet An attempt was made in the late eighteenth century to make the trumpet more flexible by adding keys, but ultimately this was achieved by introducing the **valve.**

laudi or **laude** (Ital. 'praises') Popular religious songs in the vernacular, which greatly influenced the rise of **oratorio** in Italy.

libretto (Ital. 'little book') The words of an opera or **oratorio** set to music by the composer.

lied pl. **lieder** (Ger. 'song') Most widely taken to denote the Romantic poem set to music with piano accompaniment by Schubert and others.

liturgical music, liturgy Strictly music for the Christian Eucharist or **Mass** (including the **Requiem Mass**) and services such as **Matins** and **Vespers**, though in its widest application may be taken to include canticles such as **Te Deum** and **Magnificat**, special psalms such as the **Miserere**, antiphons such as **Salve Regina**, and sequences such as **Stabat Mater.**

madrigal An Italian secular vocal piece of music. In the earliest days it had a very precise strophic and rhyme scheme, but later became much more flexible, in which form it was used in England.

Magnificat *see* **liturgical music**

major Refers to the **key** of a piece of music. Usually creates a brighter, happier sounding atmosphere, as opposed to the **minor**.

march A characteristic kind of music rather than a specific form, identified with military music for marching.

Martenot Waves An instrument devised in the 1920s, where sound is generated through the interference between a fixed and variable oscillator.

masque A courtly or aristocratic entertainment combining words, music and dance, with lavish settings and costumes, usually with symbolic or allegorical content.

Mass The central service of worship in the Christian church. Much of the service stays the same throughout the **liturgical** year and is called the Ordinary, comprising the Kyrie, Gloria, Credo, Sanctus, Benedictus and Agnus Dei. The Proper is the variable part of the Mass and is made up of the Introit, **Gradual,** Offertory and Communion.

Matins *see* **liturgical music**

mazurka A Polish national dance in **triple time**, originally also sung, and developed by Chopin and others into a piano **solo**.

melody or **melodic inflection** A succession of notes which is usually less formalized than a tune, though the distinction is a fine one. Melodic inflection denotes a small portion of a melody with a particular or unusual character.

Minnesänger German mediaeval poets who sang of courtly love.

minor Refers to the **key** of a piece of music. Often taken to characterize the sadder, more mournful nature of music, as opposed to the **major**, though Purcell, for example, wrote some of his sprightliest tunes in a minor key.

minuet European court dance, in triple time, of the seventeenth and eighteenth centuries .

Miserere *see* **liturgical music**

monodrama A play for one performer, in which the text is declaimed over music.

monody Music for a single voice with a restricted instrumental accompaniment, evolved during the Renaissance.

monophony Music for one voice alone (p.12).

motet In the Middle Ages and the Renaissance the chief form used by composers for **polyphonic** vocal music, either sacred or secular, though later it became almost entirely sacred and might be for one voice rather several.

movement A self-contained section of a **concerto**, **sonata** or **symphony**.

musique concrète Music made with pre-recorded sound.

Neo-Baroque A term used to describe the return to the earlier Baroque style in music, especially in the twentieth century.

Neo-Classical Basically the same phenomenon as **Neo-Baroque**.

nocturne (Fr. 'A night-time piece') Essentially a slow piano piece created by John Field, and taken up by Chopin, though earlier examples exist for other instruments, especially under the Italian form **notturno**.

notated and **notation** The practice and form, respectively, of writing music down in such a way that it gains the widest possible diffusion and that the largest number of people may read and understand it.

notturno *see* **nocturne**

obbligato (Ital. 'necessary') Indicates that an instrumental or vocal part is essential for the performance of the music.

octet A composition for eight singers or instrumentalists.

ode Originally a chorus in a Greek play, it came to denote an extended poem which, when set to music, usually celebrated an event of importance, similar to a **cantata**.

offices *see* **liturgical music.**

opera buffa (Ital.) Comic opera, as opposed to **opera seria**.

opéra-bouffe Basically the French version of **opera buffa**, though by the time of Offenbach it had come closer to **operetta**.

opera seria (Ital.) Serious opera, especially in the seventeenth and eighteenth centuries.

operetta (Ital. 'little opera') Originally a short opera, it is now used for musical comedy of the Viennese and Parisian type.

opus (Lat. 'work') Used in conjunction with a number to identify the works of composers chronologically.

oratorio (Ital.) Sacred drama originating in Italy, and developed in England by Handel when **opera seria** declined.

orchestral colour *see* **colour.**

orchestrate or **orchestration** The composer's practice of choosing instruments, or a particular combination of instruments, at any given moment in a piece of music for particular effect.

organum The earliest form of **polyphony**, where the **cantus firmus** was accompanied by other parts at fixed **intervals.**

overture The opening piece of instrumental music for an opera or **oratorio**, but also in the later Romantic period an extended composition in its own right.

panharmonicon A mechanical orchestra invented by Mälzel, for whom Beethoven wrote *The Battle of Victoria* in 1813.

partita (Ital.) A **suite** or **air** with **variations**, usually written for **keyboard.**

Passion A musical form based on the Gospel account of the suffering and death of Christ.

pastorale or **pastoral** A stage performance, often including ballet, on a pastoral theme taken from Classical literature.

percussion Family of instruments which sound when struck.

phrase A short section of melody.

pitch The sound of a note governed by its vibrations, fixed by international agreement at 440 per second for the A above middle C, to which all other notes are related.

plainsong The unison singing of **liturgical** texts, often unaccompanied, before the advent of singing in parts.

polonaise A traditional Polish dance in **triple time**, with the character of a **march**.

polychoral Music written for several groups of voices and or instruments.

polyphonic Music in several parts, or for several voices.

polytonality A modern practice of superimposing more than two **tonalities** on top of another. Classical music usually employs only one **tonality** at a time.

prelude In element the same as an **overture**, though in the piano music of Chopin and Debussy the term has virtually no specific connotation.

prepared piano An instrument introduced by Cage based on a conventional piano with objects inserted between the strings.

quartet A composition for four voices or instruments.

quintet A composition for five voices or instruments.

rag or **ragtime** Jazz music usually composed for the piano, in which the rhythmic element is more prominent than the **melody.**

recitative A passage in opera or **oratorio** in which the story unfolds, against a minimum of accompaniment, in contrast to the **arias**, which usually express emotional reaction to the story. *See* **secco recitative.**

Requiem *see* **liturgical music**

rhapsody (Gk.) A vocal or instrumental composition in free form.

rhythm (Gk.) The organization of sounds in time.

ricercar (Ital.) An instrumental piece which often featured imitation on the lines of **fugue** and **canon**.

ritornello (Ital. 'little return') In the Baroque and Classical periods denotes an instrumental passage which is repeated, though it had more specific connotations in early music.

round A short **canon** for voices, such as 'Three Blind Mice', and also a round dance.

Salve Regina *see* **liturgical music**

scale A succession of notes consisting of twelve semitones which traditionally give the **key** to a piece of music. When semitones are ignored in favour of whole tones, then a **whole-tone scale** is created.

scherzo (Ital. 'joke') A light instrumental piece, used by Haydn and Beethoven to replace the **minuet** as the third **movement** of symphonies, and in other compositions.

score The copy of a composition showing all the various parts together, whether they be vocal or instrumental, or a combination of both.

secco (Ital. 'dry') **recitative** A form of **recitative** where the voice is accompanied only by a succession of **chords**, and moves along swiftly.

septet A vocal or instrumental composition for seven performers.

serenade Essentially evening music, either vocal or instrumental.

serenata (Ital.) Used to designate a form of the **cantata** and also an instrumental **suite**.

serialism A method of composition elaborated by Schoenberg in which a row of notes is used as the point of departure, always in the same order, both in **chords** and as **melody** and **counterpoint**.

serpent An obsolete wind instrument with a cupped mouthpiece, part **brass** and part **woodwind**, with finger holes or keys.

sextet A vocal or instrumental composition for six performers.

shake see **trill**

sinfonia (Ital. 'symphony') An instrumental passage used to introduce a work on the lines of the **overture**.

singspiel (Ger. 'sing-play)' A sung musical stage work with spoken dialogue.

solo A vocal or instrumental composition for one performer.

solmization A system devised to aid sight-reading by naming the notes of the **scale** with syallbles (p.13).

sonata (Ital. 'sounded)' Originally an instrumental composition either for sacred or secular use, then elaborated into a work for one or two instruments in more than one **movement**.

sonatina (Ital. 'little sonata') A short version of the **sonata**.

song cycle see **cycle**.

sonority Sound in the widest sense, but also used for denoting individual effects produced by instruments.

soprano The highest human voice or instrument.

Stabat Mater see **liturgical music**

stave The lines on which music is written.

strings The members of the violin and viol family ◈ (p.39) among others.

suite An extended instrumental composition consisting of a number of pieces, usually dances, though more recently almost any succession of **movements** not adhering to the plan of **concerto**, **sonata** or **symphony**.

symphonic cycle see **cycle**

symphonic poem or **tone poem** An extended orchestral composition, usually in one **movement**, and very often following a narrative or programme.

symphonic suite A large-scale orchestral composition in several **movements** on the scale of a symphony, though not adhering to the form.

symphony A large-scale orchestral work, usually in four **movements.** Usually in eighteenth-century symphonies the first **movement** is fast, sometimes preceded by a slow introduction; the second **movement** is slow; the third a **minuet** and **trio**; and the last **movement** fast. In the nineteenth century the third movement was often replaced by a faster and more light-hearted one.

tablature A system of **notation**, especially for instruments such as the lute, which requires a somewhat different treatment from, for example, the piano.

Te Deum see **liturgical music**

tempo (Ital. 'time') The speed at which a passage is to be played.

tenor (Lat. 'to hold') Originally the **cantus firmus** in early **polyphony,** now used to describe the highest-pitched male voice, and very often the instrument of a family fulfilling a comparable function.

theme The **melody** or tune which is used as the point of departure for a set of **variations**, or to identify a concept or character in an opera or similar work.

thorough or **through bass** Another term to designate what is otherwise known as **continuo**.

timbre The **tonal colour** of an individual instrument.

toccata (Ital. 'touched') A showy, rapid keyboard composition of no particular form.

tonal colour see **colour**

tonality A term describing the use of organized **keys** in a piece of music. If a work is in two different **keys** it is **bitonal** and the abandonment of **key** as a system of organization is described as **atonality.**

tone A note of music, and more specifically the distance encompassed by two semitones.

tone poem see **symphonic poem**

transcription The arranging of a work for an instrument (especially **keyboard**) or instruments other than those originally envisaged by the composer.

trill or **shake** An ornament in vocal or instrumental music in which one note alternates rapidly with the next, to give a 'shaking' effect.

trio A vocal or instrumental composition for three performers. In eighteenth-century **symphonies** the third movement often took the form of a **minuet** and trio, where the latter was a second minuet, in contrast to the first. Possibly it earned its name from early works where it was written for only three instruments.

trio sonata A Baroque **sonata,** usually in four **movements,** normally for two violins, cello and harpsichord. Only the three **string** instruments are counted in the title, the harpsichord as an inevitable accompaniment during this period, being taken for granted.

triple time The rhythm of a piece of music where the beat is essentially in three, as opposed to two (**duple**) or four (quadruple).

twelve-note serialism A system largely evolved by Schoenberg where each of the twelve semitones in the **scale** is given equal importance. A twelve-note piece of music thus has no key in the traditional sense.

valve trumpet An invention which made the trumpet much more flexible and adapatable than the **key trumpet**, and so assisted its assimilation into the orchestra.

variations A practice of extended composition by a series of elaborations of a **theme** or **melody** by varying rhythm, **tempo**, **key** (**major** or **minor**) and similar means.

verset Originally the verse of a psalm during which the singers remained silent, the organ played, and the congregation meditated on the words which they repeated to themselves. Other parts of the **liturgy** may be treated in the same way.

Vespers see **liturgical music**

vibraphone A twentieth-century percussion instrument. Its metal tubes have lids which open and close under power from an electric motor, thus vibrating the sound produced.

virtuoso pl. **virtuosi** (Ital.) Singers or instrumentalists who have attained a particularly accomplished degree of technical and interpretational excellence.

whole-tone scale see **scale**

waltz A dance, in triple time, which was very popular in nineteenth-century ballrooms.

woodwind The members of the flute, oboe and clarinet families when they constitute a section of an orchestra or wind band.

xylorimba An American form of the xylophone.

Star Performers of the Twentieth Century

This short list is merely a selection of the many performers who, since the development of recording techniques, have contributed to the joy of countless music-lovers. It may serve as a preliminary guide to those confronted with the vast choice of recorded music now available.

CONDUCTORS

Barbirolli, Sir John (1899-1970) British conductor and cellist of Italian/French parentage. Long associated with the Hallé Orchestra.

Beecham, Sir Thomas (1879-1961) English conductor who introduced to the UK the Ballets Russes and works by Richard Strauss, founded London Philharmonic Orchestra, championed Delius and excelled in French music.

Bernstein, Leonard (1918-1990) US conductor, pianist and composer of both popular and serious music.

Boult, Sir Adrian (1889-1983) English conductor. After his appointment as Director of Music to the BBC in 1930, he formed the BBC Symphony Orchestra.

Davis, Sir Colin (b.1927) Principal Conductor of BBC Symphony Orchestra 1967-71 and then Music Director of Royal Opera House, Covent Garden. First British conductor to appear at Bayreuth.

Haitink, Bernard (b.1929) Dutch conductor. Principal Conductor of London Philharmonic Orchestra 1967-79, Glyndebourne and Royal Opera House, Covent Garden.

Karajan, Herbert von (1908-89) Austrian conductor of Vienna Philharmonic and then Berlin Philharmonic, with which he was closely identified. His forceful interpretation was legendary.

Klemperer, Otto (1885-1973) German conductor who left Europe for the USA in 1933 and became an international figure, associated especially with the music of Mahler.

Monteux, Pierre (1875-1964) French conductor of many Ballets Russes premières in Paris, where he founded the Orchestre Symphonique 1929-38, then settled in America.

Ozawa, Seiji (b.1935) Japanese conductor who has made a career in Western Classical music, and since 1973 has been Principal Conductor of the Boston Symphony Orchestra.

Prévin, André (b.1929) US conductor and pianist who has done much to bridge the gap between Classical and popular music.

Rattle, Simon (b.1955) English conductor chiefly associated with the City of Birmingham Symphony Orchestra, internationally famed for his Mahler interpretations.

Solti, Sir Georg (1912-97) Hungarian- born British conductor renowned for his work in opera, especially Mozart, and the major symphonic repertoire, particularly Beethoven.

Stokowski, Leopold (1887-1977) British conductor of Philadelphia Orchestra 1912–36 and several others in the USA. Famous for his flamboyant orchestral arrangements.

Toscanini, Arturo (1867-1957) Italian conductor of several Puccini premières, who also appeared at Bayreuth, Salzburg and in the USA. One of the most intransigent yet most respected persons ever to have mounted the podium.

Walter, Bruno (1876-1962) Highly distinguished German conductor driven out of Vienna in 1938, succeeded **Toscanini** with New York Symphony Orchestra. His love of humanity shone through his work.

INSTRUMENTALISTS

CELLO

Casals, Pau (1876-1973) Spanish cellist who settled in France, founded a distinguished trio with **Cortot** (piano) and Thibaud (violin) and became probably the most famous cellist of the century.

Du Pré, Jacqueline (1945-87) British cellist (wife of **Daniel Barenboim**) who died tragically young; recognized above all as a brilliant exponent of Elgar's Cello Concerto.

Piatigorsky, Gregor (1903-76) Russian-born cellist smuggled out of his homeland in 1921 and discovered in Berlin by the pianist Artur Schnabel. He took US citizenship in 1937.

Rostropovich, Mstislav (b.1927) Russian cellist, pianist and conductor, husband of the soprano Galina Vishnevskaya, and close associate of Benjamin Britten.

CLARINET

Peyer, Gervase de (b.1926) British clarinettist, especially associated with the Melos Ensemble.

FLUTE

Galway, James (b.1939) Irish flautist who worked with the Berlin Philharmonic before establishing an international career as a recitalist and performer of both the Classical and popular repertoire.

GUITAR

Segovia, Andres (1893-1987) Spanish guitarist, the most famous of his generation, and possibly the most influential figure in the renaissance of the instrument in this century.

HARP

Robles, Marisa (b.1937) Spanish-born virtuoso harpist, resident in Britain, from where she pursues an international career.

HARPSICHORD

Landowska, Wanda (1877-1959) Polish harpsichordist, initially a pianist, revived interest in a nearly forgotten instrument, inspiring works from De Falla and Poulenc.

HORN

Brain, Denis (1921-57) Virtuoso English horn player, killed tragically in a car crash at the height of his career.

LUTE

Bream, Julian (b.1933) English guitarist and lutenist who has been largely responsible for the revival of interest in the lute music of Dowland and his contemporaries.

OBOE

Holliger, Heinz (b.1939) Swiss oboist (and composer) of international status.

ORGAN

Demessieux, Jeanne (1921-68) After winning first prizes for harmony, piano, fugue and organ at the Paris Conservatoire, she became one of the best known exponents of the French organ repertoire.

Hurford, Peter (b.1930) English organist, renowned for his interpretations of Bach's organ music, which he has recorded in its entirety.

PIANO

Arrau, Claudio (1904-91) Chilean pianist, who made his début in Berlin at the age of ten, and played the whole of Brahms's piano music from memory. His long and distinguished career fulfilled his early promise.

Ashkenazy, Vladimir (b.1937) Russian pianist and conductor, who has enjoyed a long-standing working relationship with the violinist **Itzhak Perlman.**

Barenboim, Daniel (b.1942) Argentinian-born pianist and conductor, since 1991 Principal Conductor of the Chicago Symphony Orchestra.

Brendel, Alfred (b.1931) Austrian pianist, exponent of the Classical and Early Romantic repertoire, especially Mozart, Haydn, Beethoven and Schubert.

Cortot, Alfred (1877-1962) French pianist, conductor and teacher of wide musical culture, but remembered especially for his interpretation of Chopin, Schumann and Debussy.

Curzon, Sir Clifford (1907-82) English pianist. Already Professor at the Royal College of Music at the age of nineteen, he abandoned teaching for an international career as a performer, particularly of the works of Mozart.

Horowitz, Vladimir (1904-89) Russian-born pianist. His relentless search for perfection made him reject many of his recordings and severely restrict the number of his appearances.

Larrocha, Alicia de (b.1923) Spanish pianist of great refinement and sensitivity who excels in the works of the Spanish Romantics and Ravel.

Lipatti, Dinu (1917-50) Romanian pianist and composer, pupil of **Cortot.** During his brief career Lipatti made an indelible impression on those who heard him play, particularly with his interpretations of the music of Bach.

Moiseiwitsch, Benno (1890-1963) Russian-born pianist in the tradition of the great virtuosi, renowned for his interpretation of Chopin and Russian piano music.

Moore, Gerald (1899-1987) English pianist who became the most distinguished accompanist of the century for singers who included **Maggie Teyte, Elisabeth Schwarzkopf, Victoria de los Angeles** and **John McCormack.**

Parsons, Geoffrey (1929-95) Australian pianist who has largely become the successor to **Moore.**

Rubinstein, Artur (1886-1982) Polish pianist acclaimed throughout the world for his performances of Chopin, De Falla and Stravinsky.

TRUMPET

Hardenberger, Håkan (b.1961) Norwegian virtuoso trumpet player.

VIOLA

Primrose, William (1904-82) British viola player, pupil of Ysaÿe, who suggested that he take up the instrument, on which he became an international virtuoso.

VIOLIN

Bell, Joshua (b.1967) American violinist whose elegant and sensitive interpretation of the classics, and unassuming nature, have won him many admirers.

Chung, Kyung-Wha (b.1948) Korean-born violinist, a pupil of Ivan Galamian, she first came to fame in 1970 playing the Tchaikovsky concerto for a London charity gala.

Kreisler, Fritz (1875-1962) Austrian who became the most famous international concert violinist of the first half of the century, much loved by the public, though considered by many critics to lack taste.

Heifetz, Jascha (1901-87) Lithuanian-born violinist, youngest student ever to be admitted to St Petersburg Conservatory, and thought by some to have the most influence on his profession since Paganini.

Menuhin, Yehudi (1916-99) US-born violinist, already internationally famous when he recorded Elgar's violin concerto with the composer as conductor in 1932. A musician of deep humanity and sensitivity.

Oistrakh, David (1908-74) Russian violinist appreciated for his beauty of tone. His son Igor also became a distinguished violin virtuoso.

Perlman, Itzhak (b.1945) Israeli violinist of Polish descent, a pupil of Galamian, he has made a remarkable international career, despite being confined to a wheelchair. Has worked closely with **Ashkenazy.**

Stern, Isaac (b.1920) Russian-born American violinist, a close associate of **Casals** and Galamian, his profound musicianship causes him to be regarded as the doyen of violinists.

Zukerman, Pinchas (b.1948) Israeli violinist discovered by **Casals** and **Stern,** a pupil of Galamian. Has worked closely with **Barenboim** and **Perlman.**

SINGERS

BARITONES

Evans, Sir Geraint (1922-92) Welsh baritone, one of the first British singers to achieve worldwide recognition in the twentieth century, and remembered particularly for his role as Falstaff in Verdi's opera.

Fischer-Dieskau, Dietrich (b.1925) German baritone renowned chiefly for his performances of the German lieder repertoire, though also with a distinguished career in opera.

Gobbi, Tito (1915-84) Italian baritone remembered for the dramatic quality of his appearances in the operas of Verdi.

Souzay, Gérard (b.1921) French baritone whose career has been chiefly dedicated to the concert repertoire, especially the French chansons of Fauré, Debussy and Ravel.

Terfel, Bryn [Bryn Terfel Jones] (b.1965) Welsh baritone whose performances of a wide repertoire from Handel to Verdi and modern musicals draw their freshness chiefly from close attention to the text.

BASSES

Chaliapine, Feodor (1873-1938) Russian bass, one of the most famous of all time, with a magnificent stage presence and, after **Caruso,** the most popular singer of his day.

Christoff, Boris (1919-93) Bulgarian bass who came rapidly to fame with his interpretation of the great roles in Russian opera.

Robeson, Paul (1898-1976) US bass and actor, whose first concert appearance was singing spirituals. His repertoire ranged from opera to musicals.

CONTRALTO

Ferrier, Kathleen (1912-53) British contralto whose purity of tone and exceptional personal qualities made her untimely death all the more felt.

MEZZO-SOPRANOS

Baker, Dame Janet (b.1933) British singer who, after starting as a contralto, found her role as a deeply committed mezzo-soprano opera singer and recitalist.

Bartoli, Cecilia (b.1966) Italian singer whose flamboyant personality and lively, committed performances of the late Baroque and Classical roles from Vivaldi and Handel to Mozart have delighted her audiences.

Berganza, Teresa (b.1935) Spanish mezzo-soprano who made her début in 1957 and rapidly achieved international fame.

Fassbaender, Brigitte (b.1939) German mezzo-soprano who sings in opera, oratorio and on the concert platform.

Ludwig, Christa (b.1928) German mezzo-soprano equally at home in operatic roles or with the lieder repertoire.

SOPRANOS

Ameling, Elly (b.1938) Dutch soprano whose purity of tone and sensitive interpretation have made her a much admired recitalist.

Angeles, Victoria de los (b.1923) Spanish soprano with a wide repertoire, at home both in the opera house and on the concert platform.

Caballé, Montserrat (b.1933) Spanish soprano who excels in the *bel canto* repertoire.

Callas, Maria (1923-77) US soprano of Greek origin who achieved great fame through her dramatic performances of the coloratura *bel canto* operatic repertoire, and was for many the archetypal prima donna.

Cotrubas, Ileana (b.1939) Romanian dramatic soprano who made an international career in opera and retired in 1990.

Crespin, Régine (b.1927) French soprano, with an internationally distinguished career as a prima donna and recitalist.

Flagstad, Kirsten (1895-1962) Norwegian soprano with a remarkably even voice throughout the register, and a flawless interpreter of Wagnerian roles.

Freni, Mirella (b.1935) Italian soprano whose clear tone, supported by profound musicianship, makes her ideal for Mozart and some of the Puccini roles.

Lehmann, Lotte (1888-1976) German soprano, equally at home with the operas of Beethoven, Strauss and Wagner or the lieder of Schubert, Schumann and Wolf.

Nilsson, Birgit (b.1922) Swedish soprano, regarded by many as a natural successor to **Flagstad** in Wagnerian roles.

Norman, Jessye (b.1945) Possibly the greatest prima donna of the later part of the twentieth century, above all in the Romantic repertoire, and especially on the concert platform.

Schumann, Elisabeth (1891-1952) One of the greatest German sopranos, in opera and oratorio, but especially in the lieder of Schubert.

Schwarzkopf, Elisabeth (b.1915) German soprano, most associated with the operas of Mozart, and Strauss's *Der Rosenkavalier*, but also a consummate lieder recitalist.

Söderström, Elisabeth (b.1927) Swedish soprano with a wide repertoire of lieder and operatic roles.

Sutherland, Dame Joan (b.1926) Australian soprano whose pure, even tone throughout the vocal register was admirably suited to the *bel canto* repertoire.

Te Kanawa, Dame Kiri (b.1944) New Zealand-born soprano with a wide repertoire, including popular music, whose quality of voice is ideal for Mozart and Strauss.

Teyte, Dame Maggie (1888-1976) English soprano chosen by Debussy to be the first Mélisande in his opera *Pelléas et Mélisande*.

TENORS

Björling, Jussi (1911-60) Swedish tenor whose light but warm tone and purity of line were ideal for the standard operatic Italian and French repertoire.

Carreras, José (b.1947) Spanish tenor associated with **Montserrat Caballé** who greatly encouraged him on his path to an international career.

Caruso, Enrico (1873-1921) Italian operatic tenor, one of the greatest tenors of all time.

Domingo, Placido (b.1941) Spanish tenor whose rich, even tone and deeply committed approach to opera roles make him one of the greatest tenors of the late twentieth century.

Gigli, Beniamino (1890-1957) Italian tenor who was the highest paid singer in the world during his twelve seasons at the Metropolitan Opera House in New York.

McCormack, John (1884-1945) Irish tenor who first appeared at Covent Garden in 1907 but gradually abandoned opera for concert work. His income from gramophone records was second only to **Caruso's.**

Melchior, Lauritz (1890-1973) Danish-American tenor who excelled in Wagnerian roles.

Pavarotti, Luciano (b.1935) Italian tenor, possibly the most famous and most successful of his generation, who has done much to popularize some of the tenor operatic repertoire.

Tauber, Richard (1892-1948) Austrian-born British tenor who, after specializing in Mozart opera, made a worldwide reputation in the lighter operatic repertoire.

Vickers, Jon (b.1926) Canadian tenor whose début was at Bayreuth in 1958, and is deeply respected for the integrity of his performances.

Top 100 Classical Recordings

This list is not a 'starter collection' of CDs, but is as representative a choice possible from the many recordings available. Some have been chosen because of an advantageous pairing, but all the recordings are recognized as being of the highest quality. If CD numbers differ in the USA, these are given in parentheses. Some companies withdraw recordings and reissue them, sometimes in a slightly different format and with a new number.

KEY TO ORCHESTRAS:

ASMF	= Academy of St Martin-in-the-Fields
BERSO	= Berlin Radio Symphony
BPO	= Berlin Philharmonic
BSO	= Bamberg Symphony
BRSO	= Bavarian Radio Symphony
BSO	= Boston Symphony
CHSO	= Chicago Symphony
CSO	= Columbia Symphony
EBS	= English Baroque Soloists
ECO	= English Chamber
LCO	= London Chamber
LCP	= London Classical Players
LPO	= London Philharmonic
LSO	= London Symphony
MSO	= Montreal Symphony
NPO	= New Philharmonia
NYPO	= New York Philharmonic
PO	= Philharmonic
PRSO	= Polish Radio Symphony
RCO	= Royal Concertgebouw
RLPO	= Royal Liverpool Symphony
RPO	= Royal Philharmonic
SCO	= Scottish Chamber
SRSO	= Swedish Radio Symphony
VPO	= Vienna Philharmonic

1 Albinoni: *Sonatas a 5, Op.2/3, and Op.2/6.* **Corelli:** *Concerto grosso, Op.6/9.* **Vivaldi:** *Concertos RV121 and RV156, and Sonata (Al Santo Sepolcro), RV130.* ECO, Raymond Leppard
Classics for Pleasure CD-CFP 4371
See also No.**95**

2 Allegri: *Miserere.* **Palestrina:** *Litaniae de Beata Virgine Maria in 8 parts; Magnificat in 8 parts; Stabat Mater,* and other motets. Choir of King's College, Cambridge, David Willcocks
Decca CD 421 147-2

3 Bach, J.S.: *Arias from: Mass in B min., St John Passion and St Matthew Passion.* **Handel:** *Arias from: Judas Maccabaeus, Messiah and Samson.* Kathleen Ferrier, LPO, Adrian Boult
Decca CD 433 474-2

4 Bach, J.S.: *Violin concertos No.1, BWV1041; No.2 BWV1042; Double violin concerto, BWV1053; Double concerto for violin and oboe, BWV1060.* Arthur Grumiaux, Hermann Krebbers, Heinz Holliger; Les Solistes Romandes, Arpad Gerecz, NPO; Edo de Waart
Philips CD 420 700-2

5 Bach, J.S.: *Orchestral suites Nos.1-4, BWV1066-69.* Liszt Chamber Orchestra, Janos Rolla
Hungaroton HCD 31018

6 Bach, J.S.: *Organ works: Adagio in C from BWV565; Fantasia and fugue in G min., BWV542; Fugue in E flat (St Anne), BWV552; Passacaglia and fugue in C min., BWV582; Toccata and fugue in D min., BWV565,* and three *Chorales,* incl. *Wachet auf, BWV645.* Peter Hurford
Decca CD 417 711-2
See also Nos. **23, 91, 94** and **95**

7 Barber: *Adagio for strings.* **Copland:** *Quiet city.* **Cowell:** *Hymn.* **Creston:** *Rumor.* **Ives:** *Symphony No.3.* ASMF, Neville Marriner
Argo CD 417 818-2

8 Bartók: *Concerto for orchestra; Music for strings, percussion and celesta.* MSO, Charles Dutoit
Decca CD 421 443-2

9 Beethoven: *Piano concerto No.5 (Emperor) and Choral fantasia, Op.80.* Melvyn Tan, Schütz Choir, LCP, Roger Norrington
EMI CDC7 49965-2

10 Beethoven: *Violin concerto, Op.61; Romances Nos.1, Op.40, and 2, Op.50.* Wolfgang Schneiderhan, BPO, Eugen Jochum. David Oistrakh, RPO, Eugene Goossens
DG 427 197-2

11 Beethoven: *Triple concerto for violin, cello and piano, Op.56.* **Brahms:** *Double concerto for violin and cello, Op.102.* David Oistrakh, S. Knushevitzy, Lev Oborin, PO, Malcolm Sargent
EMI CDZ7 62854-2

12 Beethoven: *Symphony No.3 (Eroica); Grosse Fuge, Op.133.* PO, Otto Klemperer
EMI CDM7 63356-2

13 Beethoven: *Symphonies No.5, Op.67, and No.8, Op.93; Fidelio overture.* BPO, Herbert von Karajan
DG 419 051-2

14 & 15 Beethoven: *Symphonies No.6 (Pastoral), Op.68, and No.9 (Choral), Op.125.* VPO, Karl Boehm, Jessye Norman, Brigitte Fassbaender, Placido Domingo, Walter Berry, Concert Singers of the Vienna State Opera
DG 413 721-2 (2)

16 Beethoven: *Piano sonatas Nos.14 (Moonlight), Op.27/2; 21 (Waldstein), Op.53; 23 (Appassionata), Op.57.* Vladimir Ashkenazy
Decca CD 425 838-2

17 Bellini: *Norma (highlights).* Joan Sutherland, Marilyn Horne, John Alexander, LSO, Richard Bonynge
Decca CD 421 886-2

18 Berlioz: *Song cycle: Nuits d'été, Op.7; La mort de Cléopâtre; Les Troyens.* Janet Baker, NPO, John Barbirolli, LSO, Alexander Gibson
EMI CDM7 69544-2
See also No.**38**

19 Bernstein: *Chichester Psalms;* **Poulenc:** *Gloria;* **Stravinsky:** *Symphony of Psalms.* John Bogart, Camerata Singers, NYPO, Leonard Bernstein
CBS MK 44710

20 Bizet: *Carmen (highlights).* Tatiana Troyanos, Placido Domingo, Kiri Te Kanawa, José van Dam, LPO, Georg Solti
Decca CD 421 300-2
See also No.**97**

21 Borodin: *Prince Igor: Polovtsian dances;* **Rimsky-Korsakov:** *Scheherazade.* Beecham Choral Society, RPO, Thomas Beecham
EMI CDC7 47717-2

22 Brahms: *Piano concerto No.2, Op.83; Intermezzi Op.116/5 and Op.117/2; Rhapsody, Op.79/2.* Artur Rubinstein, RCA Symphony Orchestra, Josef Krips
RCA RD 85671

23 Brahms: *Vier ernste Gesänge, Op.121, other Brahms songs.* **Bach:** *Cantata No.82: Ich habe genug.* Hans Hotter, Gerald Moore (piano)
EMI CDH7 63198-2

24 Brahms: *German Requiem, Op.45.* Margaret Price, Samuel Ramey, Ambrosian Singers, RPO, André Previn
Teldec/WEA 2292 43200-2
See also No.**61**

25 Britten: *Song cycle: Les Illuminations, Op.18; Nocturne, Op.60; Serenade for tenor, horn and strings, Op.31.* Peter Pears, Barry Tuckwell (horn), ECO, wind soloists, strings of the LSO, the composer
Decca CD 436 395-2

26 Bruckner: *Symphony No.9.* CSO, Bruno Walter
CBS MYK 44825

27 Canteloube: *Chants d'Auvergne.* Jill Gomez, RLPO, Vernon Handley
EMI CD-EMX 9500
[Angel CDM 62010]

Charpentier: See No. **94**
Cherubini: See No.**99**

28 Chopin: *Ballade No.1, Op.23; Barcarolle, Op.60; Fantaisie-Impromptu, Op.66; Mazurkas, Op.7/1, Op.33/2; Nocturnes, Op.9/2, Op.15/2, Op.27/2, Op.37/1; Polonaises, Op.40/1, 53; Waltzes, Op. 34/1, Op. 64/1 & 2.* Artur Rubinstein
RCA GD 87725 [7725-2-RG]

Copland: See No.**7**
Corelli: See No.**1**

29 Debussy: *Jeux; La Mer; Prélude à l'après-midi d'un faune.* LPO, Serge Baudo
EMI CD-EMX 9502
[Angel CDM 62012]

30 Debussy: *Violin sonata in G min.; Sonata for flute, viola and harp.* **Franck:** *Violin sonata.* **Ravel:** *Introduction and allegro.* Kyung Wha Chung, Radu Lupu, Osian Ellis, Melos Ensemble
Decca CD 421 154-2
Delibes: See No.**99**

31 Delius: *On hearing the first cuckoo in spring; Walk to the Paradise Garden,* and other pieces. ASMF, Neville Marriner
Decca CD 412 390-2

32 Donizetti: *Arias from: Don Pasquale; Lucia di Lammermoor; Maria Stuarda,* etc. Luciano Pavarotti, various orchestras and conductors
Decca CD 417 638-2

33 Dvořák: *Serenade for Strings, Op.22; Romance, Op.11.* **Wagner:** *Siegfried Idyll.* Jaime Laredo, SCO, Laredo
Pickwick PCD 928

34 Dvořák: *Piano quartets Nos.1, Op.23 and 2, Op.87.* Domus
Hyperion CDA 66287

35 Elgar: *Cello concerto, Op.85; Sea Pictures, Op.37.* Jacqueline Du Pré, Janet Baker, LSO, John Barbirolli
EMI CDC7 47329-2

36 Elgar: *Introduction and allegro for strings, Op.47; Serenade for strings, Op.20.* **Vaughan Williams:** *Fantasia on Greensleeves; Fantasia on a theme of Thomas Tallis; The lark ascending.* LCO, Christopher Warren-Green
Virgin VCy 790819-2
Enesco: See No.**97**
Falla: See No.**97**

37 Fauré: *La chanson d'Eve, Op.95 and other Fauré songs.* Janet Baker, Geoffrey Parsons (piano)
Hyperion CDA 66320

38 Franck: *Symphony in D min.* **D'Indy:** *Symphonie sur un chant montagnard français.* **Berlioz:** *Overture: Béatrice et Bénédict.* CHSO, Pierre Monteux
RCA GD 86805 [6805-2-RG]

39 Gershwin: *An American in Paris; Rhapsody in Blue.* **Grofé:** *Grand Canyon suite.* NYPO, Leonard Bernstein; and CSO, Bernstein (piano and conductor)
CBS MK 42264

40 Gluck: *Arias from: Alceste; Armide; Orfeo ed Euridice,* etc. Janet Baker, ECO, Raymond Leppard
Philips 422 950-2
See also No.**95**

41 Grieg: *Piano concerto, Op.16.* **Schumann:** *Piano concerto, Op.54.* Murray Perahia, BRSO, Colin Davis
CBS MK 44899

42 Handel: *Music for the Royal Fireworks* (original wind scoring); **Holst:** *Military band suites Nos.1 & 2.* Cleveland Symphonic Winds, Frederick Fennell
Telarc CD 80038

43 Handel: *Coronation anthems; Chandos anthem No.9.* Choir of King's College, Cambridge, ASMF, David Willcocks
Decca 421 150-2

44 Handel: *Messiah (highlights).* Kiri Te Kanawa, Anne Gjevang, Keith Lewis, Gwynne Howell, CHSO and Chorus, Georg Solti
Decca CD 430 098-2
See also Nos.**3** and **95**

45 Haydn: *Trumpet concerto in E flat,* and trumpet concertos by other composers. Håkon Hardenberger, ASMF, Neville Marriner
Philips CD 420 203-2

46 Haydn: *Symphonies Nos.82 (The Bear), 83 (The Hen) and 84.* Orchestra of the Age of Enlightenment, Wieland Kuijken
Virgin VC7 90793-2

47 Holst: *The Planets.* **Ligeti:** *Lux aeterna.* BSO and Chorus; Steinberg. North German Radio Choir, Helmut Franz
DG 419 475-2
See also No.**42**
Khachaturian: See No.**97**

48, 49 and 50 Leoncavallo:
I Pagliacci ; **Mascagni:** *Cavalleria Rusticana;* and intermezzos from other operas. Joan Carlyle, Carlo Bergonzi, Fiorenza Cossotto, Michel Schwalbé (violin). Chorus and Orchestra of La Scala, Milan, Herbert von Karajan
DG 419 257-2 (3)

51 Liszt: *Piano concertos Nos. 1 and 2; Totentanz, G126.* Krystian Zimerman, BSO, Seiji Ozawa
DG 423 571-2

52 Liszt: *Piano sonata in B min., G178; Les jeux d'eau à la Villa d'Este; Hungarian rhapsody No.15 (Rácóczy march), G244;* and other pieces. Mikhail Pletnev
Olympia OCD 172
See also No.**98**

53 Lutoslawski: *Postlude No.1; Symphonic variations.* **Busoni:** *Doktor Faustus: Sarabande and cortège.* **Schmidt:** *Variations on a Hussar's song.* PRSO, Witold Lutoslawski
EMI CDM7 69840-2

54 Mahler: *Symphony No.5.* NPO, John Barbirolli
EMI CDM7 69186-2

55 Mahler: *Lieder eines fahrenden Gesellen,* and other songs. Janet Baker, Geoffrey Parsons (piano)
Hyperion CDA 66100

56 Mendelssohn: *Violin concerto, Op.64.* **Tchaikovsky:** *Violin concerto, Op.35.* Kyung Wha Chung, MSO, Charles Dutoit
Decca CD 410 011-2

57 Mendelssohn: *Overtures: Calm sea and prosperous voyage, Op.27; The Hebrides (Fingal's Cave), Op.26; A Midsummer Night's Dream, Op.21,* etc. BSO, Claus Peter Flor
RCA RD 87905 [7905-2-RC]

58 Monteverdi: *Sacred vocal and instrumental music.* Emma Kirkby, Ian Partridge, David Thomas, Parley of Instruments
Hyperion CDA 66021

59 Mozart: *Piano concertos Nos. 21, K467,* and *25, K503.* Stephen Bishop-Kovacevich, LSO, Colin Davis
Philips 426 077-2

60 Mozart: *Symphonies Nos.35 (Haffner), 36 (Linz) and 38 (Prague).* BPO, Karl Boehm
DG 429 521-2

61 Mozart: *Clarinet quintet, K581.* **Brahms:** *Clarinet quintet, Op.115.* Gervase de Peyer, Melos Ensemble
EMI CDM7 63116-2

62 Mozart: *Requiem Mass, K626; Kyrie in D min., K341.* Soloists, Monteverdi Choir, EBS, John Eliot Gardiner
Philips CD 420 197-2

63 Mozart: *The Marriage of Figaro, K492* (highlights). Kiri Te Kanawa, Lucia Popp, Frederica von Stade, Samuel Ramey, Thomas Allen, Kurt Moll, LPO, Georg Solti
Decca CD 417 395-2

64 Mussorgsky: *Pictures at an Exhibition* (orchestrated Ravel). **Stravinsky:** *The Rite of Spring.* BPO, Herbert von Karajan
DG 429 162-2
Nielsen: See No.**79**
Palestrina: See No.**2**
Poulenc: See No.**19**

65 Prokofiev: *Piano sonata No.6, Op.82.* **Ravel:** *Gaspard de la nuit.* Ivo Pogorelich
DG 413 363-2

66 Puccini: Arias from: *La Bohème; Madama Butterfly; Manon Lescaut; Tosca; Turandot,* etc. Mirella Freni, Luciano Pavarotti, Elizabeth Harwood, Renata Tebaldi, Sherrill Milnes, Montserrat Caballé, Franco Corelli, Birgit Nilsson, Joan Sutherland, Maria Chiari
Decca CD 421 315-2
See also Nos. **48-50, 88** and **96**

67 Purcell: *Ode on St Cecilia's Day (Hail! Bright Cecilia).* Soloists, EBS, John Eliot Gardiner
Erato/WEA 2292 45187-2
See also No.**94**

68 Rachmaninov: *Piano concerto No.2, Op.18.* **Tchaikovsky:** *Piano concerto No.1, Op.23.* Van Cliburn, CHSO, Fritz Reiner; RCA Symphony Orchestra, Kirill Kondrashin
RCA RD 85912 [RCA 5912-2-RC]
See also No.**69**

69 Ravel: *Piano concerto in G.* **Rachmaninov:** *Piano concerto No.4, Op.40.* Arturo Benedetti Michelangeli, PO, Ettore Gracis
EMI CDC7 49326-2
See also Nos.**30** and **65**

70 Rossini: Overtures: *The Barber of Seville; The Thieving Magpie; William Tell,* etc. CHSO, Fritz Reiner
RCA GD 60387 [60387-2-RG]

71 Rossini: *Stabat Mater.* Helen Field, Della Jones, Arthur Davies, LSO Chorus, City of London Sinfonia, Richard Hickox
Chandos CHAN 8780
See also No.**99**

72 Schoenberg: *Variations for orchestra, Op.31; Verklärte Nacht, Op.4.* BPO, Herbert von Karajan
DG 415 326-2

73 Schubert: *Symphony No.8 (Unfinished), D759.* **Schumann:** *Symphony No.3 (Rhenish), Op.97.* PO, Sinopoli
DG 427 818-2

74 Schubert: *Fantasia in C (Wanderer), D760; Impromptus, D899/3 and 4; Piano sonata No.21, D960.* Artur Rubinstein
RCA RD 86257 [RCA 6257-2-RC]

75 Schubert: *Song recital.* Janet Baker, Graham Johnson (piano)
Hyperion CDJ 33001
See also No.**98**

76 Schumann: *Arabeske, Op.18; Etudes symphoniques, Op.13; Papillons, Op.2.* Vladimir Ashkenazy
Decca CD 414 474-2

77 Schumann: Songs: *Dichterliebe, Op.48; Liederkreis, Op.39.* Olaf Bär, Geoffrey Parsons (piano)
EMI CDC7 47397-2
See also Nos.**41, 73** and **98**

78 Shostakovich: *Symphony No.15, Op.141; Song cycle: From Jewish folk poetry, Op.79.* LPO, Bernard Haitink; Elisabeth Söderström, Ortrun Wenkel, Ryszard Karcykowski, RCO, Haitink
Decca CD 425 069-2
See also No.**97**

79 Sibelius: *Violin concerto, Op.47.* **Nielsen:** *Violin concerto, Op.33.* Cho-Liang Lin, Esa-Pekka Salonen, PO; SRSO
CBS MK 44548

80 Sibelius: *Symphonies Nos.4, Op.63, and 6, Op.104.* BPO, Herbert von Karajan
DG 415 108-2

81 Smetana: *Má Vlast: Vlatava; From Bohemia's woods and fields; Vysehrad; The Bartered Bride: overture and dances.* VPO, James Levine
DG 427 340-2

82 Strauss, Johann Jr, Johann Snr and Josef: *New Year Concert in Vienna, 1987.* Kathleen Battle, VPO, Herbert von Karajan
DG 419 616-2
See also No.**100**

83 Strauss, Richard: *Death and Transfiguration, Op.24; Metamorphosen for twenty-three solo strings.* BPO, Herbert von Karajan
DG 410 892-2

84 Strauss, Richard: *Four Last Songs* and other orchestral songs. Elisabeth Schwarzkopf, BRSO and LSO, George Szell
EMI CDC7 47276-2
Stravinsky: See Nos.**19** and **64**

85 Sullivan: *A Gilbert and Sullivan Gala.* Soloists, Bournemouth Sinfonietta, Kenneth Alwyn and Northern Sinfonia, Richard Hickox
EMI CDC7 47763-2

86 Tallis: *Spem in alium,* and other motets. Tallis Scholars, Peter Phillips
Gimell CDGIM 006

87 Tchaikovsky: *Nutcracker suite; Sleeping Beauty suite; Swan Lake suite.* BPO, Mstislav Rostropovich
DG 429 097-2
See also Nos.**56, 68** and **97**

88 Verdi: Arias from: *Aida; Don Carlos; Nabucco; Il Trovatore.* **Puccini:** Arias from: *Manon Lescaut* and *Turandot.* Placido Domingo with various orchestras and conductors
DG 413 785-2

89 Verdi: Arias from: *Aida; Un ballo in maschera; La Traviata; Il Trovatore;* and other operas. Leontyne Price with various orchestras and conductors
RCA RD 87016 [RCD1 7016]
See also Nos.**48-50, 96** and **99**

90 Vivaldi: *The Four Seasons, Op.8 Nos.1-4; Triple violin concerto, RV551;* *Quadruple violin concerto, RV580.* Salvatore Accardo, I Solisti di Napoli
Philips CD 422 065-2
See also No.**1**

91 Vivaldi: *Gloria, RV589.* **Bach, J.S.:** *Magnificat in E flat, BVW243a* (original version). Christ Church Cathedral Choir, Oxford; Academy of Ancient Music, Simon Preston
Oiseau-Lyre CD 414 678-2

92 Wagner: Excerpts from: *Rienzi; The Flying Dutchman; The Mastersingers of Nuremberg; The Valkyrie; Lohengrin; Tannhäuser; Tristan and Isolde.* Kirsten Flagstad, Birgit Nilsson, Gwyneth Jones, James King, George London, Tom Krause, VPO, Hans Knappertsbusch, George Solti
Decca CD 421 877-2
See also Nos.**33** and **97**

93 Weber: Overtures to: *Euryanthe; Der Freischütz; Oberon,* etc; *Invitation to the dance, Op.65* (orch. Berlioz). Hanover Band, Roy Goodman
Nimbus NI 5154

Collections:
94 London Gabrieli Brass Ensemble: Music by: **Bach, Charpentier, Clarke, G. Gabrieli, Holborne, Locke, Pezel, Purcell, Scheidt, Stanley** and **Susato**
Academy Sound and Vision
CDQS 6013

95 Stuttgart Chamber Orchestra, Karl Münchinger: Music by: **Albinoni, Bach, Boccherini, Gluck, Handel, Mozart, L.,** and **Pachelbel**
Decca CD 417 781-2

96 Great Love Duets: **Puccini:** *Madama Butterfly; La Bohème; Tosca; Manon Lescaut.* **Verdi:** *Otello; La Traviata.* Joan Sutherland, Mirella Freni, Luciano Pavarotti, Renata Tebaldi, Franco Corelli, Margaret Price, Carlo Cossutta
Decca CD 421 308-2

97 Cincinnatti Pops Orchestra, Erich Kunzel: Bizet: *L'Arlésienne, Farandole.* **Chabrier:** *España.* **Enesco:** *Romanian Rhapsody No.1, Op.11.* **Falla:** *Love the Magician.* **Khachaturian:** *Gayaneh, Sabre dance.* **Shostakovich:** *Festival overture, Op.96.* **Tchaikovsky:** *Marche slave.* **Wagner:** *Ride of the Valkyries,* etc.
Telarc CD 80170

98 Vladimir Horowitz, piano recital: Liszt: *Impromptu (Nocturne) in F sharp; Valse oubliée No.1.* **D.Scarlatti:** *Sonatas Kk145 and Kk135.* **Schubert:** *Impromptu in B flat, D935/3.* **Schubert/Tausig:** *Marche militaire, D733/1.* **Schumann:** *Kreisleriana, Op.16.* **Scriabin:** *Etude, Op.812*
DG 419 217-2

99 Maria Callas: Operatic arias by: **Botio, Catalani, Cherubini, Cilea, Delibes, Giordano, Meyerbeer, Rossini, Spontini** and **Verdi**
EMI CDC7 47282-2

100 Elisabeth Schwarzkopf sings Viennese operetta. PO and Chorus, Otto Ackermann
EMI CDC7 47284-2

Bibliography

List for further reading

General works:

Abraham, G., *The Oxford Concise History of Music*, Oxford 1979
A comprehensive survey with sections on non-European Classical music and an extensive bibliography.

Grout, D.J., *A History of Western Music*, rev. edn, London and New York, 1973

Harman, A., and W. Mellers, *Man and His Music*, London 1962

Headington, C. (ed.), *The Bodley Head History of Western Music*, London 1974

Hindley, G. (ed.), *The Larousse Encyclopedia of Music*, London 1971

Kendall, A., and M. Raeburn (eds.), *Heritage of Music*, 4 vols, Oxford and New York, 1989

Works on specific periods or topics:

Anderson, N., *Baroque Music*, London 1994

Arnold, D., *Monteverdi*, 3rd rev. edn., London 1991

Braunbehrens, V., trans. T. Bell, *Mozart in Vienna*, Oxford 1991

Chissell, J., *Schumann*, Master Musicians series, rev. edn, London 1989

Dahlhaus, C., *Schoenberg and the new music*, Cambridge 1989

Gal, H. (ed.), *The Musicians' World: Letters of the Great Composers*, London 1965

Griffiths, P., *Bartók*, Master Musicians series, London 1984

—*Modern Music: A Concise History*, rev. edn, London 1994

—*Stravinsky*, London 1988

—*The String Quartet: A History*, London 1986

Hopkins, A., *The Nine Symphonies of Beethoven*, London and Seattle 1981

—*Understanding Music*, London 1979

Horton, J., *Grieg*, Master Musicians series, rev. edn, London 1979

Hughes, R., *Haydn*, Master Musicians series, rev. edn, London 1989

Hutchings, A.J.B., *The Baroque Concerto*, rev. edn, 1973

Jolly, J., *The Gramophone Good CD Guide*, London 1994

Kennedy, M., *Britten*, Master Musicians series, London 1993

Landon, H.C. Robbins, *Beethoven: His Life, Work and World*, London 1992

—*Handel and His World*, London 1984

—*Vivaldi: The Voice of the Baroque* London 1993

Landon, H.C. Robbins, and David Wyn Jones, *Haydn: His Life and Music*, London 1988

Mitchell, D., *Mahler*, 2 vols, London 1958, 1976

Nattiez, J.-J., trans. and ed. R. Samuels, *The Boulez-Cage Correspondence*, Cambridge 1993

Norris, G., *Rakhmaninov*, London 1993

Orrey, L., and R. Milnes, *Opera: A Concise History*, London 1987

Raeburn, M., *The Chronicle of Opera*, London 1998

Rosen, C., *The Classical Style*, rev. edn, London 1976

Steiner, G., *The Death of Tragedy*, London 1961

Warrack, J., *Tchaikovsky*, London 1973

Whitall, A., *Romantic Music*, London 1987

The most comprehensive English-language reference work is:

Sadie, Stanley (ed.) *The New Grove Dictionary of Music and Musicians*, fully rev. edn., London 2000. Articles from the original 1980 edition have been published, including:

Abraham, G., et al., *Russian Masters 2: Rimsky-Korsakov, Rakhmaninov, Skryabin, Prokofiev, Shostakovich*, London 1986

Abraham, G., T. Searle and N. Temperley, *The Early Romantic Masters 1: Chopin, Schumann, Liszt*, London 1985

Arnold, D., et al., *The Italian Baroque Masters: Monteverdi, Frescobaldi, Cavalli, Corelli, A.Scarlatti, Vivaldi, D. Scarlatti*, London 1984

Brown, D., et al., *The Russian Masters 1: Glinka, Borodin, Balakirev, Musorgsky, Tchaikovsky*, London 1986

Cooke, D., et al., *Late Romantic Masters: Bruckner, Brahms, Dvořák, Wolf*, London 1985

Dean, W., *Handel*, London 1982

Deathridge, J., *Wagner*, London 1984

Gossett, P., *Masters of Italian Opera*, London 1983

Griffiths, P., et al., *The Second Viennese School: Berg, Schoenberg, Webern*, London 1983

Kerman, J., *Beethoven*, London 1983

Köhler, K.-H., et al., *Early Romantic Masters 2: Weber, Berlioz, Mendelssohn*, London 1985

Sadie, Stanley, *Mozart*, London 1982

Tyrrell, J., et al., *Turn of the century Masters: Janáček, Mahler, Strauss, Sibelius*, London 1985

Wolff, Christoph, *The Bach Family*, London 1983

Acknowledgments

Sources of quotations

31 Filippo Vitali's *L'Aretusa*: from *L'Aretusa. Favola in musica di Filippo Vitali rappresentata in Roma in casa di Monsignor Corsini et dedicata all'Ill.mo et Rev.mo Sig. Cardinale Borghese*. Soldi, Rome 1620

35 Selden on declining standards: Milward, R. (ed.), *Table Talk – being the Discourses of John Selden Esq*, London 1689

36 *Arianna*: Printer's dedication to the libretto of *Arianna*, by Ottavio Rinuccini, Bariletti, Venice 1640

41 Evelyn on French music: Bray, W. (ed.), *Memoirs...of John Evelyn... comprising his diary from the year 1641 to 1705-60*, London 1818

43 The city of Venice: *Il cannocchiale per la finta pazza, dilineato da M[aiolino] B[isaccioni] C[onte] di G[enova]*. Surian, Venice 1641

46 Molière on Lully: preface to Molière's *L'Amour médecin*, 1665

47 Evelyn on Louis XIV: Bray, W. (ed.), *Memoirs...of John Evelyn...comprising his diary from the year 1641 to 1705-60*, London 1818

49 *Il pomo d'oro* in Vienna: Heer, F., *The Holy Roman Empire*, London 1968, a shorter version of *Das Heilige Römische Reich*, London 1967

53 Madame de Sévigné on *Atys*: Madame de Sévigné, *Correspondance*. Bibliothèque de la Pléiade, II, 1974

54 North on Corelli: North, R., *Notes of Comparison between the Elder and Later Musick and Somewhat Historicall of both*, 1728

57 Decree for gift to Legrenzi: Caffi, F., *Storia della Musica Sacra nella già Cappella Ducale di S. Marco in Venezia dal 1318 al 1797*, I, Venice 1854

64 Handel: Mattheson, J., *Grundlage einer Ehren-Pforte*, Hamburg 1740, ed. M. Schneider, Berlin 1910, repr. 1969.

66 Bach at Arnstadt in 1706: Geiringer, K. *Johann Sebastian Bach*, rev. edn 1978.

68 Handel's *Rinaldo*: Richard Steele in *The Spectator*, No.14, London 16 March 1711

70 Uffenbach on Vivaldi. Preussner, E., *Die musikalischen Reisen des Herrn von Uffenbach*, Kassel and Basel, 1949

71 Female musicians of Venice: Charles de Brosses to M. de Blancey, letter of 29 August 1739; Colomb, R., *(ed.), Le président De Brosses en Italie: lettres familières d'Italie en 1739 et 1740*, Paris 1858, repr. 1931, Vol. I

72 Reincken on Bach: Agricola, J.F. and C.P.E. Bach, *Denkmal dreier verstorbener Mitglieder der Sozietät der musikalischen Wissenschaften*, in L. Mizler, *Musikalische Bibl.* IV/1, Leipzig 1754, reprinted as *Nekrolog auf Seb. Bach vom Jahre 1754* in Bach Jahrbuch, Leipzig 1920

74 Handel letter, 20 February 1719: Deutsch, O.E., *Handel: a Documentary Biography*, London 1955, repr.1974. German edition, *Händel-Handbuch IV: Dokumente zu Leben und Schaffen*, Leipzig 1985

75 Bach competes for a post: Mattheson, J., *Der musikalische Patriot*, 1728; quoted in Blom, E., *The Music Lover's Miscellany*, London 1935

78 Burney, 5 May 1726, on the rivalry of singers: Burncy, C., *A General History of Music from the Earliest Ages to the Present Period*, London 1776-89; ed. F. Mercer, London 1935, repr.1957
The Royal Academy, 11 November 1727: Delany, M., *Autobiography and Correspondence of Mary Granville, Mrs Delany*, London 1861-2. (Mary Delany née Granville was Mrs Pendarves before she married again to become Mrs Delany.)
Vivaldi and Charles VI: letter from Abbé Conti, 23 September 1728, *Lettres de M. L'Abbé Conti, noble vénitien, à Mme. de Caylus*, Venice, Biblioteca Marciana

80 Mayor of Leipzig on Bach: Geiringer, K., *Johann Sebastian Bach*, rev. edn 1978

83 Bach letter to Erdmann: Müller von Asow, E., *Johann Sebastian Bach: gesammelte Briefe*, Regensburg 1938, repr.1950

85 Aaron Hill letter to Handel: Deutsch, O.E., *Handel: A Documentary Biography*, London and New York 1955

87 Goldoni on Vivaldi: Carlo Goldoni, Prefazione al Tomo XIII dell'Edizione Pasquali, Venezia 1761, in *Tutte le opere*, a c. di Giuseppe Ortolani, Milano, s.d., vol. I

88 Beethoven on Handel: *Harmonicon*, January 1824. In English, Thayer, A.W., *Beethoven*, Princeton 1967, Vol. II

91 Bach obituary: Agricola, J.F., and C.P.E. Bach, *Denkmal dreier verstorbener Mitglieder der Sozietät der musikalischen Wissenschaften*, in Mizler, I., *Musikalische Bibl.* IV/1, Leipzig 1754, reprinted as: *Nekrolog auf Seb. Bach vom Jahre 1754* in Bach Jahrbuch, Leipzig 1920

93 Frederick the Great's correspondence with his sister: *Oeuvres*, Berlin 1850, and *Mémoires de Frédérique Sophie Wilhelmine de Prusse, Margrave de Bareith [sic]*, 2 vols, Paris 1811

93 The orchestra at Mannheim: Burney, C., *A General History of Music from the Earliest Ages to the Present Period*, London 1776-89; ed. F.Mercer, London, 1935

96 Baron Grimm, *Correspondance littéraire, philosophique et critique*, 1757, Paris 1877-82

97 Bach, C.P.E., *Versuch über die wahre Art das Clavier zu spielen*, Berlin 1753; ed. W. Niemann, Leipzig, 1906. In English translation as *Essay on the True Art of Playing Keyboard Instruments*, ed. W.J. Mitchell, New York 1948

99 Haydn on Esterháza: Griesinger, G.A., 'Biographische Notizen über Joseph Haydn', *Allgemeine Musikalische Zeitung* XI, Leipzig 1809

100 Leopold Mozart letter, December 1763: Anderson, E., *The Letters of Mozart and his Family*, 3rd edn, London 1985; letter No.75 in Deutsch, O.E., W.A. Bauer and J.H. Eibl (eds.), *Mozart: Briefe und Aufzeichnungen*, Neue Mozart-Ausgabe, Kassel 1962-75

102 Diderot, D., *Le Neveu de Rameau*, Paris 1891

104 Mozart letter 7 January 1770: Anderson, E., *The Letters of Mozart and his Family*, 3rd edn, London 1985; letter No.153 in Deutsch, O.E., W.A. Bauer and J.H. Eibl (eds.), *Mozart: Briefe und Aufzeichnungen*, Neue Mozart-Ausgabe, Kassel 1962-75

107 Gluck letter: *Mercure de France*, Paris, February 1773
Gluck's manifesto in *Alceste*, 1769: Strunk, O., *Source Readings in Music History*, London 1952

108 Grimm on Mozart: Leopold Mozart's letter to Wolfgang of 13 August 1778 in Anderson, E., *The Letters of Mozart and his Family*, 3rd edn, London 1985; letter No.476 in Deutsch, O.E., W.A. Bauer and J.H. Eibl (eds.), *Mozart: Briefe und Aufzeichnungen*, Neue Mozart-Ausgabe, Kassel 1962-75

109 Gluck on Italian opera: preface to the French version of *Alceste*, Bureau d'abonnement musical, Paris, 1776

111 Mozart letter 9 June 1781: Anderson, E., *The Letters of Mozart and his Family*, 3rd edn, London 1985; letter No.604 in Deutsch, O.E., W.A. Bauer and J.H. Eibl (eds.), *Mozart: Briefe und Aufzeichnungen*, Neue Mozart-Ausgabe, Kassel 1962-75

112 Neefe on Beethoven, 2 March 1783: Cramer's *Magazin der Musik*, Hamburg, Vol. I, quoted in Thayer, A.W., *Beethoven*, 3rd edn, Leipzig 1917, Vol. I; English-language edn, Princeton 1967

115 Leopold Mozart letter: 16 February 1785, Anderson, E., *The Letters of Mozart and his Family*, 3rd edn, London 1985; letter No.847 in Deutsch, O.E., W.A. Bauer and J.H. Eibl (eds.), *Mozart: Briefe und Aufzeichnungen*, Neue Mozart-Ausgabe, Kassel 1962-75.

117 Da Ponte's preface to *The Marriage of Figaro*: Sonneck, O., *Catalogue of Opera Librettos printed before 1800*, Washington 1914, Vol. I; quoted in Deutsch, O.E., W.A. Bauer and J.H. Eibl (eds.), *Mozart: Briefe und Aufzeichnungen*, Neue Mozart-Ausgabe, Kassel 1962-75

118 Haydn on Mozart, December 1787: *Allgemeine Musikalische Zeitung*, Leipzig, 19 December 1798, Vol. I, quoted in Blom, E., *et al.* (trans.), *O.E. Deutsch, Mozart: a documentary biography*, London 1965, repr.1990

119 Criticism from *Wiener Realzeitung*, 11 July 1786, No.28; Raeburn, C., in *Österreichische Musikzeitschrift*, Vienna July–August 1957

120 Mozart mentioned: Schubart's *Vaterlandschronik*, Stuttgart, 1788, 1st half-year, p.30, quoted in Deutsch, O.E., W.A. Bauer and J.H. Eibl, (eds.) *Mozart: Briefe und Aufzeichnungen*, Neue Mozart-Ausgabe, Kassel 1962-75

125 Anderson, E., *The Letters of Mozart and his Family*, 3rd edn, London 1985; Deutsch, O.E., W.A. Bauer and J.H. Eibl (eds.), *Mozart: Briefe und Aufzeichnungen*, Neue Mozart-Ausgabe, Kassel 1962-75

127 Haydn on *The Creation*: Griesinger, G.A., 'Biographische Notizen über Joseph Haydn', *Allgemeine MusikZeitung* XI, Leipzig 1809

132 Beethoven on the *Eroica* Symphony: Thayer, A.W., *Life of Beethoven*, Princeton 1967, Vol. I

135 Letter first published in the *Athenaeum für Wissenschaft, Kunst und Leben*, Nuremberg, January 1839; quoted in English in Thayer, A.W., *Life of Beethoven*, Princeton 1967, Vol. I

136 *Il giornale Italiana*, Milan 1813

144 Boïeldieu letter to Charles Maurice on Rossini, 16 December 1823: Favre, G., *Boïeldieu: Sa Vie – son oeuvre*, 2 vols, Paris 1944–45, Vol. I

145 Cipriani Potter's 'Recollections of Beethoven' (1818) in *The Musical World*, 1836, reprinted in *The Musical Times* in 1861

146 Berlioz on living to 140: Berlioz, H., *Mémoires*, 1848 *et seq.*, Paris 1870

149 Berlioz's Paris: Berlioz, H., *Mémoires*, 1848 *et seq.*, Paris 1870, Chapter 14

157 Schumann on Mendelssohn's Op.49 piano trio. Schumann's writings on music and musicians are collected in *Gesammelte Schriften über Musik und Musiker*, Leipzig 1854

165 Rossini's sleepless night: Michotte, Edmond, *Une soirée chez Rossini à Beau-Séjour (Passy), 1858*, Brussels *c.* 1910

166 Gustave Flaubert on Offenbach: *L'Autographe*, Paris, December 1864

170 Berlioz in 1864: Berlioz, H., *Mémoires*, 1848 *et seq.*, Paris 1870

175 Schumann on Brahms: *Neue Zeitschrift für Musik*, October 1853

178 Tchaikovsky letter to Modest from Bayreuth, 14 August 1876. Von Meck, G., *P.I.Tchaikosvsky, Letters to his Family: An Autobiography*, New York 1981

181 Debussy on the Prix de Rome, in *Monsieur Croche, antidilettante*, Paris 1921

184 Critic on Bruckner: Göllerich, A., and M. Aucr, *Anton Bruckner*, 4 vols, Regensburg 1922-36

189 Tchaikovsky's Florence diary: from Diary Number Ten (the original is in the Tchaikovsky Museum at Klin, near Moscow), Lakond, W. (trans.), *The Diaries of Tchaikovsky*, New York 1945.

191 Verdi on Tadolini in letter to Cammarano of 1848. Luzio, A., *Carteggi verdiana*, 4 vols, Rome 1935-47

194 Bruckner's Te Deum: Göllerich, A., and M. Auer, *Anton Bruckner*, 4 vols, Regensburg 1922-36.

203 Debussy on the Paris Opéra and the Prix de Rome: Debussy, C., *Monsieur Croche antidilettante*, Paris 1921

211 Gertrude Stein, *The Autobiography of Alice B Toklas*, Baltimore/New York, 1933 © Random House, Inc. Stravinsky, *Chroniques de ma vie*, Paris 1935-36

212 Ravel on Spain: Jourdan-Morhange, H., *Ravel et Nous*, Geneva 1945

213 Jourdan-Morhange, H., *Ravel et Nous*, Geneva, 1945; the article from which it is taken originally appeared in the *Revue musicale*, December 1938, a special issue devoted to Ravel, 'Hommage à Maurice Ravel'

216 Stravinsky on Nijinska's production of *Mavra*: Stravinsky, I., *Chronicle of my Life* (English translation of *Chroniques de ma vie*), London 1936

224 Roland-Manuel, *Ravel*, Paris 1938

226 Stravinsky, I., *Chronicle of my Life*, London 1936

229 Gertrude Stein, *Paris France*, London 1940. © Peter Owen

231 Gershwin in 1926: Kimball, R. and A. Simon, *The Gershwins*, New York 1973

235 Copland in an interview with Philip Ramey in 1980: quoted by Peter Dickinson in Kendall, A., and M. Raeburn (eds.), *Heritage of Music*, Oxford and New York 1989, Vol. IV

240 Peter Pears on Zhdanov: Pears, P., *Moscow Christmas: December 1966*, privately printed 1967

243 Hindemith: Introduction to *Elementary Training for Musicians*, 2nd rev. edn., London 1949

List of Illustrations

LIST OF ILLUSTRATIONS

Index

Numbers in italics refer to captions:
those in bold to extended references and biographical details